Housing and Local Government

Cogen, Holt and Associates is a professional consulting organization specializing in the planning, funding, evaluation, and management of community development, housing, health, human resource, and other urban programs. The firm is located in New Haven, Connecticut.

Housing and Local Government

A Research Guide for
Policy Makers and Planners

Harry J. Wexler
Richard Peck
Cogen, Holt and Associates

With the assistance of
Robin Hamill
Judith Stoloff
Doris Zelinsky
Leonard Bogorad

Lexington Books
D.C. Heath and Company
Lexington, Massachusetts
Toronto   London

Library of Congress Cataloging in Publication Data

Wexler, Harry J.
    Housing and local government.

    Bibliography: p.
    Includes index.
    1. Housing—United States. 2. Cities and towns—United States. I. Peck, Richard, joint author. II. Title.
HD7293.W47   301.5'4'0973   75-22494
ISBN 0-669-00218-6

Copyright © 1975 by Cogen, Holt and Associates

All rights reserved. No part of this publication may be reproduced or transmitted in any form or by any means, electronic or mechanical, including photocopy, recording, or any information storage or retrieval system, without permission in writing from Cogen, Holt and Associates.

This work was prepared with the support of National Science Foundation Grant No. GI-39279. However, any opinions, findings, conclusions, or recommendations expressed herein are those of the authors and do not necessarily reflect the views of the National Science Foundation.

Published simultaneously in Canada.

Printed in the United States of America.

International Standard Book Number: 0-669-00218-6

Library of Congress Catalog Card Number: 75-22494

Contents

	List of Figures	ix
	List of Tables	xi
	Preface	xiii
	Acknowledgments	xv
Part I	*Introduction*	
Chapter 1	**Purpose and Scope of Study**	3
	Introduction	3
	Terms of the Study	4
	A Framework for Evaluation	13
	Project Design	17
Part II	*Evaluation of Research Findings*	
Chapter 2	**Housing Plans, Urban Renewal Programs, and Information Systems**	25
	Introduction	25
	Comprehensive Planning	25
	Urban Renewal and Renewal Planning	29
	Information Systems and Policy-related Research: Housing Abandonment as Case in Point	35
	Conclusions	45
Chapter 3	**Codes and Regulations**	47
	Introduction	47

	Land-use Regulation	48
	Building Codes	53
	Housing Codes	56
	Rent Control	60
	Conclusions	67
Chapter 4	**Real Property Taxation**	69
	Introduction	69
	Conventional Property Tax	69
	Abatement and Incentive Programs	80
	Restructuring to Site-Value Taxation	82
	Conclusions	89
Chapter 5	**Housing-assistance Programs**	91
	Introduction	91
	Housing-subsidy Programs: Supply vs. Demand	92
	Large-scale Rehabilitation	100
	Self-help Programs	110
	Conclusions	112
Part III	*Evaluation of Research Methodology and Context*	
Chapter 6	**Research Methodology and Institutional Context**	117
	Introduction	117
	Methodology of Policy-related Research: A Paradigm	118
	Methodological Problems: A Critical Analysis	121
	Availability, Presentation, and Applicability of Research Findings: Diminished Utility	133
	The Relationship of Researcher to Policy Maker: Two Noteworthy Models	136
	Conclusions	143

Part IV	Conclusions	
Chapter 7	Conclusions and Recommendations	147
	Introduction	147
	Problems of Quality	148
	Problems of Utility	153
	Problems of Access and Distribution	155
	Policy-related Research and the Problems of Decision Making	158
Part V	Appendixes and Bibliography	
Appendix A	Housing Information Sources and Needs of Local Housing Policy Makers and Advisers: Survey Findings	165
Appendix B	Evaluating Local Housing Programs Using Cost/Benefit Analysis: An Overview	181
Appendix C	Sample Evaluation Forms	205
Appendix D	NSF Research Program Note	223
	Bibliography	227
	Acquisition of Housing Studies	293
	Name Index	303
	Subject Index	305
	About the Authors	311

List of Figures

1-1	The Housing Process: Major Participants and Influences	6
1-2	Types of Research	11
1-3	Policy Instruments and Housing Problems: An Analytic Framework	14
1-4	Project Design	18
1-5	Research and Other Information Flows to Local Policy Makers: Relative Strengths	21
A-1	Research and Other Information Flows to Local Policy Makers: Types	168
A-2	Research and Other Information Flows to Local Policy Makers: Relative Strengths	170
A-3	Sources of Information Used Often by Housing Policy Makers	172
A-4	Elements of Training and Experience	174
A-5	Details on Sources of Information Used by Policy Makers	175
A-6	Utility of "Housing Studies" to Policy Makers	177
A-7	Reasons Housing Policy Makers Find It Difficult to Use Housing Studies	178
A-8	Sources of Information Used by Policy Makers to Keep Informed of Current Developments in Housing	179

List of Tables

2-1	Findings of Policy-related Research on Abandonment	40
2-2	Indicators on Which Information May be Available	45
6-1	Process of Policy-related Research	119
7-1	Quality of the Research: Summary	149
A-1	Survey of Policy Makers: Response Rate	166
A-2	Survey of Policy Advisers: Response Rate	167

Preface

This study of policy-related research on local housing services was funded by the National Science Foundation in 1973. The study is especially timely because of the transfer to state and local governments, under the Community Development Act, of major responsibility for housing production and rehabilitation.

Evaluated here are policy-related research findings in the areas of housing plans, urban renewal programs, and information systems; codes and regulations; real property taxation; and housing assistance programs. Another section discusses research methodology and its institutional context and, among other things, has subsections that critically analyze current methodological problems and the relationship of the researcher to the policy maker.

This book can help in several ways to improve local housing policy making. It identifies a vast body of research that can be valuable to officials and their advisers, synthesizes and evaluates current research findings in four key housing areas, suggests ways to overcome drawbacks in research designs and methodologies, and recommends means of improving the value and dissemination of housing research. Thus, the book combines two different levels of evaluation—rigorous evaluation of individual works of research and a broader evaluation of the institutional contexts in which policy-related research is conducted.

The book concludes that policy-related research has largely failed to play a significant role in the formulation and execution of local housing policy for at least four reasons: (1) Its overall quality is poor; (2) its utility is marred by the fact that it does not consider the critical constraints on the local policy maker; (3) it is inadequately disseminated; and (4) the local decision maker tends to rely on his own training and experience in the housing field.

In view of these problems the book offers a series of recommendations for shoring up and improving the quality of policy-related housing research and for making its products more useful and more accessible to policy makers and their advisers. The recommendations call for the Department of Housing and Urban Development (HUD) and the National Science Foundation (NSF) to provide grants to support the research agendas of institutes in the field, close coordination of this research with the federal Office of Management and Budget and the Bureau of the Census to provide more useful data stocks, and encouragement by HUD and other primary funders of systematic explorations of the impacts or side effects of specific local housing policies.

Some valuable studies may have eluded our search. Constraints of time prevented us from assessing recent efforts by HUD to fill research gaps and improve dissemination practices. Nonetheless, the conclusions of this study have stood up under scrutiny and its recommendations warrant deliberation and action.

Acknowledgments

We acknowledge the assistance of our many colleagues at Cogen, Holt and Associates in conceiving and carrying out the study that led to this book. Robin Hamill developed the bibliography and conducted the extensive search for studies. Judith Stoloff, Doris Zelinsky, Len Bogorad, and Robin Hamill shared with us the task of evaluating the many research studies. Joel Cogen, Kathryn Feidelson, and Hugh Price gave substantial time and personal attention to the study. They reviewed the evaluation forms, tightened the survey questionnaires, commented on intermediate project reports and working papers, and worked through several drafts of the final report. At various stages of the project we were also assisted by Michael Johnston, Drake Pike, Eve Sundelson, and David Davies.

We are indebted to William J. Stull, a member of the economics faculty at Swarthmore College, for his evaluation of cost/benefit analysis as applied to municipal housing services, which appears as Appendix B of this study.

Woodruff Ford of Fordesign Inc. prepared our figures and tables, and Eric Sandahl and William Cahn provided editorial advice.

Many housing analysts and scholars, who themselves have contributed to the store of policy-related research on local housing, made valuable suggestions over the course of the project. We single out for special thanks Janet Pack of the Fels Center of Government, Peter Marcuse of the City Planning Faculties at UCLA and Columbia, Arthur Solomon of the Joint Center for Urban Studies of MIT and Harvard, and John Quigley of the Institution for Social and Policy Studies at Yale.

We are grateful to John Surmeier, program manager in the Division of Advanced Productivity Research and Technology at the National Science Foundation, for his helpful comments on earlier drafts and his encouragement throughout the project.

Our thanks as well go to all the municipal officials, public housing executives, and policy advisers who responded to our surveys and in conversation or correspondence helped us in our work.

Finally, we acknowledge a special debt to Mary LaTorraca and Gail Fulop, our typists, whose energy and good cheer seemed as endless as the pages of manuscript we provided them.

**Part I:
Introduction**

1 Purpose and Scope of Study

Introduction

The purpose of this book is to present the results of an 18-month evaluation of policy-related research on local housing services. It is addressed to several audiences: researchers who conduct and disseminate the research, local policy makers and their advisers who need such research, and representatives of foundations and others who provide funds for research.

The book comes at a propitious moment: the housing industry faces its most severe crisis in a generation. A combination of runaway construction costs, inflated land prices, high interest rates, and scarce mortgage funds has reduced new housing production to a trickle. Increasing attention is being focused on the preservation and maintenance of existing housing stock—traditionally an important function of local government. In addition, through enactment of the Community Development Act in August 1974, Congress transferred major responsibility for the production and rehabilitation of housing from federal to state and local government. This has precipitated a critical debate among housing experts and policy makers over the role local government can and should play in determining what kind of housing should be built, for whom, of what quality, and where.

Factors that influence the production and preservation of housing are many and diverse. The local policy maker, however, has direct control over a very limited number of these factors. In view of the prevailing economic situation, the disfavor into which categorical housing-subsidy programs have fallen, and the likely withdrawal of a strong federal presence from the housing sector, local policy makers must learn to use their limited powers over the improvement of local housing more wisely and efficiently than ever before.

This book takes a first step in this direction. In assessing the research literature on local housing services, the book may be used to improve the quality of local policy making in several important ways:

1. It identifies a vast body of policy-related research on housing of potential utility to local officials and their advisers.
2. It synthesizes current research findings of necessary interest to local policy makers in four critical housing-related areas, assesses the validity of this research, and identifies research gaps that need to be filled (Chapters 2, 3, 4, and 5).

3. It reviews and analyzes shortcomings in research designs and methodologies employed by those who conduct policy-related research, suggesting how the conduct of current research can be improved (Chapter 6).
4. It recommends a strategy for improving both the utility and dissemination of housing research on the basis of this overall evaluation and our survey of information sources on which local policy makers rely in making decisions about housing (Chapter 7).
5. At the end of the book a body of housing research aids is provided—an extensive bibliography, a list of bibliographic and abstracting services, and an explanation of how cost/benefit analysis is applied to housing programs.

The book has two facets: First, it assesses a complex, uneven, and quite disparate set of research efforts on local housing. To do so with any consistency and insight, we had to devise a framework of analysis—a conceptual approach—that would place these seemingly independent pieces of research within a larger and more coherent pattern. Using this framework we were also able to detect major gaps in the research. Second, it explores various strategies for improving this research, not only by noting qualities of the research that at present greatly mar its validity, but by pointing to ways in which the basic institutional arrangements through which such research is produced can be improved so as to make it more useful to the local policy maker.

This is a difficult undertaking. The conduct of research is a complex matter. It cannot be improved by heavy-handed tinkering or insensitive prescriptions. Many of the shortcomings of policy-related research on housing are beyond easy remedy. They reflect our limited knowledge of the underlying mechanisms of the housing market, particularly the secondary and tertiary consequences of public interventions. They also reflect a limited public commitment to improve the quality of our local housing stock and the services required to maintain and preserve it. And they reflect researchers' limitations in taking adequate account of such local factors as political climate, private-sector commitment, economic vitality, and others that invariably influence the transferability and applicability of research findings and conclusions to particular communities.

In spite of these limitations, this book is critical and timely because it enhances the capacity of local decision makers to evaluate and make effective use of such research, while assisting researchers and funding sources to understand decision makers' needs.

Terms of the Study

In this introductory chapter we take some pains to explain how we went about defining the task put to us by the National Science Foundation (NSF)—to evaluate policy-related research on municipal housing services. Specifically, what aspects of the housing process must be investigated to understand the function and role of municipal housing services? Through what specific local policy instruments are municipal housing services provided? What is policy-related research? How does research on local housing differ from other categories of housing research or policy analysis? And how does one devise an analytic framework through which research on these instruments can be evaluated so as not to lose sight of the broader policy objectives that a municipal housing program should pursue? In responding to these initial inquiries, we specify the basic terms of the study.

The Housing Process

The term "housing" is ordinarily used to refer to a community's physical stock of dwelling units. In this book we look at housing as a set of activities related to the production, distribution, and servicing of this physical stock. More particularly, we focus on the means available to local chief executives (mayors, first selectmen, and city managers), housing-agency executives, and local legislators to influence this housing process through the specific public programs and controls (hereinafter referred to as policy instruments).

Our focus is best understood by referring to Figure 1-1, an adaptation of a chart prepared by the President's Committee on Urban Housing [688].[a] The figure depicts how local officials interact with other participants over the entire range of activities that influence the major phases of the housing process.

The figure reveals dramatically several basic characteristics of the local housing process:

First, it is dynamic. The four phases described along the center of the chart depict the life cycle of the housing stock—preparation, production, distribution, servicing, redistribution (through subsequent sales), renovation, etc.

Second, it is complex. The lower half of the chart lists the jungle of institutional rules, regulations, and laws that influence the effectiveness of the process. It also helps to explain how any one public intervention can be diffused in the backwash of so many other influencing factors.

Third, municipal officials are but part of a multitude of persons who directly participate in the process. What the chart does not show is that municipal officials are among the least influential participants in comparison with private developers and owners, lending institutions, and the federal government (through its income-tax laws, mortgage guarantees, and the expenditures of its various housing-assistance programs).

Fourth, the housing process is unusually vulnerable to nationwide economic trends over which none of the participants has control. Housing is expensive to

---
[a]This and all subsequent citations refer to the designated entry in the complete bibliography at the end of this book.

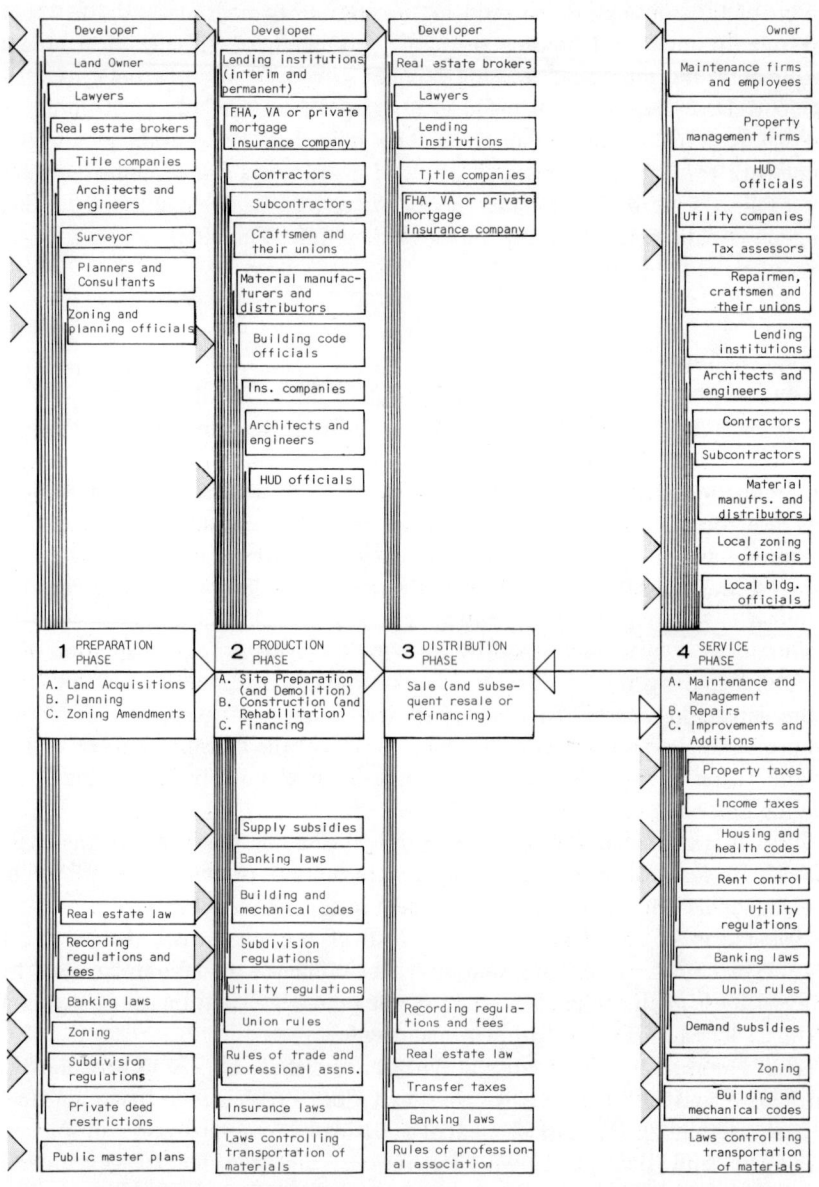

Source: Adapted from *The Report of the President's Committee on Urban Housing* [688], Table 4-1.

Figure 1-1. The Housing Process: Major Participants and Influences.

produce and expensive to purchase. It represents the largest single portion of most family budgets. Homeowners and owners of rental housing make purchases on credit. When interest rates are high or savings-institution funds are in short supply, the housing process grinds to a halt. During such periods intervention by municipal officials and agencies is of little avail. In other words, the efficacy of municipal housing services is tied not only to the health of the local housing sector but to the vigor of the national economy as well.

As indicated on the chart, we have been necessarily selective in deciding which of the many participants and influences require study. To some extent this selectivity is a function of what the research literature provides. But our scope of study was also dictated by other factors. We selected for study those policy instruments that directly influence housing production and that fall within the control—total or partial—of the municipal policy maker. Some topics we excluded simply to keep the study within manageable limits. We chose not to include research literature on highway design and location, or on the provision of sewers, water, gas, and electricity, though these services have important consequences for housing. We also chose, with some reluctance, to exclude the substantial research literature on minority-housing opportunities and fair-housing laws. Thus, we focus on the phases of preparation, production, and servicing of housing, and pass over lightly the phase of distribution, leaving that topic to other NSF evaluation teams studying the particular issues of land-use controls.[b]

Local Housing Policy Instruments

As Figure 1-1 shows, local-government officials influence the housing process through their decisions in such areas as planning, zoning, housing and building codes, subdivision, rent control, property taxes, loans, and grants. Through deliberate and coordinated decision making, local government can encourage the construction of new housing units, promote particular kinds of dwelling units to meet the needs of special groups, such as the poor and the elderly, and direct housing activity into specific neighborhoods. Likewise, local government can discourage the rate of new housing activity through restrictive regulations. Or, by inactivity or haphazard application of codes and regulations, it can leave the direction and intensity of housing efforts entirely to the private market.

It is the sum effect of these separate interventions by local government in the housing process that constitutes municipal housing policy. In this book we refer

---

[b]University of North Carolina, Center for Urban and Regional Studies, Edward M. Bergman, principal investigator; The Potomac Institute, Herbert M. Franklin, principal investigator. These and other evaluations commissioned by NSF are listed in the NSF Research Program Note, Appendix D.

to the various mechanisms through which these interventions are achieved as housing-policy instruments.

The impacts of the policy instruments we chose to examine are not necessarily confined to any one phase of the housing process. It is a measure of the complexity of local-housing policy that any one policy instrument—say urban renewal or the real property tax—will affect to varying degrees each phase of the housing process. Consequently, for purposes of clarity and convenience of analysis, we identify four basic categories of policy instruments: (1) planning and urban renewal tools; (2) codes and regulations; (3) real property taxation; and (4) housing-assistance programs. The policy instruments that comprise these categories are listed below, together with a brief explanation of their purpose and function.

Planning and Urban Renewal Tools

Comprehensive Planning. The blueprint for present and future physical-development activity, the comprehensive plan generally includes a housing element that reflects judgments of the local government as to the desired volume, density, and location of housing development within the community. In the past localities could ignore this exercise; now, any locality applying for community-development funds under the 1974 act must submit a housing-assistance plan.

Urban Renewal. This is both a planning and an operational tool. We consider the various decisions local officials make as to when and where to begin an urban renewal project and what mode of renewal to employ in the context of planning tools. The types of renewal programs considered include clearance and new construction, rehabilitation, code enforcement, and a combination of all three approaches. Specific housing-subsidy programs and code-enforcement techniques are considered separately under housing-assistance plans.

Housing-information Systems. Such systems, which only a few cities in the nation are operating, are gaining increasing attention as a means of monitoring changes and trends in the local housing stock—an early-warning system for housing problems, particularly vacancies and abandonment.

Housing Codes and Regulations

Land-use Regulations. Zoning and subdivision codes have been the policy instruments used chiefly by local government to control the density and location of housing since the first model codes were formulated in the 1920s by the U.S. Department of Commerce.

Building Codes. Local government uses detailed building-code regulations to attempt to ensure the structural and mechanical integrity of housing construction and rehabilitation. Although the content of these codes is strongly influenced by national fire-insurance underwriters, local building inspectors exercise discretion in applying them, and thereby influence the cost and location of housing.

Housing Codes. Through the enforcement of housing codes in response to specific complaints or on an areawide basis, local government regulates the quality of multifamily housing accommodations—persons per room, sanitation facilities, level of ongoing maintenance. Research has focused on the impact of codes on landlord investment and rent levels.

Rent Control. New York City's experience with rent control has produced valuable research of interest to other municipalities concerned with the impact of rising rents on low- and moderate-income families. We examine this policy instrument as one of the few local attempts to deal directly with the price of rental housing in areas where the housing supply has not kept pace with the demand.

Real Property Taxation

Conventional Property Tax. Most of the nation's municipalities are forced to rely on property taxes (levied on both land and improvements) as the chief support of local-government services. This tax falls heavily on lower income housing and encourages harmful competition among localities for "good ratables" that produce more revenue than the cost of the services they consume.

Special Tax-abatement and Incentive Programs. To encourage private developers to build housing for the poor and other special groups, local government has employed special abatement and incentive programs that reduce the tax burden of a building on the owner.

Site-value Taxation. Ever since the publication of Henry George's writings on the single tax, there has been substantial interest in restructuring the local property tax as a tax on land value alone, so that it will not discourage development. Graded-tax schemes in Pittsburgh and Honolulu, among others, have been studied in the absence of examples of true site-value taxation.

Housing-assistance Programs

Supply and Demand Subsidies. The federal government has directly influenced local housing activity ever since the public housing legislation of the 1930s provided for federal payment of the entire cost of debt service on local housing authority bonds. Since the early 1960s a series of federal subsidy programs directed at private developers has increased the supply of lower income housing. More recently the federal government has shifted its attention to various forms of demand subsidies—housing allowances and leased housing, for example. Without examining these many programs in detail, we review the impact of alternative forms of federal subsidy programs on the capacity of local government to meet the needs of lower income families.

Large-scale Rehabilitation Loans and Grants. We pay particular attention to various local attempts to improve declining neighborhoods through large-scale rehabilitation of substandard dwellings. In particular, Chapter 5 focuses on the experience of locally assisted nonprofit-housing organizations. Local-government support, in the form of technical assistance and code enforcement, is integral to the success of these efforts.

Self-help Programs. In the absence of federal categorical-grant programs, and until revenue-sharing programs are operational, local government must help housing consumers to help themselves through novel forms of transfers-in-kind and technical assistance. Chief among these innovative local programs is urban homesteading and assistance to tenant groups who desire to assume co-operative ownership and control of abandoned multifamily dwellings. Although research studies on these programs are scarce, we examine this topic because of its current importance to local government.

Policy-related Research Studies

Much has been written over the past decade on the purpose and exercise of the foregoing policy instruments. Most of this literature, however, is simply descriptive or expository. Only a small number of these housing studies can be characterized as policy-related research.

What is this category of policy-related research? When we began our study, we defined policy-related research in broad terms as studies that brought the methods of social science to bear on housing problems confronting the local policy maker. As we developed and refined our search and evaluation process, we specified such research in more operational terms: policy-related research involves studies that submit ideas or hypotheses about a local housing problem or policy to some form of rigorous testing for the purpose of generating findings and conclusions that are (1) valid in social science terms, (2) applicable to more than one community, and (3) administratively, financially, and politically feasible.

But there are costly trade-offs between validity and utility, and between utility and transferability. Few studies that we examined could satisfy each of the three criteria. In general, the more rigorous the methodology, the more qualified and equivocal were the conclusions. Similarly, the more generalizable the conclusions, the more trivial they proved. And the studies that paid most attention to the constraints of feasibility tended to be the least rigorous in methodology and, consequently, of questionable generalizability.

The characteristics of policy-related research are more understandable when this research is placed in the larger context of ongoing research activity. A useful way to grasp the significance of this larger research effort is to distinguish types of research inquiry along two dimensions—the extent to which the research is oriented toward action as opposed to understanding, and the extent to which it concerns itself with specific programs as opposed to general principles.

As Figure 1-2 shows, we distinguish among three types of research inquiry that for purposes of this discussion we call pure social science, policy-related research, and policy analysis.

Much has been written about social science and about policy analysis [408, 438]. Policy-related research is a hybrid form drawing on both pure social science and policy analysis. It is appropriate, therefore, to define these more familiar forms first, and then to state precisely what we mean by policy-related research before we discuss its limitations and suggest how to improve it.

Pure Social Science. Pure social science emphasizes understanding rather than action. Although such conclusions are fully generalizable, they are ordinarily too abstract to be of immediate use to the policy maker. Moreover, pure social

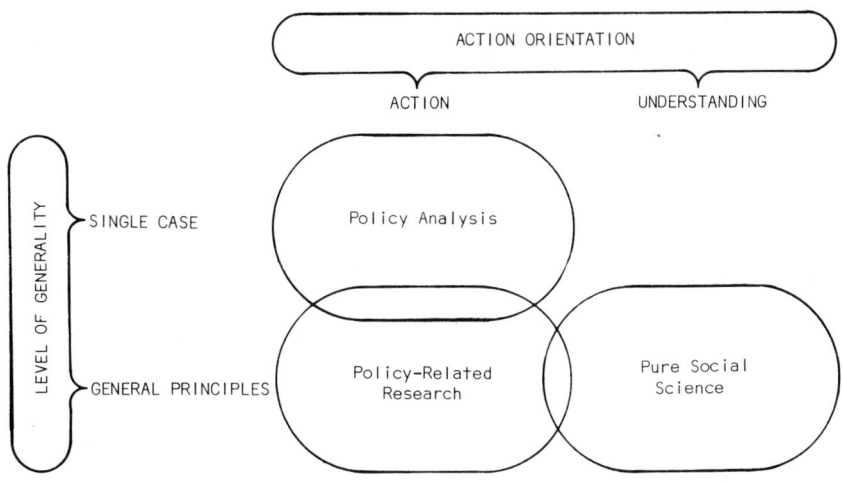

Figure 1-2. Types of Research.

science is silent on many questions that are of the greatest interest to policy makers. Too often, the social scientist is reluctant to draw conclusions because available data are not highly reliable in a probabilistic sense.

The essence of the social science approach lies in this skepticism about the validity of findings. In testing his hypothesis, the social scientist looks for alternative explanations that seem plausible. The purpose of the well designed test is to reduce the number of alternative hypotheses, leaving as the most probable the hypothesis that is being probed. The social scientist prefers to reject hypotheses even though they may be true, rather than accept something that may prove untrue. This stance has its advantages: we may feel relatively confident of hypotheses that the social science community is willing to say are well founded (laws); but the disadvantage of this approach is that it may leave us guessing in many areas where we would willingly settle for less firmly established indications of the truth if they were the best available.

Policy Analysis.[c] Policy analysis is problem-oriented in a context of action rather than pure understanding. It cannot afford the luxury of uncertainty. Where social problems and needs are pressing and require action, the policy maker needs to formulate the best possible programs.

Thus, policy analysis starts with a particular problem in a particular locale and seeks the best solution. It draws upon social science methodology when it can, or upon tools usually associated with systems analysis (mathematical programming, queuing theory, simulation, gaming, etc.). But when these methods do not succeed in answering relevant questions, the policy analyst draws upon the best indications or evidence available. Often these will be findings of social science that have not been so well validated as social science would require. They may include rules of thumb or prevailing opinion among relevant professionals. In short, policy analysis is more art than science.

The conclusions of this mode of analysis are highly specific in subject matter and are of immediate utility to one local policy maker. Unlike social science, they are limited in relevance to a single case, and will be useful in their specific findings only to policy makers concerned with a particular case. The policy analyst will make "best guesses" on relevant questions for which fully validated research findings are not available. Hence, his conclusions are as reliable as they can be, given the state of the art, but are less reliable than the results of social science. Social science may not accept as a reasonable approach to truth a conclusion that has three chances in ten of being false. But, depending upon the relative social and political costs of action and inaction, the policy maker may do better to take those odds than to rely upon hunches, stereotypes, and guesses of unknown reliability or to take no action at all for want of a scientifically proven principle.

---

[c]This is a term of art used in this study to refer to specific applications of system analysis and to single program evaluations. It does not refer to broad assessments of alternative policy options as the term "policy approach" is used by Daniel P. Moynihan [566].

Policy-related Research. Someplace between the lofty realms of pure social science, with its abstract theories and laws, and program evaluation, with its nitty-gritty applications and particularistic conclusions, resides policy-related research of the type to which this book is devoted.

Policy-related research, as we define it, involves empirical analysis of the application of a public-policy instrument in more than one limited setting. It is therefore devoted to action rather than to pure understanding, and in this sense is distinct from pure social science. But it is devoted to action in a broad variety of settings rather than to a particular action; in this sense it is distinct from policy analysis.

We believe policy findings of limited reliability and applicability derived from policy-related research on housing can still be of help to the housing policy maker. Indeed, they may be the best information available. But this will not excuse the flaws of poorly designed studies or give us better reason to think that conclusions confirmed in single cases are likely to hold in other cases. The decision maker's critical need for information does not make shoddy information any better, though it may increase its value relative to the lack of better information. The policy maker, every bit as much as the social scientist, needs to be aware of possible biases and deficiencies in the information he uses. It is for this reason that we have been rigorous in our evaluation of policy-related research on housing.

A Framework for Evaluation

Local policy makers too often tend to approach local housing problems from the limited perspective of one of the various policy instruments described earlier. This perspective leads to a piecemeal and parochial approach to the solution of policy problems. Problems are quickly pigeonholed as belonging to specific housing instruments. They are labeled as problems of zoning or housing-code enforcement, of tax policy, or of housing finance. Once a problem is defined and diagnosed in these terms, the particular policy instrument is applied for the purpose of treatment. The treatment is considered successful if the specific problem is to some degree ameliorated, whether or not other problems have been exacerbated in the process. Unfortunately, this perspective is reflected in the research literature, particularly where the researcher's purpose is to examine a specific policy instrument.

We challenge this conventional perspective in our book. As the nature of the local housing system is more clearly understood—in part through social science research—it becomes increasingly possible for local housing officials to broaden their approach to policy making and to address clusters of related problems. This may be encouraged by the transfer of local housing functions from separate municipal agencies to a single housing department or by more coordinated use and combination of the policy instruments currently employed.

There is clear historical precedent for this view. Zoning, for example, emerged in the 1920s as a more comprehensive response to the problems of incompatible neighborhood uses (conflicts among industrial, commercial, and residential activities) than the jumble of individual lawsuits that had been brought under the public-nuisance doctrine. Similarly, urban renewal agencies emerged in the 1950s as a means of combining planning, public condemnation powers, and housing-code enforcement under one roof and within one comprehensive program package. More recently, the Model Cities program further extended the comprehensiveness of urban renewal by requiring local coordination of housing and human-resource programs (job training, health, education, etc.) by one local agency within the confines of the target neighborhood.

Because we believe the current ad hoc approach of local housing officials is insufficient but amenable to change, we sought to create a framework for evaluating housing studies that would direct attention to the broader policy implications of the use of local housing-policy instruments. This framework or checklist is illustrated in Figure 1-3. The matrix links two sets of housing concepts: the housing-policy instruments we examine (which are listed down the

	HOUSING PROBLEMS									
	PROBLEMS OF QUALITY				*PROBLEMS OF QUANTITY*			*PROBLEMS OF COST AND DISTRIBUTION*		
POLICY INSTRUMENTS	Poor Private Maintenance and Management	Declining Public Services	Poor Planning and Location of New Units	Poor Construction of New Units	Insufficient Production of Public Housing	Insufficient Production of Private Units	Abandonment of Sound Units	Rising Cost of Housing Production	Rising Cost of Operation	Insufficient Income of Tenants
PLANNING AND RENEWAL TOOLS										
COMPREHENSIVE PLANNING										
HOUSING INFORMATION SYSTEM										
URBAN RENEWAL										
CODES AND REGULATIONS										
LAND USE REGULATIONS										
BUILDING CODES										
HOUSING CODES										
RENT CONTROL										
REAL PROPERTY TAX										
CONVENTIONAL PROPERTY TAX										
SPECIAL TAX ABATEMENTS AND INCENTIVES										
SITE-VALUE TAXATION										
HOUSING ASSISTANCE PROGRAMS										
SUBSIDIES										
LARGE-SCALE REHAB										
SELF-HELP PROGRAMS										

Figure 1-3. Policy Instruments and Housing Problems: An Analytic Framework.

side of the matrix); and the range of problems that threaten the health of the local housing sector (which are listed along the top of the matrix).[d]

We divide the range of problems that plague the local housing sector into three broad categories: (1) problems of housing quality, (2) problems of housing quantity, and (3) problems related to the cost and distribution of housing. Each of these categories provokes specific lines of inquiry that we use in subsequent chapters to organize the research findings, to disclose research gaps, and to assess the ultimate utility of the findings in any one policy area to the local policy maker. These more specific questions, listed below, vary with the policy instrument under scrutiny. Their purpose, however, remains the same—to broaden the frame of reference from the specific policy instrument to the underlying problems and issues of the local housing sector.

1. Problems of quality
   a) What factors account for the poor quality of private management and maintenance of housing? How can local government raise the level of private skills in these areas?
   b) What accounts for declining levels of public services (police, fire, trash removal, etc.) in certain neighborhoods? To what extent is this a problem of declining municipal financial resources? How does housing suffer? How can the level of public services be raised?
   c) What are the impacts of poor location and site planning upon the costs and availability of public services to housing? How can the public review of these private decisions be improved? With what likely effects?
   d) What impact do poor housing design and construction quality have on housing residents? Should design and construction standards be raised? How can public review of these decisions be improved?
2. Problems of quantity
   a) What accounts for shortages in local housing stocks? To what extent can local government meet these shortages through public and publicly assisted housing?
   b) By what measures can local government increase the supply of private housing?

---

[d]A matrix of this design is a flexible tool of analysis. Its principal use during the evaluation phase of this project was as a research tool, to focus attention upon the relationships—actual and potential, primary and secondary, intended and unintended—between policy instruments and housing problems. The matrix can also serve effectively to summarize the results of an evaluation of the research on a specific topic. For example, in focusing on the problem of poor private maintenance and management (the first column of the matrix), the evaluator quickly determines from the research literature that certain policy instruments, like rent control or the property tax, are more likely to aggravate the problem than to ameliorate it. But the matrix has certain limitations. It cannot easily display the more subtle and changing relationships between policy instrument and housing problem that depend upon such factors as local context and how the instrument is exercised. It is best used to explore issues and relationships and to suggest solutions or strategies. For this reason, the matrix in Figure 1-3 is presented with its cells left blank.

c) How can local government prevent the abandonment of sound housing?
3. Problems of cost and distribution
   a) What can local government do to hold down the rising costs of housing construction?
   b) What control can local government exercise over rent levels and the costs of housing operation? What are the impacts of such control in housing production?
   c) Through what measures can local government assist families with low or declining incomes who cannot afford decent housing? At what cost? With what effect on housing production?

Clearly, local policy makers cannot solve the housing problems described above with the policy instruments and resources now at their disposal. Nonetheless, they can coordinate more wisely the use of the policy tools they do control to ensure that the actions of separate local departments and agencies will complement rather than conflict with one another. The exercise of housing and land-use policy at the local level is too often characterized by mutually conflicting actions of separate agencies and departments. Case studies have frequently disclosed how the exercise of one policy instrument in treating one type of problem has nullified the effect of another policy in a related area. For example, property tax reassessment procedures may nullify special incentives for investment in rehabilitation; the zoning of undeveloped land at restrictive density levels will discourage or prevent construction of public or publicly assisted housing. Good policy-related research can tell the policy maker where these conflicts are likely to occur, how to avoid them, how to coordinate the exercise of various policy instruments so as to produce mutually supportive actions, and where basic institutional changes (the merger of existing agencies) are needed.

We sought to identify and evaluate housing studies that would serve the information needs of the policy maker in this fashion. Too often housing analysts pass over these problems entirely, focusing on too narrow a range of problems, or ignoring the broader implications of the exercise of specific policy instruments. Employing the policy framework we devised, we have occasionally synthesized the limited findings of diverse studies and have suggested the broader impacts that are likely to be associated with various policy tools.

Nonetheless, we present the research evaluations and syntheses of the following chapters with caution and qualification. Research on the policy instruments we selected to examine is widely diverse in its focus, intended audience, methodology, and general quality. The policy framework we devised imposes some degree of order on this literature. But this orderliness can be deceptive. The policy framework does no more than suggest the complex network of likely relationships between specific policy instruments and local housing problems that should be explored. It cannot improve upon bad research or relate apples to oranges; it can only help explain why the research is inadequate and point out gaps to be closed. Similarly, as a tool for the policy maker, the policy framework simply suggests that any one intervention has significant impacts upon a range of problems as well as the one causing immediate concern. It cannot tell what these impacts are or what their cumulative effect will be. For this, the policy maker must rely on his training, experience, and, we suggest, good policy-related research.

Project Design

In the two preceding sections we have discussed the general terms of our study and the framework we devised to organize our evaluation effort. In this section we explain how we actually conducted the project, specifically how we collected the research and evaluated it. In Figure 1-4, a flowchart, we present the sequence of tasks that led to the final project report.

Literature Search

While several excellent bibliographies on housing are available, none deals exclusively with research studies. We therefore launched an extensive search process to develop an entirely new bibliography, composed of writings whose titles or journal location suggested they conformed to our definition of policy-related research. The search consisted of parallel efforts to locate both the standard (in existing bibliographies and in libraries) and fugitive (largely unclassified contract research) literature on the topics selected for review and analysis.

As an initial effort we reviewed all existing standard bibliographies on housing. Several of these are published. In addition, the Council of Planning Librarians produces "Exchange Bibliographies" on selected subtopics of planning, including housing. Every work subsumed under one of our designated "policy instrument" topics was included in this original selection.

We scanned in detail the newly published shelf list of every document in HUD's (Department of Housing and Urban Development's) vast Washington, D.C. library. This library includes nearly all the studies produced under contract to federal agencies or commissions. To supplement this list of government-sponsored documents, we reviewed the HUD publication, *A Compendium of Reports Resulting from HUD Research and Technology Funding*, containing the names of persons or institutions currently performing contract research. A personal letter went to each name on this list, soliciting information about the type of research currently under way, and any other housing research performed by the person or institution during the past decade.

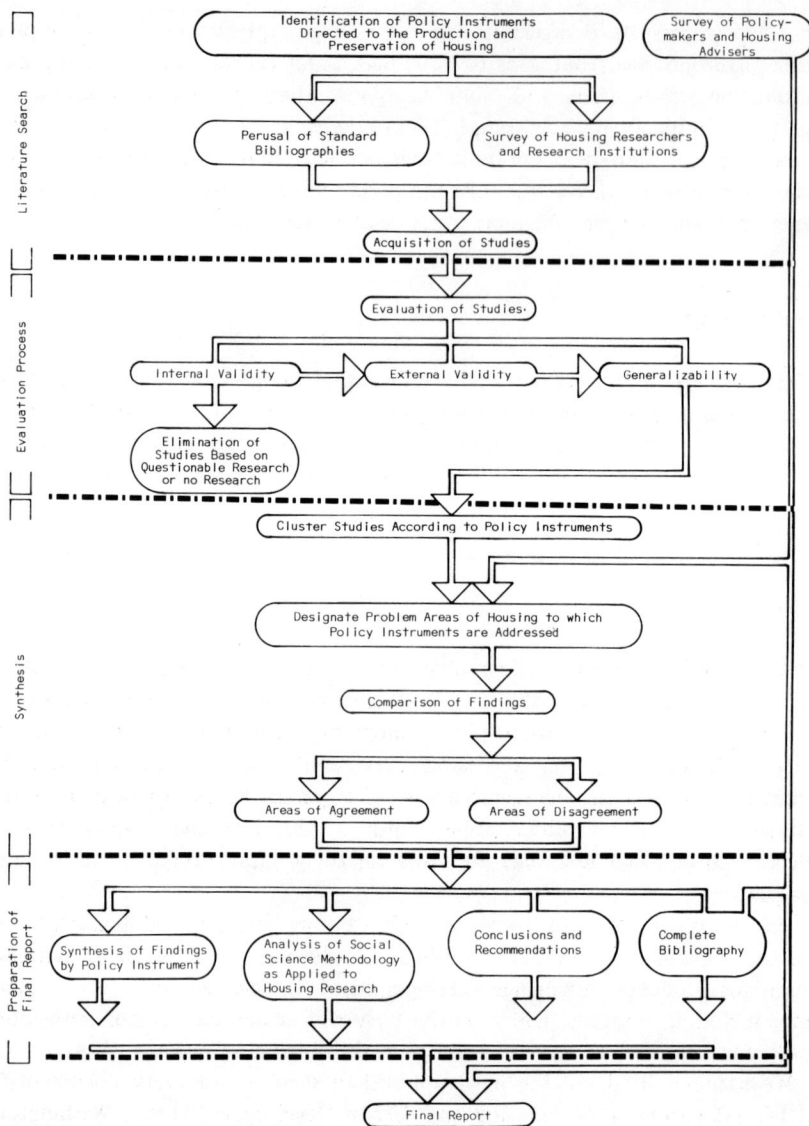

Figure 1-4. Project Design.

Indexes over the past decade were systematically searched for every social science and planning journal that might contain pertinent studies on housing. The primary resource was the Yale University Library system with its many specialty libraries on economics, the social sciences, law, and art and architecture. Journal articles thus obtained were perused for references and footnotes that were also added to the growing bibliography list.

These search efforts were supplemented by an extensive survey of all persons and institutions besides those listed in the HUD compendium known to have conducted housing research over the same ten-year period. A letter was sent to each, briefly explaining the purpose of our project, and requesting assistance in expanding our bibliography. Those addressed included governmental agencies, university research institutions, private research institutions, and individuals operating privately or through one of these institutions.

Those surveyed were asked to provide us with publication lists of housing studies. Over 200 letters were mailed. Approximately 130 responses were received. In some cases respondents sent copies of actual studies. In other cases a follow-up letter was sent requesting copies of specific studies. As a result numerous publishers transmitted copies of their studies, or let us borrow copies of publications they knew to be in short supply.

As a final effort in the bibliographic search, each of our staff researchers identified all references and footnotes cited in the particular writings they evaluated that might be germane to any of the policy instruments under study.

Unfortunately, a major bibliography on housing, produced by Virginia Paulus of Rutgers University, was published too late (May 1974) to be useful in the initial stages of our bibliography compilation. We did, however, refer to Ms. Paulus' contribution as a final check on the thoroughness of our efforts. The bulk of the bibliography search was conducted prior to February 1974. Items that came to our attention after that date had to be excluded, unless they were made immediately available to us for evaluation.

Many items in the complete bibliography were not evaluated. Most of these works did not appear to be precisely on the topic or appeared, from their titles or sources of publication, unlikely to be the results of empirical research. In other instances, however, listings quite appropriate to our study were simply unavailable, search as we might. Staff members visited libraries in New York City and Washington, D.C. (Library of Congress and the HUD Library) and utilized the resources of the Yale University libraries. But many items were either out of print or in journals not catalogued by any of our resource libraries. We were able to obtain copies of some such studies from the individuals or institutions that had written them.

Evaluation Process

The evaluation process was designed to apply principles and criteria of social science research to the studies we chose to examine. A detailed, three-part, 28-item evaluation form was designed to guide each evaluation and to ensure consistency among evaluators. Part One, the Summary Page, elicited basic bibliographic data and required only that the study fall generally within one of the policy-instrument subtopics. Part Two, the Basic Form, was used to screen out studies that did not meet our definition of policy-related research. It eliminated from further evaluation studies that were primarily historical or expository, legal-case analysis case studies that deal with a single community experience, and largely theoretical works with little or no empirical research. Finally, through the use of Part Three, the Full Form, we subjected each study that had not been eliminated in Part One or Part Two to a rigorous examination of its methodology, its assumptions, its objectives, and the validity of its conclusions. These forms are reproduced in Appendix C.

The results of this evaluation process furnished the information base for Parts II and III of this book. Part II is a synthesis of research findings within the four policy areas; Part III is an evaluation of the methodologies employed in this research, the manner in which the research findings are presented, and the institutional contexts from which this research springs.

We initially intended to exclude from discussion and synthesis any study that failed to survive the rigorous examination of the Full Form. This proved too restrictive an objective. As we explain in Part III, few studies of housing meet the criteria of good social science research. Most of the studies are flawed, some severely, others only in part. Nonetheless, many of the flawed studies were, in our view, sufficiently provocative to warrant inclusion in Part II. These findings are therefore not drawn from studies whose internal validity we can always warrant. However, internal flaws in the housing study under discussion are noted wherever appropriate.

In Part III we review the same body of research from a different perspective—shortcomings in the research process itself. This examination was based on a rigorous analysis and interstudy comparison of methodological flaws in the 68 studies cited in Chapter 6 and subjected to the criteria of the Full Form.

Thus, the evaluation process yielded these results: (1) an evaluation of each individual work; (2) an overall synthesis of findings respecting each of the 13 policy instruments; and (3) an intensive review of methodological flaws common to one or more of the studies evaluated.

Survey of Local Policy Makers and Advisers

One further element of the project design warrants comment—our surveys of the housing-information needs of local policy makers and their advisers.

On the basis of previous experience of individual project team members as housing consultants, city employees, redevelopment officials, policy advisers to mayors, and teachers of city planning, we had reason to believe that much of the available research on housing was written by academics primarily for other academics, and that it was largely ignored by local policy makers. We decided to test this hypothesis as directly as possible by surveying the policy makers themselves. The purposes of this survey were several: to identify the information sources and channels on which policy makers ordinarily rely; to assess the role of policy-related research in the local decision process; and to identify the most fruitful ways to bring the better housing research to the attention of local policy makers. Figure 1-5 presents in schematic form the results of these surveys. It lists the sources of information on housing we identified and shows the relative strength of the channels that carry this information to the local policy maker. The design, content, and results of these surveys are reported in detail in Appendix A.

We mailed questionnaires to 621 policy makers in 258 cities throughout the country, including 254 mayors, 159 city managers, 208 housing-agency executives, and 228 persons whose names were given us by the policy makers as persons on whom they rely for advice or research on housing (policy advisers). To clarify further the sources of published housing information used by local

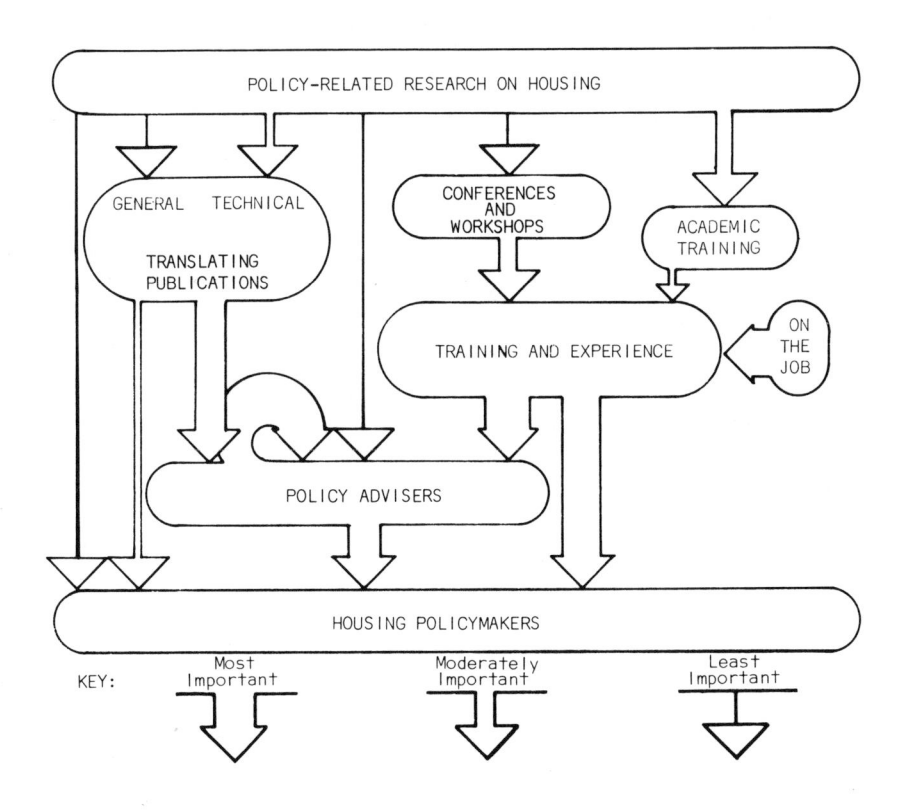

Figure 1-5. Research and Other Information Flows to Local Policy Makers: Relative Strengths.

policy makers and to ascertain the extent to which local officials rely on their own training and experience in housing, we sent follow-up questionnaires to two large subsets of our respondents.

As Figure 1-5 shows, the surveys strongly confirmed our initial hypothesis, revealing a wide gap between the production of policy-related research and its use by policy makers. A large proportion of policy makers responding to our survey make very little direct use of housing research, either in its published form, in journals that abstract or "translate" research findings into policy terms, or through other channels, such as conference or workshop sessions. Nor do the advisers whom policy makers consult often draw upon any of the research channels we identified.

There are alternative explanations for the infrequent use of policy-related research, all of which are partially valid:

1. Policy makers and their advisers rely heavily on their own training and experience in making decisions about housing.
2. No effort has been made to disseminate the findings of the better research studies to local policy makers in appropriate form.
3. With some notable exceptions, the quality of policy-related research is so poor as to discourage both its broader dissemination and its application.
4. Most policy-related research represents rather preliminary and tentative efforts of analysts to formulate theories that can explain and hopefully predict the changes that occur within the local housing sector. While this research should be closely monitored, it can hardly furnish prescriptions for public intervention.

We explore these alternative explanations at some length in our concluding chapter, in which we synthesize our findings and recommend various ways to close the gap between policy research and public actions in the local housing sector.

**Part II:
Evaluation of Research
Findings**

2

Housing Plans, Urban Renewal Programs, and Information Systems

Introduction

Comprehensive and urban renewal plans as well as related information systems are often overlooked as policy instruments with distinct impacts on the quality and quantity of local housing stocks and services. It is more common to view planning and information-gathering tasks simply as necessary but only preliminary steps taken by policy makers before they make more visible and substantive interventions in the local housing market through codes and regulations, tax measures, and housing-assistance programs.

In this chapter we take a closer look at these plans and information systems by reviewing policy-related research that has examined, directly or by implication, the present or potential impacts of these instruments upon local housing. We look at comprehensive planning, urban renewal programs, and housing-information systems in that order.

Comprehensive Planning

Comprehensive Planning and Housing Services

The topic of comprehensive planning is noteworthy for its failure to attract policy-related research. In view of the importance attributed to planning by state and federal funding sources, this neglect is not only unfortunate, but costly. We should emphasize that most public agencies and private firms engage in planning of one sort or another—program planning, day-to-day operational planning. We focus here on long-range or development planning.

The comprehensive or general plan has been defined by T.J. Kent, Jr. as "... the official statement of a municipal legislative body which sets forth its major policies concerning desirable future physical development" [420]. Most commentators have cited three essential characteristics of the plan: it is comprehensive, general, and long range.

The comprehensive plan has three objectives that directly relate to housing:

1. To serve as a guide for the zoning and other land-use control decisions of local governmental bodies
2. To serve as a guide for decisions on municipal capital expenditures—such as

for transportation, water and sewer facilities, and public buildings—that determine the location and pace of housing construction
3. To provide a reservoir of data regarding market trends, forecasts, and public policies that may increase the probability that related private decisions will be made more rationally

In this last regard, William Wheaton, a noted housing authority, has argued:

If we had better plans, which exposed their factual background, the reasons for the forecasts, and the reasons for the recommendations, and if we had plans which demonstrated with reasonable clarity that the plan was in fact obtainable, such plans could have an enormously valuable unifying effect upon the behavior of autonomous actors in the development decision processes. [908]

Few plans have satisfied Wheaton's demand. To the contrary, there has been a notable trend away from major plan efforts by municipal government on the grounds that they are too costly, necessarily vague in statement, and prematurely obsolete. One response to these criticisms has been to continue comprehensive planning but to dispense with major plan documents, emphasizing process in lieu of plan, or to shift entirely to more piecemeal, project-oriented plans.

Questions for Policy-related Research

Within the context of this debate, one would expect policy-related research to address a number of important questions concerning comprehensive planning, among them:

1. To what extent is comprehensive planning capable of improving the quality of public housing decisions and commitments? What effect does it have on the quality of private sector housing decisions?

More specifically:

2. How effectively do public plans identify and clarify community goals and objectives?
3. How realistic are their forecasts and projections?
4. To what extent do they serve as guides for the location and scheduling of public improvements?
5. To what extent do plans constrain other public agencies?
6. To what extent do public plans improve private development decisions, especially the poor design and location of new units?
7. Do plans provide more reliable market data and better long-range forecasts than the developer would otherwise obtain?

8. To what extent do public plans have unintended negative effects upon the housing market, such as discouraging investment flows or encouraging land speculation?
9. To what extent to plans enhance or impede the effectiveness of other policy instruments?

Paucity of the Literature

Most of the writing that relates to the comprehensive plan is not policy-related research as we define it. Rather, it is expository or theoretical, although in many cases highly provocative and useful. To the extent that studies have been based on original research, they have generally examined only one or a few cities, and thus may have limited generalizability.

One of the most influential studies of comprehensive planning as a housing-policy instrument is the case study of a controversy over the location of public housing units involving the Chicago Housing Authority in the 1950s—*Politics, Planning and the Public Interest* by Martin Meyerson and Edward Banfield [544]. Published in 1955, the study framed the terms of subsequent debate over the efficacy of long-range planning and systematic research by public operating agencies, such as local housing authorities.

Meyerson and Banfield examined a sequence of decisions involving how much and what kind of public housing a city should have and where it should be located. The case-study form is enlivened by the special insights that Meyerson, a principal actor in the case, brings to the narrative.

Unfortunately, the study has limited value as policy-related research. It is significant primarily for the clarity with which Banfield defines the concepts of "politics," "planning," and "the public interest," and fits them within a single conceptual scheme. These concepts are further refined in Banfield's subsequent works [44, 45]. In fact, the study yields no important policy conclusions. Instead, it concludes with Banfield's note on the conceptual scheme, underlining the fact that it is essentially an attempt to refine a set of analytic concepts for use by other analysts.

This focus on an academic peer group rather than on the policy-making community is typical of the literature in general. Policy conclusions, where they exist at all, must be pruned from the text. Among the more provocative implications of the Chicago study are the following: Comprehensive planning assumes a capacity to subordinate public and private decision makers to a single intention—an impossibility so long as power is widely dispersed and power holders have conflicting ends; the best a public agency can do is gather up what information it can about the intentions of others, private and public, and use this information to negotiate as much voluntary coordination among diverse power holders as possible.

The Chicago study is also significant for the support it lends to our survey of how policy makers use research (see Appendix A). The authors observe that the knowledge needed by the authority was not the kind that social scientists as such could supply.

> There was no reason to believe that a social scientist, or a planning technician using social science, would be better equipped, or even as well equipped, as an administrator ... to chart the agency's opportunity area, to clarify and order its end-system, to delineate the alternative courses of action that were open to it, or to identify and evaluate the consequences that would probably attend each course of action. *Social science, when it could be used at all, could probably be best used to support and make more definite some general conclusions to which the administrator had already come.* [544, emphasis added]

In sum, Meyerson and Banfield found that comprehensive planning, as such, had little value in the eyes of Chicago Housing Authority officials. And what value it did have was more symbolic than instrumental. Politics—the negotiation of agreement among competing power holders—took precedence over long-range planning, requiring a more flexible set of goals and objectives than was congenial to the planner.

In *The City Planning Process: A Political Analysis* [19], the most rigorous of the case studies on planning to follow the Chicago study, Alan Altshuler studied four cases of planning activity in Minneapolis and St. Paul. The case study that is most relevant to this discussion examines the preparation of a St. Paul comprehensive plan, on the basis of which Altshuler concludes:

1. The plan was not based on any comprehensive or carefully articulated vision of a good city.
2. The planners did not determine priorities or systematically analyze costs.
3. The plan was a cautious document that focused on what the planners believed to be consensus objectives, avoiding specific proposals for change.
4. Few political or civic leaders paid any attention to it, disillusioning the planners who had worked on it.

On the basis of these and other empirical conclusions, Altshuler argues that experienced planners believe that comprehensive planning cannot be effective without strong political support. This, he says, is one reason why planners choose to adapt to the political system in which they work rather than pursue more imaginative though controversial activities.

No doubt, the absence of inventive planners and the timidity embodied in most housing plans explain, in part, the lack of attention paid in policy-related research to comprehensive planning. This may well change as policy makers utilize plans to express their policies and views on such controversial subjects as the amount and allocation of low-income housing units within a metropolitan area.[a] The paucity of policy-related research is probably due as well to methodological problems. It is difficult to design research studies to measure the degree to which specific housing outcomes are influenced by comprehensive planning, rather than by policy tools that tend to have a more immediate and direct effect, such as regulations or subsidies. An alternative is to focus on the impact of plans on attitudes. It would be useful, for example, to examine the impact of more recent housing plans embracing "limited growth" policies on the attitudes of public officials charged with the conduct of such regulatory activities as zoning, subdivision control, and utility extension. The general research literature abounds with studies concerning the impact of recent criminal-law decisions by the Supreme Court on the attitudes of local law-enforcement officers. These impact studies draw upon research methods and measurement techniques that can be used to analyze the impact of comprehensive planning.

Urban Renewal and Renewal Planning

Definition and Description of Urban Renewal

Urban renewal combines "middle-range" planning (as compared with the long-range planning of most comprehensive plans) with a wide array of tools for implementing the renewal plan. It is the most multifaceted program for dealing with housing-related problems that we shall review in this study. We chose to examine the general process of urban renewal in this chapter, and to save for Chapter 5 a more intensive evaluation of policy-related studies that focus on the specific forms of housing subsidies and large-scale rehabilitation programs that form the complex of instruments most often referred to as urban renewal.

A program of urban redevelopment, since renamed urban renewal, was initiated as Title I of the Housing Act of 1949. Urban renewal depends upon the availability of powers of eminent domain for acquisition of blighted, deteriorating, or nonconforming property, and includes provisions for relocation, code enforcement, and rehabilitation programs. Urban renewal programs can be carried out in different parts of the city for different purposes. We examine research studies that analyze the success of urban renewal in creating new housing or improving existing housing and neighborhood facilities in residential neighborhoods.

The urban renewal program is implemented through a series of contractual relationships between the local renewal agencies and the federal government.

---
[a]A recent example of such a plan is the Miami Valley Regional Commission's *Housing Needs in the Miami Valley Region 1970-75* [545].

Local activities eligible for federal grant assistance include:
1. Land-use and resource planning
2. Use of eminent domain to acquire land and properties at fair value where redevelopment plans indicate the need for clearance or for rehabilitation costing more than present owners can or will finance
3. Concentrated efforts in code enforcement
4. Assistance in relocating displaced persons in standard living quarters at affordable rents or sales prices
5. Providing payments to displaced families, individuals, and businesses for moving expenses and additional costs that help hasten transfers to new quarters
6. Property-management activities from the time of acquisition until relocation is accomplished and subsequent clearance or rehabilitation is initiated
7. Encouraging and assisting community organizations and citizen participation in redevelopment and rehabilitation plans and actions
8. Providing guidance and technical and financial assistance for rehabilitation of private substandard properties by their owners when the condition and location of the properties indicate that such treatment will restore their physical and economic soundness
9. Installation, expansion, or improvement of public areas such as streets, sidewalks, and similar sites; and encouraging provision of supporting services through the use of noncash grants-in-aid credit
10. Disposition of cleared or improved land at prices appropriate to its new use without regard to the actual costs incurred in acquiring it and preparing it for resale

The major federal financing tool—the "land write-down"—allows the local agency to purchase and clear land and sell it to private or public redevelopers. The sale price is consistent with its reuse value. It is generally less than the cost of purchase and clearance combined, and is contingent upon redevelopment of the land in conformance with the renewal plan.

Conventional urban renewal begins with the selection and definition of the project area, extensive surveys of project conditions, and the formulation of a renewal plan.

The urban renewal plan is a detailed proposal for the improvement of a project area through demolition of structures, clearance of land, installation of public utilities and facilities, marketing of the project land, and code enforcement and rehabilitation. The plan designates the buildings to be saved and rehabilitated and those that are to be replaced by new construction. It establishes structural, aesthetic, and density standards in accordance with program requirements.

Urban Renewal—Questions for Housing Research

Urban renewal is a means of dealing with most of the housing-related problems identified in Chapter 1, particularly:

1. The high costs of housing production, particularly costs of land assembly and clearance
2. The deterioration of housing, particularly of lower priced stock
3. The decline of public services and facilities
4. The abandonment of sound units
5. An insufficient stock of public and private housing

Urban renewal is intended to deal with these problems by encouraging new construction and rehabilitation of housing and by eliminating housing of poor quality through condemnation.

Urban renewal is presumed to have two principal advantages over private market forces working on their own in addressing these problems. First, the urban renewal plan and the city's commitment to it are supposedly capable of convincing private entrepreneurs that the urban renewal neighborhood is going to be upgraded in such a way that additional investment becomes warranted. (The governmental power of eminent domain that lies behind the urban renewal process presumably heightens the developer's faith that the plan will be realized.) Second, through various subsidy tools, including land write-down, below-market interest-rate subsidies, and rehabilitation loans, the private costs of development and rehabilitation can be substantially reduced.

One looks to policy-related research to determine whether in fact urban renewal in its various forms—clearance, rehabilitation, code enforcement—is an effective and efficient means of dealing with the housing-related problems considered above. Consideration also has to be given in this research to other positive and negative effects of urban renewal. For example, what effects do renewal programs have on the strength of other housing-policy instruments? Furthermore, what are the likely effects of urban renewal programs upon factors outside the housing market, such as the revenue-raising powers of the locality, the social and political composition of the central city, and the population of local schools? Shifting our perspective, we might also want to identify the particular characteristics of those neighborhoods in which urban renewal is most likely to be an effective housing strategy.

Game-theory Analysis

A seminal work which attempts to answer some of these questions is Otto A. Davis' and Andrew B. Whinston's "The Economics of Urban Renewal" [176]. Although this analysis is entirely theoretical, it suggests many avenues for empirical policy-related research. The article adds focus and depth to the analysis of urban renewal and housing investment through the introduction and application of the economic tools of game theory and cost benefit analysis.

Davis and Whinston use game theory—which predicts the behavior of interacting parties under alternative sets of conditions—to consider what the rational actions of owners of blighted property would be under various circumstances. The authors conclude that situations clearly exist where the rational decision of an individual landlord may not result in socially desirable investment in the upgrading or redevelopment of urban properties. If the landlord acts unilaterally he may often be unable to raise the rent level in his building to cover his redevelopment costs. Instead, the benefits of his investment will accrue to his neighbors, whose properties will be enhanced at the investor's expense. In other words, there are cases where an individual investor would be better off financially if all investors in the neighborhood, including himself, upgraded their properties; but he would be worse off if he upgraded his property unilaterally.

This paradox of rationality, nicely uncovered by game-theory analysis, is called the "prisoner's dilemma." The investor, like one of two prisoners who decides to confess his crime and get a lighter sentence rather than await trial (for what if the other prisoner confesses first?), is constrained to cut his possible losses at the expense of his neighbors and the community-at-large.

According to the authors, urban renewal should be used by local policy makers to resolve this "prisoner's dilemma" where the following circumstances exist:

1. Whenever strictly individual action does not result in redevelopment
2. Whenever the coordination of decision making by some means would result in redevelopment
3. Whenever the sum of benefits from renewal could exceed the sum of the cost

Based on their theoretical analysis, Davis and Whinston reach several soundly reasoned conclusions as to how code-enforcement measures and urban renewal can be employed to resolve the investor's dilemma. They suggest that building-code standards and levels of enforcement can be used to force the coordination of investment decisions in a mutually profitable manner. The writers also emphasize that urban renewal, defined as the assembly of land, demolition, and the sale of property subject to plan restriction, removes the possibility of price gouging during the assembly stage and of windfalls resulting from piecemeal development.

Davis and Whinston then argue that choices between alternative urban renewal projects as well as decisions as to whether to undertake a specific project should and can be made on cost/benefit grounds. In fact, their analysis leads them to the rather controversial conclusion that public agencies should limit their intervention to the coordination of investment decisions through enforcement of minimum property standards. From the standpoint of the efficient allocation of resources, no federal or state subsidy—including the land-write-down subsidy—should be required for urban renewal purposes since renewal should only be undertaken when investors are willing to renew their properties without financial inducements which lower their private development costs.

Implicit in this position is Davis' and Whinston's selection of the private cost/benefit calculus as the criterion for choosing between alternative renewal projects. Regrettably, the authors do not explore in depth the possibility that social benefits, which are not included in the private investor's decision making, may exceed social costs, such as federal and state subsidies; thus, many renewal programs that appear undesirable when a private cost/benefit calculus is employed may appear optional or even attractive when social costs and benefits are added.

The Davis and Whinston analysis clearly pointed to the need for empirical research to apply game-theory and cost/benefit analysis techniques to actual urban renewal situations. Unfortunately, there has been little empirical application of game-theory techniques to urban renewal or to investor behavior in general. We still need to know how to induce socially beneficial investment decisions by private individuals.

Max Neutze's study [608], discussed in the next chapter, underscores Davis' and Whinston's suggestion that investment decisions can be encouraged and coordinated through the enforcement of property regulations. However, the empirical data presented in Neutze's study offer little evidence for the author's support of Davis' and Whinston's thesis. There have also been some useful analyses of investor behavior, particularly George Sternlieb's abandonment studies [826, 830], discussed below. Regrettably, there have been few analyses of this sort and little effort to use such empirical studies to test the Davis and Whinston model or other predictive theories.

Cost/Benefit and Budget Techniques

Davis' and Whinston's recommendation that cost/benefit techniques be applied to urban renewal has been followed in several studies. The primary purpose of most of these studies, however, has been to refine cost/benefit methodology rather than obtain reliable findings about the workings of urban renewal. Although there have been important methodological advances as a result of this emphasis, there have yet to be any significant findings derived from cost/benefit analysis. No study examines or supports the theoretical conclusion of Davis and Whinston that urban renewal can be induced without substantial public investment.

Three studies—by James C.T. Mao [519], Jerome Rothenberg [735], and Stephen D. Messner [542]—refine the cost/benefit and capital-budgeting techniques first advanced by Davis and Whinston. Mao and Rothenberg offer numerical examples of their techniques, but their studies are based upon questionable data. Messner adopts Rothenberg's technique and actually applies it to five urban projects in Indianapolis, although he, too, is forced to use estimated data for some variables. Of the three, only Messner's study meets the criteria of policy-related research. The other two are essentially excursions in methodology.

Basically, Rothenberg computes the difference between total resource costs and the increased productivity of the site land as a result of urban renewal. To the extent that the former is greater than the latter, no project is warranted unless other benefits and/or decreased social costs associated with slums exceed that margin of cost difference. Rothenberg tentatively concludes, on the basis of an examination of five Chicago urban renewal projects, that there are economies of scale in redevelopment projects. In the largest projects studied, the increased productivity of the land surpassed the total cost of renewal even before the other benefits were calculated. Furthermore, he believes that the other benefits would give additional weight to the conclusion that such projects are worthwhile.

Using similar techniques, Messner comes to contrasting conclusions about the Indianapolis projects that he studied. He concludes that in Indianapolis the increased productivity of the land did not surpass the total redevelopment cost and hence only the reduction in social costs associated with slums could justify the expenditures of resources. Furthermore, in contrast to Rothenberg, Messner argues that the potential of urban renewal as a tool to reduce these social costs is limited by the fact that many displaced slum dwellers relocate in housing that is not only more costly, but is of the same low quality as the housing they left.

Mao's study is no more conclusive. He uses sophisticated capital-budgeting techniques to evaluate an urban renewal project in East Stockton, California, but acknowledges that further application of this tool is necessary before generalizable results can be offered.

In view of the increasing use of cost/benefit analysis by municipal agencies, it is important to consider a critique of cost/benefit analysis by Robert P. Kessler and Chester W. Hartman [421], based on a case study of the Yerba Buena urban renewal project in San Francisco. This critique focuses upon the neglect by too many analysts and project promoters of the equity effects of urban renewal. Kessler and Hartman conclude that the revenues/expenditures calculation actually used by the project sponsors for Yerba Buena involves narrow private benefits and general public costs, that the revenues are overstated, and that the bulk of the cost falls regressively upon lower income families and the general public. These conclusions point to significant distortions and omissions in the cost/benefit methods urged by Davis and Whinston and practiced by Rothenberg, Mao, and others.

Of related interest are a number of sociological studies that have examined the human cost imposed by renewal on many residents of renewed neighborhoods. Herbert J. Gans, in one of the most important of these studies, *The Urban Villagers* [266], concludes on the basis of intensive study of Boston's West End that severe, unanticipated social costs were imposed as a result of the redevelopment of a valuable working-class community. Like Kessler and Hartman, Gans argues that the severity of the social costs and the distribution of costs and benefits should be given considerable weight in any analysis of urban renewal, even if these factors are difficult or impossible to quantify.

In spite of the polemical nature of much of the literature that discusses the negative effects of urban renewal, such effects are real and should be the subject of more policy-related research. For example, many urban renewal programs lie dormant; yet, the initial announcement of the plan resulted in reduced investment in capital improvement and maintenance, quick sales and abandonment of sound structures, concomitant reduction of city services, a shift in the character of tenantry to lower income families, and insuperable relocation problems. Such effects have been the subject of little if any study.

Research Gaps–Limitations of Analysis

Few of the housing-research questions listed earlier have been adequately analyzed in the studies we have reviewed. Instead, analysts have suggested tools for predicting the impacts of urban renewal planning on private investors—such as game-theory analysis—that remain largely unused. Or they have taken pains to reveal the measurement problems of the tool chiefly used to assess the benefits of urban renewal outcomes—cost/benefit analysis.

Although the results of these cost/benefit studies are of little value to policy makers at this point, further use of these techniques appears to offer some hope of determining whether or not urban renewal is an appropriate means of dealing with housing-related problems. Furthermore, the cost/benefit methods explored in these studies offer promise of use by municipal decision makers in determining whether or not to carry out particular urban renewal projects, how much they will cost, who will bear the costs, and who will benefit from them. For this reason, we provide in Appendix B a more comprehensive analysis of cost/benefit techniques as applied to housing and explain how the policy maker can make more intelligent use of this tool in spite of its present limitations.

Information Systems and Policy-related Research: Housing Abandonment as Case in Point

In spite of the existence of regional and citywide-information systems throughout the country and the increasing interest of policy makers in developing such data resources, we found virtually no policy-related research addressed to the topic. The literature tends to deal almost exclusively with the technical design of automated data systems, rather than with the more substantive question of how such systems might improve the quality of public policies and interventions in sectors like housing.

For proper planning, policy makers need information on important aspects of the housing market. Traditionally, the information readily available to policy makers for planning has been at best inadequate. This includes small-area census data, neighborhood-condition data collected to support urban renewal or model cities designation, and an occasional housing survey done by an outside consultant. An information system that would permit a ready monitoring of the housing market in the city would be of great help to local policy makers.

It is worth some speculation as to why local data on housing remain so poor. One reason is clearly the absence of strong theories, or models, or even frameworks for analysis of the local housing market that might identify the important variables on which data should be gathered in such information systems.

As we elaborate in Chapter 6, only a small proportion of the policy-related research studies we reviewed had a good theoretical backing. For the most part, theories were borrowed from economics and only modified in minor respects for the housing situation. These theories deal primarily with relatively narrow areas within the housing market. Rent control and the property tax are the prime subjects. Theory that would show the dynamics of the housing market in a more general framework is simply not available.

The lack of theory, however, is no excuse for ignoring the potential of housing-information systems. There are persuasive arguments underlying the view that good theory cannot develop in the absence of adequate data bases. Analysts and researchers are often deterred from studying problems that require prohibitive investments simply to acquire the relevant data. Moreover, while the present weakness of theory may discourage the design of large-scale, automated housing-data systems (since the substantive payoffs are still problematic), it should not discourage the development of data on a department-by-department basis, the pulling together of data sources that already exist, or the use of this data to monitor development of the more critical problems that beset local housing stocks.

We therefore decided to explore the potential utility to local policy makers of an information system for a limited though vital purpose—early public intervention to arrest large-scale housing abandonment. We selected the topic of abandonment for several reasons: There is a growing body of policy research on the subject; it is certainly among the most critical and demanding problems the local policy maker faces today; and the utility of an information system on one aspect of the housing process might suggest the potential utility of information systems on other aspects.

Policy-related Research on Abandonment

Like so many problems we have examined, the treatment of housing abandonment is hindered by the absence of theoretical insight into its causes. As two of the better analysts of the problem recently observed:

The reality of abandonment is challenging the theoretician's capacity to explain the phenomenon or predict its growth. Analysts of the reasons for the decline of blighted areas and of their prospects for renewal have brought their entire theoretical arsenal to bear on the subject but the dynamics have evaded the state of the art.... While the social costs of the decay of blighted areas have been recognized as potentially enormous, useful policies for coping with the processes at work are elusive. In part, this results from theory running behind market reality. [830, pp. xii-xiii]

The problem of abandonment has nonetheless elicited several very impressive research efforts. Particular researchers, of course, have chosen to focus their efforts differently. Two studies attempted to analyze the causes of abandonment through a comparative analysis of several cities. The Center for Community Change and the National Urban League drew upon the experience of seven cities [129]; and Linton, Mields and Coston, Inc. dealt with four cities [482]. The diffusion of effort necessitated by the comparative approach (apparently under severe time constraints) led these researchers to rely extensively upon informants and secondary sources. Their results, however, give valuable indications of the nature of the process. These results have been modified and given greater precision in studies that have concentrated on single cities.

George Sternlieb and his associates have clearly been the leaders among those who concentrated upon single cities in their analysis of abandonment. In a follow-up to the early and extensive study of tenement landlords in Newark [826], George Sternlieb and Robert W. Burchell have addressed the problem of abandonment more closely [830]. In addition, Sternlieb considered the question of abandonment in the course of his massive analysis of rent control in New York City [828].

The housing market in Baltimore has been studied in depth by William G. Grigsby and his associates in a study that is to date available only in summarized form in HUD's *Abandoned Housing Research: A Compendium* [873]. Michael Stegman, however, relied extensively upon the data and analysis of this compendium in his excellent study *Housing Investment in the Inner City* [814].

All of these reports undertook extensive surveys of participants in the housing markets in the single cities they studied. The work of Sternlieb, in particular, seems the model of modern case-study analysis.

One further study, Arthur D. Little's *Property Taxes and Urban Blight* [28] (also published—in a somewhat better written report—as Peterson, et al., *Property Taxes, Housing, and the Cities* [671]) focused on a more limited question than the general issue of abandonment. (For a detailed discussion of this study see Chapter 4.) But in the course of their analysis of the impact of the property tax in ten cities, the authors also addressed themselves more broadly to the question of blight.

The complex nature of the problem of abandonment and the lack of progress in the development of theory has meant that policy-related research studies on the problem have been somewhat unfocused. The common strategy of all of the studies on the specific problem of abandonment has been to cast the net wide in order to examine a variety of possible explanations of the phenomenon. These studies have not succeeded in isolating causes. William T. Nachbaur [583], in fact, defends this approach. He argues that there is indeed no single cause of abandonment and that only a comprehensive treatment strategy at the neighborhood level can arrest the process. This conclusion can hardly be supported on the basis of one neighborhood case study. Like those of Nachbaur, most research efforts have been addressed to the threshold problem of identifying the "syndrome" of abandonment in all of its possibly pertinent detail. Only the Arthur D. Little study of property taxes and urban blight addresses itself with any precision to the putative causes of abandonment.

Abandonment—Research Gaps

In spite of the attention paid to the subject, three principal gaps in the policy-related research on abandonment remain:

1. The most crucial is the lack of a social science theory concerning abandonment. This theory, which would certainly want to draw upon the empirical findings of the studies discussed here, might sharpen the focus of empirical research that should come later.
2. Too little attention has been paid to the early stages of the processes of urban blight that lead eventually to abandonment. These stages seem the least well understood.
3. There has been far too little research assessing the impacts of various public interventions in the housing market upon the blighting process. This research must address three central issues: First, what policy instruments are likely to arrest the processes leading eventually to the abandonment of socially valuable structures in our cities? Second, what are the costs of these policies? Third, what policy instruments have unintended negative effects and speed up the process of urban blight?

Indicators of Abandonment—A Tool for Planners

Although research literature on housing abandonment seems to present more questions than conclusions, there has been impressive agreement among the authors whose works we evaluated on the nature of the abandonment process in its broad outlines, and on some of its variables. Accordingly, we can begin to identify potential indicators of abandonment. Planners trying to develop housing-information systems can use these indicators as a basis for gathering and coordinating appropriate data. This would be a useful and relatively simple tool for most communities.

In Table 2-1 we have synthesized the findings of policy-related research on abandonment. We identify variables that have been associated by several of the policy-related research studies on abandonment with the declining health of the housing market and with eventual abandonment. For the purpose of a housing-information system, we need not be concerned with the fact that the theory and the research have not succeeded in separating causes from the concomitant efforts of private and public individuals to arrest the decline of local communities. Any variables associated with the phenomenon can be potentially valuable indicators of the failing health of the housing market. Particularly in the absence of a theory indicating which are the crucial indicators, the policy maker will want to be aware of as many as possible. Variation in a similar direction of a number of these crucial indicators might then give a more certain indication of the state of health of the market.

We imposed some structure on the list of variables by separating those that can be expected to influence primarily the demand side of the market from those that can be expected to influence the supply of housing. Under each of those categories the variables are further arranged according to the scope of the impact that the research suggests they may have. Thus, the chart divides the variables into those which apply to particular blocks, those which apply to neighborhoods, those which can be expected to influence the entire city, and those which have effects beyond the city itself.

Relying on these studies, we attempt to provide some measure of the usefulness of the variables by asking three questions:

1. How useful is it as an indicator of the health of the city's housing market?
2. Is it likely to provide an early warning of the declining health of the housing market in the city?
3. Are current data pertinent to the variable likely to be available?

Of course, different kinds of variables present different problems in data gathering. An information system of the most comprehensive kind might include periodic surveys of landlords, tenants, building conditions, financial institutions, or housing transactions. Such an information system, if the surveys were to be even moderately adequate, would be expensive. A promising minimal system, or a minimal start toward such a more comprehensive system, might profitably attempt to coordinate bits of information which are already in the files of city or state agencies. The chart indicates our best guesses about which variables might be measured by such available bits of information. The availability of such information will vary from city to city and from state to state; but we have indicated variables on which data might reasonably be expected to be available in most settings.

The chart presents our findings on these three questions.

The most interesting result of our analysis is the number of pertinent

Table 2-1
Findings of Policy-related Research on Abandonment

Variables Identified in Research Literature as Important to Abandonment	Useful Indicator Yes	Useful Indicator No	Warning Stage Early	Warning Stage Late	Warning Stage Current	Availability of Data Infrequently Collected[a]	Availability of Data Not Available
I. Demand side							
A. Block characteristics							
1. Rent paying ability of tenantry							
a. concentrated welfare tenantry	X		X		X		
b. income of tenants	X		X			X	
2. Race of tenantry							
a. concentrated minority tenantry	X		X			X	
b. racial tension between tenant and landlord	X		X				X
3. Tenant practices							
a. overcrowding in occupied units	X		X			X	
b. frequent rent skipping and arrears	X		X				X
c. high vacancy rate	X		X			X	
d. high turnover rate	X		X				X
4. Psychology							
a. bad tenant-landlord relationships	X		X				X
b. strongly antisocial tenant attitudes	X		X				X
5. Lack of resident ownership	X		X			X	
B. Neighborhood effects							
1. Racial and/or economic change, including:							
a. concentration of low-income nonupwardly mobile families	X		X				X

b. increasingly low-income all-black neighborhoods					X	
c. increasing levels of unemployment	X	X	X			
d. concentrated welfare tenantry	X	X	X			
2. Social pathology						
a. increased vandalism	X	X	X			
b. increased crime rate	X	X	X			
c. increased fire incidence	X	X	X			
d. riots	X	X	X			
3. Low reputation of neighborhood	X	X				
4. High overall vacancy rate, but low vacancies in occupied buildings	X	X				
C. Citywide indicators						
1. Outflow of upper and moderate-income households	X			X	X	
2. Inflow of low-income households	X			X	X	
3. Inflow of welfare recipients	X		X			
4. Absolute population decline	X			X		
D. Broader than city						
1. Changes in national migration patterns	X					
2. Demographic changes, for example, in household formation rates	X					
3. Loss of function by city	X					
II. Supply Side						
A. Block characteristics						
1. Ownership characteristics						
a. absentee white owners	X		X			X

Table 2-1 (cont.)

Variables Identified in Research Literature as Important to Abandonment	Useful Indicator Yes	Useful Indicator No	Warning Stage Early	Warning Stage Late	Warning Stage Current	Availability of Data Infrequently Collected[a]	Availability of Data Not Available
b. owner-inherited buildings	X		X		X		
c. small-investor owners	X		X				X
2. Owner attitudes							
a. bad landlord-tenant relationships (including racial antagonism)	X		X				X
b. prior unachieved desires to sell	X		X				X
c. low expectations of future value	X		X				X
3. Building characteristics							
a. older buildings	X		X		X		
b. resale value declining, very low, or nonexistent	X			X			X
c. overassessment	X		X				X
d. property vandalized	X			X	X		
4. Financing							
a. noninstitutional financing, or none	X		X				X
b. speculation and overmortgaging	X		X				X
5. Management							
a. decreased maintenance expenditures	X		X				X
b. "arms length" professional management	X		X				X
c. lack of insurance	X		X				X
d. mismanagement	X		X				X
e. negative cash flow	X			X			X
f. weekly rent collection	X			X			X

g. property tax arrearage
h. foreclosures by city or financial institutions

B. Neighborhood effects
  1. Impact of nearby buildings
     a. adjacent abandonment
     b. foreclosures by city or financial institutions
     c. concentration of substandard buildings
     d. declining rate of homeownership
     e. adverse effects of nearby public works or renewal projects
  2. Institutional impacts
     a. redlining by financial institutions
     b. decreased public services
     c. redlining by insurance companies
     d. exploitative real estate practices

C. Citywide indicators
  1. Rising costs
     a. increased cost of maintenance services
     b. risk premium on workmen's fees
     c. rising property tax
  2. Housing availability
     a. increased alternatives for minority and moderate income families to live outside the ghetto
     b. prior overbuilding

Table 2-1 (cont.)

Variables Identified in Research Literature as Important to Abandonment	Useful Indicator		Warning Stage			Availability of Data	
	Yes	No	Early	Late	Current	Infrequently Collected[a]	Not Available
D. Broader than city							
1. Rising costs							
a. general inflation		X					
b. increasing insurance rates		X					
c. increasing utility rates		X					
d. increasing interest rates		X					
2. Income tax provisions (depreciation deduction, etc.)		X					
3. Suburban development		X					
4. Negative social image of slum landlord		X					
5. Loss of function by the city		X					

[a]This information is collected by the Bureau of the Census at ten-year intervals.

Table 2-2
Indicators on Which Information May be Available

Variable	Indication	Public Source
Concentrated welfare tenantry, by block and neighborhood	early	Welfare
Level of unemployment by neighborhood	early	Labor
Vandalism, fire, crime, riots, by neighborhood	early	Police, fire
Inflow of welfare recipients to city	early	Welfare
Owner-inherited buildings, by block and neighborhood	early	Land records
Age of buildings, by block and neighborhood	early	Building
Vandalized property, by block and neighborhood	late	Police, fire
Property tax arrearage, by block and neighborhood	late	Tax
Foreclosure by city or financial institutions, by block and neighborhood	late	Land records
Concentration of substandard buildings, by neighborhood	early	Planning
Decreased public services, by neighborhood	early	Public works

variables it shows on which current data may be available. Most of these variables could provide early indications of the failing health of the city's housing market. These variables are singled out in Table 2-2, together with the name of the municipal agency most likely to have the appropriate data.

Gathering this data and putting it into a form appropriate for use in a housing-information system that would assist the policy maker would not be simple. Sources of such data may vary from city to city or not be available at all. But there is every indication that much potentially useful information is available. Those planning a housing-information system need not start entirely from scratch. Whether an information system based on these variables would provide an adequate picture of the health of the housing market is an open question. It would surely be an improvement on the information now typically available to the local policy maker. And, to the extent that the development and refinement of strong theory depends on the analyst's access to good data, this effect should advance understanding of the abandonment process and of the general housing system.

Conclusions

The foregoing survey of the research literature on the three related policy instruments—housing plans, urban renewal programs, and information systems—demonstrates the paucity of research on point. We cannot even say that the research satisfies the observation quoted earlier from the Meyerson and Banfield study [544] —that the research supports or makes definite some general conclusions to which policy makers have already come. With one exception [542], the studies we discuss fail to meet the criteria of policy-related research. They are discussed because they advance or refine some relevant theory or methodology, or because they have something provocative to say. The policy maker cannot look to the sources for valid and transferable conclusions as to how to use the policy instruments in question more wisely. In short, the studies we surveyed are addressed primarily to the housing analyst, not the housing practitioner.

The research agenda is broad. Theory enabling the analyst to relate the use of housing plans or information systems to specific housing outcomes is at best rudimentary. Attempts to measure the costs and benefits of the outcomes of urban renewal programs need much refinement. Case-study conclusions based on participant-observation research must suffice for the present. These conclusions—to the extent that they are drawn from the specific context of the study—are of limited generality. Comparative case-study analysis of the type discussed in Chapter 6 may be a partial answer, though an expensive one.

Inadequate theory seems to be the nub of the problem. There is little evidence that housing analysts have identified the key variables that account for changes in housing quality, quantity, cost, or distribution in the local community. This is best illustrated by the research on housing abandonment. There are several exhaustive studies of the abandonment process, but they do little more than list the outward indications of the abandonment syndrome. There is a significant distinction between a list of indicators and a designation of the key variables that account for changes—a distinction that can be drawn only when an explanation of the process of change is formulated. This, again, is essentially a call for helpful theory.

3

Codes and Regulations

Introduction

Policy-related research on land-use regulations, building and housing codes, and rent control is a principal focus of this study. These instruments regulate the planning, design, construction, operation, and maintenance of housing, and they afford considerable latitude for discretion by local decision makers. They form a continuum ranging from the most general guidelines that loosely regulate the relationships between land and buildings to the most specific strictures detailing conditions of occupancy and rent levels of housing units.

In spite of some overlapping, most of the codes focus on different aspects of the development process: Zoning regulates the type and density of housing that can be placed on a parcel of land; subdivision codes deal with the division of land into building lots and the design of supporting site improvements; building codes deal with construction standards and materials specifications; housing codes regulate occupancy factors relating to the health of tenants and the structural conditions of existing housing; and rent control deals with rent levels.

These regulations fall within the state's general mandate under the police power to promote the public health, safety, and general welfare. State enabling legislation is typically general. It sets minimum standards and leaves the locality with relatively broad discretion in the drafting and application of standards. An exception to this general rule exists for municipalities subject to state building codes. Even in those cases the enforcement of such standards may still vary widely from place to place within the state. In total, these codes are the principal instruments localities use to control the quality, quantity, and location of housing, and thereby strongly determine the physical character of the community.

This system of regulation, characterized by local flexibility and autonomy, results in a wide variety of codes and ordinances. Administrative regulations and staff practices and requirements also vary significantly between municipalities. The resulting diversity of land use and building standards has prompted a call from the federal level for reform and reorganization. This is essentially a call for the transfer of land-use function from the municipality to broader governmental jurisdictions—metropolitan, county, regional, state—so as to reduce the costs of diversity and to achieve more uniform and equitable land-use controls over larger geographic areas.[a]

---

[a]This reshaping of institutional authority is discussed at length in the Report of the National Commission on Urban Problems (Douglas Commission) [588], especially on pp. 235-53.

By and large, land-use regulations and building and housing codes aim at improving the quality of private housing, coordinating decisions in developing areas, and maintaining the existing character of residential neighborhoods and estates in relatively undeveloped areas. Exclusionary zoning—the exercise of zoning to exclude low-income families and minority-group members from a town—is an extreme example of the latter. Increasingly, however, social scientists have emphasized that the exercise of zoning and subdivision power has additional unintended negative effects upon the housing market. In particular, the enforcement of regulations and codes often exacerbates the problems of insufficient housing production and rising costs of production and operation, frequently counteracting the effect of other policy instruments designed to alleviate these conditions. The better research on housing codes and regulations has looked carefully at the unintended negative effects of code enforcement and the trade-offs made by policy makers and housing officials, expressly or by implication, when they attempt to resolve problems of housing quality at the expense of quantity, cost, and distribution.

In the following sections we review the research literature under the following headings: land-use regulation, building codes, housing codes, and rent control. Falling outside the scope of our study is research on fair housing laws and the racial impacts of zoning practices, although these subjects are clearly relevant.[b]

Land-use Regulation

Nature of the Literature on Land-use Regulation

There is extensive literature analyzing zoning codes and other forms of regulation. The bulk of this literature—largely surveys and reports—has been descriptive and exhortative rather than analytic. These surveys and reports have heightened public awareness of the issues and have generated interest in resolving outstanding problems. They do not, however, constitute policy-related research. Only a handful of studies has attempted to measure the impact of these instruments on the major problems that confront local policy makers, for example, the impact of zoning and subdivision standards on housing costs or of zoning practices on the location, quality, and quantity of housing units.

There are several possible explanations for the paucity of empirical research on local land-use regulations. First, most of the funding for major research projects comes from the federal government and large national foundations that focus on issues of nationwide import. In this respect the wide variety of local regulations discourages research and makes generalizations to the national level difficult.

Second, the multiplicity and variety of regulations demand extensive and

---
[b]See earlier explanation and footnote b, Chapter 1.

costly survey and data collection. This has been undertaken in part by the National Commission on Urban Problems (hereafter referred to as the Douglas Commission) through its technical reports on the content and administration of codes and ordinances throughout the United States. Several of these reports are discussed below.

A third possible explanation for the relative absence of research on this subject is the role local regulations play in the politics of our urban areas. The formulation and administration of local codes and regulations involve a delicate balance of the most powerful interests on the local scene: homeowners, developers, construction trades, lenders, town and city government, among others. Many analysts view the reform of these codes as more of an exercise in political statesmanship than a technical problem.[c]

Questions addressed by studies of zoning and other land-use regulations generally pertain to some aspect of the broad question of how existing codes affect the production and conservation of housing. Of particular interest is the question of whether local regulations have had an adverse effect on the development of an efficient, large-scale construction industry or have otherwise raised housing costs. These questions are raised with respect to both the substance of the regulations and the way they are administered.

The most comprehensive and influential study of these questions is contained in the staff report of the Douglas Commission [588] and its separately published research studies. The staff report, *Building the American City* [588], concludes that zoning and subdivision regulations are among the chief barriers to the efficient production of housing through a modern, large-scale construction industry. On the basis of this finding, the commission suggests that local control and its resulting complexity be reduced and greater power be given to regional, state, or federal agencies. The research studies, particularly American Society of Planning Officials (ASPO) [21] and Alan D. Manvel [515], provide the policy maker and potential researcher with perhaps the most useful catalog of current code elements and practices. In the course of its deliberations, the commission staff also weighed the opinions of leading participants in the housing field (builders, representatives of government agencies, planners, architects, etc.), held public hearings, and conducted field visits to urban areas.

Unfortunately, like many other influential reports on housing policy, for example, President's Committee on Urban Housing [688] and Anthony Downs [199], the Douglas Commission report defies proper evaluation. Its sampling procedures, the reliability of its research methods, and the types and modes of analysis are rarely exposed to view. The report is more like a good legal argument, a Brandeis brief, than an example of policy-related research. We refer to its findings where appropriate in this and succeeding sections, but with a general caveat as to their reliability.

---
[c]This point is advanced by John Mollenkopf and Jon Pynoos [558].

Effects of Zoning

A major study of the effects of zoning and other land-use regulations on housing costs, *Zoning and Housing Costs*, was conducted by Lynne Sagalyn and George Sternlieb in 1973 [747]. Their objective was to determine the degree to which such controls decrease the supply of available housing by raising the purchase price of new single-family homes. In an examination of new subdivisions in New Jersey, the authors compare differences in the selling price of new houses with (1) selected zoning and subdivision provisions of the township, such as minimum lot size and dwelling-area requirements; (2) various building regulations, such as minimum thickness of exterior walls and foundations; (3) the scale of the builders' operation; and (4) other factors, such as the density of the subdivision and the socioeconomic characteristics of the local population.

Sagalyn and Sternlieb conclude from this analysis that a variety of zoning and subdivision regulations—particularly those concerning floor area, lot size, and frontage—have a large and significant impact on the price of new housing. Therefore, the authors argue that reductions in these minimum requirements would increase the production of lower priced housing. Their analysis showed that the socioeconomic status of the community and the developer's scale of operation are somewhat less important factors but significant nonetheless in explaining price variations.

On the other hand, variations in building codes among New Jersey townships explain little of the variance in housing costs. Therefore, the study provides no basis for arguing that changes in building-code requirements would have a significant impact upon the price of new housing.

The influence of zoning administration on land costs and the intensity of housing development is one of the many issues considered by Max Neutze in *The Suburban Apartment Boom* [608]. This is essentially a study of the causes behind the boom in suburban-apartment construction in the 1960s. In the process, the study looks closely at the role of land speculators and their relation to public officials. Neutze relates variations in the proportion of building permits issued for new apartments in the Washington, D.C. metropolitan area to changes in demographic factors, building costs, tax provisions, consumer tastes, and zoning policy. He concludes that demographic factors, such as the increase in smaller families, are the prime causes of the variations in suburban-apartment construction. However, the willingness of zoning administrators to rezone suburban areas to higher densities, thereby providing a source of relatively inexpensive land for apartment developers, is also a dominant factor in attracting new apartments to the suburbs. This factor accounts for the vulnerability of suburban zoning commissions to undue developer influence for zone changes, since substantial windfall profits are involved. This has been a major source of litigation in the suburban communities Neutze surveyed.

Interestingly, Neutze is one of the few analysts to consider the proposition of

Otto A. Davis and Andrew B. Whinston [176] that public bodies can influence the actions of private developers without resorting to substantial subsidy, simply by reducing uncertainty about the future use of land. Neutze argues that this uncertainty can be reduced and land-use decisions coordinated more effectively by more purposeful public investment in roads, sewers, and schools and public control over private utility extensions. Public planning, in his view, should include both public capital-budget commitments and forecasts of private land-use activity. The more reliable the forecasts, the better they would function as deterrents to private-investment decisions that fall outside the mainstream, that is, that run counter to the public interest as expressed in public plans. And opening the zoning process to public scrutiny by subjecting plans and forecasts to public debate can deter collusion between developer and zoning officials.

Once again, the problem with this argument is that it is essentially exhortative. There is little evidence that the outcome of public land-use planning has in fact been salutary. Neutze has no basis for assigning such an expanded role to the public sector or thinking it can be performed well other than his recognition that there is no effective way for the private sector to compensate the public for the injurious external effects of land speculation. Neutze concludes his study by acknowledging that his propositions require empirical testing. As we discussed earlier, this is not an easy task. Except for some work in welfare economics and public finance, the literature on land-use planning and the housing market lacks a theoretical framework.

In a study somewhat similar to that of Neutze, Frederick Buttel [116] relates the percentage of land converted to urban use at higher than the prescribed zoning densities to several social, economic, and land-use characteristics of towns in South Central Connecticut. Although he does not distinguish between housing and other uses, we can assume that housing was his focus. The towns he studied are primarily residential and the majority of zoning conversions are to high- or medium-density housing. Buttel concludes from his study that less developed towns, those characterized by higher proportions of vacant and unsubdivided land, are less apt to rezone land to higher densities than are developed towns. This suggests a process by which the integrity of a zoning district undergoes routine, and not necessarily detrimental, subversion when the town has nearly exhausted its available land resources—but not before.

Research on Zoning and Property Tax Issues

There are two additional topics related to the impact of zoning on housing costs that have attracted policy-related research—zoning for fiscal purposes and exclusionary zoning. Research on fiscal zoning deals with the municipal costs and tax revenues of alternative forms of housing development. One purpose of these studies is to identify good "taxables"—those forms of development that do not require heavy municipal outlays for services. Several research studies have addressed this issue, among them the New Jersey study by George Sternlieb and his associates [829]. Because this research involves issues of municipal-property tax policy as well as zoning, we defer discussion and evaluation of these studies to the next chapter.

There is also an increasingly important body of research on the causes and effects of "exclusionary zoning." This term refers to the use of zoning powers by suburban communities to prevent an influx of low-income families or minorities. As explained earlier (p. 7), we did not feel that we could survey and evaluate this research literature adequately within the confines of this book on municipal housing services. Nonetheless, in the context of our discussion of research on the property tax we do evaluate a recent study by Eric J. Branfman, Benjamin I. Cohen, and David M. Trubek [85] on the relative impact of racial and fiscal factors in motivating zoning policies.

Research Gaps

Additional research is still needed on the subjects discussed and analyzed in these studies, since each study attempts to draw broad conclusions from the analysis of a limited geographical area. We need some confirmation that Lynne B. Sagalyn and George Sternlieb's conclusions about zoning hold true beyond New Jersey. We also need more studies that hold other factors constant, such as building codes and/or market conditions, in order to isolate the effects of zoning from other influences.

It is clear from the few research studies we have surveyed that zoning has a substantial impact upon the principal problems associated with housing quality, quantity, cost, and distribution. In addition, zoning practice undermines land-use planning and thwarts other programs, such as housing subsidies, designed to combat inequities in the supply of housing. In view of the disturbing lack of research studies that examine these effects of zoning, we recommend a rather extensive research agenda to fill this gap. The research should address one or more of the following questions:

1. Are neighborhoods zoned for a single use with few variances and nonconforming uses maintained better or worse than areas of mixed use?
2. What impact, if any, does density have on levels of housing maintenance?
3. How effectively does conventional zoning channel housing to specific neighborhoods, prevent overbuilding, and promote more efficient types of development?
4. Do the more flexible forms of zoning—floating zones, cluster provisions, planned residential development districts—promote more efficient types of development in terms of the ultimate costs to the occupant and the

municipality? Do the potential savings offset the added costs of administration? Do such zoning innovations hinder or promote the development of lower cost housing?
5. What factors are most influential in promoting more uniform and equitable zoning administration?

Additional questions one should pose relate to the impact of zoning on the municipal tax base—fiscal zoning policy. These questions are raised and discussed in the following chapter on real property taxation.

Building Codes

Purpose of Building Codes

The general purpose of building codes is to guarantee the structural and mechanical integrity of new construction, including its fire resistance. Model codes for each region of the United States have been promulgated by various national organizations, chiefly the Building Officials Conference of America, the International Conference of Building Officials, and the American Insurance Association. These codes have been adopted in about 1,600 communities. Although the standards of the principal model codes are considered adequate, local regulations are often more stringent. Problems also tend to arise in the local administration of building codes because of either inadequate size and skill of staff or the deliberate subversion of regulation.

Impact of Codes on Costs

Debate on building codes has not concentrated upon the primary intention of the policy—to prevent the construction of unsafe housing—largely because the codes work fairly well in this regard. Instead, the debate has centered on the extent to which the codes raise construction costs and thus limit the supply of housing, particularly low-cost housing.

The conventional wisdom on the impact of building codes on the costs of housing construction is expressed in the technical studies and final report of the Douglas Commission. These reports argue that the diverse requirements of local building codes prevent the development of an efficient housing market in three ways: (1) The costs of materials required by many of the codes exceed the costs of safe, available substitutes; (2) the stipulations of codes discourage experimentation and development of new materials and building techniques; and (3) the diversity of materials required by various codes prevents builders from broadening their markets and thus restricts the development of a broad-based industry with competing suppliers.

The commission concludes that the effect of diverse standards upon the ability of developers to broaden their markets is substantial. It estimates that the requirements imposed by local jurisdictions in excess of model-code requirements would cost a prefabricated home manufacturer nearly $2,000 per home if he attempted to market in each of the 20 states surveyed [588]. The reliability of this calculation is questionable, however, for it is based on estimates by prefabricated home manufacturers with large multistate markets who consequently have a substantial stake in promoting code uniformity and reform.

Other reports, using somewhat more objective methods and considering the total costs of housing—including costs of land assembly, construction materials, labor, builder, and homeowner's financing—have reached conclusions that contradict the commission's position. As mentioned, Sagalyn and Sternlieb [747] found, in their analysis of code provisions and actual sales prices, that provisions of local building codes emerged as a relatively insignificant element in the determination of total housing costs. This finding must be qualified by the fact that building-code standards are uniformly high in New Jersey, the study area; thus, differences among local code provisions are small and cannot account for differences in housing cost.

In their study, the *Effects of Constraints on Single-Unit Housing Costs* [580], Richard F. Muth and Elliot Wetzler also conclude that the costs imposed upon builders as a result of local departures from national code standards are small. Their study compares sales prices in selected standard metropolitan statistical areas using as variables regulations, enforcement practices, market size, availability of supplies, and unionization of work force. They found unionization to be the most significant variable. The sample here is broader than in other studies, but the difficult task of operationalizing the complex variables limits the acceptability of these conclusions.

A student article in the *Columbia Journal of Law and Social Problems* dealing with building codes and residential rehabilitation [106] also concludes that construction cost rises are not due to the technical provisions of codes. However, this study relies on the opinions of agency administrators as the basic source for conclusions.

While we do not have sufficiently reliable data to reach a final conclusion on this issue, we give greatest weight to those studies that relate actual market-cost increases to specific elements of building-code regulation. Similarly, we give greater weight to those that attempt to collect a variety of opinions, however poor their sampling procedures, than those that rely on the opinions of a single class of respondent. By these criteria, the Sagalyn and Sternlieb and Muth and Wetzler studies present more objective data than does the Douglas Commission. Likewise, the Douglas Commission findings are more convincing than the *Columbia Journal* article. Thus, while no final conclusion can be reached, the more reliable studies conclude that the technical provisions of building codes are not a major determinant of housing costs. Again, this is not to say that substantial reductions in building-code standards would fail to have a major effect on housing costs. They most certainly would. The question—not yet addressed by research—is whether reductions are warranted. Put another way, to what extent do existing code standards reflect the desires of the building-materials industry rather than the requirements of health and safety?

Impact of Codes on Quality

Another major subject of interest to decision makers is the impact of codes upon the quality of new construction. Although codes are designed to ensure structural integrity, there have been contentions that deserve serious investigation to the effect that codes have obstructed the introduction of new and possibly superior technology. The Douglas Commission has concluded that the greatest hurdle to overcome in the product-approval process is the local building code. The commission stated that the model codes themselves provide sufficient flexibility, but that variations among local codes create a chaotic situation. A survey conducted among home manufacturers for the International City Management Association (ICMA) *1971 Municipal Yearbook* [231] further confirms the conclusions of the commission. Again, both conclusions are flawed by the potential bias of the informants.

Fairness of Administration

Questions are also raised by the Douglas Commission, the *Columbia Journal* note, and the *Municipal Yearbook* article concerning ways in which codes are administered. The fairness of administration and the quality and size of code-agency staffs may also have an impact on the costs of construction and the introduction of possibly superior technology. The commission concluded that current administrative practices have detrimental effects upon housing quality and raise costs. In contrast, the respondents to the *Columbia Journal* survey did not feel that code administration had any negative impact on housing quality or costs. Again, these works are based primarily on interviews with informed respondents.

Another problematic aspect of code administration is that building permits are frequently granted or denied on political grounds. The impact of permits granted to structurally unsound housing undermines the intended purpose of building codes—the protection of housing quality. Permits are also denied as a last-ditch effort to prevent or discourage the development of low or moderate-income housing. In the latter case, code administration adds to the problem of inadequate supply of low-cost housing. Problems in acquiring evidence of political tampering in code administration make it difficult to measure the overall impact of such unscrupulous practices.

Research Gaps

There is a direct connection between building codes and housing codes. Research might investigate the relationship between housing condition, measured by numbers of code violations, and the technical and administrative provisions of building codes. For example, does the encouragement of certain types of building materials lead to higher subsequent maintenance costs, thereby increasing the chances of housing-code violations and contributing to the future abandonment of sound housing units?

The implicit trade-offs made by policy makers when they attempt to set high safety standards at the expense of lower cost housing production must also be examined. For example, the use of mandated building materials may decrease the risk of fire to the integrity of the structure only slightly; yet, the increase in material costs may be substantial enough to price new units beyond the reach of low-income groups. A cost/benefit approach might be used to examine whether the small decline in risk is worth the large drop in housing production for low-income tenants. General theoretical approaches to risk have been developed in the analysis of portfolio investment, and these suggest a possible methodology for a study of building-code trade-offs.

There is also a need for longitudinal studies comparing the condition of housing built under performance-standard codes with those subject to specification codes. The former set standards for compliance; the latter specify actual materials. Research of this nature would provide the local decision makers with basic information needed to make and justify code revisions. The administrative costs associated with different types of codes require research as well.

The secondary impact of codes upon housing-subsidy programs, particularly those that encourage technological innovation, is another area that could be profitably studied. Reports on Operation Breakthrough and on various rehabilitation programs assert that codes do significantly impede these programs, but the findings are inconclusive. A study on the impact of building-code provisions upon mobile-home manufacture would also be timely, since mobile homes may well be the best example of acceptable low-cost housing. Code provisions and administrative practices have a significant impact upon the success of self-help programs that attempt to involve new participants in the production of housing. This also needs study. Like zoning, building codes are a fertile but neglected area for rigorous research.

Housing Codes

Purpose of Housing Codes and Enforcement Programs

Housing codes set minimal standards of health and safety relating to the quality of basic facilities, level of maintenance, and occupancy of a housing unit. The most widely used code, first published in 1952, was developed by the American Public Health Association (APHA) and the U.S. Public Health Service (USPHS) and includes elements from the housing codes of the model-building-code groups.

Housing codes originated as codifications of common-law nuisance concepts. The requirements of the Housing Act of 1954 encouraged their adoption by cities and towns throughout the country. This act required that communities seeking urban renewal funds and other federal aid must adopt a "workable program for community improvement." The administrative regulations of the act interpreted the requirements to include adoption of building and housing codes and formulation of a plan of enforcement. While many cities had building codes at the time, no more than 100 cities had housing codes. Due to the workable program requirement and the incentives described below, about 5,000 local governments had adopted housing codes by 1968.

Incentives were introduced in the 1965 Housing Act through the provision of code-enforcement grants. The grants covered two-thirds of program costs in cities with populations of 50,000 and above, and three-quarters of the costs in cities with populations under 50,000. The money was to be spent on general program administration, administration of rehabilitation programs, and public improvements. To qualify for code enforcement aid, an area had to be primarily residential (with code violations in no less than 20% of the buildings) and of such a nature that the program could be expected to eliminate violations and to arrest decline in the area.

Housing Codes—Issues for Research

Housing code-enforcement programs are a response to the problems created by poor private maintenance and management of the existing housing stock that, in turn, are often a function of rising costs of operation and the insufficient income of certain classes of tenants. The basic issues suitable for research include the relevance and adequacy of existing standards, the degree to which housing-code enforcement has improved housing conditions, the potential effectiveness of enforcement programs, the impact of these programs on the costs of operation and the likelihood of abandonment, the effect of these programs upon the supply of housing units for particular income groups, and the negative effects of code enforcement upon other housing policies and programs outside the housing sector.

We found no rigorous empirical studies treating housing codes or the costs and effectiveness of code-enforcement programs. The state of that art is presented by the Douglas Commission [588, pp. 273-307] and in the supporting technical reports [288, 515, 561] —that housing-code standards are inadequate; that there are no generally agreed-upon definitions for such key terms as "adequate," "in safe condition," and "in good repair"; and that the code is frequently unenforced. The commission recommends a total revamping and enlargement of the local code-administration function through the creation of housing-services agencies. This agency would provide information and technical assistance to public and private developers and managers of housing.

Equally important, the Douglas Commission acknowledges the need to reformulate the basic standards for a "decent home," and suggests that an Institute of Environmental Sciences be established to conduct the research, testing, and processes required for such an effort. In this regard, the commission notes that the APHA study, *Planning the Home for Occupancy* [25], over 25 years old, is still considered the most thorough analytic work on the effects of housing upon health.

Several works besides the Douglas Commission studies, while not strictly research studies, deal with the merits of code-enforcement programs. The Department of Housing and Urban Development (HUD) [872] conducted an evaluation of the concentrated code-enforcement program, but, again, the evaluation was based primarily on interviews and site visits. This evaluation concludes that the majority of programs have been successful in improving physical conditions, stabilizing neighborhoods, prolonging the economic life of structures, and reducing abandonment. However, no valid measures are developed to determine how much improvement is derived for each subsidy dollar expended, nor is any satisfactory definition of stability proposed.

Frederick E. Case's study of code enforcement in urban renewal [123] is a methodological analysis of the costs and benefits of code enforcement. The author tentatively concludes that code enforcement is acceptable to homeowners, but burdensome on renters to whom the costs of enforcement are passed. In terms of its effects on municipal costs, Case does not feel that code enforcement will reduce short-term public-service expenditures such as police, fire, and trash removal in a neighborhood, although it is likely to increase building assessments and, consequently, property tax revenues.

Code Enforcement—When to Use

One of the most productive works on the relative merits of code enforcement is Bruce Ackerman's article, "Regulating Slum Housing Markets on Behalf of the Poor..." [10]. In this theoretical work, Ackerman manipulates an economic model of the slum-housing market to determine appropriate preconditions for an effective code-enforcement program.

Ackerman concludes that in a variety of situations a code-enforcement program accompanied by a special housing subsidy to either landlord or tenant can generate more benefits to the poor than a negative income tax or income-maintenance program of comparable dimension. A government dollar spent on a housing subsidy in support of code compliance benefits not only the direct recipients of the subsidy but other poor tenants who, under Ackerman's analysis, would receive improved housing with no increase in rents. A government dollar spent on a negative income tax or income-maintenance program lacks this scope and leverage. Ackerman's analysis also suggests that the effectiveness of code-enforcement programs may depend upon the structure of ownership in the target neighborhood. In slum neighborhoods where buildings are controlled by relatively few landlords who coordinate pricing policies, code enforcement can generate greater benefits to poor tenants than comparable programs conducted in slums where ownership is divided among a large number of competing landlords.

Ackerman's conclusions are dependent upon a series of assumptions about the structure of the slum-housing market and the nature of the code-enforcement program. For example, he assumes a fairly low level of interest among slum residents in paying additional rents for improvements, little interest among people outside the slum in moving into the area if code standards are enforced, uniform code enforcement in the entire slum area, and sufficient government funds to prevent a decline in the supply of slum housing when code standards are enforced. The realism of some of Ackerman's assumptions, especially the latter two, is questionable. This weakens the usefulness of his analysis for local policy makers.

Ackerman's propositions counter the conclusions of Case [123]. Ackerman posits a world in which owners pass on to their tenants only a small share of the costs of bringing their buildings up to code standard. There is only one empirical study on this point—the Douglas Commission research report by the Boston Municipal Research Bureau [77]. The BMRB study reports that owners absorbed a portion of the amortized repair costs incurred under a code-enforcement program and passed the rest of the costs (slightly less than half) on to their tenants. The sources of BMRB data on this point are unverified reports from two project areas; thus, the data is suspect. Whether the Case or Ackerman model more aptly describes other slum markets, and whether the costs of specific code-enforcement programs in select municipalities are likely to be borne by owners or tenants and in what proportion—these questions remain to be answered by empirical research.

Code Enforcement and the Housing Supply

Several studies of housing abandonment also touch on code enforcement as one of several market variables. The Center for Community Change/National Urban League's *National Survey of Housing Abandonment* [129] finds that code-enforcement programs have not resulted in maintaining or increasing the number of available standard-housing units in many of the cities studied. Lack of specificity about the sources for this conclusion weakens its strength, however.

Similarly, the Linton, Mields and Coston, Inc. study of abandoned housing [482] concludes that certain steps must be taken in the design of code-enforcement programs to reduce rather than encourage abandonment. Among the specific elements in such a well-designed program are: (1) continuous enforcement; (2) establishment of standards that will not encourage abandonment (reduced standards may be called for); and (3) adequate program staff.

These studies, both somewhat marred in their methodology, indicate that code enforcement can tip the balance in a landlord's marginal economic situation, and thereby substantially reduce the supply of housing in a local community.

Research Gaps

All of the aspects of the code-enforcement programs discussed above need far more rigorous empirical research to determine whether the programs meet their objectives, whether their costs—including the costs of the programs' unintended effects upon other housing and social programs—are reasonable in terms of their achievements, and whether there is a way to redesign enforcement programs to make them more effective. In addition, we need to know whether changes in the administration of code-enforcement programs would improve their effectiveness. Such changes might include decentralization of program responsibility, improved site selection criteria, better accounting methods and larger or better trained staff. This has not been examined.

In addition, current housing-code standards have not generally been derived from empirical research. Instead, they have been based on the judgments of public-health experts. This topic therefore requires careful scrutiny. How do the existing standards affect the physical and mental well-being of occupants? To what extent do code standards reflect the cultural norms of the middle class, possibly those of several generations ago, rather than minimum health standards? What are desirable social criteria for minimum health standards? This research can build to a limited extent on an older (pre-1964) literature that discusses and measures the effects of crowding on social pathology.[d] However, these studies have focused on fairly broad-stroke international comparisons.

Rent Control

The Nature and History of Rent Control

Unlike the literature on land-use controls and building and housing codes, the subject of rent control has attracted solid policy-related research. This is largely

---
[d]For example, see Robert C. Schmitt [766].

because the subject is more suited to conventional economic analysis. Also, through an anomaly discussed below, ample data have been made available to analysts.

In essence, rent control is a program under which rents on all or some portion of a city's rental housing stock are restricted to a level below the "normal" market rate. The program was used widely as part of the federal wartime price-stabilization controls, but in recent years it has been retained in only a few cities, principally New York City. Meanwhile, other cities, including Hartford, Connecticut and Cambridge, Massachusetts have considered adopting or have adopted similar measures. Rent control therefore remains potentially relevant to a municipal decision maker in the field of housing.

As an instrument of housing policy, rent control addresses itself primarily to the problem of an insufficient stock of low-cost housing for individuals and families who cannot afford to pay market rents. Rather than attempting to increase the stock of such housing, rent control attempts to ensure that rising rents will not place the existing stock out of the price range of lower income households. This goal is frequently characterized as making housing more readily available to those groups in society that are most disadvantaged in seeking housing, for example, members of minorities, the elderly, and large families.

Although the entire rent-control program was originally under federal control, in New York City it has passed progressively to state control and later to city control. At present the program is within the discretionary powers of municipal decision makers. Should similar programs be adopted in other cities, they undoubtedly would be under municipal control as well.

Research on Rent Control

Policy-related research on rent control has been quite extensive, and on the whole, well done. The theoretical treatment of rent control, with minor modifications, has been subsumed under the more general standard price theory of microeconomics. Edgar O. Olsen's "The Effects of a Simple Rent Control Scheme in a Competitive Housing Market" [643] is a good example of such theoretical works. There is, therefore, a well-articulated theory available upon which policy-related research studies on rent control can draw.

Because of a peculiarity in the New York City rent-control law, there is an unparalleled data base upon which these studies can draw. The New York law requires, as a condition of the continuance of the program, that extensive surveys of the New York housing market be undertaken periodically to demonstrate that a housing crisis continues to exist. The U.S. Bureau of the Census has mounted ambitious special surveys of New York housing for the city in fulfillment of this requirement. Data gathered in these special surveys have provided the basis for most of the studies of rent control reviewed here. Partially as a result of the ready availability of this data, however, each of the studies of rent control that we evaluated dealt only with rent control in New York City. Although the theoretical backing of these studies gives us reason to believe that the effects of rent control found for New York should apply for rent control elsewhere, the data are, strictly speaking, drawn only from a single case of rent control.

Rent Control in New York City

Since the literature focuses on New York City, a description of rent control there is in order.

In the New York City version of rent control, all buildings built before 1947 were subjected to rent control, while structures built (or converted) after that date were not. Rents on controlled units were held to pre-1947 levels with increments legislated from time to time. In an effort to promote rehabilitation of controlled units, rent increments are regularly permitted in several circumstances. For example, rent increases are allowed in four cases: (1) where there is an increase in services or facilities; (2) where there are major capital improvements; (3) where there are cases of financial hardship of the landlord; or (4) where there is a turnover of tenantry. It is important to note that rent increases are not allowed when ongoing costs, such as the price of heating fuel, increase unexpectedly.

Since 1969 a new version of rent control (the rent-stabilization program) has been applied to the newer housing stock in New York as well. Previously, however, the New York City housing stock was divided into two distinct segments—a segment of older buildings subject to rent control, and a segment of newer buildings not controlled. A number of studies of the effects of rent control have adopted the simple expedient of comparing these two segments in an attempt to ascertain the effects of rent control.

Basic Questions for Research

The basic questions addressed by studies of rent control concern the effectiveness, efficiency, and equity of this instrument in meeting its goal of providing low-cost housing to households that need it most. Although rent control is in a sense a regulation, it is considerably more illuminating to consider it a subsidy to households living in controlled housing, financed in large part by a tax upon the landlords of controlled buildings. To some extent the subsidy will also be financed by the taxpayers of the city because of its effects on the assessments of controlled buildings. Rent control will lower the rental income from the controlled buildings, and hence lower the value of the buildings through the process of capitalization. As assessments for tax purposes take this reduced value into account, the taxes that the city collects on these buildings will also fall somewhat. Hence, the city as a whole pays for part of the subsidy to occupants of rent-controlled dwellings.

The issues of effectiveness, efficiency, and equity are basically related to the distribution of the benefits, the distribution of the costs, and the relative magnitudes of the costs and benefits of the program. These calculations are complicated by several unintended consequences of the rent-control program that are discussed below.

Distribution of Benefits

Rent control in New York City does provide benefits to certain tenants, but the program is poorly targeted. The benefits of rent control do not accrue mainly to the specific population the program is supposed to assist—low-income households in need of low-cost housing.

The studies of rent control confirm that the program does provide benefits to the occupants of controlled units. Ernest M. Fisher [235] found that households not in controlled housing pay a larger percentage of their income for housing than do those in controlled units. And the RAND study [491] found that although rent-controlled housing is of poorer quality on the average than noncontrolled housing, it is nevertheless a bargain to its tenants. Most interesting is a perspective and finding suggested by Olsen [643]. The subsidy to tenants provided by rent control is in essence an increase in the income of those tenants, but that increase in income is tied to their continued occupancy of the rent-controlled apartment. Thus, tenants will not increase their consumption of housing services as they might do if they were to receive an untied increase in income. As a result, paradoxically, tenants of rent-controlled units consume on the average fewer housing services than would be expected given their income and relevant personal attributes (e.g., family size). Thus, rent control functions primarily to subsidize the consumption of nonhousing goods financed by a tax upon landlords (and by the city in general through lowered tax revenues).

Studies of rent control in New York City (e.g., Fisher [235], Rapkin [704], Olsen [642], RAND [491], Sternlieb [828]) suggest that groups of tenants who should benefit from the program (those relatively disadvantaged in the competition for housing) do tend to benefit from it in greater proportions than do others. Yet, all studies agree that the program is poorly targeted. Many of those who should benefit from the program do not, and many of those with no special claim to public assistance do benefit from the program. The RAND study emphasizes that rent control rewards occupants without regard to their need but merely based on their length of tenure. And Sternlieb's evidence indicates that rent increases, resulting from lease turnover, deleteriously affect minority tenants more than they do whites.

Distribution of Costs

That the costs of rent-control programs are borne primarily by the landlord is rarely justified in the literature, and never well justified. Presumably the justification would have to be phrased in terms of windfall profits accruing to landlords in tight housing markets. Sternlieb's extensive documentation of the plight of the central-city landlords of both controlled and noncontrolled buildings in New York, however, goes far toward dispelling myths about profiteering landlords [828]. Other studies not addressed specifically to rent control, such as Sternlieb's studies on Newark [826, 830] and Michael A. Stegman's on Baltimore [814], enrich and lend confirmation to this picture in other settings.

Unintended Consequences

The question of the efficiency of the program of rent control—the relative magnitude of costs and benefits—is considerably clouded by unintended consequences of the program which introduce hidden social costs. Olsen's [643] work suggests that even if one ignores these hidden costs, the rent-control program in New York is highly inefficient. Olsen's estimates suggest that the direct benefits to tenants are approximately $270 million, while the direct costs to landlords are of the order of $514 million. The costs of administering the program probably add another $7 million to the considerable waste suggested by these figures.

Misallocation of Space. One deleterious consequence of rent control is a misallocation of the available housing space. Since rent control rewards long tenure in the same apartment, one would expect to find households remaining in apartments larger than their current needs, thus keeping much underutilized space off the market.

Policy-related research has found some evidence of misallocation, but rarely finds it to be as bad as might be expected. Ernest Fisher, RAND, Chester Rapkin, and George Sternlieb all agree that there is little evidence of serious misallocation of space to be found in the New York rent-control program. Fisher, however, finds that it does distort the age pattern of occupancy somewhat; Sternlieb finds the controlled facilities slightly less crowded than the noncontrolled; and Rapkin suggests that one and two-person households do use a bit more space under the rent control program than they might in noncontrolled units.

Other undesirable consequences alleged to result from rent control are better supported by the policy-related research on the topic. Undermaintenance and the withdrawal of rental units from the market are two such consequences that reduce the amount of available housing.

Reduction Through Undermaintenance. Most serious, and best supported by the research, is the adverse effect of rent control upon the maintenance level of controlled buildings. If landlords of uncontrolled units are not reaping profits above a normal return on their investments (as the studies detailing the "plight of the landlord" mentioned above would suggest), then landlords of equivalent units who are required by rent control to rent their units at rates below the market rates will reap less than the going market return on their investments. With a return on investments below normal, they would be expected to attempt to compensate by reducing their own costs. Reducing their expenditures on maintenance and repairs is virtually the only alternative available to them, although it is a drastic measure and can lead to serious deterioration of buildings.

If the landlord expects that rent control will be lifted in the future, he may prefer to suffer his losses in the meantime, and to preserve his assets. But in general, one would expect to see the level of maintenance reduced in rent-controlled units. John C. Moorhouse [563] gives an excellent theoretical demonstration of this effect, and supports it with some evidence from New York. In general, policy-related research suggests that this is in fact a real problem in New York City.

Empirical examination of the effect of rent control upon maintenance is complicated to some extent for New York City by the fact that the rent-controlled housing stock is older and in worse condition on the whole than the noncontrolled stock. Nevertheless, the empirical results reported by Moorhouse, Sternlieb, and RAND show that rent control does lower the level of maintenance of buildings, all other things (including age and condition) being equal. Specifically, Sternlieb found, for example, that deterioration is more advanced in controlled buildings because of their age. Therefore, necessary repair expenditures are higher. But those repair expenditures that are elective are lower, on the whole, in the rent-controlled than in the noncontrolled buildings. Surprisingly, present rent-control policy in New York may exacerbate the problem even more than one would expect. Sternlieb's findings suggest that the New York program, by allowing rent increases when there is a turnover of tenantry, provides landlords with an added incentive to maintain rent-controlled buildings poorly. Declining maintenance levels encourage turnover, allowing landlords to establish rent increases, and eventually raising the rents in their controlled buildings to near-market levels. Thus, in the hope of reaping a near-market return on their investments, the owners of rent-controlled buildings may attempt to encourage rapid tenant turnover by establishing progressively lower levels of maintenance.

Thus, by promoting the deterioration of rent-controlled buildings and reducing the quality of the housing units found in them, rent control in effect reduces the quantity of housing services available in the City.

Reduction Through Withdrawal of Units. Fisher has argued, and presented some weak empirical evidence in support of his argument, that rent control may act in another way to reduce the stock of rental housing available in the city. Owners of one- and two-family homes who previously rented them out may be led to sell them to owner-occupants to get out from under rent-control requirements. Recent newspaper reports buttress Fisher's argument. Within the last two years several New York landlords have sold large apartment buildings as condominium units, apparently to escape the rent-control regulations.

Research Gaps—Effects on Noncontrolled Stock

The most serious gaps in the research on rent control and its effects have to do with the effects of rent control upon buildings in the city that are not subject to control. Most of the research seems to be based on the assumption that rent control affects only rent-controlled buildings. Olsen's theoretical treatment corroborates common sense in suggesting that, in the short run at least (and probably in the long run as well), there will also be an influence upon the uncontrolled housing stock. As rent control influences the deterioration of controlled stock, that stock will come into competition with the poorer units among the uncontrolled stock. Thus, it has the tendency to drive down rents on these units (and perhaps exacerbate tendencies toward disinvestment and eventual abandonment by landlords holding these properties).

Conversely, occupants of controlled units willing to pay for higher quality housing may elect to move out as their controlled unit is allowed to deteriorate. This, in turn, may drive up prices of the better quality dwellings among the uncontrolled stock. Fisher suggests, but offers weak evidence in support of the suggestion, that developers of new rental apartments will avoid competition with the artificially depressed rental levels of the lower quality rent-controlled units by building for the top of the market. This trend is already evident in New York City.

These effects on the noncontrolled stock have not been examined satisfactorily by the policy-related research on rent control, and hence there are no real findings of relevance here. It is striking, however, that all of the alleged effects of rent control upon the uncontrolled stock are deleterious.

Rent Control—Summary of Findings

In summary, even without taking into account possible effects of rent control upon uncontrolled buildings, the policy-related research on rent control suggests that it is an exceedingly poor instrument for keeping housing available to those most handicapped in obtaining it. While the program has some of the distributive effects that it should have, it produces them at the cost of tremendous waste and considerable inequity. Moreover, by its broader effects it worsens the very problems that it is intended to solve.

One is led to wonder why rent-control programs enjoy any popularity, and why they are proposed from time to time as solutions to housing problems. Other programs seem better able to achieve the same goals and do so without the deleterious consequences of rent control. Virtually any form of demand subsidy—perhaps accompanied by, and partially financed by, a tax upon possible "windfall gains" enjoyed by landlords—should work better. One suspects that the popularity of rent control derives in large part from its political expediency. Landlords have fewer votes than tenants; the costs of rent control to the taxpayers in general are well hidden; myths of profiteering landlords make the program seem more equitable than it is; and the effects of the program upon the housing stock are not immediately apparent.

Conclusions

The research literature on housing codes and regulations, rent control aside, does not support firm policy conclusions. It does, however, invite some concluding thoughts on the policy implications of research in the very complex area of local controls, particularly on the interplay of regulations and housing costs. We discuss these implications and the research gaps they reveal in this concluding section.

Several analysts have asserted that zoning standards—particularly minimum-lot-size and dwelling-area requirements—play a dominant role in raising the price of new housing. Minimum dwelling-area requirements have little or no justification other than to exclude smaller, lower priced housing. Similarly, lot-size requirements have little merit when they exceed the minimum requirements of public health to ensure proper separation between septic systems and water sources. In the end, the local policy maker must maintain a fine balance between the social and fiscal concerns of the community and the need for lower priced housing.

Much of the literature understandably exhorts the policy maker to strike this balance in favor of lower priced housing. The role of policy-related research is less to exhort the policy maker than to identify the relationship between zoning actions and housing costs and to measure the magnitude of these effects. On the basis of the evaluated studies, particularly Sagalyn and Sternlieb [747], it appears that reductions in lot-size and building-area requirements would in fact reduce housing costs. However, the magnitude of such reductions remains in issue.

Similarly, the research has not adequately analyzed the costs and benefits of private land speculation. There is evidence that in the absence of reliable public planning and investment, it is the private developer who must decide where and what to build. The routine subversion of local zoning through variances and zone changes, as reported by Max Neutze [608], Frederick H. Buttel [116], and others, may simply reflect a more accurate assessment by the developer of changes in market demand and housing need. One can even argue that lower priced suburban housing is possible (in the absence of public subsidy) only to the extent a developer is able to purchase land cheaply—meaning land zoned at low densities—and then persuade the zoning boards to grant a zone change to accommodate his plans. In fact, however, there is little incentive for the developer to build for lower income families; middle-class couples, young and elderly, have been the chief beneficiaries of the suburban apartment boom of the 1960s. More flexible forms of zoning that limit increases in density to developments of superior design quality may have the same ultimate impact on housing costs for the consumer as large-lot requirements.

In sum, there is no reason to believe that housing costs can or will be reduced if local policy makers use the zoning or subdivision instruments more wisely. Municipal and developer self-interest and the bluntness of these tools in promoting specific kinds of housing development stand in the way. Problems of housing cost and distribution require more powerful tools and deeper resources than localities now possess. We examine these issues in Chapter 5 under the topic of housing-assistance programs.

There is less to say about the policy implications of research on building and housing codes. These instruments do not require the same balance of fiscal and social concerns that zoning does. The better studies on building codes conclude that they are not a major determinant of housing cost. This may be true in general, but not for specific cases. For example, in spite of the bias in the study samples, it is most likely true that both the diversity of local building codes and the suspicion with which new technologies are greeted by local building inspectors deter the home manufacturer, if not the conventional tract developer, from testing new and less expensive methods and materials. The most logical response to this problem falls outside the scope of local action. It is to transfer responsibility for the formulation of code standards to the state level, as several state legislatures have already done. It is surprising that no researcher has attempted to assess the outcomes of code administration under the two systems—municipalities administering state codes and those with local codes.

Research on housing codes presents a different problem—the failure of enforcement. Code enforcement is an unpopular program with salient costs and less obvious benefits. Bruce Ackerman's theoretical analysis [10] of the likely benefits of code enforcement when coupled with housing subsidies should be tested. One approach is a HUD sponsored demonstration program, like the housing-allowance demonstrations discussed in Chapter 5. Such demonstrations could be designed to permit ongoing assessment of the scope and magnitude of the benefits associated with code-enforcement subsidy programs.

Finally, the results of research on rent control are relatively clear: The benefit of keeping some rents down is achieved at tremendous cost and with considerable inequity.

4 Real Property Taxation

Introduction

The property tax is the principal system by which municipalities raise the revenues that support their municipal expenditures. Hence, the main objective of the property tax has little to do with housing problems or goals. The main objective is the raising of revenues.

However, the property tax does have a considerable impact upon housing. As the property tax is currently structured, its effect on housing is generally believed to be detrimental. This impact may derive from the manner in which the property tax is administered or from the basic structure of the tax. In this section we review the policy-related research that explores the impact of the current property tax upon various housing problems. Both administrative and structural aspects are discussed.

A number of reforms aimed at reducing the pernicious effect of the property tax on housing have been suggested. Some of these have been tested in practice. Such reforms may even permit the tax to be used specifically to promote housing goals. Possibilities for using the tax in this manner include programs that leave the basic character of the tax unchanged but make adjustments within that structure (incentive and abatement programs). They also include major restructuring and creation of an alternative system of property taxation such as site-value taxation, which might provide better incentive effects for improving housing.

This chapter addresses research on the following topics: (1) housing implications of the present property tax, both in its administration and in its basic structure; (2) tax incentive and abatement programs; and (3) site-value taxation.

Conventional Property Tax

The Effects of Administration

A substantial portion of the detrimental effects of the property tax on housing may derive from problems in its administration. Dick Netzer, an expert on the property tax, draws very pessimistic conclusions about its administration:

My view is that the quality of administration of the property tax is universally worse than the quality of administration we have come to expect in connection with income and sales taxes. . . . In some jurisdictions, the quality of property tax administration is only moderately worse than the quality of good nonproperty tax administration; in others, it is abysmally worse. But nowhere does it really match nonproperty tax administration. [605, pp. 386-87]

The effects of assessment practices have probably been the most neglected aspect of the property tax in the policy-related literature. A number of studies (A.D. Little [28], Schaaf [755], Linton, Mields and Coston [482], Davis and Wertz [174], Price Waterhouse [691], T.R. Smith [788], Oldman and Aaron [638]), primarily case studies, have found that central city properties are typically overassessed. Surely this relatively high tax burden aggravates the problems of housing in such areas. Nonetheless, no policy studies exist that measure the effects of overassessment relative to other blighting factors. A.H. Schaaf [755], for example, attempts to test the proposition that over-assessment fosters slums, but the data he has gathered from Northern Alameda County, California are insufficient to resolve the issue.

Similarly, there is some evidence from the T.R. Smith and the Oliver Oldman and Henry Aaron studies that single-family homes are typically underassessed in both central-city and suburban neighborhoods. But again there are no studies to show the magnitude of any effects that this underassessment might have.

If the deleterious effects of the property tax upon housing are primarily due to administrative problems in the property tax, efforts devoted to establishing uniform assessment practices might reduce these effects. There is no lack of suggestions as to how such practices might be established. However, there seem to be no studies to show how this is best done. Furthermore, it may be that the property tax is simply incapable of being administered well. Netzer [604] has argued that the difficulty of knowing the value of infrequently traded assets like houses imposes serious limits on the possibilities for improvement in the tax. The political calculations that undoubtedly underlie many assessment practices may impose similar limits as well.

Tax Administration—Research Gaps

We are left, then, with several questions about the administration of the property tax on which further policy-related research is needed:

1. What effects do current property-tax assessment practices have on the construction and rehabilitation of housing?
2. What are the most effective methods of improving assessment practices to minimize the negative impact of the property tax upon housing?
3. What are the practical and political limitations on the improvement of property tax assessment practices and their impact on housing?

Efforts to improve property tax assessment to benefit housing may be largely futile if the detrimental effects of the property tax upon housing primarily derive from the structure of the tax itself. There is strong theoretical reason to believe this may be the case. Policy-related research has not gone very far, however, in corroborating conclusions suggested by the theoretical literature.

Effects on Housing of the Current Structure of the Property Tax

Theory, and to a lesser extent empirical research, suggests several problems in the current structure of the property tax that may have detrimental effects upon the location, construction, maintenance, and rehabilitation of housing. The defects commonly charged to the property tax as currently structured are:

1. It has a regressive impact on housing consumers.
2. It acts as a sales tax on housing, raising the price and reducing effective demand.
3. It acts as a tax on capital invested in residential buildings, driving capital into higher yield investments.
4. It reduces the cash available to landlords for maintenance and improvements.
5. It adds to past capital losses and helps lock current owners into properties they would prefer to sell and are unlikely to maintain.
6. It promotes fiscal competition among jurisdictions and encourages exclusionary zoning, which may reduce the supply of low-income housing.

While the research literature on the impact of the property tax has grown substantially in the last decade, most of it has involved the application of highly abstruse and technical econometric theories. An understanding of this theoretical literature is critical if sense is to be made of the policy implications of these studies. Since the technical nature of the literature makes it less accessible to the urban analyst and policy maker than the balance of policy-related research on housing, we take special pains to synthesize its analyses and conclusions. In this section, we consider the findings of research on the property tax concerning each of the preceding six assertions.

Regressivity. The prevailing view for many years has been that the property tax is regressive, falling upon the poor more heavily than upon the rich when taken as a proportion of income.

While this view still dominates the political forum, there is a growing literature in economics that suggests that the overall effects of the property tax may be proportional and perhaps even progressive. Building on Arnold Harberger's classic analysis of the corporate income tax [322], this new literature suggests that when all the effects of the property tax are considered, the progressive impact of the tax may more than offset the regressive effects that traditionally have been emphasized [1]. Although the new literature relates primarily to questions of general equity rather than the impact of the property tax on housing, no review of research on the property tax can ignore the force of its argument. We therefore summarize the basic terms of the debate on regressivity below.

Both the new literature and the more traditional analyses agree that the regressive impact of the property tax depends on the extent to which the tax is borne by housing occupants. In the conventional literature it is presumed that the tax is largely borne by the consumers of housing. In more technical terms conventional economists have assumed that the demand for housing is relatively unresponsive to increases in rents, while the supply of housing is fairly flexible. Thus, they postulate that a substantial portion of the property tax is shifted to tenants in the form of rent increases. Home owners are presumed to bear the property tax burden directly in their capacity as owner-occupants [569].

The more recent body of economic literature acknowledges that a portion of the property tax is borne by housing consumers, hence the tax has some regressive effects. However, the regressive effects do not arise from monopolistic owners shifting the tax to renters. Rather, they result from a redistribution of investment funds away from housing to other sectors of the economy. Moreover, the regressive effects of the tax on housing consumers are offset by the progressive impact of the tax upon investors.

The new literature assumes that the property tax, by slicing into the profits of landlords, leads to an outflow of investment funds from housing to other sectors of the economy. This redistribution of investment continues until the net returns earned by investors are equalized across sectors of the economy. By making crucial assumptions about the ability to substitute labor and capital in production and about the responsiveness of savings to interest rates, the new literature suggests the major burden of the property tax is shouldered by the owners of investment funds through reductions in the rate of return on investment. It is assumed that individuals own an increasing share of such funds as they move into higher income groups. Therefore, the total effect of the property tax—including its regressive effect on housing consumers and its progressive effect on the owners of capital—is at least proportional and probably progressive.

Unfortunately, no empirical studies support either the traditional view that the property tax is highly regressive or the new theory that the incidence of the tax may well be progressive. There has not been an empirical estimate of property tax incidence. Moreover, we do not know whether the housing market is as noncompetitive as presumed by much of the conventional literature or as competitive as the new literature suggests.

While empirical evidence is scanty, several studies suggest that the literature which holds that the housing market is fairly competitive may more accurately portray the real-world supply and demand for housing. George Sternlieb's studies of Newark [826, 830] suggest that, at least in one inner city, owners of low-income rental units do not earn the profits that we would expect of a market as noncompetitive as is conventionally presumed. Bruce Ackerman's analysis of the high mobility of low-income families [10], which contends that such families do a great deal of "shopping around" for the best housing available, also suggests that the demand of the poor for housing is more responsive to rent increases than economists and policy makers have traditionally assumed.

The problem of empirically testing the two diverse theories of property-tax incidence is not simple. It is complicated, in part, by a lack of systematically collected and readily available data. The estimation of the incidence of the property tax is further complicated by the fact that although permanent income (the income stream with temporary fluctuations smoothed out) is better than current income as a measure for calculations of the tax's burden on housing consumers, data on current income are much easier to obtain. Households experiencing temporary setbacks do not immediately reduce their housing expenditures. So, incidence calculations based on current income (which for these families will be lower than permanent income) overstate the regressivity of the tax. Because of the difficulty of generating data on permanent income, however, current income is most commonly used in calculations of the incidence of the tax.

At the moment the nature of the property tax burden is open to considerable debate. While more empirical support is needed before we can conclude that the impact of the tax is proportional or progressive, the conventional assumption that the property tax unequivocally burdens the poor more heavily than the rich should no longer be accepted as a sine qua non by policy makers.

In any case discussion of the possible regressivity of the property tax is related primarily to questions of general equity rather than to the effects of the property tax on housing. It is pertinent to housing problems to the extent that regressivity reduces the effective demand among housing consumers. The conventional analyses and the new literature agree that the property tax has some regressive effects on housing consumers; the tax plays some role in diminishing the demand for housing among the poor.

The Property Tax as a Sales Tax on Housing. To the extent that the property tax is passed on to tenants rather than being borne solely by property owners, the tax acts as a sales tax on the consumption of housing. This can be expected to raise the price and reduce the quantity of housing consumed.

For owner-occupants of single-family homes, of course, the issue of whether the tax is shifted from owners to tenants does not occur. These households are both owners and tenants. They bear the burden of the property tax regardless of shifting considerations.

In some instances the property tax is a direct function of the level of public services. Education is the clearest example. In such instances the tax acts as a hidden price for these services. Hence, it may not reduce the amount of housing consumed or, in balance, raise the cost of housing per se.

Theoretical results based on highly restrictive assumptions show that when the property tax is directly related to the level of public services, housing consumers can "vote with their feet" by choosing to live in the locality with the mix of tax costs and public-service benefits that they prefer. Some empirical results of good internal validity obtained by Edward M. Sabella [745] and W.E. Oates [634], but deriving from limited samples, support this possibility. The theoretical conclusions depend upon a market model including a multiplicity of taxing jurisdictions with different tax/services packages, and a clear relation in each jurisdiction between the level of taxes and the extent of services.

The competitive market characteristics that are assumed in this model are not likely to be found in the central city. Thus, for single-family homes in the central city, one may expect that the property tax will act in part as a sales tax on housing. For other types of dwellings in central cities the extent of tax-shifting from owners to tenants will determine the extent to which the tax deters housing consumption.

The theory of tax incidence argues persuasively that that portion of the property tax that is levied on the land under the structure will be borne by the owner of the property. Some portion of the tax levied on the structure itself will be passed on to the occupants of the structure, but the extent of the shifting depends on the responsiveness of the occupants' demand for housing to increases in rent.

Unfortunately, there has been very little empirical confirmation of this conclusion. In fact, the best study addressing this question [652] finds that even the tax on the structure seems to be borne substantially by the owner of the property. Larry L. Orr based his study on data limited to the Boston metropolitan area. Sampling problems and problems in the operationalization of some of the variables weaken the conclusions of his study. Moreover, the tax differentials to which the study was addressed were differentials among taxing jurisdictions rather than among the tax burdens on particular properties. (See Heinberg and Oates [354], and Orr [653].) The extent of shifting of taxes on structures is still very much an open question.

For single-family homes in the central city, the property tax will act in part as a tax upon the consumption of housing. This holds true for rental units as well if there is a forward shifting of property taxes. The tax on consumption reduces the effective demand for housing and thus, in the final analysis, reduces the amount of housing provided and consumed. Coupled with the possible regressivity of the property tax, this could have a serious effect on lower income housing in the central city.

The theoretical basis for the argument that the tax will raise the price and lower the quantity of housing consumed is well established by Netzer [602], among others. But the magnitude of the effect is not known. One would surely want to know how serious the effect is before adopting alternative tax measures, particularly if there are costs and disadvantages to the alternatives as well. If the effect of the property tax on the cost of housing is substantial, the possible long-range effects of this tax may be serious. In particular, by increasing the cost of lower income housing, the tax may promote overcrowding and thereby speed deterioration, further reducing the supply of low-income housing.

Even if the property tax on structures is not shifted to the occupants of rental units, its effects may still be detrimental to housing.

The Property Tax as a Tax on Capital. That portion of the property tax which is not passed on to tenants of rental units becomes in effect a tax upon the owner's capital. One would expect that this tax would reduce the amount of capital that is put into real property. Owners of capital will presumably find lower tax, higher yield uses for their capital. With minor exceptions, the amount of urban land available will not change whatever the tax upon it, as our later discussion of site-value taxation explains. But the level of improvements can change. The existing housing might be deprived of maintenance funds and allowed to deteriorate, or investors might refrain from investments they might otherwise have made in new construction, rehabilitation, or capital improvement of buildings.

The theory on the capital-disincentive effect of the property tax is unassailable. L.A. Dougharty [197], Dick Netzer [604], George E. Peterson [669], and James Heilbrun [347] all argue that this effect should continue as long as there is a tax upon capital invested in real-property improvements that is higher than the tax on other uses of capital. Policy-related research has not, however, addressed this question in such a way as to derive estimates of the magnitude of the effect on the level of improvements.

One very specific aspect of this capital-disincentive effect concerns the marginal disincentive to invest in remodelling or renovations that derives from the incremental nature of the tax on capital improvements to residential structures. We do have some reasonably good empirical results on this effect in a study done by Arthur D. Little, Inc. [28]. This study contains several flaws in sampling, but on the whole seems reasonably reliable. Its sample of ten cities is a minimal basis for generalizations intended to apply to all United States cities, but there seems no particular reason to think that the results are not more broadly applicable.

The Arthur D. Little study found that in practice the property tax should not deter investment in renovations or remodelling because improvements to existing structures do not usually result in increased assessments. With no incremental increase in effective taxation, there should be no disincentive effect. However, the Little study and work by Sternlieb [826] indicate that because property owners cannot be sure what improvements are allowable without new assessments and because many owners share a widespread misconception that improvements will invariably lead to higher assessments, the property tax does reduce the level of improvements on existing properties.

The Little study and the Sternlieb work suggest the magnitude of the property tax's disincentive effect on remodelling or renovation of existing structures. Neither study, however, offers any empirical estimates of the disincentive effect of the tax on capital invested in real estate improvements in general.

The Impact of the Property Tax on Cash Flow. To the extent that the property tax cannot be shifted to tenants and must be borne by the landlord, it reduces the cash flow of the landlord. It may thereby contribute to reduced maintenance and repair outlays and to the eventual deterioration of the buildings.

The theories of taxation have not really dealt with this effect of the property tax. But many studies of abandonment problems, chief among them studies by the Center for Community Change/National Urban League [129], Linton, Mields and Coston [482], Michael A. Stegman [814], and Sternlieb [826], have stressed the cash-flow problems of landlords in central cities. They have also documented that the property tax takes a large bite out of the cash flow of the typical central-city rental-housing unit, and that this is in general an increasingly large bite.

What is not at all clear is the relative impact of the property tax as compared with other factors in contributing to the problems of declining buildings. If the property tax were entirely removed from these buildings, it seems highly likely that other neighborhood problems and problems specific to the buildings would remain. The cut of the property tax into the cash flow may hasten the end. But the end may arrive soon even without the property tax, as George E. Peterson [670] argues.

The Property Tax and the Locking-in of Landlords. Most of the arguments presented so far about the detrimental effects of the property tax on the housing supply have been based on standard economic assumptions concerning rational investor behavior. These assumptions may not be realistic when applied to the housing market. In particular, economic rationality would imply that losses previously incurred should be ignored in current decisions. Only present realities and future expectations of profitability should influence current operating decisions. Historical losses should have no influence.

The owner of central-city property is not likely to agree with this proposition. The abandonment literature referred to earlier suggests that many owners are deterred from selling their properties by the disparity between original purchase prices (plus later capital investments in the structures) and the much lower prices that can be obtained in central cities currently. These same considerations may deter owners from making further capital improvements which might raise their selling price. Current owners are not likely to "throw money down a rathole" in spite of the possibility that it may make it a more marketable "rathole." The Sternlieb [826] and Little [28] studies indicate that owners consider themselves locked in both by the low current selling prices of properties in central city areas and by their own disinclination to take the significant capital losses implied by a sale at those prices.

Economic theory holds that the part of the property tax that is borne by the landlord will be capitalized. Lower property taxes should therefore result in higher selling prices. Peterson [670] has argued that if property taxes on central-city properties were lowered, the resulting increase in the selling price might make owners of "ratholes" more willing to sell them. By this reasoning the new purchasers might be more willing to expend funds for maintenance and repair since they would not have the history of past losses that discourages present owners from making improvements.

The argument is interesting and is consistent in part with what we know about housing markets and motives of landlords in the central city. It is not, however, a strategy that has been tried. Hence, we have no empirical findings on the efficacy of the proposal or estimates of the extent of improvements that might result. Since the program obviously has a cost—foregoing the tax revenue—an assessment of the benefits would be crucial. Likewise, it would be helpful to analyze who reaps the benefits of this policy and whether the benefits outweigh the disadvantages that alternative tax policies might create.

Fiscal Competition and Exclusionary Zoning. Another effect of the property tax on housing arises from local control of property taxes and the fragmentation of taxing jurisdictions. Local control results in efforts by municipalities to compete for land uses that add more to the general fund in revenues than they consume in public services. The fragmentation creates incentives for towns to engage in fiscal competition through their zoning policies.

The policy studies discussed in this chapter assume that localities shape their zoning largely in response to taxing and spending considerations. A recent study by Eric J. Branfman, Benjamin I. Cohen, and David M. Trubek [85] questions this assumption and suggests that fiscal motives may be much less important than other factors in shaping the zoning practices of local policy makers. The cross-sectional study, which sampled areas comprising over one-half of the metropolitan population of the United States, concludes that zoning is not typically imposed to increase the taxable value of real property in the locality or to exclude low-income residents who would heavily burden public services. Instead, zoning appears to be motivated by other variables, most notably racial factors. While the group's findings are provocative, the conclusions of the study are tentative and subject to many qualifications. More research is needed before the traditional assumption that zoning is typically enacted for fiscal reasons can be discarded.

To the extent that fiscal zoning does exist, it inhibits the most efficient use of land and a rational geographic distribution of housing. At least one author, Bruce W. Hamilton [319], has argued that it may reduce the amount of low-income housing available by reducing the overall amount of land available for low-income housing construction.

One must add, however, that although fiscal zoning is a result of the local property tax, it is unlikely to be corrected by municipal decision makers who must continue to operate within the constraints of a fragmented system. In fact, the local decision maker is more likely to want assistance in competing for "good taxables" than to support proposals for passing control of property taxation to a higher level of government and achieving more uniformity of tax levels.

Some policy-related research has been done that may be useful to local officials trying to increase revenues at a greater rate than public-service costs. The most impressive and reliable of these studies was conducted by Sternlieb and his associates [829]. This is a detailed and careful examination of housing developments of various types in New Jersey. Using sophisticated analysis of systematically gathered data, the authors reach the conclusion that an index based on the number of bedrooms in each home is still the best method of estimating the additions that a housing development can be expected to make to the population of school-age children (and hence to education expenditures) and to the total population (and hence to the cost of other municipal services). Other characteristics of the developments were not found to add much in predictive value.

This impressive study also lists the actual "bedroom multipliers" that apply to various types of housing units, and one would have every confidence in the validity of the multipliers presented—so long as one wanted to apply them to New Jersey. How useful the actual figures might be in other settings has not been determined. But these multipliers may be better than rules of thumb for assessing costs of new developments outside New Jersey. Fortunately, the authors make an extensive presentation of the methodology they used, thereby allowing analysts in other settings to develop results that take account of differing local factors.

Two further studies are addressed to the related question of whether the single-family home pays for its share of local services. Unfortunately, both are relatively weak studies. One of the studies, Ruth L. Mace and Warren J. Wicker [499], concludes that the single-family home pays its own way everywhere except where the local tax rate has to support nearly all educational expenditures. The study is based on three cases chosen to represent extremes in the balance between local and state support for education. As explained in the methodological discussion of Chapter 6, this is not a satisfactory technique. The internal validity of the study may be adequate, but we are left with the limited conclusion that in two of the three locations considered, a hypothetical single-family home would pay its way. The generalizability of that conclusion is dubious.

The second study on this topic, by Metro Metrics [543], considers only one case, and so must be considered even less generalizable. Moreover, the reporting of the methodology in the Metro Metrics study is so vague that it is not possible to judge the validity of the conclusion—that the single-family home in Fairfax County, Virginia does indeed pay its own way—even for the single case studies. The fact that the study was done under contract to the Northern Virginia Builders Association raises some questions about the objectivity of the report that are not at all dispelled by the reporting of the methodology.

Impacts of the Property Tax—Research Gaps

In sum, our review of policy-related research on the detrimental effects of the structure of the property tax upon the supply of housing has left us with a series of unanswered questions:

1. To what extent is the property tax borne by property owners, and to what extent is it shifted forward to tenants? What specific conditions determine the extent of shifting?
2. To the extent that the property tax acts as a tax on the consumption of housing, how serious an effect does this have upon the effective demand for housing? To what extent does the possible regressivity of the property tax focus this effect on the effective demand for low- and moderate-income housing?
3. To the extent that the property tax acts as a tax on capital invested in residential structures, what effect does it have upon the construction, maintenance, and rehabilitation of housing?
4. What independent influence on the condition of buildings can be attributed to the effect of the property tax in reducing the owner's cash flow?
5. What effect might a reduction of central city property taxes have in facilitating the transfer of properties from locked-in owners to new owners who may improve the properties?
6. What effects does the incentive toward exclusionary zoning provided by local control of the property tax have on the supply of low-income housing?
7. What are the effects of various sizes and types of housing developments upon municipal tax revenues in settings other than New Jersey?
8. In the light of these questions, what are the most effective changes that can be made in the structure of the property tax? To what extent will these changes minimize the negative impact of the property tax on housing? Who will reap the benefits of new policies, and who will bear the costs that alternative methods of raising the shortfall of local revenue will involve?

While our review of the policy-related research has left us with virtually no firm empirical findings, we have found an extensive theoretical literature that can serve as an excellent basis for future empirical testing and analysis of the issues.

Abatement and Incentive Programs

Changes in the structure of the property tax intended to reduce its detrimental effects upon housing might involve minor reforms or radical restructuring. Most nonradical efforts to reform the property tax system involve tax abatements that may be given to qualified investors contemplating new construction, improvements, or rehabilitation. So far there has been very little research dealing with the effectiveness, costs, or other consequences of these various schemes.

The basic idea of abatement and incentive schemes is simple. If the presence of a tax on particular uses of capital discourages those uses of capital, the removal of that tax should eliminate the disincentive. If the result is a tax that is lower than the average on competing uses, then the removal should be an incentive to the use in question. The reasoning does not tell us, however, how much of an influence a change in the tax is likely to have. That is the crucial question.

Unfortunately, there has been very little research devoted to this question. One may surmise, however, that tax abatement is likely to have little influence in and of itself on housing in the later stages of decline. George Sternlieb and Robert W. Burchell [830], in their study of the housing market in Newark, arrive at this conclusion on the basis of some of their interview results. Owners in the worst areas, when asked if they would improve their parcels given tax relief, replied in large numbers that it simply would not be worth it. From this Sternlieb and Burchell conclude that tax abatement is at best "merely an enabling act."

The attractiveness of abatement schemes may be reduced by the added administrative burden they impose. Netzer [604] has argued that this burden may be considerable. But, once again, no policy-related research seems to have addressed this question.

Other consequences of tax-abatement schemes are worth considering. Since some portion of the property tax is probably shifted to tenants, abatements will result in inequities between tenants in buildings that qualify and those in buildings that do not. One reasonable assumption might be that buildings in areas of contagious abandonment will not be seen as worth additional investment by their owners regardless of abatements. Hence, abatements may benefit primarily middle-income households in borderline neighborhoods and do little for lower income residents in blighted areas. There are no empirical findings on this question, but it is worth further consideration.

Finally, it should not be forgotten that the primary purpose of the property tax is to raise revenues. Abatements are likely to result in tax revenues rising more slowly than they might otherwise. If the shortfall is made up by other taxes, what disadvantages will the alternative taxes have?

We have seen virtually no policy-related research addressed to abatement schemes. A major problem with analyzing the effect of tax abatements, is that programs vary considerably. Most programs combine tax abatement with other incentives. Hence, the effects of abatement cannot be separated from those of the other incentives. Peterson [670] argues that the only evidence presented by those who urge abatement as a solution to housing problems comes from New York City, where abatement is a relatively small part of a package of incentives. He argues, in fact, that the impact of the package on the housing stock may come primarily from the other subsidy elements, such as low-interest loans. Morris Beck [51] seems to corroborate this general impression in a report on the influence of property taxation on urban renewal that is more an anecdotal report of the experience of one program than a true research report. Beck found that the marketing problems of the project he studied were so huge that they smothered any marginal impact the abatement program might have had.

Main Study of Abatement

The principal study on tax abatement was done by Price Waterhouse and Company [691]. This is essentially a series of case studies of nine cities chosen because they had distinctive types of property tax innovations that seemed worthy of consideration. But only one of the three abatement programs is to be found in more than one city. The other two are each found in only one city. In addition, for each of the cases, the sample of respondents was rather small and did not seem to be representative. Because this research is based on evidence drawn from a case study, the authors' ability to disentangle effects of various policy instruments that work simultaneously is questionable. Nevertheless, this study represents the best evidence available on the effects of abatement programs.

The most common type of tax abatement considered by the Price Waterhouse study is abatement granted on properties developed by urban renewal corporations. Under this program, property tax concessions are given to owners who choose to develop their property through limited-dividend corporations. Price Waterhouse found that considerable construction has been accomplished under the auspices of these corporations, although little of this was low-income housing. The study suggests, however, that it is difficult to attribute much of this construction to the particular incentive of property tax concession.

Two other types of abatement programs considered in Price Waterhouse were found only in New York City and in Boston. In New York a program of exemptions and abatement was used to encourage the rehabilitation of substandard dwellings to bring them up to code standards. In Boston, officials were willing to enter into informal preconstruction tax agreements with prospective developers. This appears to have been quite successful in promoting construction. The authors' ability to evaluate the Boston program was severely limited, however, by the fact that the informal agreements are not open for public inspection. Their information, therefore, is imprecise, and in most cases second-hand. For the New York program, however, they are able to report estimates of the cost of the program.

Given the lack of precise data on the Boston program and the mix of two instruments—code enforcement and tax concessions—in New York City, it is hard to draw firm generalizable conclusions from the Price Waterhouse study about the specific costs and impacts of tax abatement. The best that can be said is that in some instances tax abatement can contribute to the amelioration of housing problems, either as a separate policy instrument or in conjunction with other programs such as code enforcement.

Overall, tax-abatement schemes are not likely to have a very large positive effect in and of themselves. But in the absence of more profound restructuring of the property tax, it may make sense to use them as part of a broader mix of instruments. Our conclusion, unfortunately, is not well founded in the research we have reviewed. In particular, the research fails to identify the best mix of policy instruments in which tax abatement may play a part.

Tax Abatement—Research Gaps

Once again, we are left with a series of questions about tax abatement programs that policy-related research could profitably address:

1. What independent effect can tax-abatement programs have upon the construction, maintenance, and rehabilitation of housing?
2. What effect can tax-abatement programs have upon the abandonment of sound housing units?
3. What are the administrative costs of various tax-abatement programs?
4. How equitable are various tax-abatement programs?
5. What are the direct costs of tax-abatement programs in terms of property taxes foregone?
6. What are the disadvantages of alternative means for raising revenues foregone?
7. In what combinations of programs are tax-abatement programs most effective?

Restructuring to Site-value Taxation

There is widespread agreement in the economic literature, principally Arthur P. Becker [54], James Heilbrun [347], George E. Peterson [669], and Dick Netzer [605], that the detrimental effects of the conventional property tax described earlier are not shared by a tax levied entirely upon the value of the land. It is argued, in fact, that such a site-value tax would have beneficial effects on land use but that it has not been possible to confirm this empirically. There has been considerable research on the effects of hypothetical switches to site-value taxation in various localities, but much of it seems to miss this basic point. And virtually none of the literature tries to estimate the size of the benefits that might flow from site-value taxation. Given the obvious costs of a tax change of such magnitude, the absence of such an estimation is regrettable.

The theoretical arguments in favor of site-value taxation are based upon the simple fact that, unlike prospective development, land is tied to one location. If one taxes it heavily, there is no risk that it will move to a place where the taxes are lower. Thus, the supply of land in the city is essentially constant. If taxing land reduces the yield on money invested in the land, the owner may decide to sell it and put his money elsewhere. Upon sale, the landowner will discover that the increased tax has been capitalized into a lower price for his land. At the reduced price the new purchaser will find that his return on the purchase price should yield him an adequate return on his investment. Hence, the best a landowner can do in the face of higher site taxes is to put the land to its most productive use.

The thrust of the argument is that site-value taxation will promote the best and most intensive use of the land. But again we have no estimates of the size of this effect. As persuasive as these arguments are, better answers are needed to the following questions before a switch to site-value taxation can be recommended:

1. What intensity of land use is desirable?
2. How effective is site-value taxation relative to other policies in promoting its main objective—better planning and location of new housing?
3. What are the administrative problems and costs of site-value taxation?
4. What are the administrative difficulties of a transfer to site-value taxation from the current system? The equity effects?
5. What are the equity effects of site-value taxation itself?
6. What is the revenue-producing capacity of site-value taxation?
7. What compromise solutions are available between site-value taxation and the current system? What are the advantages and disadvantages of these systems?
8. What short-term and long-term effects might a changeover to site-value taxation have upon social and demographic characteristics of different neighborhoods?

We consider in turn each of these questions and the answers the research can give to each.

Intensity of Land Use

The theory of property taxation suggests that the site-value tax should promote the most intensive use of land. In these days of concern with the environment and the quality of life, the matter of what land-use intensity is desirable has become an important question. It is a mixed empirical and value question. The empirical aspects specify the various social consequences of intensive land use, and the value aspect determines society's choice among these consequences. In its broadest aspects, this is a question for local governing bodies and for city planners in general.

Should the community prefer a less intensive use, a judicious combination of zoning and site-value taxation might provide incentives that promote the favored intensity. Clearly, coordination of the zoning instrument and the tax would be crucial. Unfortunately, virtually no empirical studies of site-value taxation address these questions.

Planning and Location of New Units

The question of effectiveness has rarely been researched in policy-related studies. There is an extensive evangelical literature on this question that harks back to Henry George and his single-tax movement. The most current examples are A.M. Agapos and Paul R. Dunlap [12]. Dale Bails [41], Steven Cord [154], Mason Gaffney [255], [258], [259], [261], [262], Arthur L. Grey [299], Richard W. Lindholm [480], and Walter Rybeck [740]. This theoretical work argues for the existence of incentives in this direction, but says little about their strength. Research that seems to address the question proves on closer examination to have missed the point. In fact, the question is addressed directly only by a few nearly anecdotal case studies.

A number of studies, particularly those of T.R. Smith [787], Dean O. Popp and Frederick D. Sebold [683], and Steven Cord [155], have addressed the effects of hypothetical transfers to site-value taxation in various localities. The technique in most cases is the same. Properties in some area are assessed and the incidence of the tax burden on each property is calculated under two assumptions: that the tax would be levied on the site value only, and that the total revenue yield for the locality would remain the same as under the current system.

Typically the researchers ignore possible capitalization effects. Although a high tax burden on a valuable site should be capitalized into a somewhat lower value for the site, these studies calculate the tax burden using the site value under the current tax structure. The results are reported by type of land use aggregated in various ways, and usually depending upon the nature of the data available to the researcher. Nearly all these studies conclude that the switch to site-value taxation would benefit property more intensively developed at the expense of sites with less valuable improvements.

In a variation on this technique, T.R. Smith [788] calculated the various rates of return to property owners in Hartford, Connecticut, under several assumptions, including the current yield of property subject to a site-value tax. He found that for several underdeveloped parcels the increased tax burden would exceed the existing income stream.

In another variation, A.H. Schaaf [755] considered the income groups of occupants of properties in Northern Alameda County, California. He concluded that a shift to site-value taxation would increase the tax burden on sites occupied by lower income groups. The implied conclusion that this would increase the regressivity of the tax rests upon two assumptions: the tax would be substantially shifted forward to tenants and, at least in the short run, properties would not be abandoned by owners. The assumption that landlords could shift the increased tax burden to tenants is rather curious when applied to a site-value tax. Writers who have developed and refined property tax theory insist that the site-value tax is borne entirely by the owner and is not shifted forward.

It is difficult to draw very useful conclusions from such general studies. They demonstrate only that much valuable urban land is currently underutilized. This finding will surprise few observers of the urban scene.

Some empirical evidence on the effects of modified versions of site-value taxation is available in the Price Waterhouse study [691] cited earlier. In the course of their case-by-case analysis of several tax-incentive programs, the authors considered two instances each of a graded-tax system (Pittsburgh and Honolulu), a property tax system emphasizing land values (Southfield, Michigan and Arlington, Virginia), and one case of a simulated site-value tax system (Fairhope, Alabama). None of these is true site-value taxation. Under the graded tax land values are taxed at a higher rate than the rate on improvements. The emphasis on land value in the two other cases is essentially an attempt to make sure that the assessed land value accurately reflects true land value within the context of a standard property tax. In the Fairhope case there has been an attempt to simulate site-value taxation through a system of rents.

The methodology of the Price Waterhouse study is not particularly strong, as we indicated earlier. Nevertheless, this study represents the closest approach we have to research on the effects of tax systems incorporating aspects of site-value taxation.

In general, Price Waterhouse finds no instance of positive effects on the intensity of development that can be unambiguously attributed to the incentives presented by the site-value aspects of these tax systems. In neither Pittsburgh nor Honolulu did they find evidence that supported the theoretical claims that site-value taxation could, by itself, spur an intensive development of urban land. In fact, the authors concluded that in Pittsburgh the existence of a graded-tax system could not prevent the blighting of many local neighborhoods. While the authors acknowledged that the two systems in which there was an emphasis on land value showed explosive growth, they attributed this growth largely to socioeconomic and geographical considerations, not to the site-value aspects of the tax. And in the case of Fairhope's simulated site-value tax, the authors concluded that capital considerations of the lessees were more important than the simulation of site-value taxation in generating the upsurge in redevelopment.

With no more than two cases for any of the three variations on site-value taxation, it is not possible to factor out the independent effects of the tax system. The authors are correct in their argument that the effects cannot be attributed to the tax system alone. Yet, it is not clear from this evidence that the tax system lacks an independent effect. Perhaps the only conclusion that can be drawn is that the partial site-value taxation represented in Pittsburgh's graded tax does not alone suffice to prevent blight.

Administrative Problems—Costs

There is virtually no policy-related research on this question. Experience in some foreign countries where the site-value tax has long been used indicates that it is administratively feasible. It can be argued that assessment task may be harder for site-value taxation than for general real-property taxation. Sites without improvements are rarely sold, particularly in the central city, so there is little market data for assessment. But there is virtually no pertinent evidence from this country.

On the other hand, one could argue that assessment for site-value taxation is certainly easier than it is for a graded tax in which buildings and land are assessed separately. There is some evidence that pertains to the administration of a graded tax in this country. Price Waterhouse [691] reports that the Honolulu assessor's office has encountered no difficulty in operating under the graded-tax system. Similarly, the Pittsburgh assessor's office thought it no more difficult to operate under a graded tax than under the conventional tax system.

The evidence thus suggests that assessment for site-value taxes is at least possible. But there are no studies which address the question more closely.

Administrative Problems—Equity Effects

Clearly, the effects of an immediate switch to site-value taxation would be disruptive. As Dick Netzer, a proponent of the site-value tax system, has put it:

Rapid conversion of the existing property tax into an ideal one would be one of the most radical and destabilizing changes in fiscal institutions imaginable. [604, p. 14]

There is, however, no real evidence on what those effects might be. Given the most probable expectations about the seriousness of these effects, we are not likely to undertake the experiment that would be necessary to generate such evidence. This may be the strongest argument against the switch to site-value taxation; but its strength may be weakened by a more gradual shift through the intermediate stages of a graded-tax system.

On the equity effects of a shift to site-value taxation, one might presume that those holding underdeveloped property would be hardest hit. Given the capitalization of future taxes into present value, they would bear the brunt of future effects, that is, an increased tax on unimproved properties would be capitalized into a lower present value of those properties. The equity questions this raises have not been addressed in the literature. But they are tied to the question to which we turn next.

Equity Effects in General

The evangelical literature on site-value taxation has made much of the argument that the tax has desirable equity effects because it operates as a tax on socially created wealth. A tax on wealth is generally held to be desirable in its own right; site-value wealth is viewed as even more justifiably taxable. The argument is that in general the value of land in particular locations is not created by the holder of the land, but rather by society. A site becomes more valuable because of expanding transportation networks, neighboring land uses, public services, parks, and so forth. Hence, society is justified in taxing back part or all of the wealth that it created.

The argument reduces to a question of social values, and as such could hardly be resolved by policy-related research. Such research could, however, establish more carefully the incidence profile for site-value taxation. This has not been done well in the research literature. The Schaaf study [755], the one study that does address the question of incidence, makes the crucial and probably erroneous assumption that the entire tax will be shifted to the occupants. Its conclusions therefore cannot be accepted.

An interesting relationship between the equity question and the question of the effect of the site-value tax on development should be noted. Some site values are not socially created. The developer of a large development may be able to capture most of the neighborhood effects of his development within the development itself, that is, the value of individual parcels within the development may increase because of the improvements placed upon neighboring parcels. This increase in land values within the large-scale development will form part of the incentive to the developer to undertake the investment in the first place. To the extent that site-value taxation would tax away part of this increased land value, it might deter the development of large-scale projects such as planned neighborhoods and communities.

Revenue Producing Capacity

We cannot forget that the basic point of the property tax is not to provide incentives for housing development, but rather to provide revenues for local government. Clearly the question of whether the site-value tax can provide sufficient revenues for municipal government is crucial. It has hardly been touched by the policy-related research, however. Perhaps the closest that such research has come to dealing with the question is the assumption, in the various studies using a hypothetical shift to site-value taxation, that the revenue yields for the localities in which they do their research would have to be the same under the site-value tax as they are under current practice. That this assumption does not yield internally contradictory results in these studies may indicate that the yield of the site-value tax can be made as adequate to the city's needs as are the yields of the current tax. But we are left without any strong empirical evidence on the issue.

In general, then, the theoretical literature on taxation makes a very strong case for the desirability of site-value taxation. But little of this theoretical work is supported by good policy-related empirical research.

Compromise Solutions

Some cities have adopted systems of graded property taxation that tax land more heavily than improvements in an attempt to strike a compromise between site-value taxation and the current system. Unfortunately, we also have very little research reporting on these systems. The Price Waterhouse study [691] of Pittsburgh and Honolulu represents the only evidence we have on the graded tax. And, of course, the same questions that apply to the site-value tax can be addressed to the graded tax.

Consequences of Conversion

Unfortunately, there is no available research that focuses on the impact of site-value taxation upon the relative value of different land parcels and the social and demographic characteristics of different neighborhoods. How will a changeover to site-value taxation affect the availability of low-income housing projects in suburban areas? Will a graded local tax system have a major impact upon the viability of middle-income residential neighborhoods in the central city? These and other issues must be analyzed before the full costs and benefits of a changeover to site-value taxation can be measured.

Conclusions

There is an extensive literature on the effects of the property tax on housing. Much of this material, however, is of little help to the local policy maker interested in using the conventional property tax to support certain housing policies or to ameliorate certain housing problems. The literature is highly theoretical. There is almost no empirical evidence as to the actual impacts of the current tax or the consequences of reform measures, such as tax abatement programs and site-value taxation, on housing investments or expenditures. Furthermore, the literature only identifies the detrimental effects of the property tax on housing. It does not measure the magnitude of these effects nor the costs and benefits associated with alternative tax proposals.

Studies concerning the conventional property tax agree that the administration of the present tax is detrimental to housing. Several of the studies indicate that the tax as it is currently administered aggravates the problem of urban blight because central city properties are typically overassessed while single family homes are often undervalued. These analyses suggest that changes in current assessment practices should improve the possibilities for dealing with urban blight. However, none of the studies measures the impact of assessment practices relative to other blighting factors. There is also an absence of analysis concerning how assessment practices can best be changed.

Much of the literature regarding the property tax addresses problems in the current structure of the tax that have detrimental effects upon housing. This literature identifies six basic effects of the tax that impede local housing policies designed to stimulate the construction, maintenance, and rehabilitation of housing: the tax has a regressive impact upon housing consumers; it acts as a sales tax upon housing; it acts as a tax on capital invested in housing; it reduces the cash available for maintenance and improvements; it contributes to the "locking in" of current owners; and it promotes fiscal competition and exclusionary zoning.

There is almost no empirical evidence concerning any of these six effects. The few analyses that are available suggest to policy makers that the property tax in its role as a sales tax on housing has a more detrimental effect on the housing market in the central city than in suburban communities. Studies by Arthur D. Little, Inc. [28] and Sternlieb [826] also suggest that local policy makers can reduce the detrimental effects of the property tax upon investment in renovations and remodelling by conducting a vigorous information campaign among landlords. These two studies indicate that many owners share a widespread misconception that improvements on their properties will invariably lead to higher assessments.

Analyses of the effect of the property tax on a landlord's cash flow suggest that the relative impact of the property tax upon the deterioration of specific buildings and neighborhoods is small. Consequently, the evidence indicates that local policy makers will not significantly stop urban blight if they remove the property tax from deteriorating buildings, but do little else to address the social and economic problems of blighted neighborhoods.

Peterson's analysis [670] suggests that the policy maker, by lowering property taxes in central cities, can induce the "locked in" owners of deteriorating properties to sell to purchasers who will be willing to expend more funds on maintenance. Peterson's suggestion is provocative. Unfortunately, there are no empirical findings on the efficacy of his proposal or on the costs of alternative taxes that must be levied to replace the tax revenue foregone on central city properties.

Policy-related research to guide local officials in promoting housing that increases tax revenues is sparse. Sternlieb's analysis [829] concludes that the number of bedrooms in each home is the best indicator for assessing the public-service costs associated with new developments: the more bedrooms, the higher the costs. Two other studies indicate that single-family homes (three and four bedroom) do not consume more in services than they generate in taxes except where the local tax rate supports nearly all educational expenditures. Much more empirical analysis is needed before these results can be applied by policy makers with confidence to their local communities.

There is very little evidence available concerning alternatives to the conventional property tax—tax-abatement programs and site-value taxation. The few available studies indicate that both tax abatement and site-value taxation in and of themselves are not likely to retard urban blight. Tax abatement, which has been studied more extensively, appears to work best in conjunction with other housing policy tools, such as code enforcement and consumer subsidies. However, more research is needed before the local policy maker can identify the particular mixes of policy instruments—tax and other—that are most appropriate in dealing with the particular housing problems he faces.

5 Housing-assistance Programs

Introduction

Although state housing-finance agencies are beginning to play important roles, subsidy programs in the field of housing have traditionally been funded and administered by the federal government. There are two general categories of federally assisted housing serving low- and moderate-income families: publicly owned housing; and privately owned, publicly assisted housing. The former, generally referred to as the public housing program, is administered by the Housing Assistance Administration within the Department of Housing and Urban Development (HUD). The latter includes a variety of subsidy programs covering both rental housing and home ownership and has been administered by the Federal Housing Administration (FHA) within HUD, the same agency that in the 1950s insured the mortgages of countless young, suburban-bound middle-class families.

Within the past several years the design and administration of these programs have come under increasing criticism from many sources—academics, local and state policy makers, recipients of federal housing assistance, and more recently, HUD itself. The programs have been criticized as inefficient, unresponsive to consumer needs, and administratively unwieldy. At the date of this writing many of these categorical housing-assistance programs are suspended, their funds impounded, while the federal government reassesses its role in this area.

For several important reasons we review the policy-related research on housing-assistance programs even though, with the exception of certain self-help programs, local officials have had relatively little control over their design or administration.

First, of all the policy instruments thus far discussed, these programs have had the most direct and substantial impact on the quality, quantity, cost, and distribution of housing for low- and moderate-income families. From 1968 through 1971, following passage of the National Housing Act of 1968, federally assisted housing has constituted over 18 percent of conventionally built housing (nearly 15% of all new units including mobile homes). And federally assisted housing was more widely dispersed than under previous subsidy programs. In fact, a significant proportion of privately owned, federally assisted housing constructed since 1968 is located in the ring of suburbs that circle the large metropolitan centers that, in the preceding decade, were the principal beneficiaries of public housing and urban renewal funds.

Second, the local policy maker can hardly ignore the impact of these programs since he must provide and pay for the many supportive services housing requires. These include schools, police and fire protection, sewage and trash removal, parks, playgrounds, and the like. It is the responsibility of local public officials to absorb and service federally assisted housing within the local community. In the case of public housing programs, local public authorities have extensive responsibility for the design, construction, and operation of new and existing units as well.

Third, the local policy maker needs to understand the successes and failures of these programs to date so he can make more effective use of the funds now available under the community development and assisted housing provisions of The Housing and Community Development Act of 1974 to promote housing construction and rehabilitation activity.

In this chapter we address three general issues:

1. Should a housing-assistance strategy consist primarily of supply subsidies, demand subsidies, or a combination of both?
2. To what extent should a housing-assistance strategy be tied to the large-scale rehabilitation of substandard units?
3. In the absence of funds, should local government promote forms of self-help such as urban homesteading and tenant cooperatives?

Housing-subsidy Programs: Supply vs. Demand

Alternative strategies of housing assistance have been widely debated but inadequately analyzed. As in several policy areas discussed in prior chapters, the literature tends to be either highly theoretical or narrowly empirical. We have not attempted a comprehensive review of all the policy-related research on subsidy programs, since much of it is addressed exclusively to the federal policy maker. Instead, it is our intention to convey the general character of the research literature in this area and to report selectively on studies that may be of interest to the local policy maker.

In dealing with the issue of housing-subsidy programs, the more theoretical research studies explore two related questions: What are appropriate methods for measuring the direct tenant benefits of housing-assistance programs? What is the relative efficiency of alternative forms of subsidy in terms of these measures of cost effectiveness? These studies are essentially the explorations of academic economists. With few exceptions they tend to focus on the quantifiable benefits of housing-assistance programs and rely upon standard economic assumptions concerning the profit-maximizing behavior of participants in the housing market. And with few exceptions they conclude that demand subsidies, particularly unrestricted cash grants, are far more efficient than supply subsidies, and are capable of reaching a far broader segment of the poor. Few of these propositions have been empirically tested and thus they are of limited reliability as guides to the local policy maker, however well reasoned the economic arguments.

A second group of studies, principally those of Arthur P. Solomon [798, 799, 800] and Anthony Downs [199], gives weight to the direct and measurable benefits of alternative subsidy programs, but considers as well the broader social and political objectives of these programs. It is the consensus of these studies that a balance of supply and demand subsidies is the most viable housing strategy.

In the remainder of this section we assess those research studies on housing subsidies that should be of general interest to the local policy maker. Since the largest number of these studies are program evaluations, we have organized them around the principal form of subsidy they examine: first, supply-subsidy programs—public housing and interest-reduction subsidies; second, demand subsidies—housing allowances and leased-housing programs.

Since the 1930s the principal strategy for helping poor families secure adequate shelter has been to reduce the construction and operating costs of new or rehabilitated housing. These supply subsidies may take a variety of forms: paying the debt service on public housing bonds; providing loans at below the market interest rate to builder or home purchaser; and establishing rent supplements that are tied to specific housing units; among others. These subsidies are aimed at expanding the supply of housing and bringing its cost within reach of the lower income consumer. Not surprisingly, supply subsidies are the favorite of the home-building industry, which has been instrumental over the years in formulating the contents of housing legislation through the lobbying efforts of such organizations as the National Association of Home Builders, National Association of Mutual Savings Banks, and United States Savings and Loan League.

An alternative set of strategies seeks to augment the demand for housing by increasing the income of those who buy or rent housing. This strategy differs from supply subsidies in that the funds go directly to the consumer and are not necessarily tied to a predesignated housing unit. These demand subsidy programs are relatively new, and include programs like rent supplements and leased public housing. Some are now in the planning stage. These include general income-maintenance programs advanced as welfare-reform proposals and housing-allowance programs that differ from the welfare-reform proposals in requiring a minimum level of cash expenditures on housing.

Supply Subsidies

Public Housing. Richard Muth presents a classic critique of public housing in *Public Housing: An Economic Evaluation* [576]. The work is largely theoretical and marred by the author's reliance upon standard economic assumptions, for example, that a perfect market prevails in low-income housing with competing suppliers and informed, mobile consumers. Muth's analysis demonstrates that the average unit cost of public housing is higher than that of comparable housing on the private market. And not only is public housing relatively inefficient, but its benefits reach only a small fraction of families eligible for public housing assistance.

The Muth critique accords with conclusions reached by Eugene Smolensky [794] and Robert L. Bish [70] in two earlier studies. Applying standard welfare-economics theories, Smolensky concluded that it would be far more efficient to give families eligible for public housing a cash subsidy so long as they continued to occupy standard housing. Drawing upon Smolensky's estimate of the resource cost of public housing, Bish provides an elaborate analysis of the direct benefits that accrue to families in public housing and concludes that costs exceed these benefits by a significant margin.

A subsequent study undertaken by HUD [875] to serve as the basis for new housing policy recommendations for 1975 reaches similar conclusions. Several statistical measures are designed to analyze each of three basic effects of the major supply-subsidy programs:

1. How do the benefits generated by these programs compare with the costs incurred?
2. Are the subsidized housing programs serving the appropriate people?
3. Are the programs having the desired effects on those served, and on the community at large?

The writers conclude that each of the major supply-subsidy programs—rent supplements, low-rent public housing, interest-subsidy programs, and rural-homeownership assistance—makes low-rent housing available only at the cost of serious inefficiency and inequity. While certain problems could be remedied through legislative changes, the writers maintain that many of these changes would create or aggravate other problems that characterize supply-subsidy programs. The HUD group also concludes that changes in administration are not likely to mitigate these significant problems that, they maintain, are inherent in the structure of a supply-subsidy program.

Regrettably, these findings are of little immediate use to the local policy maker choosing among alternative housing strategies. The HUD analysis is based upon samples derived from highly aggregated national data and the results are dependent upon computer simulations. Consequently, the authors' findings concerning the magnitude of inefficiency and inequity associated with a particular type of supply-subsidy program are not necessarily applicable to specific localities or projects.

Edgar O. Olsen and James R. Prescott [647], in a study for the RAND

Corporation, also attempt to formulate a meaningful measure of net tenant benefits attributable to government-assistance programs, particularly public housing. Their study goes slightly farther than the previous three, which rely principally on aggregate data from HUD, in that it tests this measure on a sampling of public housing tenants. Unfortunately, the sampling procedure relied upon is not at all clear from the study.

Olsen and Prescott find that the average public housing household sampled spends less on housing than it would have on the private market in the absence of subsidy. Put another way, the lower rent available to the public housing tenant permits him to spend more on nonhousing items such as food, clothing, and recreation. Pursuing this finding in an independent study, Olsen [646] demonstrates that only the rent-subsidy portion of the public housing program actually increases the aggregate quantity of nonhousing items consumed, if temporary effects are ignored. The construction-subsidy portion, which is the principal focus of the public housing program, has no such effect.

Richard F. Muth's analysis [576] leads him to recommend lump-sum rental certificates, a demand subsidy, over conventional public housing because of their relative efficiency, equity, and ease of administration. Eugene Smolensky [794] favors conditional cash grants—a similar form of demand subsidy. In another theoretical analysis, Larry L. Orr [654] perceives conditional cash grants as clearly more efficient than traditional public housing. Orr concedes, however, that the policy decision between conditional cash grants and public housing must rest on a broader base than the relative efficiency of the two programs. The ultimate policy choice will depend upon the value one ascribes to the fact that public housing provides more than the minimal housing services a cash-grant recipient may opt to purchase.

In a comparative analysis of conventional public housing, leased public housing and rent-supplement programs, operating in the Boston area, Arthur P. Solomon [800] reaches beyond the limits of the previous studies in measuring the programs against four social objectives: maximizing aggregate consumption of housing services, promoting equal residential opportunities, reducing the number of residents in substandard units, and redistributing the consumption of housing services more equitably. He concludes that leased housing, a consumer-oriented strategy, is less costly, more equitable, more responsive to consumer choice, and more conducive to racial and economic integration. However, his analysis also indicates that certain production-oriented programs, particularly rent supplements for new construction, supply tenants with better-quality units than those provided under consumer-oriented programs.

Generalizing from these findings, Solomon concludes that the existing dominance of supply subsidies, like public housing, is inappropriate. He recommends that federal housing policies provide a balance between supply and demand strategies. For our purposes, this means that local policy makers should thoroughly compare the economic and social costs and benefits associated with each program, and then carefully select a program package reflecting the priorities of their communities.

In sum, the studies on public housing and related programs for low-income families are largely theoretical with limited empirical bases, or attempts to refine methods for measuring benefits. Since this is an area of critical concern to local policy makers, more empirical studies of the sort undertaken by Solomon are essential.

Interest-reduction Subsidies. The most telling defense of interest-reduction subsidies is made by Anthony Downs in his comprehensive analysis of federal housing subsidies. The Downs study [199] is curious in that his data and analysis are not available in the published report. Too often one must guess what the sources of his information are, as well as the analysis on which his conclusions are based. Nonetheless, his analysis is forceful and influential. Downs is careful to show the numerous and sometimes conflicting objectives of federal housing-subsidy programs—encouraging home ownership, stimulating the housing industry, improving the quality of deteriorated neighborhoods, and encouraging housing innovation, among others—that preclude application of any single criterion of effectiveness.

Downs' study is primarily a defense of the two principal interest-subsidy programs (Sections 235 and 236 of the National Housing Act of 1968) that were severely criticized by the Nixon administration as too costly, geared too exclusively to new construction, badly administered, and inequitable.[a] Downs disputes these findings point by point.

Challenging the kind of economic analysis presented by Muth, Downs argues that a program of supply subsidies is required whether or not income strategies are adopted, because housing supply—like the supply of other consumer services—responds sluggishly to increased consumer demand. In support of his argument, Downs cites federal experience with medical-demand subsidies. He contends that housing—like medical services—will not grow sufficiently in response to the increased income of consumers. Therefore, in the absence of supply subsidies, a program that increases consumer income will only increase the price of existing housing services.

Muth and several other economists disagree with the Downs' position. Muth argues that the price elasticity of supply approaches unity, except in the short run. Put another way, the supply of housing services will expand by an amount equal to the expansion in consumer demand for housing—even in the absence of supply subsidies. This is an important issue that needs to be empirically tested. Even if the supply of housing services is only sluggish in the short run, as Muth contends, the short-run impacts of increased consumer demand upon prices and

---

[a]These arguments are summarized in the report of the National Housing Policy Review, *Housing in the Seventies, Part I* [368]. Part II of the HUD report, containing technical and background papers, was not available for evaluation.

rents of existing units could very well make demand-subsidy programs politically infeasible over the long run.

Downs also argues that conventional public housing is fundamentally a sound instrument for providing decent physical dwelling units to households with low incomes. He contends the effectiveness of the program in meeting this objective has been distorted because our society has used public housing as an instrument for coping with general problems of poverty and racial discrimination.

Whether or not his research methods can pass muster, Downs succeeds in focusing debate on the social and political complexities of housing-assistance programs. He argues that any effective subsidy program must involve some combination of three main variables: income-maintenance and social service delivery programs, capital-investment programs to upgrade innercity neighborhoods, and programs for dispersal of low- and moderate-income families throughout the metropolitan area. Once these variables are considered along with the more quantifiable objectives of cost effectiveness and equity, it is difficult to challenge the conclusions Downs reaches. He favors a mix of housing subsidies containing a balance of supply and demand features.

One is tempted to challenge the objectivity of the Downs report, since it was commissioned by the very organizations which are accused of exploiting supply-subsidy programs in their role as intermediaries in the housing process, namely the National Association of Home Builders, the National Association of Mutual Savings Banks, and the United States Savings and Loan League.

Once again, the research on supply subsidies, both public housing and mortgage interest-reduction subsidies, is notable for the absence of strong and convincing empirical studies. Analysts seem to agree that the dominance of supply over demand subsidies as instruments of federal housing policy has been inappropriate—that they are less efficient and equitable than consumer-oriented strategies. Several analysts, however, argue with some force that a sudden shift to demand subsidies would have severe inflationary impacts on housing prices, and that a balance of supply and demand subsidies may be required. On this pivotal issue—the short-run impacts of increased consumer demand on prices and rents of existing units—careful empirical research is lacking.

Demand Subsidies

As evidenced in the studies discussed above, demand subsidies, whether conditional (subsidy must be spent on housing) or unconditional (subsidy can be spent at the discretion of the recipient), are thought to have several advantages over supply subsidies:

1. Recipients are permitted much the same freedom of choice exercised by the rest of society, thereby eliminating the paternalism implicit in any transfer-in-kind strategy.

2. Costly dependence on housing intermediaries is largely eliminated.
3. Families receiving help are not limited to designated projects or locations.

Much of the research on demand subsidies and their putative advantages is theoretical, largely because there have been few demonstration projects to evaluate. We discuss below those studies that explore aspects of demand subsidies that may be of special interest to local policy makers.

Housing Allowance. Arthur P. Solomon [799] has conducted one of the few empirical studies that examines a demand-subsidy program in operation. His objective was to assess the impact of the Kansas City housing-allowance experiment on rent levels, landlord behavior, tenant behavior, and tenant aspirations. As policy-related research the study has the limitations of most program evaluation. Based largely on interview data and lacking a control group, this is at best a case study of limited generalizability.

Solomon found evidence to support the advantages of housing allowances in the Kansas City experiment. His findings show that recipients improved their housing conditions (larger units, less overcrowding, and better facilities), as well as the comparative status and service level of the neighborhood in which they located. He goes beyond his data base and specific findings, however, in concluding that a larger percentage of each subsidy dollar is likely to reach the target population in housing allowances than in any alternative existing subsidy program.

Solomon's findings bear out the propositions of several other economists (specifically Olsen [645], Tullock [869], Lowry [487], and Wehner [896] who constructed largely theoretical arguments on behalf of housing allowances.

Marilyn Langford Reeves' study of Philadelphia's rent-subsidy program [712] deserves mention as one of the very few studies of a locally funded housing-assistance program. Reeves finds—as would be expected—that rent subsidy does not work well in a tight housing market. Augmenting the purchasing power of the low-income family during periods of tight housing supply merely inflates rents charged for existing units.

Reeves' study suffers from the limitation of the case study. It is reported here to highlight an issue that needs further investigation before rent-subsidy or housing-allowance programs can be given unqualified support.

Leased-housing Program. Through the leased-housing program, local housing authorities lease dwellings from private owners and make them available to low-income families at below-market rents. The program imposes substantial responsibility upon the local housing authority, which is charged with enrolling landlords, inspecting participating units, selecting and interviewing tenants, and mediating disputes between landlords and tenants. In some important respects leased housing occupies a halfway ground between income-assistance (demand)

and supply-side subsidy programs. Where new units are constructed by a developer on the strength of a long-term lease guarantee from the local housing authority, the program has the features of a supply-subsidy program.

Solomon distinguishes between the supply and demand features of the leased-housing program in another significant study [800] and poses the following questions: What is the least expensive method of providing housing to low-income families? What proportion of total cost is subsidized by the government? What proportion actually reaches the tenant? What proportion goes to administrative overhead? And how much local-government revenue is lost because of assorted tax concessions under the various programs? Solomon's analysis indicates that the leasing of existing units is substantially less expensive than leased housing with new construction or with rehabilitation. And leased-housing strategies are far less expensive than either public housing or other production subsidies such as rent supplements. Though Solomon relies exclusively on Boston development data, there is reason to believe that his methodology would yield similar results elsewhere.

In a more recent study [801] Solomon draws heavily upon Boston program data to construct a means of comparing and ranking alternative federal housing strategies. Solomon concludes that although leased housing compares poorly with other housing programs on the basis of conventional cost/benefit criteria, it ranks higher than other programs on the basis of broader measures of economic efficiency as well as measures of social and environmental impact.

Solomon's study makes two major methodological contributions to the policy analysis of alternative housing strategies. First, the formal model of economic costs and benefits that he has constructed attempts to evaluate in one measure both the efficiency and the distributional effects of different housing programs. He does so by attaching a special weight to benefits received by such target groups as the poor, minorities, and large families.

Second, Solomon develops an ordinal scale to gauge the nondollar benefits of housing programs. This ordinal ranking is necessarily subjective and Solomon applies it to only five categories of noneconomic benefits: consumer sovereignty, racial and economic dispersal, stabilizing low-rent housing markets, adaptability to changing local market conditions, and ability to provide an "acceptable" residential environment. In spite of these limitations Solomon's methodology is an important first step in developing a more comprehensive and explicit means of evaluating the extensive costs and benefits associated with alternative housing strategies.

In a less analytic piece, Frank deLeeuw and Sam H. Leaman [184] compare the leased-housing program with standard public housing and turnkey alternatives. This is basically a survey, marred by the failure of the authors to reveal their sampling procedure. The survey results show that for several understandable reasons, scattered-site leased housing is greatly preferred to project housing. It is generally located in better neighborhoods, provides more bedrooms for large families, and spares tenants embarrassment by assuring their anonymity. The survey also indicates that program costs per unit are lower than for conventional or turnkey units. The single disadvantage noted by the authors is that scattered locations and diversity of housing type can generate higher administrative costs per unit than the more conventional high-rise public housing projects.

Research Gaps

Substantial research obviously remains to be done on alternative forms of housing subsidy. The research literature is sketchy. Sound empirical studies are few. Many propositions from the more theoretical studies remain untested. Questions addressed by The Urban Institute in 1970 to the housing-allowance experiment are still ripe for inquiry: How will rent levels change as a result of likely changes in tenant income? What will tenants get in the way of housing services for increased rents they might pay? What part of the rent increase will be reflected in improved housing services and what part will be swallowed by inflation? What are the advantages of different forms of administering these programs?

One must be careful in assessing income strategies to recognize the interaction between this policy instrument and other local-government policies and services. For example, it is unlikely that housing allowances can succeed in assuring standard housing, especially in tight housing markets, without intensified code enforcement. As studies of code enforcement and abandonment have revealed, however, anticipated rental income must equal or exceed operating costs before landlords will invest in maintenance or needed capital improvements. This necessitates second-order calculation of the minimum level of income assistance required to assure improvement in the quality of housing services.

Questions related specifically to the consequences of a shift to income-assistance strategies are important to local policy makers because there has been so little experience with such programs. Thus far, the debate has centered on the issues of cost effectiveness of alternative subsidy forms. No studies have considered the indirect costs imposed upon local government by these programs. There is certainly some question as to whether local housing-authority staffs have the capacity to provide the market analyses and property-inspection and tenant-counselling services that leased-housing and housing-allowance programs require.

Large-scale Rehabilitation

The Promotion of Rehabilitation

We turn now from an examination of alternative forms of housing to an assessment of the research on one kind of housing-assistance strategy—large-scale rehabilitation of existing units.

Downs [201], among others, directly addressed the question of the priority that should be given to the creation of additional housing units through extensive rehabilitation. As the research studies assessed above indicate, in areas of tight housing supply, income-assistance strategies may be inappropriate or, at the least, prohibitively expensive. Efforts to increase the supply of housing over the short-run must be undertaken, especially for families that are not ordinarily served by the private market: large low-income families, racial minorities, and the elderly, among others.

If a balanced strategy involves the continuation of supply subsidies, what priority should be given to the large-scale rehabilitation of existing units, one of the principal foci of supply-subsidy programs over the last decade?

The federal rehabilitation initiative in the broad context of neighborhood rejuvenation began in the middle 1950s with the establishment of mortgage-insurance programs for multifamily housing in urban renewal areas. Rehabilitation had previously been undertaken—if at all—on a house-by-house basis. Renewal activities consisted primarily of clearance and new construction. It was in reaction to the disruptive aspects of clearance projects that rehabilitation was promoted.

Subsidies earmarked for the rehabilitation of dwellings began in the 1960s. Section 312, introduced by the 1965 Housing Act, provides low-interest loans generally intended for the rehabilitation of one-to-four-unit buildings by owner-occupants, or absentee owners of houses in urban renewal or federal code-enforcement areas. Section 115, introduced the same year, provides rehabilitation grants to families with incomes under $3,000 annually. The two programs have been used in tandem for families with incomes above the Section 115 limits, but for whom the carrying charges from a 312 loan amount to more than 25 percent of income.

In the face of slow production of rehabilitated units, the federal government made several attempts to help develop a large-scale housing-rehabilitation industry. It was believed that only through large-scale activity could savings be realized and passed on to low-income consumers of housing. Several major demonstration programs were undertaken in Chicago, Philadelphia, New York, and Boston. The latter effort, the Boston Rehabilitation Project (BURP), produced a large number of rehabilitated units and has been the focus of two studies that will be discussed below. BURP provided the framework for the largest federal rehabilitation program, Project Rehab.

Project Rehab began in 1969 as part of the federal government's attempt to gear up to meet the nation's housing needs. The rehabilitation goal was two million units over the decade following 1968—one-third of the estimated production of subsidized housing. The rehabilitation goal was soon lowered to one million, but Project Rehab has failed to reach even the lowered production level.

Rehabilitation has many apparent advantages. It saves structurally sound buildings and the network of physical and social infrastructure that has been developed in older neighborhoods. Many venerable buildings also have certain amenities that are not duplicated by current construction: large rooms, high ceilings, large units, hardwood trim, etc. Presumably rehabilitation also reduces the need for relocation. Residents may possibly remain during the process, or buildings can be repaired in several stages. Since at least the shell of the building remains, rehabilitation should be cheaper and faster than new construction. Rehabilitation is especially well suited for marginal neighborhoods with patchy areas of deterioration.

By definition, rehabilitation is addressed to existing housing. The focus generally is in older inner city neighborhoods. The housing rehabilitated with the assistance of government programs is more often than not occupied by low- or moderate-income families. Frequently they rent their units from owners who may or may not live in the building. The fact that the buildings are not kept in repair by their owners suggests that there are larger social and economic problems associated with the poor condition of the housing. Many experts believe that rehabiliation is most appropriate for neighborhoods where housing conditions are declining, but where housing is still generally sound.

Nature of the Literature

A great deal has been written about the local operation of federal rehabilitation programs. These studies have generally combined some quantitative evaluation of program performance with more subjective analysis—impressions as to the role of various program participants and beneficiaries, estimates of the future of specific programs and of rehabilitation in general, and a variety of prescriptions for improving rehabilitation as an alternative to clearance and new construction.

The diverse methodologies and small sample or case-study nature of most of the works reviewed here prevent us from making any well substantiated general statements about rehabilitation.

In addition, most of these evaluations were made either during the operation of a program or shortly after its completion. A few studies look retrospectively at earlier programs. Base-line data for purposes of before and after comparisons are generally lacking; no attempts were made to isolate control neighborhoods. Although these retrospective opinions are not vigorously supported, a somewhat consistent pattern in the life cycle of the specific rehabilitation program under study emerges—one of high expectation and low performance.

Clearance and Construction vs. Rehabilitation

One of the major issues public agencies face is the choice of renewal mode—in what cases to choose (a) clearance and new construction, (b) rehabilitation, to one or another standard, or (c) concentrated code enforcement, generally in conjunction with rehabilitation.

In an impressive research study, D. Gordon Bagby [37] provides the most clear-cut empirical results on the choice between clearance and new construction and rehabilitation. Because of the limitations of his sample, his results are not clearly generalizable beyond particular types of buildings in a particular neighborhood in Philadelphia at a particular time. Nevertheless, the study is well done and the conclusions are certainly striking. As such they are of considerable interest.

Bagby develops cost estimates for particular sizes of buildings for new construction, urban renewal (defined as clearance of existing structures and new construction), and total rehabilitation. He concludes that total rehabilitation is somewhat less costly (by 12%) than new construction; and substantially less costly (by 22-24%) than clearance and new construction. Not surprisingly, he concludes from this data that rehabilitation is the most appropriate housing strategy whenever "least cost" is the sole criterion.

However, Bagby convincingly notes, along with A.H. Schaaf [753] and others, that a least-cost construction criterion biases policy decisions in favor of rehabilitation over new construction by overlooking key factors such as differential life expectancy of the structure, differences in efficiency in furnishing housing services (e.g., adequate light and air), and differences in future maintenance and operating expenditures.

Bagby does not test these factors directly. Instead, he tests the hypothesis by comparing the amount that consumers will pay for new housing with the amount they will pay for comparable rehabilitated housing. He finds that the Philadelphia consumers will pay substantially more for new housing. He then compares the "profit" (defined as the sales price of the unit less the development cost) from clearance and new construction with the "profit" from total rehabilitation. Clearance and new construction proved considerably more profitable. Bagby argues that such evidence of consumer preference for new homes as compared with rehabilitated units should be respected by government and other nonprofitmaking bodies.

It should be noted, however, that these conclusions do not necessarily apply to less costly alternatives than complete or "gut" rehabilitation, nor are they necessarily generalizable to other situations.

The theoretical basis for comparing the costs and benefits of rehabilitation and new construction, and of various levels of rehabilitation, has been more fully elaborated by Schaaf [753] in this country and Lionel Needleman [596] in Great Britain. Schaaf offers a theoretically convincing technique for determining the optimum renewal standard for a particular building or neighborhood. The technique requires knowledge of the renewal cost, the structure life, the expected average annual future maintenance cost, and the life expectation and expected average annual market-rental value both for units renewed to various standards and for new units.

Through conventional economic analysis, Schaaf can determine, for example, the comparative feasibility of new construction as against rehabilitating a structure to code standard three times (now, 10 years from now, and 20 years from now) and then rehabilitating to a higher "modernization" standard. Rehabilitation is feasible if the present value of any investment situation involving long-term rehabilitation exceeds the value of immediate new construction.

Schaaf suggests that his equations be used in any given renewal area in the following manner:

1. As a first step it must be determined that no major areawide changes in land uses or residential densities are desirable since rehabilitation in such circumstances is not feasible.
2. Having decided that rehabilitation is a possible choice for at least some of the structures in the area, the various renewal standards must be established and fully specified, with the two limiting cases ordinarily consisting of minimum code compliance and new construction.
3. When the various renewal standards have been specified, the cost of meeting these standards can be estimated for each study property, or for representative examples of properties.

Schaaf's analysis depends on the selection of an appropriate discount rate to calculate the present value of future rehabilitation investments. Choosing such a discount rate is difficult, and the question of which rate to apply to different future investment and earning streams has long been a lively topic of conversation among economists.

It would also be difficult for a local policy maker to apply Schaaf's methodology in analyzing programs for his locality because much of the data required would be difficult and costly to obtain for any given project area. More studies along the lines of Bagby's, preferably dealing with alternative standards of rehabilitation, should test the reliability of "ersatz" measures of the factors Schaaf identifies. Consumer preference, as reflected by sales prices and rents, is but one of these.

Large-scale Rehabilitation—The Boston Program

Perhaps the most useful project to the policy maker, albeit a discouraging experience in large-scale rehabilitation, is the Boston Rehabilitation Program (BURP). Two independent evaluations of the program were conducted, one by Urban Planning Aid (UPA) [877], an advocacy planning group, the other by Langley Keyes [423] for the Joint Center for Urban Studies. The two analyses are in substantial agreement about details of the project. In fact, UPA used some of the research compiled by Keyes in its analysis, and Keyes quotes extensively from the findings of UPA's survey of conditions in BURP rehabilitated structures.

The studies agree that the program achieved the goal of speeding production. They also find that speed was achieved at the expense of quality. UPA conducted a survey of 11 percent of the BURP units and found a pattern of substandard materials and shoddy workmanship that did not meet FHA's own specifications. Keyes expresses certain reservations about UPA's admittedly skewed sample (most buildings in the sample were chosen because of tenant complaints), and UPA's failure to distinguish between completions approved by FHA and de facto completions. However, he also concludes that the quality of BURP housing is inferior to other rehabilitation work. The two studies also agree that the program dealt inadequately with the problems of relocation and community involvement. Training for low-skilled local people should have been included in the program but was not.

Another program flaw alluded to in both studies is that relatively expensive buildings were rehabilitated. In their eagerness to do the job quickly, contractors did not search for less expensive buildings, probably in poorer structural condition. Keyes suggests that it would have been possible to produce more quality rehabilitation by spending less on acquisition and more on rehabilitation. Such a strategy would have provided a greater overall improvement of the low-cost housing stock.

The only significant point of contention between the two works is their respective political and economic philosophy. UPA includes some recommended revision in the structure of the housing market (most notably a more vital role for community development corporations) that Keyes finds are unnecessarily argumentative and peripheral issues.

UPA concludes that BURP is a failure; Keyes is not sanguine about the life expectancy of the physical improvements.

Emily Achtenberg, a member of the UPA project staff that evaluated BURP, published a further study [9] critical of the impact of rehabilitation loans and grants. She found that an average of one-third of the rehabilitation activity in the study neighborhoods was financed by public programs. In addition, many of those assisted by the loan program were not those most in need, and in at least one neighborhood the program caused a decline in the amount of low-cost housing available.

In an earlier study for the Douglas Commission, which generally supports Achtenberg's findings, the Boston Municipal Research Bureau examined nationwide experience with these loan and grant programs in the context of code-enforcement activity [77]. The bureau found that the increase in market value of houses improved through the use of loan and grant funds generally does not exceed the actual costs of rehabilitation. It also concluded that the maximum grant (at that time, $1,500) was not sufficient to bring houses up to code standards, and that this resulted in administrators' approving work that was not adequate.

The bureau also collected and assessed the available information on federal programs, other than concentrated code enforcement, designed to upgrade substandard dwelling units. This included supply-subsidy and related welfare and OEO programs. Although the information on actual performance under these programs is scanty and drawn largely from federal-agency reports, the bureau concluded in its 1968 report that rehabilitation programs had not been effective. Estimates of work completed or underway in 1968 accounted for no more than 3 percent of the units identified in the July 1966 housing census as substandard and in need of rehabilitation.

On the basis of these findings the bureau did not suggest that the rehabilitation loan and grant programs be jettisoned or even radically revised. Instead, in a series of recommendations it called for broadening the program to include citywide eligibility, increase maximum grants and income-eligibility limits, and accept insurance and taxes as eligible expenses for refinancing purposes.

The bureau report is typical of many of the technical studies that were sponsored in the 1960s by the major housing commissions—Kaiser and Douglas. The assessment of past experience under federal housing programs is largely critical. The response to this experience is to urge the commitment of increased resources. This may be justifiable. Nonetheless, insufficient attention is paid to the comparative efficiency of alternative approaches to the upgrading of the housing stock.

Community-based Housing Development Corporations

Much of the success, or lack of it, of the large-scale rehabilitation projects has been attributed to various program factors, particularly the competence of the operating or sponsoring organization. Several studies have examined the role of the community-based housing development corporation.

In his study, *The Dynamics of Housing Rehabilitation* [483], David Listokin attempts to determine the elements that account for the relative success of the Camden Housing Improvement Projects (CHIP) as compared with programs like BURP. Listokin reports that CHIP, using federal interest-subsidy programs for home owners, produced good quality rehabilitation.

While almost all of Listokin's conclusions are based on interviews, they are provocative. He says that CHIP avoided many problems by working only on vacant buildings. It did not have to relocate people, or deal with problems of eligibility of former tenants. Other advantages of CHIP were strong support from influential local corporations, experienced staff, support from neighborhood residents, exclusive focus on housing, and strict selection criteria for new tenants. Listokin feels that CHIP's pattern is unlikely to be repeated because other rehabilitation efforts will lack either the resources, expertise, or concentration.

Several other case studies of community experiences with nonprofit housing corporations have been published and deserve brief mention, in spite of their limited generalizability.

In a somewhat polemical study of housing development corporations operating in the South End of Boston [367], the Housing and Community Research Groups argue that efforts to activate neighborhood organizations and to develop housing often conflict, leading to high resident expectations and low performance levels. Not only did the efforts of the corporations under study have no significant impact on neighborhood housing, but, in the author's opinion, may have deflected attention from more basic remedies—changing the profit-oriented structure of the housing industry.

Paul Niebanck and John Pope [617] examine a Philadelphia rehabilitation effort, the Queens Village, Inc. (QVI) housing development corporation. This group did not achieve its production goals and had difficulty selling units. The authors feel that the critical problems were the inexperience of sponsors and contractors and a lack of special rehabilitation-construction methods. Inexperience caused the sponsors to undercapitalize the program and misjudge the market.

John Kenower's report on MICAH [419], a group of nonprofit housing development corporations, reaches somewhat more optimistic conclusions. While the MICAH effort in Providence failed for reasons similar to those that plagued QVI, the effort of an associated MICAH in Springfield, Massachusetts fared considerably better. Kenower accounts for Springfield's success in terms of the neighborhood, FHA cooperation, an effective tenant-relations policy, and sufficient subsidy. Unfortunately, the author's conclusions are largely speculative.

These accounts, while provocative, are impressionistic and speculative, rather than rigorous and objective. More systematic research and analysis are required before conclusions can be drawn from CHIP's reported successor or the failures of other programs that would benefit local policy makers.

Rehabilitation and New Technology

Among the basic objectives of federally supported rehabilitation efforts was to introduce cost-saving technologies to a sector of the construction industry noted for its relative stagnation and diseconomies of scale.

One rehabilitation program that stood out in its emphasis on new technology was the "Instant Rehab" project carried out in New York City in 1967. This program was evaluated by New York's Institute of Public Administration (IPA) [378]. The project tested the cost effectiveness of using off-site, industrialized building elements in a 48-hour (instant) rehabilitation effort. IPA's principal conclusion was that both the speed and the techniques generated costs that exceeded those of standard rehabilitation or new construction. Prefabricated plumbing cores, for example, thought to be a major technological breakthrough, proved unsatisfactory and difficult to install and stack because of variations in building dimensions and setting patterns.

In spite of, or perhaps because of, the discouraging experiences with housing rehabilitation in the late 1960s, the federal government mounted Project Rehab, an attempt to promote a large-scale rehabilitation industry. The staff of Arthur D. Little, Inc. prepared the monitoring report on Project Rehab [30] and confirmed many of the findings of earlier rehab programs. They found no evidence of technical or administrative breakthroughs for rehabilitation in the near future. They tentatively concluded that large-scale rehabilitation is not necessarily less costly or less disruptive than new construction.

A.D. Little reported that no one has found a way to transfer a successful rehabilitation program from one city to another. They speculate that the complexities and uncertainties of rehabilitation may severely limit the volume of construction. Thus, rehabilitation may not be profitable for large firms with high overhead costs. Other difficult problems were likely to discourage development of a large-scale rehabilitation industry. They included tenant relocation, flexible selection criteria for structures, interagency cooperation, need for training funds, identification and financing for minority contractors, execution within tight program-cost limits, and community support.

Organizing a Renewal Effort

The performance of these large-scale rehabilitation efforts cannot be considered apart from the renewal process—a point brought home by several researchers who treat questions of neighborhood organization and renewal decision making. Keyes [424] attempts to deal with this question by means of case studies of residential renewal efforts in three Boston neighborhoods.

Keyes bases his analysis upon the theory of an "ecology of games" in the local community, borrowing from Norton Long's important formulation in *The Polity* (Chicago: Rand McNally, 1962). Hypothesizing a rehabilitation-planning game in which the redevelopment authority must negotiate with the other players, principally neighborhood residents, Keyes comes to the following interesting conclusions:

1. The composition of the renewal team, based on the socioeconomic dynamics of the community, determines which groups are excluded from the bargaining process and, consequently, most severely penalized by the effects of renewal.
2. The composition of the local renewal team, as a reflection of the distribution of power in the community, is more determinative than objective physical or planning conditions in predicting how the renewal plan will deal with such items as the relationship between rehabilitation and clearance, housing for low-income relocatees, and the cost of rehabilitation to renters and owners whose homes are preserved.
3. Decentralized renewal decisionmaking poses extreme difficulties for local

residents and institutions that are politically unacceptable, and often ignores future considerations and the relation of the project area to the broader city system.

The study and its conclusions are clearly of interest to local decision makers involved in organizing urban renewal efforts, although the study's generalizability is, as with all case studies, problematical. Another acknowledged limitation of this study is that its examination of each neighborhood goes no further chronologically than the adoption of the renewal plan. This makes it difficult to relate Keyes' conclusions to the actual success of the renewal projects in dealing with the problems that urban renewal addresses.

Summary

A large amount of investigation has been addressed to the problems and effects of various local rehabilitation programs. However, few studies have examined neighborhoods after completion of the renewal program or have analyzed the effects of rehabilitation upon other programs that concern local policy makers.

There is consensus that there is a shortage of experienced, capable rehabilitators, without whom the programs cannot succeed. In addition, attempts to expand the scale or increase the speed of rehabilitation have, it seems, violated the social framework of the neighborhoods in which they have been attempted.

There has been no major attempt thus far to examine and compare in a systematic and rigorous manner a wide array of rehabilitation efforts, isolating those contextual elements of the local community and specific program variables that best explain rehabilitation outcomes at the neighborhood level. Such a study would require formulation of a preliminary explanatory model as well as rigorous and comparative case study analysis. This type of policy-related research designed to produce findings of utility outside the case-study community is desperately needed in many of the housing areas we have examined. It is of particular value and timeliness on the topic of neighborhood rehabilitation. Consequently, the broad outlines of such a study are suggested below:

1. Develop a preliminary explanatory model consisting of alternative causal factors and hypotheses to guide in identifying key variables and cataloging relevant information.
2. Compile and catalog information from literature and raw data about rehabilitation programs, drawing on this project's review of the policy-related research, on the rich reservoir of unstudied data that is available in local renewal-project offices, planning agencies, and HUD area offices on the views and experiences of housing professionals in the field of blight treatment, and on-site visits to specific programs.

3. Develop diagnostic indicators to identify and organize the pertinent social, economic, political, institutional, physical, and psychological characteristics of local environments into appropriate neighborhood clusters or typologies for analysis.
4. Develop measures of success to evaluate the impact of different modes and mixes of rehabilitation programs on key social and economic conditions of the neighborhood and the city.
5. Classify strategies and examine the relationships of local characteristics to the measured success or failure of a specific program strategy.
6. Select local blight-treatment projects and analyze in depth the variables that account for the success or failure of particular strategies under certain circumstances and not under others. Computers may be used in the categorization and classification of information concerning the effectiveness of strategies and the characteristics of locales in which programs were instituted.

The likelihood of obtaining studies of this scope and rigor, requiring resource levels and methodological sophistication not ordinarily committed to problems of local housing, is discussed in subsequent chapters of this book.

Self-help Programs

Although large-scale renewal interventions of the past decade have been largely discouraging according to researchers, relatively new phenomena may be of significance to local housing policy makers. These are the urban "self-help" programs, including urban homesteading and tenant-cooperative conversions. Their attractiveness stems from the fact that they presumably involve limited public intervention and no explicit form of financial subsidy.

Urban homesteading is a method of reclaiming abandoned central city housing for residential use by transferring units to individuals who make a prior commitment to bring them up to code level. Some plans provide properties to individuals at no charge or a nominal fee. The city may arrange a rehabilitation loan or simply provide counselling on how to obtain one. Following a period of required residency the property is deeded to the homesteader.

Conversion of rental apartments to tenant cooperatives or even condominiums is another method for reclaiming abandoned housing for residential use. It may also be a way of preventing abandonment if the conversion is arranged before the landlord walks away from a marginal economic investment. Conversion to cooperative form is not always a viable option, particularly when the tenants themselves are no better able to finance or perform the tasks required to maintain the property at code level. The cooperative often requires continuing assistance from trained city personnel.

The city becomes the conduit for urban homesteading and cooperative conversion through a variety of devices that shift title of tax delinquent or abandoned buildings to the city.

Research Literature

Both the urban-homesteading and tenant-cooperative movements are in need of careful research and analysis. We could find no good research studies on either topic. Robert Kolodny [436] provides an informative analysis of low-income cooperative conversions in New York City. Although there is little basis for assuming that his case study findings are applicable outside the particular setting of his study, he does reach conclusions that may be of general interest to local policy makers. Essentially, Kolodny finds that the success of a cooperative venture depends upon strong tenant participation and initiative together with strong and continuing technical and financial assistance from city agencies. Kolodny sees cooperative conversion as a viable alternative to abandonment. His argument, however, is somewhat unconvincing, particularly in view of the relative helplessness of tenant groups in the face of the larger social and economic factors that engender neighborhood decline and housing abandonment.

The urban-homesteading movement has not yet generated research into its operation and outcome. Researchers in Wilmington, Delaware, the city that pioneered the entire urban-homesteading program, have only begun during the past year to analyze the program's costs and accomplishments. Four other major homesteading programs, in Baltimore, Philadelphia, New York City, and Washington, D.C., are in the very early stages of operation. They have therefore generated little information about the success of the homesteading approach.

Two works recently published by the National Urban Coalition [592, 593] discuss the urban-homesteading program and analyze its potential for success. Since little else has been published on the subject, we recommend them to the local housing official. The earlier work suggests an agenda for action research on homesteading.

Research Gaps

Some of the research we have evaluated in earlier sections, particularly on the housing-abandonment process, sheds light on the potential usefulness of these self-help programs. But many questions remain unanswered. What are the most viable forms of tenant control of housing? What impact does increased tenant control have upon the level of building maintenance and upon the sense of community within the larger neighborhood? What are the actual costs of those self-help programs to the municipality, such as intensive counselling and technical assistance from city agencies as well as forms of tax abatement? Should deficient properties be required to meet housing-code standards immediately upon occupancy or should these requirements be waived where a combination of occupancy and rehabilitation work is anticipated? How do self-help programs help to change or maintain the social, demographic and economic characteristics of local areas?

Conclusions

Although additional empirical analysis is needed to test the propositions advanced in the literature, it appears that a balanced program of subsidies to housing consumers and producers is the most effective strategy available to local policy makers for meeting their major economic and social objectives. These objectives include minimizing program cost, maximizing program efficiency, extending benefits uniformly to all families eligible for housing assistance, improving living standards of local residents, upgrading innercity neighborhoods, and dispersing low-income families throughout the metropolitan area.

Local resources almost always will be inadequate to fulfill all these objectives simultaneously. Even if unlimited financing is available, some of these goals may prove mutually inconsistent. Therefore, the specific combination of supply and demand subsidies most appropriate to a particular community at a specific time will depend upon which of these competing objectives appear most critical to local policy makers.

The theoretical—largely economic—analyses and the few empirical studies that are available suggest some guidelines for local policy makers who must choose among these goals. There is general agreement in the literature that consumer subsidies are less costly than production-oriented strategies, especially public housing. Richard F. Muth [576], Eugene Smolensky [794], Robert L. Bish [70], Arthur P. Solomon [800], and others also demonstrate that consumer-oriented programs distribute the benefits more evenly among impoverished families. These programs are also more conducive to racial and economic integration, more responsive to consumer choice and, except for leased-housing programs, entail less administrative costs than production subsidies.

However, Solomon's comparison of subsidy programs in Boston [800] reveals that certain production-oriented programs, particularly rent supplements for new construction, enable low- and moderate-income families to secure better quality housing than they acquire under consumer-oriented strategies. Anthony Downs' analysis [199] also argues persuasively that production subsidies are more effective in meeting the goals of income maintenance, delivery of social services, and improvement of innercity neighborhoods.

The question of whether production subsidies are also required because housing supply responds sluggishly and inadequately to increased consumer demand remains unresolved. More analysis is required before local policy makers will know whether the supply of housing services is as unresponsive to changes in housing demand, as Downs contends, or whether housing supply adjusts relatively quickly to changes in the housing market, as is argued by Muth and others.

There are a limited number of case studies that examine the costs and benefits associated with a major type of supply subsidy—the large-scale rehabilitation of existing housing. The evidence to date is discouraging; large-scale rehabilitation programs have been characterized by high expectations and low performance levels in terms of costs and efficiency. The case-study nature of the evidence, however, renders these findings questionable and inconclusive. Before local policy makers can assume that large-scale rehabilitation is not a viable form of housing assistance, it is necessary to undertake studies that apply standardized methodologies to several programs and examine the contextual factors and opportunity costs associated with large-scale rehabilitation.

New York City's experience with an "Instant Rehab" program, involving off-site industrialized building elements, suggests that housing rehabilitation with prefabricated materials is a much more costly alternative than conventional rehabilitation or new construction. Again, more research is needed before policy makers can be certain of the technical advantages, costs, speed, and administrative factors associated with such programs.

The information about urban homesteading and tenant cooperatives is even more limited. Robert Kolodny's case study of New York [436] indicates that cooperative conversion can be a viable alternative to abandonment if policy makers are prepared to extent strong and continuing technical and financial assistance to tenant groups. This finding needs to be tested in other cities. An assessment of the viability of urban-homesteading programs must also await further study.

**Part III:
Evaluation of Research
Methodology and Context**

6 Research Methodology and Institutional Context

Introduction

In Part II of this book we presented a framework for the evaluation and synthesis of research findings on local housing and related services. This framework was designed to benefit the local policy maker, particularly the housing official and his staff, by clustering related sets of findings by policy instrument and examining these findings in terms of the most critical policy problems that local policy makers confront in formulating and executing housing policy.

The evaluation presented in the four preceding chapters reveals in broad outline why this body of research fails, for the most part, to provide clear and reliable guidelines for action or decision. There are entire areas of local housing activity that have not been studied or have failed to attract competent research efforts. Strong explanatory theory is generally lacking, interdependencies among programs are dimly perceived, and findings tend to be overqualified, unsupported by data, or trivial. Furthermore, research in most areas is insufficient to allow extensive or systematic comparison and evaluation of conflicting findings.

That is not to say that policy-related research on housing should be ignored. The studies we uncovered provide the best evidence currently available as to why certain housing efforts have appeared to succeed while many others have failed. And, to paraphrase Santayana, policy makers who ignore the failures of the past are destined to repeat them.

Furthermore, we have strong reason to expect an improvement in the general quality of housing research as better research groups turn their attention from national to local housing problems and more powerful tools of analysis and explanatory theory are developed and refined. Recent studies of the Joint Center for Urban Studies of MIT and Harvard and of The Urban Institute concerning housing subsidy programs, of the Center for Urban Policy Research at Rutgers concerning residential abandonment, and of the New York City-RAND Institute concerning the issue of rent control, illustrate the value of sustained efforts by sophisticated research teams, drawing freely on the methodologies and techniques of the social sciences.

In this chapter we take a second look at the studies whose findings we have reported in the preceding four chapters, focusing on the design and presentation of the research. The purpose of this analysis is to display the general quality of policy-related research on housing and to highlight the methodological flaws that diminish the reliability of reported research findings and limit their applicability beyond the specific context in which the research was conducted. We also discuss common flaws in the focus and presentation of housing studies that limit the usefulness of this research to local policy makers. In concluding the chapter we examine two housing models of research effort in which policy makers and analysts were placed in novel and fruitful relationship to one another.

This chapter is addressed primarily to those who perform, supervise, or evaluate policy-related research on housing, although other persons who must rely on the results of housing studies may also find it of value. It is drawn from the systematic evaluation of more than 68 studies cited herein that met the criteria we established for policy-related research on local housing services.

Methodology of Policy-related Research: A Paradigm

Policy-related research on housing, as we have defined it, is the application of techniques of social science to the analysis of the housing problems that face the local policy maker. The largest number of studies listed in the bibliography of this book do not qualify as policy-related research. To further clarify what we mean by policy-related research and the standards to which we hold such efforts, it is useful to review the steps undertaken in such research, from definition of the problem to the drawing of conclusions.[a]

Process of Policy-related Research

The process of policy-related research will vary from study to study, depending upon the nature and complexity of the problem the researcher defines and the objectives of the study. The outline presented in Table 6-1 is a model or paradigm of this process. It may be foreshortened where the research draws on existing theory or data, for the purpose of confirmation or refinement; it may be elaborated where several hypotheses are pursued or difficult problems of measurement or analysis are confronted. But generally, policy-related research will proceed as described here.

Policy-related Research: The Steps Examined

Policy-related research typically begins with a problem (step 1) that is suggested

---
[a]Standards of research in the social sciences are subject to continuing debate. There is, however, some concurrence as to the basic pattern of inquiry. We draw much of the following discussion from Abraham Kaplan's classic study, *The Conduct of Inquiry: Methodology for Behavioral Science* [408].

Table 6-1
Process of Policy-related Research

Steps in Research	Resources
1. Defining problem	Practical insight
2. Formulating hypothesis	Social science theory
3. Specifying relevant variables	Social science theory; practical insight
4. Deciding upon concrete references for measurement of variables—"operationalization" or "concretization"	Social science techniques; general ingenuity

5. Devising observation or experiment ("test")
   a. Choosing the universe to be studied
   b. Choosing the sample of cases to be observed
   c. Choosing the time frame of the observations
	Social science techniques; general ingenuity

6. Considering alternative hypotheses that could survive the test	Social science techniques and theory
7. Conducting pilot or full test and gathering data	Social science techniques
8. Analyzing gathered data	Statistical techniques; logic; arithmetic; common sense
9. Drawing conclusions: Did the hypothesis survive the test? Did alternative explanations survive?	Social science techniques
10. Modifying the hypothesis, further specifying conditions under which it holds true	Social science theory

by the practical experience of those working in the housing field. To be susceptible to research, the problem usually must be defined further in more precise terms. The researcher will attempt to formulate the question in terms of a hypothesis (step 2), drawing upon practical description of the problem, and upon such relevant social science theory as can be applied. The problem may require the investigation of a number of interlocking hypotheses. But for our purposes it is easier to conceive of the process as involving a single hypothesis. The hypothesis might be phrased along the following lines: "Under these specified circumstances, adopting the program in question will raise the probability of these specified results."

Once the hypothesis is formulated in precise terms, the researcher will turn to theory for help in specifying the relevant variables (step 3). The statement of the problem, once clarified, should define the program and the desired result. But the researcher will turn to the theory (if it exists, or to common sense if it does not) to identify other variables that are likely to influence the relationship between the program and the result. These other variables may play a critical role in determining the circumstances under which the program produces the result.

With the variables identified, the researcher will seek a way of measuring them. To do this he must devise a reasonable way of linking the abstract variables used in his research design with the concrete observable events of everyday life. This process is often called "operationalization," but "concretization" is probably as good a phrase (step 4). If the hypothesis suggests, for example, that raising the level of housing-code enforcement may in certain circumstances increase neighborhood cohesion, the researcher will have to come up with some way of measuring neighborhood cohesion.

With these preliminary steps out of the way, the researcher must design an approach to his research that tests the hypothesis (step 5). A wide variety of research designs is available, each with several advantages and disadvantages.

Only rarely are true experiments possible for social science researchers. The researcher will not ordinarily find cities that are willing to raise the level of housing-code enforcement, to continue the example, just so he can observe the effect on neighborhood cohesion. Moreover, even if such cities can be found, the researcher cannot prevent other relevant variables from having effects upon the outcome that are difficult to separate from the effects of the variables he is studying. For example, the election of a neighborhood resident as mayor in one city or the election of a minority member as governor of the state may have an impact upon neighborhood cohesion that is difficult to identify or disentangle from the effect of upgraded code enforcement.

Because pure laboratory cases are not available, the researcher must choose designs in which he compares situations in which the program is already present with those in which it is absent, attempting to control for other relevant variables and looking for different levels of the supposed result.

Choices that are associated with the choice of a research design include the choice of the universe to be studied (step 5a), the selection of a sample from that universe (step 5b), and the choice of a time frame for analysis (step 5c). Since an analysis that includes all cases is usually impossible, or exorbitantly expensive, the researcher will choose a small sample of cases to investigate. His method of choosing those cases will affect his ability to draw conclusions about the whole universe of cases to which he wishes to generalize. The time frame may also be important. The researcher may choose to ignore effects that can be seen only after a long exposure to the purported causes, selecting a more limited period of observation during which the specified effect must occur.

Once the observations or tests are made, the researcher may want to reexamine his design and consider possible alternative hypotheses (step 6) that might survive the test he designed. This may lead him to revise his test in order to rule out those hypotheses as well. Similarly, the researcher may want to run a pilot test (step 7), gathering some of the data to see whether it lives up to his expectations about the kinds of information that he could obtain. The results of his pilot study may lead him to restructure his study so that he can deal with the quality of data that is actually available.

With his test designed, and his perfected measuring instruments in hand, the researcher will gather the full set of data that he needs. The information he gathers will be analyzed in accordance with the processes spelled out in his research design (step 8). If his analysis of the data permits, the researcher will conclude that his hypothesis survived the test that he designed (step 9). He might conclude, for example, that a higher level of code enforcement does in fact improve neighborhood cohesion. The researcher may well discover, however, that his hypothesis needs revision (step 10) to take account of his findings. For example, his analysis may indicate that code enforcement improves neighborhood cohesion only if there is a minimal level of neighborhood solidarity before the program is inaugurated. This mode of analysis, if carried to its logical conclusion, involves a return with a modified hypothesis to the third step of the research process and the repetition of each succeeding step (steps 3-10).

In the following pages we define the general terms of our analysis of the research methodologies that were employed in the studies we analyzed. We then proceed to examine each type of methodological failing contained in these studies—in the hope that by illuminating these failings we can promote more useful policy analysis in the future.

Methodological Problems: A Critical Analysis

A principal objective of our housing study was to identify research findings that could be applied with some confidence by policy makers outside the circumscribed study context in which these findings were drawn. In determining whether a conclusion is widely applicable in this sense, the underlying research process must satisfy three distinct sets of criteria that we defined as: (1) internal validity, (2) external validity, and (3) generalizability.

Internal validity involves the threshold question of whether the researcher observed correctly and drew correct conclusions about the cases that were analyzed. Without this minimum, conclusions of research are uninterpretable. For example, data on housing conditions are frequently taken from reports of the U.S. Bureau of the Census. These data are notoriously unreliable, based in large part on self-evaluation of housing conditions by census respondents. Structure condition surveys based on "windshield" analyses of block groups (observations while driving through a neighborhood) are equally suspect. When housing studies depend upon data from these sources we cannot be sure that we know the truth about what the researcher has seen.

If there are *external-validity* flaws in a study, we are not sure that we know the truth about what has not been seen. The question of external validity is the question of whether or not conclusions—correctly drawn about the cases observed—can be reasonably expected to hold for cases not observed but also in the universe from which the analysed cases were drawn. For example, a political poll may be right about one sample; but is it right about the entire national population? Thus, for external validity we demand that the conclusion derived by internally valid research be reasonably expected to hold for other cases in the universe that is being studied.

For policy-related research we made demands more exacting than simply those of internal and external validity. External validity requires that some generalization—from the specific sample that the study observed to the universe from which the sample is explicitly drawn—be justified. To satisfy the criterion of *generalizability* we demand that similar generalization from that universe to all comparable universes in the United States be justified.

For example, if we interview landlords in Newark using an internally valid research design, external validity asks whether we can generalize to all landlords in Newark. An externally valid study of this sort may be of great policy utility to a policy maker in Newark. But can a policy maker in another city rely upon its conclusions for his city?

Needless to say, policy-related research on housing that satisfies each of the three criteria is exceedingly rare. Such research must involve a large number of cases and is both expensive and time-consuming. The tendency has been for research designs to attempt to economize in one way or another. The result is that the principal problems inherent in policy-related research on housing are those of external validity and generalizability.

Internal Validity

Under this heading we discuss problems related to the use of theory, the specification of variables, the use of assumptions, the operationalization of variables, sampling, the use of informants, and data analysis.

Problems of Theory. On the whole, theory in the field of housing is at a very rudimentary state of development. As earlier sections on information systems indicated, there has been some agreement on variables that affect the housing market; however, much remains to be done to discover how these variables act and interact in determining the operations of that market. In housing, as in any field that lacks a strong theoretical underpinning, the absence of a well developed theory causes serious problems in the validity of the research.

In the absence of theory, the researcher himself is forced to formulate tentative concepts or working hypotheses that he can test. This appears to be the stage attained by the housing literature so far. A number of variables have been identified, a number of concepts formulated, but the interactions and effects of the variables are not clear. The absence or weakness of theory has further ramifications for research. Without some theory underlying the analysis, the researcher cannot know which facts are relevant to his question. As Abraham Kaplan has presented the problem:

The word "data", it cannot too often be emphasized, is an incomplete term, like "later than"; there are only data for some hypothesis or other. Without a theory, however provisional or loosely formulated, there is only a miscellany of observations, having no significance either in themselves or over against the plenum of fact from which they have been arbitrarily or accidentally selected. [408]

Some of the studies that we rejected were in fact so poor in theory that the researcher seemed to have no hypotheses to which his "facts" applied. Most of the research, however, had hypotheses to investigate and suggested at least nascent theory at some level of articulation. But with theory at a low level of articulation, there is usually little assurance that all of the important factors have been taken into account.

More than two-thirds of the policy-related research studies we evaluated had no coherent and well articulated theory at their bases. Of the remainder, theories borrowed or adapted from economics predominate. Most of these studies displayed some variation of supply-demand analysis from economics. A smaller number used tax capitalization and/or incidence theories.

Specification of Variables. In several of the studies important variables had not been included among the variables investigated. This inadequacy of variables was found primarily in studies that were also lacking in theory. One particularly severe example involved a study intended to determine whether building or other codes discourage rehabilitation efforts. No attempt was made to control for variations between codes, geographical differences, varied rates of construction and rehabilitation or other important variables that might influence the conclusions.

Use of Assumptions. Another result of the lack of theory in the field of housing is the introduction into housing studies of unrealistic assumptions called for by theories developed elsewhere. Several studies made standard assumptions about profit-maximizing behavior in the market, perfect information, and so forth (Olsen and Prescott [647], Bagby [37], Moorhouse [563]). Reliance upon such assumptions may be forced by the desire to keep the theory intelligible. Nevertheless, it might be possible to introduce more realism into the assumptions or to recognize the magnitude of probable bias introduced into any analysis based on such assumptions.

Models that relax some of these standard economic assumptions have been developed recently in other fields of study and offer a promising basis for future theoretical developments in the field of housing. Most of these models have modified the conventional assumption of perfect information, developing frameworks in which producers and consumers do not possess perfect knowledge about prices or quality. The classic models of markets with imperfect information, by George J. Stigler [835] and Michael Rothschild [738], have precipitated a plethora of theoretical literature concerning the effects of imperfect information upon such diverse fields as medical care, day care, nursing home services, and unemployment. These studies suggest that consumers cannot make rational choices among competing services in these fields. They make decisions based on fragments of information. The application of a similar framework in the field of housing would introduce a more realistic theoretical base to the studies in this field and, hopefully, permit more accurate predictions of the local market's response to alternative housing policies.

Much of the research we analyzed also involved controversial assumptions that were made in order to keep the scope of the research within manageable bounds. For example, studies of rent control [491, 828] frequently assumed that the presence of rent control in New York City affects only the rent-controlled dwellings. No attempts were made to consider the broader market effects of the policy.

Operationalization of Variables. Researchers working on policy problems dealing with housing face a difficult task. Data are usually not available on the variables one might want to consider, or in the detail one might hope to see. And gathering data on housing can rapidly become very time-consuming and expensive. Moreover, the difficulty is compounded by the abstractness of the concepts with which housing researchers must often deal. These are serious problems when they occur. If the researcher cannot get access to data, an empirical study is impossible. If the researcher's operationalization is not reasonable or is too subjective, he may not be investigating what he says he is.

Data availability has been a serious problem in the housing-research literature. Studies that had problems in obtaining the requisite data show us only the tip of the iceberg. Many researchers have undoubtedly been deterred from undertaking research at all because of the lack of data. For example, the issue of property tax incidence—whether the tax is progressive or regressive—remains unresolved because of the lack of systematically collected and readily available data [1]. In at least two cost/benefit analyses [542, 123], the researcher could not find all of the data he needed about the project's benefits. Edward M. Sabella [745] could find no data on "income from properties" for his property tax study and was forced to fall back upon the age of the property as a "proxy variable." Census data are often used, but nearly as often force the investigator to use an inappropriate level of aggregation [362, 580].

As the Sabella example suggests, one result of the lack of appropriate data on a topic of interest to the researcher is often a resort to a "proxy variable" of somewhat dubious worth. This is poor operationalization resulting from the lack of appropriate data. The proxy variable may be the best indication that the researcher can find of the variable he would like to study. The search for good proxy variables leaves considerable room for ingenuity on the part of researchers. But the reader is often left wondering whether the research really touches the questions that it intended to handle. Too many of the policy-related research studies we evaluated were forced upon somewhat questionable operationalizations by the lack of appropriate data (e.g., Neutze [608], Orr [653], Popp and Sebold [683], and Nourse, Phares and Stevens [632]).

Problematic operationalization also arises because of the interest of housing researchers in variables that are difficult to operationalize. For some examples: researchers who apply cost/benefit techniques usually despair at the problem of measuring intangible benefits and ignore these benefits altogether in their calculations, for example, Stephen D. Messner [542]; Richard F. Muth's and Elliot Wetzler's study [580] on building codes used the variable "stringency of local codes," which necessarily involved very subjective operationalization; "neighborly interaction" and "community solidarity" proved difficult for Donald G. Sullivan [844] to operationalize for his study of cooperative housing projects; and a study of rehabilitation programs done by Langley Carleton Keyes, Jr. [423] relied upon highly subjective data to determine "the extent to which the program goals focused solely on size and speed."

In other cases there were simply mistakes in operationalization, or results reported with so little indication of the researcher's methods of operationalization that we were left wondering whether or not the measurement of variables was reasonable. This type of problem with operationalization is the result of carelessness, usually carelessness in reporting, and is not peculiar to housing as a topic of research.

Sampling. Sample problems—problems with the way one chooses cases for observation from among the universe of cases available, and the number of cases one chooses—can weaken both the internal and external validity of research. Sampling problems can weaken internal validity when they are part of an inadequate research design that allows too many possible alternative explanations of the results observed. While the independent variable to which one attributes the results may in fact be the cause of those results, a poor design leaves open so many plausible causes as possibilities that it is impossible to draw firm conclusions.

Too many studies seemed to have sample problems. Marilyn Langford Reeves [712] and Arthur P. Solomon [799] made "after only" observations of participants in a program with no control groups. Several studies had samples too small to allow for the disentangling of co-varying variables [499, 647, 691]. The Arthur D. Little study [29] of the relative costs of conventional and modular building techniques examined ten sites spread between two cities. With so few sites it was not possible to control adequately for possible effects of location in one or the other of the cities. Three of these studies chose respondents to be "illustrative" or "typical" or to "represent the range of possibilities" on some variable. Since this technique does not rule out the possibility that other variables vary systematically across the cases in question, one never really knows what the cases studied represent.

A hypothetical study makes the problem more obvious. Suppose that we undertake to study the relationship between welfare tenantry and deterioration by examining three apartment buildings, one each with low, moderate, and high proportions of welfare tenants. If we demonstrate that they show respectively low, moderate, and high structural deterioration, would not a reviewer of our study be entitled to wonder about other important variables that have not been considered in our research? Is it possible that the buildings also differ in age? Do their owners differ as well? Their neighborhoods? Their debt structure? We have not disproved the hypothesis that welfare tenantry accelerates deterioration, but neither have we much reduced the number of plausible alternative hypotheses.

Use of Informants. Given the time and funding constraints under which several of the studies in question have operated, the use of informants has been relatively frequent. This was a technique of some importance, for example, in the Center for Community Change/National Urban League report on abandonment [129] and the Linton, Mields and Coston, Inc. report on the same subject [482].

In this approach one typically uses nonprobability sampling, and rightly so. If we want to know what considerations went into a particular zoning decision, we undoubtedly do better to interview those who seem to know most about the making of the decision than we do to take a random sample of municipal decision makers in the city. And if we have a limited amount of time and limited funds available to study the housing market in a number of cities, we may do better to seek informants in the several cities than we could do by mounting the huge studies that would be necessary to make definitive statements about those markets. But even with this orientation, considerable caution must be exercised in the statement of conclusions. The conclusions do not summarize the reality of the phenomenon in question but rather the perceptions of knowledgeable persons about the reality of that phenomenon. The argument is not that the opinions of knowledgeable persons cannot be trusted; rather it is that without knowing their methods, we cannot know how accurate their perceptions are. Even consensus may reveal widely shared stereotypes rather than objective determinations of the nature of the phenomenon.

Data Analysis. A wide variety of analytic techniques was used in the literature, ranging from simple narrative treatments to the most highly sophisticated techniques of factor analysis and discriminant analysis. For examples of the latter two approaches, see Robert Sadacca et al. [746] and George Sternlieb [828]. The literature was nearly evenly divided between preferences for sophisticated statistical techniques and less complicated approaches. Somewhat more than half of the studies relied upon narrative approaches, or used no statistical techniques more complicated than tabular presentations of figures. Somewhat fewer than half of the studies relied upon correlations, regressions, or the more sophisticated approaches mentioned above. The most favored technique among those using statistically sophisticated approaches was regression analysis. Undoubtedly this reflects the favor which this technique enjoys in the social sciences in general these days.

On the whole those who used sophisticated techniques seemed careful in their use. In a few instances we found that requisite assumptions for the application of regression techniques were not clearly met. But the careless or inappropriate use of statistical techniques did not seem to be the source of many problems of validity.

For the less sophisticated techniques, it is difficult to reach overall judgments about how well they were applied. Few strict standards can be set forth for evaluating the use of a narrative comparison of different cases, or for other narrative approaches. As long as reasonable summarizing inferences are drawn and reasonable logic is followed, these techniques probably live up to whatever minimal standards can be expected of them. Almost all one can ask is that they be persuasive.

Although we found few problems arising from the techniques of analysis used in this literature, it should be emphasized that the application of the best and most sophisticated techniques of analysis cannot turn bad data into good conclusions. Nor will the application of the computer work any wonders. Computer operators use an acronym, GIGO, that sums up the contribution of the computer to analyses based on inadequate data: "Garbage in, garbage out." The same phrase can summarize elaborate statistical manipulation of poor data. No amount of cutting facets and polishing will turn a lump of coal into a diamond.

Summary. The absence or weakness of theory pervades policy-related research on housing. Its ramifications are wide, involving indiscriminate adaptation of theories from other fields, inadequate specification of variables, use of unrealistic assumptions about the behavior of buyers and sellers in the housing market, and reliance on informants and/or proxy measures of important variables. The use of relatively sophisticated techniques of analysis, including those available through the computer, cannot correct these basic deficiencies that limit the internal validity of housing studies.

External Validity and Generalizability

In this section, we discuss sampling problems that threaten the external validity of research conclusions—the representativeness of the cases from which the study generalizes. The problems we discuss include the use of opportunity samples, typical cases, small samples, case studies, and failures to disclose sampling techniques. We also discuss the stricter criteria of generalizability—to how large a universe of cities would the rules of social science allow us to generalize—and the lessons to be drawn from this.

"Opportunity" Sample. One technique used with considerable frequency in the policy-related research on housing is something that might be called the "opportunity" sample. This is the technique of choosing the cases from which one gathers information because of the ease of obtaining information from them. For example, the researcher may obtain information on land-use planning from those towns that have such information readily available. He may interview home owners who are recommended to him as cooperative interview subjects. Or, he may interview those officials in a city who are most willing to talk with him. In each case the selection of respondents in this manner decreases the likelihood that they are representative of the wider group to which the researcher would like to apply his findings.

Sometimes a researcher is able to account for the direction and magnitude of the bias introduced by an opportunity sample when he draws his conclusions. But it usually is no more than a guess. And in the absence of a theory that may help guide the researcher, the opportunity sample makes it much too easy for the researcher, consciously or unconsciously, to build support for his preconceptions.

Eleven of the research studies we evaluated obviously or probably used an opportunity sample. These included five cases in which those from whom the information was gathered were treated as informants rather than as respondents. In these cases doubts about validity raised by the use of informants undoubtedly are as serious as those problems caused by the method of selecting the informants. The five studies were those by the Boston Municipal Research Bureau [77], *Columbia Law Journal* note [106], Center for Community Change/National Urban League [129], Bernard J. Frieden [248], and Linton, Mields and Coston [482].

Use of "Typical" Cases. The use of "typical" or "representative" cases also has very little value as the basis for external validity. Without broader sampling, and preferably random sampling, one simply cannot tell whether or not the other cases that the "typical" sample is purported to represent differ in important ways from cases that are analyzed. If there were very strong theory in the field that allowed one to conclude that no other possible variables are important, one might worry less about this possibility. But few, if any, theories in the social sciences are robust enough to bear the weight of such an assertion. In the field of housing, no such theory is to be found.

If the sample is obviously biased in one direction or another, of course, there is a prima facie case against the external validity of conclusions based upon it. Attempts to rectify a recognized bias may help somewhat. Two studies that we evaluated appeared to have samples which were biased in directions not intended by the researcher (*Columbia Law Journal* note [106] and Reeves [712]). In his abandonment study of Baltimore, Michael A. Stegman [814] recognized the bias in his sample and made serious efforts to counteract it.

Sample Size. As the size of the sample becomes larger, we become more confident about the universe from which the sample was drawn. Conversely, if the sample is relatively small, however carefully drawn, it is possible that what we observe is something peculiar to the set of individuals in the sample rather than something common to all individuals in the universe from which the sample was drawn. The case study is simply the most extreme example of the small sample.

Even without imposing the more stringent demands suggested by our desire to generalize to all United States cities, we find many studies that cannot generalize to the more limited specific universe from which their cases were explicitly drawn. For one example, the sample of four cities drawn by Linton, Mields and Coston [482] is inadequate to support a generalization to cities with critical abandonment problems. In at least nine other instances, studies had samples that were simply too small. There is no presumption that these results are misleading; it is just that there is not sufficient assurance that they are not.

Case Studies. Case studies are the most extreme example of a limited sample. No statistical technique is of help in allowing one to generalize from a single case. At best, case studies may suggest hypotheses that can be tested in future research.

In this sense true case studies on housing are rare. But there are many studies that are as unreliable as pure case studies because they limit themselves to only a single portion of the unit that is their central concern. The question of the central unit of concern is highly subjective, so we cannot claim that our count has very high accuracy. Nevertheless, we count no fewer than 26 studies that seem to be this type of quasi-case study. For some examples: Frana Summa Wendell's study of code enforcement [906], which interviews 40 parcel owners, all in the Bronx; examinations of the effects of the property tax that examine many properties, but all in one city or county (e.g., Sabella [745], Smith [788]); Arthur P. Solomon's examination of participants in the Kansas City housing allowance program [799]; John Kenower's study of 46 projects all completed by a single firm [419]; two huge studies by George Sternlieb [826], and Sternlieb and Robert W. Burchell [830] involving interviews with many landlords, examinations of records of many buildings, etc., but all intended to illumine the housing market in Newark; and each of the studies of varying levels of complexity intended to examine the effects of the rent-control scheme now in effect in New York City.

It should be emphasized that case studies can provide useful information. They may be fertile sources of hypotheses and insights. Furthermore, such analyses may be all we can ask for so early in the development of theory on housing. However, we have no scientific basis for accepting the conclusions of such studies as conclusions which can be applied to other cases.

In some instances, however, even the argument that case studies can provoke and illumine loses much of its force. Where there is already a reasonably well developed theory and a plethora of interesting hypotheses, there is little to be said for the case study. This would seem to hold for those studies of the probable effects of a hypothetical switch from the property tax to site-value taxation in a single city or county (e.g., Cord [155], Schaaf [755], Smith [787-88]). That the case studies support the theory adds little weight to the strength of the theory. In the absence of a controversy about the theory in which the case study might be helpful and suggestive there seems little justification for the effort involved.

Poor Reporting. Too many studies contained too little information about samples used for us to have much confidence about either the internal or external validity of the results. This is simply careless reporting, but it is fully as serious an error as a poor sample. In both the John C. Moorhouse [563] and the Muth and Wetzler [580] studies, the authors make use of data developed in other studies without describing the sampling techniques relied upon.

In other studies the problem is even more serious. The sources of the data are simply not given. There is little that can be said for the validity of such studies (e.g., Case [123], Davis and Wertz [174], Downs [199], Mace and Wicker [499], Niebanck [617]).

Generalizability. In the absence of strong explanatory theory, the quest for generalizable research conclusions is little more than quixotic. Nonetheless, we put the housing studies we examined to this test.

The requirement of generalizability is necessarily more restrictive than that of external validity. Many studies with good external validity do not attempt to derive generalizations which would apply to every United States city. Indeed, the quest for simple conclusions that are generalizable to such a level may well be futile. Cities undoubtedly vary among themselves on almost any dimension that one might consider relevant. Conclusions that would apply to every city would have to assume a form complex enough to take variations along these relevant dimensions into account.

For example, a conclusion that rehabilitation is cheaper than razing and rebuilding might only apply to other cities if it were recast in a more restrictive form: that rehabilitation is cheaper if the city has a large pool of skilled labor, if mortgage financing is relatively available and if the demand for rehabilitated buildings has shown itself reasonably robust.

Unfortunately, the difficulty of generalizing simple conclusions points up only too well the difficulties a decision maker might face in applying such simple conclusions to his city. In the absence of generalizable, complex conclusions the decision maker is faced with the necessity of adding the complexity to the conclusions himself. He is forced to ask himself in what relevant ways his situation differs from the situation studied, and he must estimate the effects these differences are likely to have. Although the source of the original conclusions may be exquisitely valid, the decision maker's interpretation of them can hardly be based on much more than hunches and "feel" for the situations. Neither process has much scientific standing.

For most of the policy-related research we analyzed, the decision maker is forced to fall back upon his hunches and "feel" to apply their conclusions to his case. We found only nine studies for which there seemed some basis for generalization to the entire United States [28, 85, 86, 335, 362, 580, 608, 746, 756]. Two other studies had conclusions which could be applied anywhere within one state [747, 829]. And six studies had conclusions which might be presumed to apply to any city in a particular metropolitan region [354, 653, 662, 683, 755, 800]. Most studies, however, presented little or no evidence that their conclusions might apply more broadly than to one or a few cities. And for one-fifth of the studies it was not clear that their conclusions could be relied upon even throughout one city. Six studies, for example, had conclusions that might apply at best to one or a limited number of neighborhoods within the city [118, 138, 334, 367, 583, 786]; three were restricted to particular projects [617, 647, 845], and two to particular buildings [378, 499].

A number of studies listed here were relatively modest in their attempts to generalize and were restricted to a relatively low level of generalizability by choice. Several studies, however, strove for a higher level of generalizability than we were willing to grant that they had attained. The reasons for our restrictive interpretation almost invariably had to do with the size and type of sample upon which the studies based their conclusions.

Implications for Research Design. It would be unfortunate to abandon our discussion of generalizability without attempting to draw some lessons about how the situation could be improved. We seek conclusions that can be generalized to all cities in the United States. Nine of the studies we reviewed seemed to have the evidential basis for such generalization. Do these nine present a pattern that should be emulated in future studies?

One of the nine studies was the Arthur D. Little study of property taxes and urban blight [28]. This study drew a sample of ten cities and, within each of the cities, drew a further sample of homeowners. In this particular case the technique should, perhaps, not be held up as an example. With only ten cities to represent all cities in the United States, it is at best a borderline case of wide external validity. Moreover, the ten were not randomly drawn—or at least it is not indicated in the study that they were so drawn. Hence, the presumption of external validity is greatly reduced.

The technique used by Arthur D. Little shows promise if more carefully carried out. The better approach is to control for state, regional, and local influences by sampling cities randomly, and then sampling respondents within each city in some reasonable way. Unfortunately, this can become prohibitively expensive when one addresses a question that is at all complex. Several studies attempted to use techniques that approximate this optimal approach, but they shared a common weakness—they involved such small numbers of cities, or cities chosen in such a manner, that the results had no external validity beyond the cities represented in the sample (e.g., Center for Community Change/National Urban League [129]; Linton, Mields and Coston [482]).

Two of the studies that were adequately designed to permit generalization to the United States conducted large surveys of local housing agency personnel in cities across the United States. Chester W. Hartman and Gregg Carr [335] sent questionnaires to approximately 10,000 such individuals. Their low response rate of 19 percent, however, raises some questions about the external validity of their results. Robert Sadacca [746] carefully selected a representative sample of local housing authorities, and conducted interviews in 120 of them. This approach generates data that are likely to represent well the universe of interest. Again, the principal drawback is that with complex questions it can soon become prohibitively expensive. If the mailed-questionnaire technique is used, there is a clear trade-off between the complexity of questions one can ask and the response rate one can expect. With relatively simple, well defined questions, however, this may be a reasonable technique.

Five studies attempted to reduce the prohibitive expense of data-gathering by relying upon census data, typically for standard metropolitan statistical areas [85, 86, 362, 580, 756]. If one is willing to settle for census level accuracy, this may not be a bad approach. However, it is only rarely that housing researchers find the categories of data pertinent to the questions they want to address in census materials.

One study, Max Neutze [608], used what seems a promising approach by shifting back and forth between a detailed local study of one neighborhood in Washington, D.C. and a broad overview of the United States using census data for SMSAs. This seems a reasonable way of combining generalizable conclusions with conclusions that are based upon an analysis of local issues for which the census may not have data. Even so, this approach is likely to generate independent sets of conclusions. Only one set, consisting of conclusions from the local study that can be checked against census data, will be generalizable. Those conclusions of the local study that cannot be so checked may not be generalizable at all.

In sum, unless the research team commands substantial resources or is unusually ingenious in its use of census data, we are unlikely to find research conclusions that can be applied with assurance beyond the urban context in which the research was conducted. Let the local policy maker beware!

Availability, Presentation, and Applicability of Research Findings: Diminished Utility

Problems with the internal and external validity of housing research limit its value as social science and restrict the extent to which the decision maker can rely on its findings for policy guidance. Problems with the generalizability of these findings mean that officials from one city may draw from this research a general feel for the way things sometimes work, but questions about how things will work in his own city remain unanswered.

Even the most valid and generalizable research is of little or no value to the policy maker if it is not readily available, easily understood, or ignores the practical constraints that circumscribe his policy options—administrative feasibility, program costs, political benefits, and equity effects.

In our evaluation of housing research we paid particular attention to these practical issues of communication and feasibility. Unlike our assessment of validity and generalizability for which social science criteria are available, any assessment of the policy utility of research is largely subjective and imprecise. Nonetheless, we feel that these are important judgments that should be included in any study which strives to be useful to local decision makers. We summarize the results of this portion of our evaluation in the remaining pages of this chapter.

Accessibility

The project team accumulated a list of more than 1,000 promising titles from a variety of sources—standard bibliographies, publication lists of public and private research institutions, lists of government-contracted studies from federal and state agencies, references from the literature, and letter replies from the individual researchers and university faculty to whom we sent inquiries. A substantial number of the titles we chose to evaluate more closely were readily available in one of the three large library collections we consulted—Yale University Library, the Library of Congress, and the Library of the U.S. Department of Housing and Urban Development (HUD). But many titles that intrigued us proved difficult or impossible to procure. These included items presently out of print, master's and doctoral studies available only through interlibrary loan facilities (with substantial delay), contract research by private firms that could not be authorized for release, and government-contracted studies unavailable to the general public.

The studies that proved easiest to obtain were those issued by commercial publishing houses. Most elusive, unfortunately, were those conducted under contract to the federal government. Some studies had to be obtained from the sponsoring agency; in other cases, copies could be obtained from the U.S. Superintendent of Documents (requiring a lengthy waiting period) or from the National Technical Information Service (NTIS) of the U.S. Department of Commerce.

In the case of background or technical studies conducted for a national commission, for example, National Commission on Urban Problems [588], President's Committee on Urban Housing [688], any one of several agencies of the federal government might have a supply, but rarely were all such documents available at one central place. In fact, acquiring documents from the various agencies and libraries of the federal government becomes very much a game of skill—one that most urban policy makers and their advisers have neither the time nor the resources to perfect.

To facilitate the search for and acquisition of policy-related research, we have included at the end of the complete bibliography a descriptive listing of the bibliographical, abstracting, and library sources we found most helpful.

Presentation

An equally disturbing program involves the time and effort required to distill the policy-related findings, conclusions, and recommendations from much of the housing research. Nearly 40 percent of the studies we evaluated have significant flaws in style and format, making the studies unreasonably difficult to read and to abstract. The point of many studies was concealed by the peculiar jargon or notations of their discipline; others were simply dense or in need of careful editing. Many authors stopped short of pulling the research findings together, leaving the reader to guess at the significance of their analyses.

Many of the problems of presentation and communication could have been eased, if not solved, by changes in format. Somewhat fewer than half of the studies we evaluated were organized so as to display their conclusions and recommendations in a prominent fashion. This is in part a matter of audience. The more academic studies were the chief culprits, indicating a tendency to value techniques of analysis more highly than conclusions. From the viewpoint of readability and presentation, the best studies were those contracted by commissions or written for more general audiences. The former were addressed to policy makers, generally federal, and provided executive summaries and/or sections devoted exclusively to conclusions and recommendations (e.g., Downs [203], Committee on Urban Housing [688]). Several of the studies written for more general audiences (e.g., Altshuler [19], Keyes [424]), showed a rare felicity of style.

Practical Application

In the course of each evaluation we considered whether the researcher dealt with a category of practical problems and issues that no policy maker can afford to ignore—administrative cost and feasibility, political feasibility, and equity effects. In Chapters 2-5 we noted instances where the failure to deal with any one or more of these problems undermined the validity of specific conclusions. Here, we deal with the problem in more general terms.

Cost. Considerations of cost will vary depending upon the subject of the research. We looked to see whether the researcher asked two basic questions about any municipal housing program: What does it cost? Who pays the bills? At a more sophisticated level additional items of cost must be considered, such as size of capital outlay vs. operating costs, fixed vs. variable costs, direct vs. indirect costs, general funding sources vs. bonding, front-end outlays vs. incremental outlays, average vs. marginal costs.

Less than half of the studies we examined paid ample attention to issues of program cost. For about one-fifth of the studies, this failure severely limited the utility of the study for policy makers.

Administrative Feasibility. This includes many vital programmatic considerations concerning the ease of understanding, staffing, managing, implementing, evaluating, modifying, and terminating the municipal housing program in question.

Only one-third of the research we evaluated fully addressed these issues. Failure to consider these questions severely reduced the utility of at least one-fifth of the studies we examined. For example, several studies concluded that housing-allowance and leased-housing programs appear more efficient and equitable than production subsidies. However, these studies ignored a critical programmatic consideration: Are local housing authorities equipped to perform the tasks that housing-allowance and leasing programs impose upon them—survey the housing inventory, inspect dwellings, negotiate leases, counsel tenants, police landlords, etc.? And if not, what strategies are required for them to become so? Another example of this failing occurs in the literature on tax reform, where few if any of the authors consider the short-term costs in time and staff resources of converting to a site-value tax system.

Political Feasibility. Political considerations certainly play a major role in municipal decisions on housing policy. To avoid the criticism of political naivete, policy-related research should examine such factors as controversiality, immediacy of results, salience of benefits, interagency or departmental conflict, likely permanence of program, impact on benefit flows, and the like. Rent-control measures have little to recommend them, except their favor with important segments of the electorate. Similarly, more open planning by public agencies is often thwarted by the politician's desire to pick the right time, place, and audience to announce a new venture.

It is not surprising that the most frequent criticism of policy-related research by municipal officials is directed at its political naivete. This criticism could be deflected if the researcher simply acknowledged the importance of these factors; too often he simply ignores them. Fewer than one-tenth of the studies we evaluated paid attention to political feasibility. We judged that the utility to policy makers of nearly half the studies we reviewed was significantly diminished as a result.

Equity. Fortunately, fully 60 percent of the evaluated studies paid attention to issues of equity, focusing upon the relation of costs and benefits to ability to pay and to need. This attests to the interest among academics, particularly welfare economists, in the distributional impact of alternative public policies. In only a small number of studies did we feel that the failure to consider these issues diminished the utility of the research.

Summary—Communication and Feasibility

Studies can be flawed in ways unrelated to the formulation and testing of hypotheses, and the drawing of conclusions. They can be flawed by the manner in which the research findings are presented and by the researcher's indifference to practical issues of cost, feasibility, and equity. Flaws in the conduct of research destroy or reduce the validity of the research; flaws in the presentation and distribution of the findings, or in dealing with the practical problems of program implementation diminish the utility of policy-related research for one of its principal beneficiaries—the policy maker.

In short, the researcher must become more sensitive to the unique needs of the policy maker. He must learn to communicate to the policy maker as effectively as he presently communicates to his peers in the research or academic communities. This is less a matter of training than one of exposure and experience. Thus, we turn briefly to an examination of the relationships between the researcher and the policy maker that show promise of producing helpful policy-related research.

The Relationship of Researcher to Policy Maker: Two Noteworthy Models

As we discussed in our introduction, there tends to be a trade-off between (a) the validity and generalizability of research findings and (b) their utility to the policy maker. In social science research, on the one hand, the emphasis is upon validity and generalizability, although the research may well have utility for policy makers in the long run because it improves the basic understanding and methodological tools of the policy analyst. In policy analysis, on the other hand, validity and generalizability are neglected as the policy analyst concentrates upon serving the short term needs of the policy maker.

What, then, should we expect of policy-related research? At the very least, when the policy researcher formulates his research design he should be aware of the more critical constraints that confront local decision makers. He should recognize that these constraints are crucial variables in explaining the success or failure of alternative policy interventions. However, the researcher must strike a delicate balance. He should not define these specific local variables with such specificity that the conclusions of his study cannot be generalized to other communities.

It is the role of policy-related research to assess the likelihood of a policy's success for a class of cities sharing common characteristics over a reasonable period. Policy-related research should not concentrate upon identifying the success or failure of a particular neighborhood program, under the auspices of a particular sponsor, conducted in a select community, during a specific time span. Nor should policy-related research be criticized for failing to advise a specific policy maker how to administer a set of policies or make the most political capital out of their success. If and when the policy maker needs such advice, he seeks it from those whose judgment of the local scene he has come to trust.

In fact, it may often be shortsighted for those who conduct policy-related research to limit the set of policy alternatives they analyze to those the policy maker deems administratively or politically feasible. Robert Harris has argued convincingly that it is nearly impossible for the analyst or scholar to predict the seemingly rare times when any major policy change is feasible [328]. In the case of Medicare/Medicaid, Harris concluded that the premature restriction of options to those deemed politically feasible left HEW officials in the unfortunate position of improvising a large part of the new program. In two other cases, income maintenance and the volunteer army, the work of analysts had an indirect impact on shaping political feasibility.

Harris perceives an increasing willingness among federal officials to support the work of scholars or analysts for lengthy periods on seemingly unproductive studies. This creates a stockpile of research and analysis that can be drawn upon when the political or economic climate changes and policy shifts are possible.

Harris is actually probing the area of overlap between what we have labeled policy-related research and policy analysis when in using the latter term he concludes:

Much policy analysis may have to be done outside government—although that poses a severe problem of access.... The academic researcher has more freedom to consider broad options—but does not have a chance to sell, test, and refine his ideas immediately... No linkup of policy analysis with implementation will take place if the analyst assumes that the first or second rejection of a desirable policy change is final or that his work is done when he has published his paper. [328]

By what means can the scholar or analyst be free to consider broad options without sacrificing his access to the policy maker? How can he maintain this access without losing that wider perspective that renders his work of value to the larger policy-making community? Answers to these questions call for a departure from past practice. In short, researchers and analysts must be placed in a novel relationship with urban officials. There are two cases of relevance to research on local housing that offer some promise—the work of the New York City-RAND Institute and the Urban Observatory Program.

The New York City-RAND Institute[b]

The New York City-RAND Institute was established in 1968 at the request of former Mayor Lindsay to assist several city agencies, including the Housing and Development Administration (HDA), in dealing with problems of policy and resource allocation. Ira Lowry, a professor of city planning and housing analyst, organized a team of fourteen full- and part-time professionals to work with HDA. This marked a unique arrangement in municipal housing research. Unlike more standard contract research, Lowry's team worked out a broad agenda of researchable problems to tackle in conjunction with HDA personnel, and established an ongoing relationship in which the levels of effort and expenditure were renegotiated each fiscal year. As Lowry explains: "This gave us the flexibility to adjust research objectives over time to meet client needs within our own emerging sense of priorities" [488, p. 4]. This breadth of the assignment also permitted the research team to explore fully the interrelatedness of the major regulatory programs that affected housing.

Lowry's team performed assorted tasks. They compiled program descriptions and expenditure data and attempted to measure program outputs; proposed a program-budget structure that HDA tried to implement; conducted background studies on various factors of housing supply and demand; designed a conceptual framework for explaining the maintenance decisions of private landlords as a means of identifying points of leverage for public policy; conducted analyses of each of the city's principal housing management, regulation, and construction programs; and recommended ways to improve HDA's decision process.

In the course of their assignment, Lowry's team became convinced that the traditional emphasis of New York City housing policy on incremental new construction scattered throughout various neighborhoods was altogether inappropriate and unsuccessful in affecting the city's housing problems. As Peter L.

---
[b]This brief account is based on three papers by RAND analysts [488, 855, 861].

Szanton pointed out: "The problem was not to turn the faucet on harder; it was to plug the drain" [855]. With its arsenal of studies and arguments RAND was able to convince HDA, the Bureau of the Budget, and eventually the mayor's office that attention should be focused instead on saving the existing stock of housing from deterioration and abandonment.

The RAND experience is instructive on several counts. It is repeated here to indicate that it is possible under certain circumstances to combine disciplined policy-related research with client-oriented policy analysis. Unfortunately, as our bibliography reveals, too few of the RAND studies for New York City have been published. RAND had little time to refine working papers, and city officials were reluctant to risk the adverse consequences of publication. Lowry estimates that more than 90 documents of professional quality had been prepared for the client through 1970 and only two had been published. Several other studies, primarily on rent control, have been published since that time, although the majority of the research remains unavailable.

Perhaps of more significance than its record of publications—and several studies are very good—is the process of interaction between analyst and policy maker that the RAND group claims it established. Reflecting on the success and failures of this process of interaction, Lowry and his colleagues distilled several general lessons for those who contemplate similar enterprises, which we paraphrase below:

1. The staff should consist of competent scholars who are well grounded in quantitative analysis and willing to address their research to the client's problems rather than to their academic peers.
2. The research charter should be flexible; initial task-order contracts bind the analyst to a research strategy that often proves inappropriate and irrelevant.
3. The research approach should provide a steady flow of intermediate products to assure the client interim guidance while he awaits the final document.
4. There must be continual and close contact throughout the research process with the client's staff.
5. Good program evaluation must answer no less than three basic questions: What does it cost? Who gets the benefit? Who pays the bills?
6. One of the most efficient modes of communicating research findings to the clients is the well rehearsed briefing, replete with visual aids, but supported with massive documentation. These back-up documents, when they are not too sensitive for public distribution, are the stuff from which policy-related research is generated.

Unfortunately, there has been no systematic evaluation of RAND research, other than by RAND personnel. Not surprisingly, reactions to the RAND effort among public officials in New York City have been mixed. RAND analysts have been accused of political naivete, intellectual arrogance, and plain incompetence.

One high-level official at HDA has told us that in his opinion RAND's housing research and analysis was of much less utility in reforming rent control than the contributions of other research groups operating in the more traditional role of contract consultants. Towards the end of the Lindsay administration and over the past several years, RAND's level of effort in the city has been greatly curtailed, partly in response to published criticism concerning the high costs of consultant research. It is therefore difficult to conclude whether the reduction in its research output is the result of political factors alone or whether it also reflects an assessment of the utility of the research.

One can conclude, however, that the political environment of any one city is hardly conducive to stable long-term arrangements with independent consulting groups. This suggests that other institutional arrangements should be explored. Such arrangements should incorporate those characteristics of the RAND experience that permit the pursuit of policy-related research in conjunction with more focused policy analysis, but should also establish a more stable political base for such research. One recent example of such an arrangement is the County and Municipal Government Study Commission of the State of New Jersey, whose staff has worked closely with the Center for Urban Policy Research at Rutgers and officials of the New Jersey Department of Community Affairs. The commission has released a report on the fiscal and social impact of multifamily developments [610], which was released too late for us to include among our evaluated studies.

In view of the increasing tendency to transfer federal housing responsibilities to state and local levels and the senselessness of formulating urban housing policies that focus exclusively upon their impacts within one municipality, a strong argument can be made for transferring the locus of action and research to the county (where it is an operating unit), regional, or state levels.

The Urban Observatory Program[c]

An entirely different institutional base for local policy-related research is typified by the Urban Observatory Program, the second example we present, although its output of housing research has been very sparse to date.

In 1962 Professor Robert Wood of MIT, later Under Secretary and, briefly, Secretary of HUD, urged that a nationwide network of city-university linked research centers, or urban observatories, be established. "The study of urban politics," he asserted, "lags far behind the natural sciences in the treatment of the phenomena under observation." In June 1968 the Urban Observatory (UO) Program was funded by HUD on an experimental basis. The National League of Cities (NLC) was selected to serve as program secretariat, responsible for

[c]Much of the following discussion is drawn from the evaluation of the program prepared for HUD [296].

channeling funds to ten city-university consortia (Alberquerque, Atlanta, Baltimore, Boston, Cleveland, Denver, Kansas City, Milwaukee, Nashville, and San Diego).

There were three principal objectives of the program:

1. To make university resources available to local government for understanding and solving particular urban and metropolitan problems
2. To coordinate a program of continuing urban research relevant to urban management, human resources, and environmental and development problems
3. To advance university capabilities to relate research and training activities more effectively to urban concerns

Although individual observatories have substantial autonomy, each is required to pursue both a national and a local research agenda. The national agenda, coordinated by the NLC, is an exercise in comparative urban research and focuses upon a discrete set of topics, including housing policies. The experimental hypothesis from which the national agenda emerged is a familiar one—that the systematic, comparative study and analysis of urban phenomena will yield general knowledge—a science of cities. In contrast, the local agendas are meant to respond to the unique problems of the host city as perceived by the local government's chief executive.

We focus here on one component of the Urban Observatory (UO) Program— its structure, both within each city and the network among cities. According to the Greenleigh Evaluation Report, the network system appears to be the strongest and most successful element of the experiment. Unfortunately, we can not judge the specific impact of the Urban Observatory experiment on housing research. Few of the local research products we located constituted policy-related research—most were limited surveys or case studies. Furthermore, only three of the ten cities chose to include the topic of "housing policies" in their national research agendas. Dissemination of the research has been delayed until the later years of the program; the results of this research are therefore not yet available.

For the most part the Greenleigh evaluation of the program's research products confirms our earlier conclusions concerning local housing research. There was little evidence that the studies which were undertaken led to concrete problem solving; instead, the research products merely provided a more knowledgeable approach to the problem under consideration. Understandably, local officials felt that the local-agenda research projects had the greatest value and impact.

At the very least the UO Program has succeeded in bringing local universities and local governments in closer juxtaposition. The Greenleigh report indicates that in several locales a group of academicians has developed who not only have a growing expertise about local urban problems, but have won the confidence of city officials by making useful contributions to policy analysis and development. Each observatory is required to have a local policy board consisting of university and local government participants. Two observatories also experimented successfully with joint advisory committees for specific research projects. Those observatories with full-time directors with no other major academic or governmental responsibilities have been most successful.

There is less to say at this time about the network system. It has not been adequately tested. What is more, it involves a number of complex operations and relationships both within the network and between the Secretariat, NLC, and HUD. Many of these relationships have been modified and revised. There has been an attempt to reduce the autonomy of local observatories in conducting national agenda research products. The initial studies did not produce findings that could be adequately validated, compared or synthesized. Consequently, NLC was directed to centralize and standardize research procedures. To do so and to assure that comparable data and methodologies would be employed throughout the network system, NLC has retained outside research experts of high quality. The success of the endeavor has not yet been determined.

In sum, the UO program has not been entirely successful. After six years of effort, it is still difficult to assess the quality of its research products. It has failed to contribute in any concrete or meaningful way to a "science of cities." In fact, the Greenleigh report concludes that this was an unrealistic goal and recommends, instead, that the program focus on public-policy research. Though this term is inadequately defined, it appears to us that it is intended to cover the area we define as policy-related research, especially where policy-related research and policy analysis converge.[d] The UO environment has not proven congenial to pure social science research. It has also failed to tap those university resources most appropriate to "problem solving," as opposed to "understanding."

To redress the imbalance in program management that led to an undue emphasis on local research needs, Greenleigh recommends that HUD and local governments become partners in the selection of comparative-research projects. This is a sound recommendation. The UO network system remains potentially the most fruitful structure that presently exists for encouraging and managing policy-related research.

Unfortunately, the recommendations of the Greenleigh report are unlikely to be implemented or tested. Financial support of the original ten observatories by HUD terminated as of June 1974. Instead, HUD intends to continue the program in ten smaller cities with populations ranging up to 200,000. However, there will be a three-year limit on HUD funding for the new observatories, with local matching grants increasing each year.

HUD's decision bodes badly for comparative research of the kind included in UO's national agenda. HUD and NLC must take care that the UO program does

---
[d]For a review of these terms, see Chapter 1, pp. 10-13.

not degenerate into a vehicle for the production of surveys and reports of limited utility and transferability similar to those produced under the auspices of the Urban Planning Research and Demonstration Program established under section 701b of the Housing Act of 1954, as amended. One possible way to ensure that the studies conducted under the modified UO program have some broader utility is to select towns in those states that have active and competently staffed departments of community affairs. These state agencies may then play a role in the selection and management of research that the Greenleigh report contemplated for HUD.

Summary

Both the RAND-New York Institute and the Urban Observatory Program are noteworthy examples of institutional arrangements between researcher and policy maker that attempt to place in balance the often competing demands of validity and generalizability, on the one hand, and utility, on the other. Neither model is without flaws, but until other institutional arrangements are created and tested, these two models merit further examination, refinement, and extension.

Conclusions

It is the absence or weakness of theory that compromises the validity of policy-related research on housing. The use of relatively sophisticated techniques of analysis does not correct this basic deficiency.

In the absence of strong explanatory theory, the quest for transferable research conclusions is largely quixotic. To some extent broad comparative analysis of groups of cities based on random sampling procedures will increase the presumption of external validity and generalizability. We must recognize, however, that such studies are difficult to administer and expensive to undertake. An alternative approach is to place a detailed local study in the larger context of the United States, comparing local with national census data.

Studies are also flawed by the manner in which research conclusions are presented and by the researchers' indifference to practical issues of cost, feasibility and equity.

Critiques of published policy-related research or attempts to draft measures of validity or utility may miss the mark. More fruitful are efforts to establish stable and creative institutional relationships between research scholar and local policy maker, between university and city hall. The most promising examples of such research enterprises are the New York City-RAND Institute and the Urban Observatory Program. We return to this point in the conclusions and recommendations that comprise the next and concluding chapter.

**Part IV:
Conclusions**

7
Conclusions and Recommendations

Introduction

Quite frequently large-scale evaluation studies change course midway. Objectives and criteria formulated at the start of a study prove inappropriate to the material when probed in depth. Sometimes this change of direction is acknowledged and imparts to others a special insight into the difficulties and obstacles unexpectedly encountered in the field of study.

An excellent example of this in the field of housing research is the study of planned communities and new towns conducted by Edward P. Eichler and Marshall Kaplan [218].[a]

The researchers had set out to promote a particular remedy—the development of broad-based new communities along the outskirts of metropolitan areas. They concluded by questioning, if not challenging this remedy.

We too conclude by challenging certain objectives of our original research proposal. By way of review, we started with the following assumptions:

1. There was a critical need to strengthen and improve municipal programs for promoting new housing development and for preserving existing housing stock.
2. To improve these housing programs, local policy makers had to resolve thorny technical problems relating to site acquisition, land banking, development codes and controls, real estate taxes, and housing subsidies.
3. Many municipalities, particularly medium-sized cities and smaller towns, lacked the in-house technical resources to develop policy alternatives and to decide among them on a cost-effective basis.

---

[a]Their original project proposal was based on the assumption that imperfections in the housing market (particularly the fact that the poor in general and blacks in particular had little access to suburban housing) greatly exacerbated the poverty, racial separation, and fiscal inequality found within and among cities and towns of our major metropolitan areas. The major premise of their study was that these problems could be mitigated by certain public and private interventions, particularly the development of new towns. The objective of their study was to devise one or more demonstrations to spur the development of new towns along the rural fringes of metropolitan areas.

In the course of their research and interviews, the authors began to challenge the major premise and alter their objective. They found little evidence that new towns presented a viable solution to the social and economic problems they had identified. To the contrary, the accumulated evidence showed that planned communities either ignored or aggravated these problems.

4. Policy makers in these municipalities would make more rational decisions if existing research on these more technical policy problems were collected, rigorously evaluated, and disseminated.

Our central purpose, then, was to collect policy-related research on housing, evaluate it intensively, and devise ways to bring the results of this distillation to the attention of local policy makers.

Certainly, local decision making can benefit greatly if the decisions of policy makers are informed by the results of carefully conceived and executed research studies. But it is premature to begin disseminating such research to local officials without examining carefully why, until now, policy-related research on housing has been largely ignored by the local policy maker and his advisers.

In the course of our search of the literature, our evaluation of specific studies, and our surveys both of the persons who produce it—the research community—and of those who presumably apply its findings—the local policy makers—we began to grasp more clearly why the product of this research process has been of limited utility to the policy maker, and, more significantly, the extent to which the situation can be corrected.

Policy-related research of the kind we have evaluated fails to play an important role in the formulation and execution of local housing policy because of one or several of the following kinds of problems:

1. Of quality—its overall scope and reliability is poor.
2. Of utility—it fails to consider the critical constraints inherent in the political process.
3. Of access and distribution—it is inadequately disseminated.
4. Of the rigors inherent in decision making—the local policy maker tends to rely on his own training and experience in making decisions about housing.

Some of these problems, particularly those that affect quality and distribution, suggest short-run remedial actions. But many of the problems do not represent failings, Rather, they are attributes of policy-related research, and are not as easily remedied.

In the remaining pages of this book we examine in turn each of the reasons why policy-related research has failed to have direct utility for policy makers and in each case recommend actions that can alter this situation.

Problems of Quality

Conclusion 1. The theoretical base for policy-related research on local housing is insufficient; the level of empirical analysis is very low. In no single area of the research is it possible to explain or predict with confidence the impact of specific policy interventions upon local housing markets.

Table 7-1
Quality of the Research: Summary

	Theoretical Base	Empirical Analysis
A. Planning tools		
Comprehensive planning	*Insufficient*—Altshuler [19] critique remains unanswered.	*Limited*—narrow case studies. Little comparative analysis.
Urban renewal	*Limited*—Davis and Whinston [176] one of few important studies.	*Limited*—studies have concentrated on refining cost/benefit methodology rather than applying game theory and cost/benefit techniques to analyze urban renewal.
Information systems	*Insufficient*—studies concentrate on technical design of systems, not on questions of key variables and how information systems can improve the quality of public intervention in housing.	*Insufficient*—diffuse and unfocused, although some preliminary analyses of abandonment are available.
B. Codes and Regulations		
Land-use regulations	*Insufficient*—studies have been descriptive and exhortative rather than theoretical or analytic.	*Limited*—narrow case studies.
Building codes	*Insufficient*—only descriptive.	*Limited*—largely anecdotal surveys of builders.
Housing codes	*Limited*—Ackerman [10] is an exception.	*Insufficient*—some case studies.
Rent control	*Sufficient*—several good economic studies, for example, Olsen [642, 643], Rapkin [704].	*Limited*—all NYC-based, and inadequate analysis of rent control effects on non-controlled buildings.
C. Real property taxation		
Conventional property tax	*Sufficient*—an extensive theoretical literature, for example, Netzer [602], Orr [652, 653], Sabella [745].	*Limited*—research scant, in case study form only.
Special tax abatements and incentives	*Sufficient*—draws on property tax theory. See previous citations.	*Limited*—Peterson [670] and Price-Waterhouse studies [691] focus primarily on New York and Boston experience.
Site-value taxation	*Sufficient*—draws on property tax theory.	*Insufficient*—nothing besides Price-Waterhouse study [691].

Table 7-1 (cont.)

	Theoretical Base	Empirical Analysis
D. Housing-assistance programs		
Supply subsidies	*Limited*—draws on standard welfare economics, but needs further refinement.	*Limited*—conclusions are largely theoretical, based on restricted economic models.
Demand subsidies	*Limited*—same as above.	*Insufficient*—little besides Solomon [799] on Kansas City; few demonstrations to analyze.
Self-help programs	*Insufficient*—nothing.	*Insufficient*—nothing besides Kolodny [436] on NYC.

As the earlier chapters reveal in detail, the reliability of policy-related research on local housing services is poor. In the brief overview presented above, we summarize our findings about the quality of the research literature. The summary chart focuses upon the degree of theoretical backing and the extent of empirical analysis available in the research for each of the local housing policy tools discussed in Part II. This review of the quality of the research, though drawn from systematic and rigorous evaluation of the individual studies, is necessarily subjective. By "insufficient," we mean that little or no theory or empirical research exists—certainly not enough to warrant generalization. By "sufficient," we suggest that a base does exist for some generalization. Note that in no instance, however, did we find both the theory and empirical analysis on a topic to be sufficient. Finally, by "limited" we mean that general conclusions from the existing studies must be carefully qualified to acknowledge the limitations in the underlying theory or empirical analysis.

It is equally possible to assess housing research in terms of the problems it addresses, rather than the policy instruments it examines. But the result would be the same. Underlying theory is weak. Empirical analysis is spotty, and consists primarily of case studies.

Conclusion 2. Policy-related research on housing pays insufficient attention to the interdependencies among local housing programs, particularly the positive or negative impacts of one policy instrument on another in dealing with similar or related local problems.

Given the grave limitations in theory and empirical analysis, it is not surprising that the literature is so disconnected. The relationships among principal policy instruments are largely ignored. Most of the studies focus on the evaluation of specific programs and ignore broader policy objectives or problems.

Conclusions 1 and 2 are related. They reveal basic inadequacies in the conduct of research on local housing. Both failings can be remedied, though not necessarily in the short run. Advances in basic theory are sometimes as much matters of good luck or personal insight as of systematic group effort.

Nonetheless, certain preconditions to theoretical advance can be identified and supported by public funding. Theoretical advances of value to housing research involve long-term interdisciplinary efforts, essentially by economists and political scientists, to test hypotheses as to the nature of housing markets, investor behavior, expenditure patterns, multiplier effects, interdependencies, and the like. Such research requires far better data stocks than now exist, an institutional context for interdisciplinary efforts, and some way of inducing the better social scientists to contribute their skills.

It is naive, however, to believe that a credible argument can be made for giving basic research on housing a priority over other competing demands for public-policy research or for creating new institutional settings to promote such research. Rather, the institutional settings that now generate basic research of quality on housing should be supported. These are principally independent and university-related urban research institutes devoted to housing concerns. The most appropriate agencies to sponsor and fund this enterprise are the Office of the Assistant Secretary for Research and Technology of the Department of Housing and Urban Development (HUD) and the Division of Social Systems and Human Resources of the National Science Foundation (NSF). Essential to the success of such an effort is the allocation of funding to the general research arms of housing and urban institutes, rather than for specific projects. An example of the kind of agenda these institutes should be encouraged to formulate is the one developed by Morton Isler for The Urban Institute.[b]

One last set of observations concerning the economics of policy-related research on municipal issues is relevant here. Sources of support for policy-related research differ from those on which social science research or local policy analysis depend. With few exceptions social science research is conducted by academics as an integral aspect of their own professional agendas. Much of this effort is fueled by a scholarly quest for knowledge, but the added incentives of professional advancement and strong institutional support by the university cannot be underestimated. Policy analysis, on the other hand, tends to be contract research performed at substantial expense for public agencies by consultant groups—some university-related, others from private firms. Since the 1960s federal agency and commission staffs have had an opportunity to conduct rigorous in-house policy analyses. The Office of Equal Opportunity between 1965 and 1967 and the President's Commission on Income Maintenance in 1968 and 1969 are notable examples. The Office of Management and Budget and

---

[b]Morton L. Isler, *Thinking About Housing: A Policy Research Agenda* [382]. Isler describes the key housing problems that the federal government has addressed—poverty, declining housing services, faltering production, and rising prices—and places them in a common analytic framework. Drawing on this framework, he suggests procedures for investigating proposed solutions to these problems, thereby outlining a linked set of research strategies.

various congressional watchdogs have begun to concede the importance of this effort because the internal research efforts of these agencies have generated useful short-term products.

In contrast to the resources that support these research efforts, it is difficult to identify any stable sources of funding for research in the middle ground—for policy-related research. It is not the kind of research that advances academic careers or satisfies the demand for short-term products by those who watch over public funds. No wonder, then, that the research literature we reviewed is spotty in quality and limited in scope. Policy-related research is frequently a by-product of the other two research enterprises—the "policy" or "applications" paper at the close of more scholarly endeavors or the "think" piece published by the consultant at the close of more mundane assignments in policy analysis.

Policy-related research on local housing, moreover, suffers from a further and more severe liability. The local policy-making community has far less attraction than the federal arena for the scholarly mind and far fewer resources to spend on policy analysis or research of any kind.

Expanding the store of policy-related research on local housing in spite of these handicaps is not an easy task. It cannot be accomplished haphazardly through occasional "requests for proposals" by federal agencies or funding sources, or through occasional consultant contracts that specify a research product of utility to the local policy maker. The quality of policy-related research can be improved only to the extent that (a) the institutional settings for such research are strengthened and made more stable, and (b) incentives are provided to attract to problems of local housing policy those persons and organizations with the resources and capacity to conduct rigorous empirical research.

Recommendation 1. That HUD and NSF ensure a more stable institutional setting for basic research (social science and policy-related) into the underlying causes of the problems that cities face in housing, community development, and urban growth; that they do so by providing grants to support the research agendas (three to five-year programs) of housing and urban institutes, such as The Urban Institute, the Joint Center for Urban Studies of MIT and Harvard, and the Center for Urban Policy Research at Rutgers.

Recommendation 2. That to promote more useful stocks of data, the research efforts of these institutes be coordinated with the work of the Statistical Policy Division of the U.S. Office of Management and Budget in developing social indicators, and with the Bureau of the Census, U.S. Department of Commerce, in designing the decennial census of housing and special housing surveys, with particular emphasis upon the bureau's methodology for measuring the quality of housing.

It is our judgment that implementing these recommendations would alter the quality of existing housing research far more effectively than specific recommendations on what needs study or how specific research designs should be formulated. This is because they address the underlying theory, data base and methodological approach of housing research, in general. That is not to say that research funds should be limited to a few major institutions, or that implementing the recommendations in the preceding chapters cannot greatly assist individual analysts who are interested in particular problems of housing policy. But evaluation of local-housing programs has been too fragmented and too narrowly conceived and conducted. Housing researchers must be encouraged to view the local-housing process in more systematic terms. They must trace the impacts of any single policy intervention upon the array of related housing problems and determine whether the policy instrument under study complements or conflicts with the exercise of other policy instruments impinging on the area of study. Few analysts consciously pursue a narrow or fragmented research design. More frequently, they ignore the secondary or side effects of the policies under study because data are limited and measurement is difficult. Nonetheless, such exploration, even if preliminary and tentative, should be encouraged. As Jay Forrester has forcefully argued, the secondary effects of policy interventions are often counterintuitive; central city housing policies that appear sound in the short run may erode the metropolitan economic base over the long run [239].

Recommendation 3. That HUD and other primary funders of policy-related research encourage housing analysts to explore more systematically the secondary impacts or side effects of specific policy interventions upon the local housing market and upon related public policies and programs.[c]

Problems of Utility

Conclusion. Policy-related research lacks immediate utility for the policy maker because it often fails to pay sufficient attention to the constraints that limit his decisions. Issues of administrative feasibility, cost, and political acceptability are particularly overlooked in policy-related studies.

---

[c]This recommendation should not be interpreted as a demand for elaborate systems analysis as much as a recognition that competent research and experimentation in public policy must begin with a careful conceptualization of the system under scrutiny. Conceptualization need not be overly elaborate or framed in econometric terms; it should not be mistaken for technique. For examples of useful conceptualization of housing problems, in layman's terms, see, for example, Anthony Downs [199, 203], Morton L. Isler [382]. For a listing and discussion of more sophisticated models, see, for example, Maurice D. Kilbridge, R.P. O'Block, and P.V. Teplitz [427].

Drawing on the case studies of the New York City-RAND Institute and the Urban Observatory Program discussed in the previous chapter, and on our own project experience, we make the recommendations listed below. These recommendations address a different set of issues than those set forth in the previous section. The latter aim at raising the basic quality of research on housing; the following recommendations are designed to produce institutional environments in which the scholar or analyst is free to pursue broad research options in close association with the local policy maker. In our judgment the objectives of policy utility are more likely to be achieved by exploring alternative institutional arrangements or patterns of interaction between analyst and policy maker than by specifying utility criteria that the research should satisfy.

Recommendation 1. That HUD or NSF adopt a specific plan and timetable for encouraging policy-related research of relevance to local policy makers.

More specifically:

Recommendation 2. That in view of the uniqueness of the New York City-RAND Institute and the mixed assessment of its contribution to housing research, HUD or NSF commission a systematic evaluation of this enterprise, comparable in scope to the evaluation of the Urban Observatory Program.

Recommendation 3. That because the quality and utility of policy-related research cannot be divorced from the institutional arrangements from which it springs, HUD or NSF should also evaluate the efforts of county- and state-level study commissions, like the New Jersey County and Municipal Government Study Commission. These evaluations should focus on how to help states to create and lend stability to research efforts designed to produce policy-related research on local housing that is both useful and transferable.

Recommendation 4. That the national research agenda and network of urban observatories developed in the course of the Urban Observatory Program not be jettisoned, but be continued with HUD financial support and participation under the supervision of the National League of Cities. This is the best existing arrangement for encouraging comparative policy-related research on urban problems like housing.

Recommendation 5. That in the context of its proposed modification of the Urban Observatory Program, HUD consider the inclusion of state departments of community affairs or state study commissions as co-participants with smaller towns and university research personnel in the selection and conduct of research subjects.

Problems of Access and Distribution

Conclusion. Policy-related research on housing is presently listed, abstracted, produced, published, and distributed in a haphazard fashion, thereby greatly diminishing its availability and utility to the local policy maker.

The difficulties that confronted our project staff in piecing together a bibliography and collecting items of policy-related research on housing testify to the patchwork nature of the literature. Research conducted by academicians is generally the most accessible, since it tends to be published in standard periodicals or in books that are distributed by commercial or university presses. Publications of research institutes are less accessible; publication lists must be requested and items are often out of print. Contract research, except for that done under contract with HUD, is by far the most fugitive source—difficult both to identify and to acquire.

Problems related to the dissemination of research findings run deep and defy simple solutions. Many research consultants are too busy to bother about publication or distribution. The research analyst who is interested in publication frequently has a client who prefers to control the manner and timing of release. Often this implies no release. This problem is confirmed by Ira S. Lowry's account of the New York City-RAND experience:

We [RAND] have been kept too busy with new issues to rewrite and edit for publication material that we have in hand.... But it is also true that our client has been reluctant to publish some documents that we view as finished products. This is partly because almost everything we have done has visible policy implications, and our client is not always ready to respond with policy initiatives. [488, pp. 13-14]

Even when dissemination is part of the larger research assignment, it is frequently poorly designed and executed in a haphazard fashion. In its evaluation of the Urban Observatory Program, Greenleigh reported that beyond certain routine activities—quarterly meetings of participants, NLC site visits, and the distribution of finished research products to each participating Observatory— "no systematic network strategy was developed to effectuate dissemination and transfer of research products" [296, p. 18].

Lack of adequate dissemination of this research not only deprives the policy maker of potentially useful information, it also handicaps the scholar and analyst by depriving him of the necessary dialogue with his professional peers working on similar problems. This became clear in our evaluation process. We included a section in our evaluation form on "interdependence in the literature." This was to record instances in which the author of one study cited the conclusions, data, methodology or theory of other studies. We also asked the evaluator to note whether the works so cited were accepted as given, supported, refined, disputed, or rejected. With very few exceptions, this proved an exercise in futility. We found very little "interdependence" in the literature. Where novel issues were addressed or narrow housing programs evaluated, the failure to cite and discuss other works seemed justifiable. More often, however, the inadequate consideration of other related works seemed short-sighted and parochial.

Obviously, policy makers are discouraged by the many difficulties they encounter in identifying the issues that have been studied and in obtaining the research products. Respondents to our survey of policy makers and their advisers (Appendix A) said they found housing studies too hard to find, frequently out of date, too cumbersome and time consuming to read, and too complicated—in that order.

The first two complaints suggest a need for better bibliographies, publication lists, abstracting, and retrieval services. Several good services already exist and simply need to be brought to the attention of policy makers. For example, the policy advisers we surveyed, including a disproportionate number of city planners, rely most frequently on the technical bulletins and research monographs issued by the Urban Land Institute (ULI), Planning Advisory Service of the American Society of Planning Officials (ASPO), and the occasional booklets and reference materials issued by the National Association of Housing and Redevelopment Officials (NAHRO). Few seem aware or make use of the publications available through the National Technical Information Service (NTIS) of the U.S. Department of Commerce, the Urban Affairs Abstracts published weekly by the National League of Cities (NLC) and U.S. Conference of Mayors (USCM), or the Housing and Planning References issued bi-monthly by the HUD library.

This book, especially the synthesis of research findings, the bibliography, and the guide to bibliography and abstracting services will hopefully make policy advisers and decision makers more aware of the existing services.

Fortunately, others are also filling this information gap. Virginia Paulus of The Center for Urban Policy Research (CUPR) at Rutgers has issued an extensive housing bibliography—*Housing: A Bibliography 1960-72* (New York: AMS Press, 1974). In conjunction with the AMS Press, CUPR has also issued two anthologies of readings on housing [825, 833] that include selections of policy-related research. It is hoped that CUPR and other university-based research institutions will continue to issue similar anthologies annually.

In the long run journals devoted exclusively to policy-related research on housing may eliminate the need for more general anthologies. The current audience for such publications is, however, extremely limited.

It is our view that the local policy maker and his advisers on housing matters need a simpler and more direct pipeline to policy-related research than now exists. It is more feasible to run this pipeline through organizations and publications with which the decision makers have the most frequent contact than to promote new or different information sources or clearinghouses. In this regard local chief executives should be reached through the National League of Cities and U.S. Conference of Mayors (NLC and USCM), the International City Management Association (ICMA), and their state affiliates. For instance, nearly every state has a state municipal league affiliated with NLC, and each state league has an information-dissemination system. The National Association of Housing and Redevelopment Officials (NAHRO) should be used to reach housing-agency executives and various housing advisers. Similarly, municipal finance officers can be reached through the Municipal Finance Officers Association (MFOA).

To bring the existing studies to the attention of local policy makers and their advisers, we make the following recommendations:

Recommendation 1. That HUD commission an annual review of recent developments in policy-related research on local housing; the review should be suitable for publication in magazines like NLC's *Nation's Cities* and NAHRO's *Journal of Housing*.

Recommendation 2. That NLC, USCM, ICMA, NAHRO, and MFOA individually (or jointly) prepare for distribution to their members a simple reference manual on how to search for and obtain research studies on local housing. The manual should expand the listings and comments that we have appended to the bibliography at the close of this report.

Recommendation 3. That NTIS and the U.S. Government Printing Office (GPO) adopt more aggressive means for publicizing accessions of contract research on housing, including the distribution of announcements through such organizations as NLC, USCM, and NAHRO.

Recommendation 4. That the bibliographic data sheet presently used by NTIS should be modified to include a reference to the specific "user groups" to which the research study should be directed. A brief explanation of the policy utility of the research study should be included at the close of the abstract.

Recommendation 5. That the extensive catalogue and research-retrieval facilities of HUD's Library and Information Division in Washington, D.C. be made available to its regional- and area-office libraries and information programs, and through these programs to local housing and planning agencies. Priority should be given to the establishment of a sophisticated automated network to expedite the search for relevant titles and to link regional and area office libraries to HUD's central office library.[d]

---

[d]For HUD's own plans in this area, see Elsa S. Freeman [245, pp. 15-17].

Recommendation 6. That both NTIS and HUD consider systematically soliciting and cataloging nongovernmental research studies that merit wide distribution. In this manner a central depository for all policy-related research on local housing can be established and updated.

Policy-related Research and the Problems of Decision Making

Conclusion. The policy maker will rely chiefly upon his own training and experience and that of his policy advisers in making decisions about housing.

Policy-related research plays a relatively minor role today in decisions about local housing. This is partially due to the problems we have discussed at length in earlier sections of this study. But it is also a consequence of two quite independent factors: the kind of person who tends to become a local chief executive and the rigors of the decision process itself. Unless both factors are understood, attempts to direct even the most valid and useful findings of policy-related research to the local policy maker will be unsuccessful.

We conducted surveys of the chief executives and their housing policy advisers in every medium-sized city (populations between 30,000 and 300,000) in New England, and sampled at random their counterparts in more than a quarter of the remaining medium-sized cities in the United States. The sample included 254 mayors and selectmen and 159 city managers. We also surveyed 208 housing-agency executives representing public housing, urban renewal, and code-enforcement agencies. A full account of our several surveys, including methodology and findings, is presented in Appendix A of this book.

Our survey findings support five general conclusions about the way in which local decision makers formulate policy and make decisions about housing:

1. They make little use of policy-related research.
2. They rely primarily on their own training and experience and, to a lesser extent, on information gained at conferences and workshops.
3. They turn frequently to various advisers for information and counsel.
4. These advisers in turn rely primarily on their own training and experience.
5. Periodicals or reports containing housing research are not currently an important source of information for either policy makers or their advisers.

These findings are confirmed by other surveys and studies that have examined the nature and style of local elected officials. In a recent survey [43] the National League of Cities provides a revealing portrait of the local chief executive. Although there are able and dynamic chief executives, the more typical mayor fills a part-time job for which he is paid less than $5,000 per year.

There is a high turnover rate among mayors. The typical mayor is in office about four and one-half years, and either plans to run again or does not know whether he will or not. And most mayors have similar frustrations: the time he spends away from his family, the long hours required on the job, and the information glut—too much material to evaluate the most effective way to receive information about new ideas related to municipal government.

Actually, the most popular form of government for cities above 50,000 population is the council-manager plan, used in 146 of the 309 cities in this category. The profile of the city manager differs somewhat from that of the typical mayor. He frequently has had special graduate school training in an area related to urban government or administration. Recruited in a national market, his frame of reference and standard of success comes from his professional peers rather than the local community. The housing agency executive is increasingly professional in his training and outlook as well.

In spite of these differences in training and outlook, the three types of local policy maker we analyzed—mayor, city manager, housing agency executive—are essentially generalists who approach problem solving in a tough, pragmatic fashion. They rarely have adequate staff, certainly few capable of conducting or evaluating research studies. Their jobs neither attract nor reward reflection. It is challenge enough to keep up with the difficult challenges of day to day administration and operations. By temperament these officials are activist and look to others like themselves for counsel and advice. As our survey results display, it is no wonder that the policy maker and his advisers place little reliance on policy-related research.

This leads us to the second factor—the rigors of decision making. The elected or appointed official is rarely in a position to benefit directly from policy-related research, no matter how helpful it might be. The problems he must solve are generally too focused and rooted in a specific context and time frame, to justify recourse to a general body of research. For the local policy maker, the search for relevant research not only is extremely costly but is rarely worth its cost and is generally too late to help. This point has been put well by Elizabeth Wood, a noted public housing administrator, who explained:

... I have been very skeptical of the ability of research to help a housing operator solve the problems that confront him. At times I have been anti-research ... we did try to solicit the aid of research people. By the time the researchers had defined the problem, debated about proper methodology, taken their observations using the most precise techniques, made a highly refined and scientific analysis, and prepared their report, the emergencies which had given rise to the research had already reached a climax several months earlier, been handled in the best way possible by the operators, and the housing program had passed on to other problems. Not only was this research too late, but most of it was phrased in a language which was difficult to understand and apply to practical situations.

"Many of the pieces of research which have proved most useful to public housing operators, such as myself, have been beaten out hastily, using the evidence that could be accumulated quickly, in order to help formulate a policy or make a decision that could not be delayed.

"Even when available, research findings can be only one of the elements entering into a decision. For example, we once sponsored a very successful study of the relationship between income and the ability to pay rent. The question was, 'Can a family pay 1/3 of its income for rent and yet have enough left to nourish the family?' Our study showed that under such conditions fathers and children were sufficiently well nourished, but mothers tended to be undernourished. With this conclusion, we were still confronted with the perplexing problem of whether to leave low-income families in health-destroying, overcrowded slum houses or to permit undernourished mothers to starve in greater comfort! The point I want to make clear here is this: a single piece of operation cannot be implemented with a single piece of research. Implementation involves many considerations to which research can only make a modest contribution. [945, reprinted with permission.]

Policy-related research is most valuable when the decision making process proceeds in ideal terms: an official sets an objective in advance, collects and organizes all relevant information, compares alternative policies, and then makes a decision. On occasion, the official has an opportunity to frame a new program in these terms—urban renewal and model cities, for example. Even then the actual decision process is far less systematic than the ideal. More often than not, however, the official must deal with fragments of a whole. Tough decisions are forced upon overburdened and harassed local officials who must spend the bulk of their intellectual energy and resources in determining exactly what the problem is, how quickly it can be remedied and how much it will cost. In these circumstances the official has no choice but to rely on his own training and experience if he is to survive. The alternatives are too costly in time lost and decisions deferred.

If this brief analysis of a complex set of issues is correct, it is clear that the policy maker—elected or appointed—has little time to devote to books and periodicals. He is already glutted with paperwork and burdened with problems requiring immediate action. He must get the findings of policy-related research, if at all, from others, digested and in oral-auditory form. If he is fortunate enough to have adequately trained staff, he can turn to them for information and research on housing. If the city can afford it, he can demand from outside consultants the tightly organized briefings of the kind the New York City-RAND Institute claims it presented periodically to HDA officials and Mayor Lindsay. The mayors of the largest cities, like New York, can even approach the ideal model of decision making by commissioning policy analysis of housing issues before problems arise. If he is farsighted enough he will also require the consultant group to train counterpart analysts among his permanent staff.

The less fortunate and more typical local official must look to persons and institutions outside his city for briefings on housing issues. He mainly relies upon the professional organizations to which he belongs—NLC, USCM, ICMA, and their state affiliates—for ideas and information. Nearly 75 percent of the mayors and councilmen surveyed by NLC reported attendance at statewide conferences sponsored by their state municipal leagues within the previous two years. Another 25 percent had attended at least one conference sponsored by the national organization.

Given these characteristics of the local policy maker and his necessary reliance on his own training and experience, we conclude with the following recommendations:

Recommendation 1. That NLC, USCM, and ICMA, acting through or in concert with their state affiliates, bring current developments in housing research to the attention of local policy makers through their various publications. At least once every two or three years, these organizations should hold briefing sessions at conferences and workshops relating important research findings to current housing opportunities and problems. Digests of the research should be distributed to the conferees with information as to how the research reports can be obtained.

Recommendation 2. That professional organizations like ICMA, NAHRO, and ASPO provide more frequent and intensive briefings for city managers, housing agency executives, and planners. These programs should be designed to keep local officials and their advisers informed of current developments in policy-related research on housing and to apprise them of the more sophisticated methods of policy analysis.

Recommendation 3. That one or more of these national organizations provide interim assistance to chief executives and their housing advisers by stockpiling research reports, evaluating important studies, and preparing executive summaries of the better reports for distribution to their membership.

Recommendation 4. That HUD or one of the national organizations prepare for circulation a manual of alternative contractual arrangements for securing research services. This should address, among other factors, the flexibility of the research agenda, and the form and frequency of intermediate work products and briefings.

The problems of policy-related research on housing, like those of the subject matter it probes, are subtle and complex. There are no easy solutions. It is unlikely that the quality, utility, or accessibility of the research studies will improve unless the importance of research activity is acknowledged by the larger policy-making community and unless sufficient resources are deployed to support the actions we have proposed in this book.

The promotion of policy-related research on local housing is an essential element in any strategy to improve the quality of life in our cities. Local government, the principal beneficiary of such efforts, is least able to support ongoing research, and many local officials question whether such research will ease their burdens of decision. We single out state and federal agencies as well as the professional organizations to which local officials look for guidance and assistance to implement many of the changes we propose. These agencies and organizations have the stature and resources to promote research of high quality and to see that research findings reach the appropriate local audience in timely and useful fashion.

**Part V:
Appendixes and
Bibliography**

Appendix A:
Housing Information Sources and Needs of Local Housing Policy Makers and Advisers: Survey Findings

As one component of the evaluation of policy-related research on housing we prepared a series of mail questionnaires. They were designed to elicit from local policy makers and their advisers the sources of information upon which they each rely in making decisions about housing. It was also our intention to gain the perspective of a representative cross section of local officials on the utility of policy-related research on housing.

The results of these surveys, which we present in detail in this appendix, strongly suggest that local policy makers and their various advisers (city planners, real estate professionals, other city officials) pay little attention to policy-related research. If the findings of policy-related research get before housing officials at all, it is through secondary sources (popular articles and abstracts) and even tertiary ones (conferences and workshops). These sources, we suspected, are more amenable to the practical, action-orientation that characterizes these officials.

In the following pages we present our survey design, the general conclusions we draw from the survey tabulations, and the evidence (in chart form) that supports these conclusions.

Survey Design

To gain the perspective of housing policy makers we designed four separate questionnaires that were mailed out over a period of six months.

Initial Survey of Policy Makers

The initial survey of policy makers was mailed to 621 officials in 258 cities. Consistent with the terms of the larger literature study, we focused on "medium-sized cities," which we defined as cities with populations between 30,000 and 300,000, particularly those in New England. We covered 92 New England cities in this size range exhaustively. For the other 179 cities that we surveyed, we drew a random sample in the remaining 44 states of the Union.

Questionnaires were mailed to 621 local policy makers in the 258 cities. These included 254 mayors, 159 city managers, and 208 housing agency executives (representing public housing, urban renewal, and code-enforcement agencies). To keep the survey within manageable limits, we did not attempt to survey city council members, in spite of the fact that they often possess some executive as well as legislative powers. For names and addresses of these officials we drew upon the *ICMA Municipal Yearbook* and three publications of the National Association of Housing and Redevelopment Officials (NAHRO): *NAHRO Housing Directory, NAHRO Renewal Agency Directory*, and *NAHRO Code Agency Directory.*

Our sample represents 100 percent of the 86 medium-size cities in New England, 27.6 percent of the 624 in the United States, exclusive of New England, and 36.4 percent of all United States cities of medium size.

The single-page questionnaire, which we deliberately kept as brief as our ingenuity could devise, probed five areas: sources of information for housing decisions; persons on whom the policy maker relied for advice; the extent to which housing studies proved helpful; problems with housing studies; and the likelihood that the respondent would read more housing studies if these problems were eliminated. We also provided space for general comments.

The overall response rate was favorable. Thirty-three percent (203) of the 621 policy makers responded. The response rate by category was reasonably balanced (see Table A-1).

Survey of Policy Advisers

The initial survey results revealed that policy makers do indeed rely upon policy advisers in substantial proportions for information before making housing

Table A-1
Survey of Policy Makers: Response Rate

Category	Sent Out	Received	%
Region:			
New England	203	63	31
Rest of United States	418	140	33
Size of City:			
Small 30-50,000	299	86	29
Medium 50-100,000	221	75	34
Large 100-300,000	101	42	42
Type of Respondent:			
Mayors and selectmen	254	63	25
City managers	159	58	36
Housing agency executives	208	82	39

decisions. From the 203 returned questionnaires, we obtained 228 names of policy advisers to whom we sent questionnaires.

This second questionnaire was similar to the one we sent to policy makers. However, we added two questions to the advisers—one to determine the different kinds of general housing publications they consulted, and one to determine topics or issues on which policy-related research would be helpful to them.

The response rate far exceeded that of the policy makers with 55 percent (127) of the 228 persons returning questionnaires. Policy advisers include a wide range of persons, defying easy classification. The categories we defined and the respective response rates are set forth in Table A-2.

Follow-up Surveys

Two follow-up surveys were prepared to fill gaps and clarify ambiguities revealed by the earlier surveys.

The first follow-up was sent to 140 policy makers who had replied to an earlier question that they "often" or "sometimes" consulted general housing publications. We took this opportunity to ask them the two questions we had added to the policy adviser's questionnaire. Of these 140, 53 responded to the follow-up for a response rate of 38 percent.

The second follow-up was addressed to 217 policy makers and advisers who

Table A-2
Survey of Policy Advisers: Response Rate

Category	Sent Out	Received	%
Private individuals:			
Academic	15	6	40
Business	21	4	19
Others	1	1	[a]
City officials:			
Housing	58	36	62
General	102	66	65
Other specialists	5	2	[a]
Outside agencies and organizations:			
HUD	9	6	[a]
NAHRO	1	1	[a]
State, regional, county	16	5	31

[a]Base too small for meaningful percentage.

had indicated that they often relied on their own training and experience in making housing decisions. The purpose of this second follow-up was to determine the components of "training," particularly the usefulness of conferences and workshops as an element of continuing education. We also took this opportunity to pose the central question—on what sources of housing information they relied—in a different manner. Initially we had asked policy makers and advisers about sources they draw upon in "making decisions." Few respondents listed housing research or publications. In the follow-up we asked about sources they consulted in "keeping informed of current developments in housing." Surprisingly, 72 percent (156) of the 217 policy makers and advisers responded to the second follow-up questionnaire.

Channels of Housing Information

Our survey findings are most easily understood by reference to Figure A-1. As our initial responses were received this chart was designed to organize the data and suggest further inquiries to include in the follow-up surveys. The flow chart

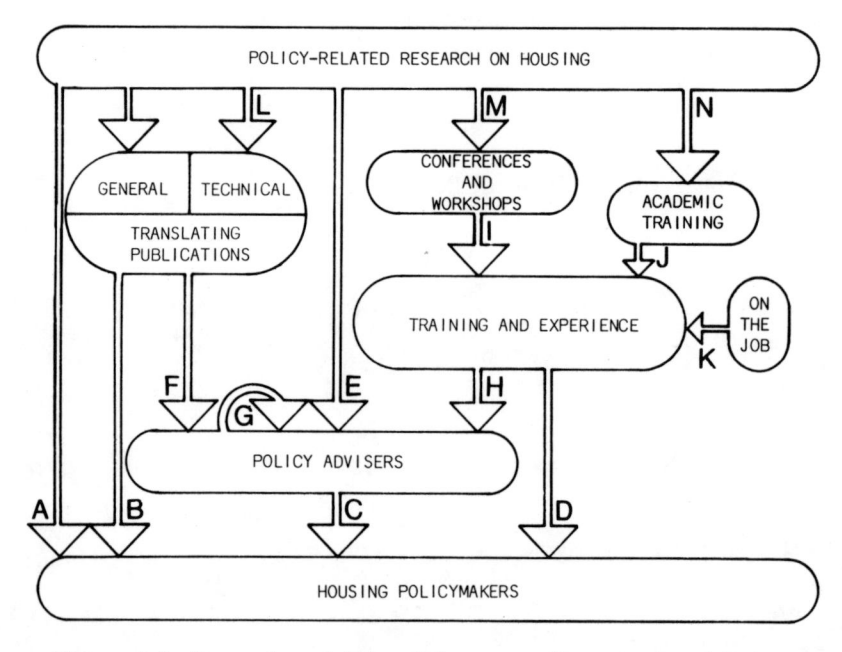

Figure A-1. Research and Other Information Flows to Local Policy Makers: Types.

also serves as a schematic and simplified model of the flow of information from policy-related research on housing to the housing policy maker.

The flow chart starts with the housing studies themselves. This focus is consistent with the purpose of the larger study: to assess the validity and utility of housing research. The point of the survey was to determine the extent to which policy makers or advisers relied directly on this source, the extent to which they drew on the findings of these studies through other channels, and the relative importance of these other channels.

The channels of information are described briefly in the following paragraphs (letters in parentheses are keyed to the letters on the chart):

Policy makers rely upon housing studies directly (A) or they read the conclusions of these studies at second hand in publications that provide summaries or "translations" of such studies (B). These are the primary and secondary channels through which research information flows. Policy makers also rely upon advisers as a source of information about housing (C). They rely as well upon their own training and experience (D).

Our first survey gave us a basis for judging the relative weights of channels A, B, C, and D. We examined in particular the impediments restricting the direct flow of information through channel A. The first follow-up clarified the components of channel B.

The same range of channels is used by the policy adviser. He reads studies directly (E), reads "translated" versions in general or technical publications (F), gains information from other persons (G), and from his own training and experience (H).

Finally, through their training and experience, policy makers and advisers draw on three additional information sources: conferences and workshops (I), academic training (J), and on-the-job training (K). The first two may impart the conclusions of housing studies; the third does not.

Through a content analysis of the technical publications named by the respondents we examined the extent to which publications they named actually present the findings of housing studies (L). Through our own background as housing professionals and the experience of the senior investigator as a former professor of city planning, we were able to assess the relative strength of two other channels of information derived from housing studies—the flow to conferences and workshops (M) and academic training (N).

Our analysis indicates that policy-related research on housing has a minimal impact on local housing decisions.

Figure A-2 presents schematically our conclusions on the relative importance of the various channels of information on which local policy makers rely in making housing decisions. The wider the channel as drawn on the chart, the more often the channel was named as an important source of information by our survey respondents.

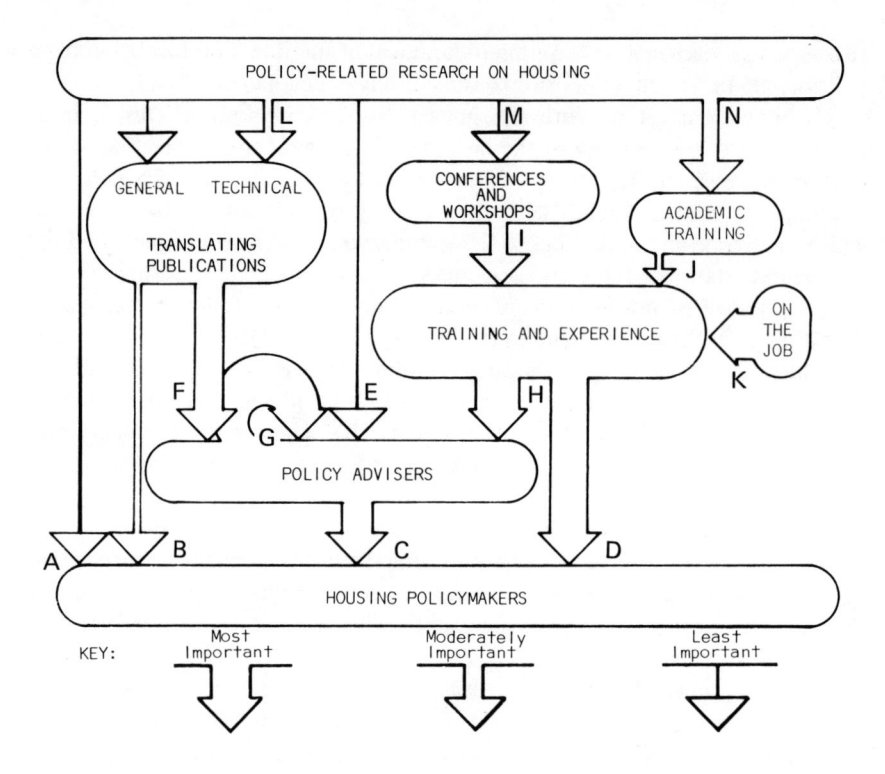

Figure A-2. Research and Other Information Flows to Local Policy Makers: Relative Strengths.

General Conclusions from the Surveys

Our conclusions are summarized below (channel designations are in parentheses):

1. Policy makers make little direct use of policy-related research on housing (A). Too often they find such research:
   a) Politically naive
   b) Hard to obtain on specific issues
   c) Out of date
2. Policy makers rely most frequently on their own training and experience (D) in making housing decisions. This consists primarily of on-the-job training and experience. To a lesser extent they cite conferences and workshops (I) and academic training (J) as sources of their training.

3. Policy makers turn frequently to various advisers for information about housing.
4. The sources of information used by these advisers closely parallel those of the policy maker. Specifically, advisers make little direct use of housing studies (E), strongly rely on their own training and experience (H), and turn frequently to other advisers (G).
5. Periodicals that occasionally "translate" technical housing studies into policy terms are not currently an important source of housing information for policy makers (B) or for policy advisers (F). On closer inspection, articles in those publications named by respondents have little policy-related research content (L).[a]

Selected Findings: Charts and Explanations

Data gleaned from the returned questionnaires were tallied and cross-referenced by category of respondent, size of city, and region. Responses proved remarkably similar across these categories, though slight variations did exist.

Figures A-3 to A-8 and explanatory text on the following pages present in summary form the principal findings for policy makers. Because the responses of the policy advisers largely confirmed the attitudes of their superiors regarding policy-related research on housing, we have not reproduced the findings of our survey of policy advisers. Instead, we refer to these findings, where appropriate, in the following discussion of policy makers.[b]

Sources of Information: General

This question asked policy makers about source of information:

Every municipal chief executive makes major decisions that directly or indirectly affect the supply and quality of housing (e.g. property taxes, zoning ordinances housing code enforcement, urban redevelopment public housing). When you are faced with such a housing decision, from what sources do you ordinarily get information? (Please check as many as apply.)

Rarely	Sometimes	Often	
☐	☐	☐	My own training and experience
☐	☐	☐	A research person in my municipal government
☐	☐	☐	An urban renewal, planning, or housing agency
☐	☐	☐	A regional housing or planning agency

[a]This finding derives from our content analysis of listed publications.

[b]For readers who want more complete findings and charts, working papers of each survey are available from the authors.

Rarely	Sometimes	Often	
☐	☐	☐	A state housing or planning agency
☐	☐	☐	An outside consultant
☐	☐	☐	Newspapers and general news magazines
☐	☐	☐	Housing newsletters, technical journals, etc.
☐	☐	☐	Other knowledgable people: bankers____ lawyers____ housing professionals____ architects____ real estate operators____ journalists____ others____ (please specify):____
☐	☐	☐	Other sources (please specify):____

See Figure A-3 below for a summary of the responses.

Reliance by policy makers on their own training and experience was unusually strong. This was perhaps due to the position of the item at the top of the list of possible sources and to the ego involvement of the respondent. But

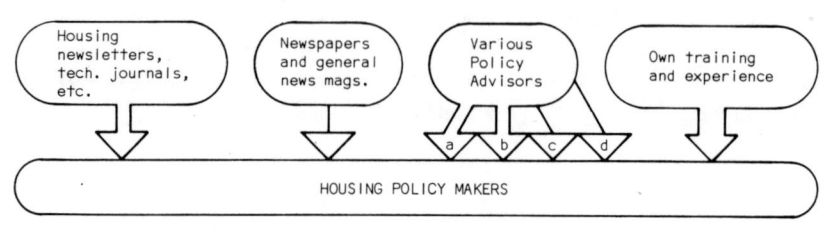

SAMPLE: ALL HOUSING POLICYMAKERS SURVEYED

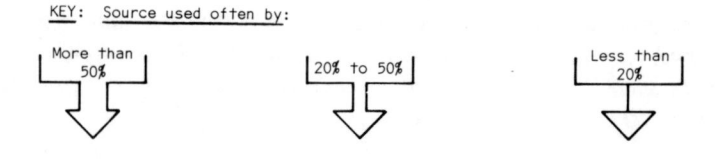

KEY: Source used often by:
More than 50%
20% to 50%
Less than 20%

Various policy advisers:
a. City housing officials
b. Other city officials
c. Private individuals
d. Outside agencies and organizations

Figure A-3. Sources of Information Used Often by Housing Policy Makers.

this response is also consistent with the notion that many aspects of housing are frequently viewed by policy makers as unique local matters (property taxes, zoning, code enforcement), amenable to solution by persons lacking special training but familiar with local conditions. In this view policy-related research on housing is hardly essential or useful to decision.

Conclusion. Policy makers rely on their own training and experience as their most frequent source of information about housing.

Reliance on Policy Advisers

Next to their own training and experience, local policy makers rely most frequently on various advisers for information pertinent to housing decisions. (Refer to previous question and Figure A-3.)

These advisers fall within four general categories: city housing officials (urban renewal and housing officials), other city officials (financial, planning and legal officers), private individuals (academic and business), and outside agencies and organizations (HUD, NAHRO, state and regional planning agencies). The primary source of policy advice, however, comes from city officials who have little special training or experience in housing—general financial, legal, and planning officials. This explains in large part why the responses of policy advisers paralleled those of policy makers so closely. Like the policy makers, who turn to them for advice, the policy advisers tend to be generalists.

Policy advisers do appear to consult journals containing policy-related research on housing in greater proportions than do policy makers. But examination of the journals actually listed by the policy advisers in response to an open-ended inquiry we put to them suggests that they consult popular journals (*Journal of Housing*) far more often than research-oriented publications (*Journal of the American Institute of Planners*).

Conclusion. Any strategy aimed at improving the flow of housing information to policy makers must include the various advisers on whom they chiefly rely. With few exceptions, these advisers have no special expertise in housing.

Sources of Information: Elements of Training and Experience

To further extend our understanding of the elements of training and experience upon which the policy makers rely, we conducted a follow-up survey of policy makers and advisers who had indicated that they rely upon their training and experience. They were asked to specify the elements of their training and experience:

How much of your housing "training" has come from:

	Most	Part	None
a. College courses	☐	☐	☐
b. Professional school courses	☐	☐	☐
c. On-the-job training	☐	☐	☐
d. Conferences and workshops	☐	☐	☐
e. Other (specify): _____			

See Figure A-4 for a summary of the responses.

Conclusions. (1) The policy maker perceives the major position of his training and experience to be on-the-job training; (2) conferences and workshops frequently provide part of the policy maker's training and experience; (3) academic training (college and professional school courses) apparently provides a smaller part of the policy maker's training and experience.

Sources of Information: General Housing Publications

Less than half of the policy makers who responded to the initial survey indicated that they make use of "housing newsletters, technical journals, etc." We directed

SAMPLE: Policymakers who rely often on their own training and experience for information for housing decisions.

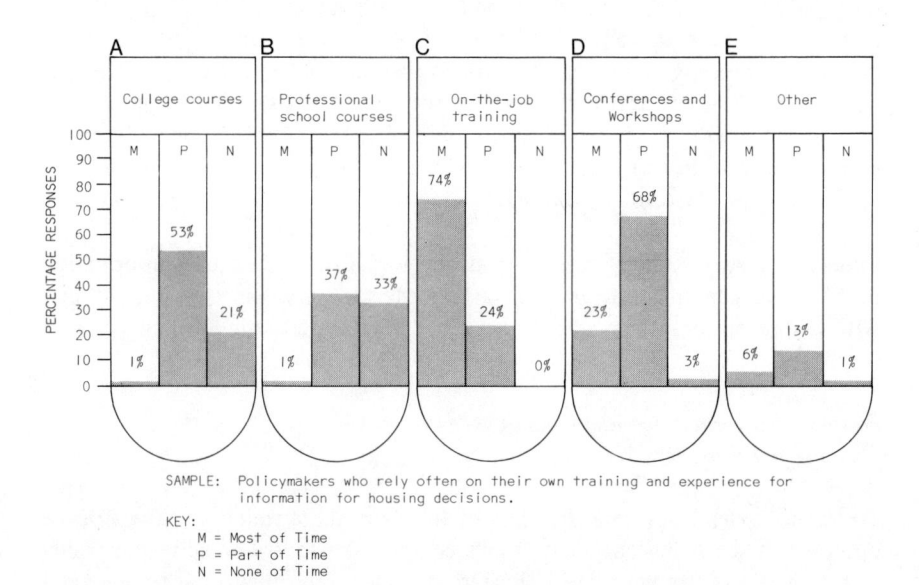

KEY:
M = Most of Time
P = Part of Time
N = None of Time

Figure A-4. Elements of Training and Experience.

a follow-up questionnaire to those policy makers who "often" or "sometimes" obtain information from "housing newsletters, technical journals, etc." This questionnaire was intended to give us a more precise indication of how policy makers gain access to policy-related research. We asked these policy makers to specify the types of "general housing publications" they consulted:

If you sometimes obtain information for major decisions affecting the supply and quality of housing from general housing publications, please indicate the sources:

Rarely	Sometimes	Often	
☐	☐	☐	Technical journals (e.g., *Journal of Housing*)
☐	☐	☐	Newsletters (e.g., *ASPO, Housing Affairs Newsletter*)
☐	☐	☐	Looseleaf services (e.g., *Housing and Development Reporter*)
☐	☐	☐	Books

Please list a few that you have recently found useful:
_____
_____
_____
_____

See Figure A-5 for a summary of the responses.

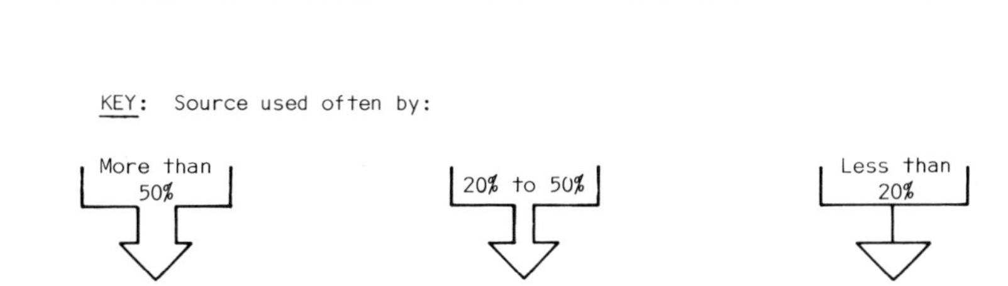

Figure A-5. Details on Sources of Information Used by Policy Makers.

Newsletters are the source most commonly consulted; technical journals are a distant second. Technical journals, however, are the source most commonly consulted if the "sometimes" and "often" responses are combined. Thus, there is evidence that policy makers are familiar with technical journals. There is little evidence, however, that they obtain policy-related research from this source. Few of the publications named in the open-ended portion of the question were publications in which we actually found policy-related research studies.

Conclusion. Although policy makers occasionally consult housing publications, they are not likely to obtain policy-related research from such sources.

Utility of Housing Studies

A question on the utility of housing studies was put directly to the policy makers:

To what extent do you find "housing studies"[a] helpful in making housing decisions:

Never _____ Rarely _____ Sometimes _____ Often _____

[a] By "housing studies" we mean research studies by housing analysts or social scientists of problems of broad significance affecting local housing policies or programs.

See Figure A-6 for a summary of the responses.

Conclusions. Based on our analysis of the responses to this and the previous question, it is obvious that local policy makers do not perceive policy-related research on housing ("housing studies") as helpful in making decisions.

Problems with Housing Studies

In view of the negative response of policy makers to the utility of housing studies, we attempted to uncover the specific problems they encountered in their "occasional" resort to these studies:

If you have found it difficult to use housing studies, please indicate the reasons. (Check as many as apply.)

☐ Too hard to find on a specific issue when I need them
☐ Take too much time to read

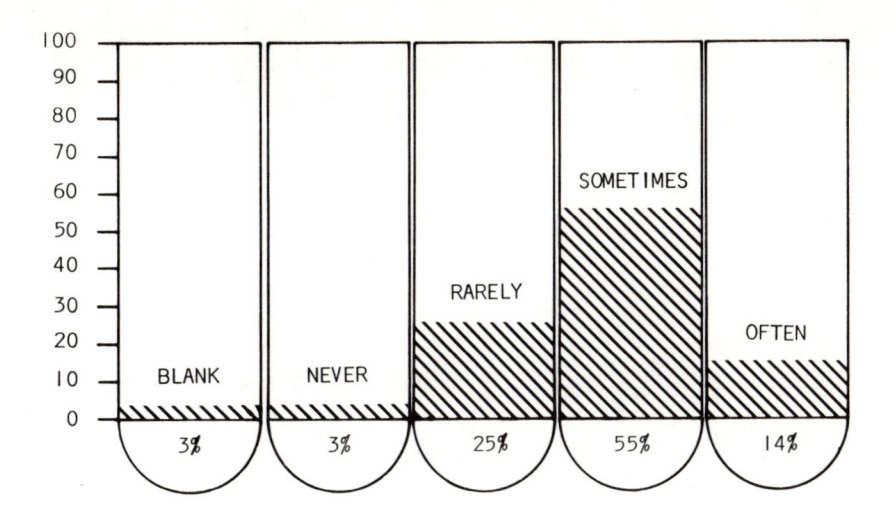

Figure A-6. Utility of "Housing Studies" to Policy Makers.

☐ Frequently out of date
☐ Too complicated
☐ Fail to take political realities into account
☐ Recommendations require more staff to implement than I have available
☐ Recommendations are too costly for my municipal budget
☐ Not enough attention to problem of who pays and who benefits
☐ Other problems (please specify): _____

_____

See Figure A-7 for a summary of the responses.

Conclusions. These problems break down into two categories—problems intrinsic to the studies and problems of dissemination.

The response led us to conclude: (1) Policy makers often find housing studies politically naive; (2) problems with specificity, accessibility, and timeliness limit the utility of housing studies to policy makers. Problems of dissemination are more amenable to solution than those intrinsic to the studies. Our conclusions suggest the need for more attention to better abstracting services, indexing, and interim research reports in the technical housing journals.

			%	0 10 20 30 40 50 60 70 80 90 100
Dissemination Problems	1)	Too hard to find on a specific issue when I need them	51%	
	2)	Take too much time to read	30%	
	3)	Frequently out of date	46%	
	4)	Too complicated	15%	
Intrinsic Problems	5)	Fail to take political realities into account	63%	
	6)	Recommendations require more staff...than I have	33%	
	7)	Recommendations are too costly for my municipal budget	41%	
	8)	Not enough attention to problem of who pays and who benefits	45%	

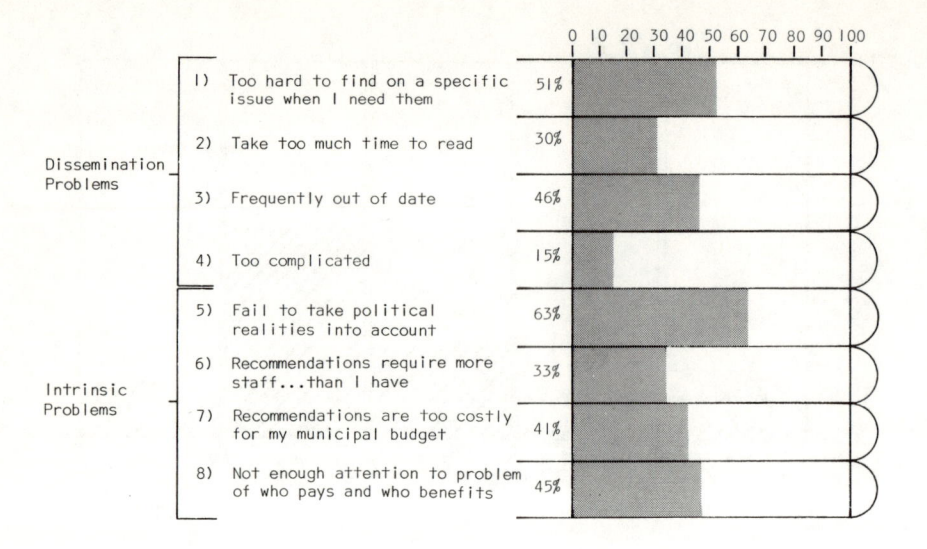

Figure A-7. Reasons Housing Policy Makers Find it Difficult to Use Housing Studies (Percent Mentioning Each Item).

Sources of Background Information on Housing

Our negative conclusion on the direct use of policy-related research by housing policy makers is tempered by one consideration. We initially asked policy makers to indicate their sources of information when they face a specific housing "decision." The possibility remains that they may still use this source of information for general background purposes. Our second follow-up questionnaire posed a question asking how respondents keep informed about current development in housing:

On which of the following do you rely in keeping informed of current developments in housing?

	Rarely	Sometimes	Often
a. General publications (e.g., newspapers & magazines)	☐	☐	☐
b. Technical publications (e.g., *Journal of Housing*)	☐	☐	☐
c. Workshops and conferences	☐	☐	☐
d. Discussions with knowledgeable people in my locality	☐	☐	☐
e. Other (specify): _____	☐	☐	☐

See Figure A-8 for a summary of the responses.

These responses indicate that policy makers frequently resort to technical publications and to conferences and workshops to stay abreast of current developments in housing. Both sources can thus play more useful roles in giving policy makers access to policy-related research. One category of policy maker, housing agency executives, appears to make frequent use of technical housing publications, principally NAHRO's *Journal of Housing*.

Conclusions. Any strategy aimed at bringing policy-related research findings to the attention of the local policy maker should include articles in housing publications and sessions at conferences and workshops.

Significance of the Surveys

These survey results are significant in determining how to bring the findings of policy-related research on housing to the attention of local policy makers and their advisers.

Research on housing presently has minimal impact on the local decision process. This is a consequence of several factors that have little to do with the quality or the availability of the research itself. For one, the local policy maker is not a housing specialist. He does not perceive his problems in the same terms as the housing analyst or researcher. He is not inclined to conceptualize the housing process. He is more apt to push ahead with familiar policy tools, dealing

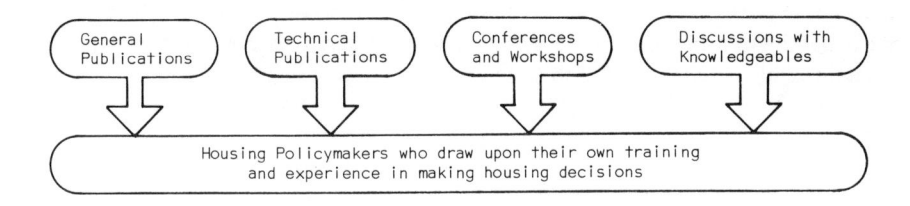

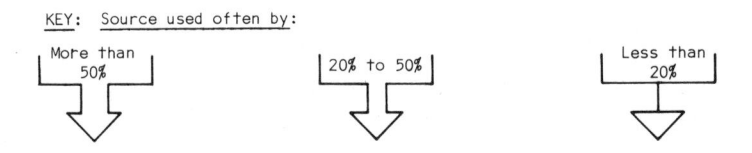

Figure A-8. Sources of Information Used by Policy Makers to Keep Informed of Current Developments in Housing.

with situations as they develop. He relies on his own experience and that of his advisers in deciding how to remedy the housing problems he confronts.

Another factor that reinforces this style of decision making is the lack of resources available to the local policy maker, especially for the elected official of the small or medium-sized town. Unlike his federal counterparts to whom most of the policy-related research on housing has been directed, the local policy maker lacks the time, the funds or the staff support to anticipate problems, consider alternative treatment strategies and their consequences, or to evaluate the effectiveness of a particular housing policy once applied.

There is no simple remedy for this state of affairs. Rather, one must recognize the constraints upon local policy makers and attempt to assist them in a number of different ways at once. Our survey findings help identify several potentially fruitful approaches. These include: presentations and discussion of pertinent research findings at conferences and workshops; annual reviews of research in the more widely read housing journals like NAHRO's *Journal of Housing*; wider local dissemination of research abstracts and digests by federal agencies (such as NTIS and the HUD Library) and professional organizations (such as NAHRO, ICMA, NLC); and greater involvement of local policy makers in the design and conduct of housing research through enterprises like HUD's Urban Observatory Program.

These strategies, spelled out in more detail in the text of this book, would make the findings of housing research studies more readily available to the local policy maker. They would also encourage the kind of dialogue between local policy maker and housing researcher that should benefit both parties. It would expose the policy maker to more rigorous and systematic approaches to problem solving. It would give the researcher a stronger and more accurate sense of decision variables, especially the political factors, that the local official must balance in the course of providing housing services. It is through this dialogue that housing research will improve in its quality and in its utility.

Appendix B:
Evaluating Local Housing Programs Using Cost/Benefit Analysis: An Overview

Brief Introduction to Cost/Benefit Analysis

History

Cost/benefit analysis is a useful tool for helping public agencies choose among competing projects. Its origins are found in a series of federal statutes, some dating as far back as 1824, that deal with water resource management. These early statutes—the River and Harbor Reclamation Act of 1902 is a representative example—required that projects proposed by the Army Corps of Engineers be evaluated by an independent committee of engineers. The reports filed by these committees had to consider, among other things, the cost of the proposed projects and the extent to which commerce benefited from them. By 1935 the idea that the direct and tangible benefits of a proposed project should be specified fully before a decision is made had established itself in several federal government agencies. Furthermore, the Corps of Engineers had developed a number of regular procedures for actually performing the relevant calculations and presenting the results. The Flood Control Act of 1936 formalized the requirement that the benefits of a project must exceed its costs in order for it to be undertaken. It also required that all benefits, "to whomsoever they may accrue," be included in the final accounting, thus recognizing that "commerce" need not be the only beneficiary of a water resource project. This language encouraged cost/benefit analysts to make estimates of the indirect and intangible benefits flowing from such projects, and by so doing it also encouraged the use of this tool in project evaluation outside the water resource area.

Since World War II cost/benefit analysis has been used in the evaluation of an incredibly wide variety of governmental undertakings. A representative list might include the following: the interstate highway system [251], urban renewal [517, 542, 735], high school drop-out prevention [901], outdoor recreation [498], air pollution abatement [724], and many more. As this list suggests, the

---

The author of this appendix is William J. Stull, Department of Economics, Swarthmore College. Appendix B, fills a gap found by the project team in the housing literature. No balanced account of the utility of this important evaluation and decision tool for the local policy maker was found to exist.

This appendix, unlike the text of this book, is addressed primarily to the housing technician.

Peter Kemper, Janet Pack, and Harry Wexler reviewed a preliminary draft. The views expressed here, however, remain the sole responsibility of the author.

applicability of cost/benefit analysis has come to be seen as limited only by the imagination and ingenuity of the analysts making use of it.

Over the same period a number of somewhat different but closely related decision-making techniques have also seen widespread adaptation. The best known of these are: cost/effectiveness analysis, systems analysis, and operations research. The differences among these techniques are largely a product of the different decision-making situations in which they are applied. Cost/effectiveness analysis, for example, is simply a variant of cost/benefit analysis, which is particularly suited for solving problems in national defense planning. Similarly, operations research and systems analysis are most correctly described as extensions of cost/benefit analysis; they are used when the alternatives being considered are highly complex "systems" made up of numerous interdependent components. Unfortunately, there is not sufficient space in this appendix to discuss any of these in detail.[a] The essential point is that the main purpose of each is identical to that of cost/benefit analysis, namely, tracing and evaluating the consequences of alternative actions in such a way that rational choices can be made. As a result of this congruence, many of the problems and procedures to be discussed below will be common to all of the above forms of analysis.

Procedure

The basic procedures followed by all cost/benefit analyses are easily understood. The decision problem a governmental unit such as a public agency or a department of city government faces when it has limited funds available from taxation and appropriation is one of allocation. It must allocate funds in a way which is most beneficial to its constituency. Cost/benefit analysis can be an important aid in making such decisions.

To define the role of cost/benefit analysis more clearly, it is useful to distinguish three different levels of local government operation. The lowest of these might be called the operational level. Decisions made at this level are of a day-to-day, routine nature and typically do not engage the energies of senior personnel in any significant way. The second is the programming level. Here the overall goals of the governmental unit in question and a set of broad programs are taken as given. Decisions are then made, usually involving junior and senior employees in consultation, that concern the best way to implement or operationalize these programs in order to achieve the specified goals. The last level is the planning level. This is the exclusive bailiwick of senior personnel, who, by choosing among alternative goals and programs, determine the scope and direction of the organization's activity over the long run.

---

[a]For a further description of these techniques and their relationship to cost/benefit analysis see Roland N. McKean [531]. Both this work and Ann Friedlander's [251] also discuss the use of cost/benefit analysis as an adjunct to program budgeting.

Cost/benefit analysis is most usefully applied at the programming level. In general, decisions made at the operations level are too insignificant in their consequences to justify the use of formal analytical techniques. At the other extreme, the planning level, the decision problems that are confronted tend to be very broad and unspecific. As a result they are not susceptible to the quantification procedures that form the heart of any complete cost/benefit study. This means, for example, that cost/benefit analysis will probably not prove very useful in helping a federal government agency or a congressional committee decide whether or not it wishes to support a particular type of national water resource management program. On the other hand, this tool can be a significant aid in helping the appropriate agency decide among alternative projects competing for the limited funds of the parent program once it is established. Similar considerations govern the use of cost/benefit analysis at the local level. When the question that must be resolved is a broad and highly political one (for instance, whether or not the community should undertake a large, multifaceted summer recreation program), cost/benefit analysis is probably not going to be very useful to the local decision maker. In contrast, when the question is narrow and well-defined (for instance, whether or not a new swimming pool should be built), a careful cost/benefit analysis can provide the informational basis for a rational decision.

Given a decision problem to which cost/benefit analysis can be applied fruitfully, the next step is the specification of the target population. It is the costs and benefits to this population that will be measured. Benefits or costs falling on individuals who are not members of this target group will be categorically excluded from the analysis. In the case of a municipal government project the appropriate target population, from the point of view of local officials, will generally be the citizenry of the municipality. This is not the only possible perspective, however. Federal or state officials looking at the same project may well have a broader conception of what the appropriate target population is, and this may have a significant effect on their decision to supplement local funding.

Once the question to be answered has been framed and the target population specified, the real work in doing a cost/benefit analysis can begin. First, the costs of the projects under consideration must be calculated. For the purposes of this study the "costs" of a project are defined to include only those cost elements that represent purchases of resources needed to implement, construct, administer, or maintain it. Costs defined in this way may be incurred by either the public or private sectors. If, in addition, the project has any adverse consequences that can be quantified (for instance, moving costs incurred by urban renewal relocatees), these are included in the benefits calculation as "negative benefits."

The next step is to identify and then measure the benefits generated by the project or projects under consideration. This is usually the most difficult task in any cost/benefit study. In some cases there is an available market price that can be used to quantify project benefits. For example, government hydroelectric projects generate electricity that is sold to private firms and households. The price at which a unit of this electricity is sold is usually thought to be a natural measure of the benefit that society derives from its use. Typically, however, no such convenient benefit measure is available because the service provided by the project has no private market counterpart. For instance, the service that air pollution abatement programs provide is the use of clean air. Since no market for clean air exists, it is necessary for cost/benefit analysts to develop special measurement procedures that are then used to obtain a rough estimate of the aggregate value of clean air to the affected population. One of the principal reasons for employing specialists to do cost/benefit studies is precisely because they have expertise in developing and using such procedures.

The benefits (and occasionally the costs) of a project do not typically accrue in only one or two years. Instead, a large initial expenditure may generate a stream of benefits that stretches several decades into the future. Consider for a moment the nature of the benefits yielded by a successful high school drop-out prevention program. Assuming high school graduates earn more than those who drop out, the benefits from a prevented dropout can be conceived of as a series of annual income increments received by the graduate above and beyond the annual incomes he would have earned had he dropped out. In this case the benefit stream may extend over the individual's entire working life, a span of 40 years or more. This creates a conceptual problem because it does not seem appropriate to put benefits that will be received in 40 years on the same footing as those that will be received this year. How then do we aggregate benefits accruing in different years to obtain a total benefit figure? The answer is that a procedure called discounting is used. An elementary discussion of discounting will be included in the next section. It suffices here to point out that discounting means that each dollar's worth of benefits accruing in the future is given less value in the final accounting of benefits than a dollar's worth of benefits accruing today. The extent of the discount depends on a parameter known as the discount rate and on the time elapsed before the benefit actually occurs.

Once aggregate benefits and costs (approximately discounted) have been obtained for the relevant project or projects, the analyst is ready to use them to make decisions. Precisely how they are used will depend in large measure on how the decision problem was initially posed. One might, for example, want to use cost/benefit analysis to evaluate a completed project (possibly a pilot project) to see if, in some sense, the government got its money's worth. Such a course of action would be desirable if additional projects or extensions of the original project were contemplated. Alternately, a full-scale cost/benefit analysis might serve as a check on the more ad hoc and less expensive information gathering and decision procedures used at the initial selection of the project. In either case a simple examination and comparison of the aggregate costs and benefits are all that is necessary for the appropriate decision to be made.

Cost/benefit analysis may also be used for project selection. If a given governmental unit has several alternative projects, usually of the same general type, that it wishes to carry out and budgetary restrictions prevent it from doing all of them, which should be chosen? Such a question might arise if an agency is considering a variety of possible sites for a public housing project. In this situation separate cost/benefit analyses should be performed on the most likely candidates. Unlike the case described above, these analyses will have to be carried out using projected rather than actual data. Therefore, a greater degree of uncertainty is involved in obtaining the final aggregate cost and benefit figures. Once these figures are in hand, they can serve as a basis for a choice among the competing projects. If all of the competing projects cost approximately the same amount, it is appropriate simply to choose the project or projects yielding the greatest excess of benefits over costs. If, however, the projects under consideration differ significantly in cost, then the benefit/cost ratio procedure must be used. Here the ratio of benefits to costs for each project is calculated and the projects with the highest ratios are chosen. This procedure guarantees that the total benefit yielded by a given appropriation is maximized because the projects selected are those that produce the largest benefit per dollar of cost.[b]

Cost/Revenue Analysis

Before examining the use of cost/benefit analysis as an aid to the evaluation of projects designed to upgrade local housing quality, it is necessary to distinguish cost/benefit analysis from cost/revenue analysis. Cost/revenue analysis is procedurally similar to cost/benefit analysis, but its focus is narrower and it is generally employed in a different type of decisionmaking situation. In particular, cost/revenue analysis is often used to help decide whether or not a community should oppose a particular private project (such as a housing development or shopping center). Its central concern is the net impact that this project will have on the municipal budget.

In the case of cost/revenue analysis, as with cost/benefit analysis, one follows three basic steps in applying the method. First, the costs of the proposed project to the municipality in the form of additional public services are calculated. In the case of residential developments, these might include costs incurred for street widening, additional police or fire personnel, sewer system extensions, or new schools. Second, fiscal benefits the project yields are measured. In general, any new development will increase the tax base of the community. The annual fiscal benefit produced by the project is thus the increase in the tax base multiplied by the appropriate nominal tax rate. Finally, a decision must be made

---

[b]If the projects under consideration are indivisible or "lumpy," this may not be strictly correct. A project with a low benefit/cost ratio may be preferred to one with a high ratio if the former exhausts the available budget and the latter does not. For a further discussion of this point see E.S. Mishan [553], Chap. 25.

based on the calculated fiscal costs and benefits. The strict logic of cost/revenue analysis requires that all private projects whose fiscal costs exceed their fiscal benefits be excluded. Another way of stating the same rule is that all private projects whose net effect on the local tax rate is positive must be excluded. In practice, nonfiscal considerations frequently enter into a community's decision to support or oppose a proposed private development. It is apparent, therefore, that cost/revenue analysis is not a fully satisfactory method for resolving even these sorts of controversies.

There is not sufficient space here for a complete evaluation of cost/revenue analysis. The critical point to remember is that the cost/revenue method by itself is not appropriate for the evaluation of public projects. Consider, for instance, a local public park. Such parks are costly to construct and maintain; yet, they are usually made available to the general public free of charge. It follows that if the cost/revenue criterion were to be applied blindly to all park construction projects, none would be built. The increase in expenditure would never be offset by an associated increase in tax revenue.[c] Such a result is clearly absurd.

Another example that shows the inadequacies of cost/revenue analysis involves urban homesteading, a much-discussed new technique for extending the life of abandoned residential structures. Under current urban homestead statutes, abandoned properties that have come into the possession of city governments through tax foreclosures are given free to qualified households subject to occupancy and rehabilitation conditions. Since the market value of many of the structures given away is close to zero, the only costs to the city are administrative and these are not likely to be high. Tax revenues, on the other hand, will rise as the properties are rehabilitated. A cost/revenue analysis of an urban homestead program is thus likely to indicate that it should be undertaken. This may in fact be the correct result, but this decision procedure in no way guarantees it. One of several problems that arises is that no weight is given to the significant private costs incurred by rehabilitation. These may be far in excess of all conceivable benefits—including those accruing to the city government in the form of increased tax revenues.

Thus, the main point is that cost/revenue analysis may not give a complete accounting of either the true costs or the true benefits of a given project. One might still want to do a cost/revenue study, for knowing a project's fiscal impact might be very important in specific instances. However, in general one would want to know more. A more comprehensive approach is needed—and this is what cost/benefit analysis is all about.

---

[c]This is a bit of an overstatement since it is possible (though not certain by any means) that property values in the neighborhood of the park will increase sufficiently to generate the needed revenues. Such "neighborhood effects" are discussed further in the next section.

Cost/Benefit Analysis of Local Housing Programs

Conceptual Framework

There is an enormous variety of government programs that can be implemented at the local level that are related to housing in one way or another. Such programs include urban renewal, public housing, code enforcement, zoning, and urban homesteading. In spite of their numerous differences, these programs generally have certain goals in common. Most, either explicitly or implicitly, seek to increase local resources devoted to housing to a level above that which would prevail in a totally free real estate market. A second and related objective common to most local housing programs is the improvement of housing occupied by the community's poor.

It is clearly impossible in the present brief report to give a detailed description of how cost/benefit analysis can be used to make decisions about each of these various types of programs. Instead, in the subsections that follow an unspecified type of local housing program designed to achieve the goals described above is discussed. The perspective taken is that of a city official wishing to use cost/benefit analysis to assist in making efficient use of the available resources. These include tax monies, bond sale proceeds and intergovernmental loans and grants. The focus is on the problems common to most cost/benefit analyses in the housing field.

A caveat is in order before proceeding. Previously it was noted that cost/benefit analysis was most appropriately used when the problem to be resolved was narrow and well-defined. This suggests that it is not the best possible tool for deciding among alternative housing programs. Suppose, for instance, that a local government official wishes to improve the housing conditions of the poor in his community. Should he initiate a policy of strict code enforcement, build public housing on vacant land near the outskirts of the city, or employ urban renewal to raze downtown slum areas and replace them with highrise apartments for the elderly? Such questions, at least in the form stated, cannot be easily answered by a formal cost/benefit analysis because they lack sufficient specificity.

This is true because programs usually must be accepted or rejected before final decisions about the specific projects to be undertaken under them can be made. Thus, when a decision maker is comparing alternative programs he is not usually comparing specific alternative projects at the same time. Instead, he is comparing alternative families of projects, each member of which has its own probability of being undertaken if the parent program is funded. Clearly, if either the number of programs or the number of projects that might conceivably be carried out under the typical program is large, the cost of doing all the necessary cost/benefit analyses will be prohibitive.

The operational significance of this is that the decision maker will probably have to commit himself at the outset to one or two types of programs solely on the basis of political considerations and personal insight.[d] Once committed to a few types of programs, it becomes feasible to use cost/benefit analysis to evaluate the projects that each will fund to ensure that the overall appropriation for housing is used in the most effective way. In the subsections that follow, it will be assumed that a commitment to some sort of housing program has already been made. What remains to be illustrated is the use of cost/benefit analysis in choosing among the individual projects through which this program will be given tangible expression.

Costs

Resources are required to complete a given project and then keep it in operation over time. These resources—which may include city government personnel, construction workers, building materials, land, etc.—are generally in limited supply and consequently are not available free of charge. It is customary in cost/benefit analysis to assume that the total market value of all of these resources is a good measure of the economic or resource cost of the project. Thus, to obtain the economic cost of a public housing project one would have to add up property acquisition costs, demolition costs (occasionally), construction costs, planning costs (usually in the form of government employee salaries), and, finally, administrative and maintenance costs.[e] (Since the last two categories represent recurring costs, the discounting procedure must be used to make them commensurate with the others.)

The economic costs of a project may be borne in whole or in part by either the public or private sector. In the case of public housing the costs fall almost exclusively on the public sector. The costs of a code enforcement project, on the other hand, are largely borne by landlords in the private sector since they are the ones who must pay for the required upgrading of their structure. Public costs in this case are essentially limited to those incurred in administering the project. It is important to note here that the private costs as well as the public costs must

---

[d]This is not to say, however, that the cost/benefit approach is totally irrelevant to this decision problem. Knowledge of the technique can help the official organize his own thinking about the choices that lay before him and thus enable him to decide more quickly and rationally. This point is discussed further in the final section.

[e]If the property for the project is assembled from many small parcels through the exercise of eminent domain, there may be a significant difference between its value before and after assembly. In such a case the appropriate property cost figure to use is the former—that is, the total amount actually paid out by the government to landlords for the land and structures it acquired.

be included in the final accounting in any cost/benefit study. Both types of cost reduce the available resources that could have been used by the target population for other purposes.

It is important here to distinguish between the economic cost of a project and what might be called its out-of-pocket cost. The out-of-pocket cost of a project is the total amount that local public and private agents actually have to pay (appropriately discounted) to bring about the desired shift in resources to the housing sector.

The out-of-pocket cost will be larger than the economic cost when otherwise unemployed resources are used to construct, administer, or maintain the project. If, for example, an urban renewal project is begun at a time when the local construction industry is in a deep slump and is expected to remain in this state for an extended period, the economic cost of all the labor and equipment used on the urban renewal site is approximately zero since employing them will in no way reduce consumption somewhere else in the local economy.[f] Out-of-pocket costs, on the other hand, will not be zero since the construction firms and their employees will have to be paid. It is also possible for out-of-pocket costs to be smaller than economic costs. This occurs when some of the costs incurred for labor, materials, or equipment are financed at the state or federal level rather than locally. Such, of course, is the case with most public housing and urban renewal projects.

The next question is which of the two cost measures that have been discussed here is the appropriate one to use in a cost/benefit analysis? The correct answer, technically, is neither. In fact, the only costs that should be included in a local government cost/benefit study are those that are both out-of-pocket and economic in nature.[g] That is to say, only those cost elements that represent the use of genuinely scarce local resources and that are ultimately paid for by the members of the target population should be included. One can, of course, arrive at the proper figure either by subtracting the price of any unemployed resources from out-of-pocket cost or by subtracting state and federal subsidies from economic cost.

In practice, most of the data needed to perform the first of these calculations are usually readily available. Projections for the public portion of the project's out-of-pocket cost will usually be generated as a result of regular planning procedures. Obtaining private out-of-pocket costs may be more of a problem,

---

[f]In less extreme circumstances (the slump, for example, might only be temporary) these resources will have some positive value but one that is still less than their market price. For further discussion of this problem see Mishan [553], Chap. 9. It should also be noted that consumption in the local economy will be reduced to the extent that the project is financed out of current property tax revenues. Thus, the statement in the text is technically only correct when all funds are obtained by borrowing.

[g]It should be noted that if the same project were evaluated at the federal level it would no longer be possible for out-of-pocket costs to be less than economic costs. In this case the appropriate cost measure for cost/benefit analysis is the economic cost.

but even here one would expect some estimates to be made in the ordinary course of events. For instance, if a local government were thinking about instituting an urban homestead program, it is likely that its planning or housing department would calculate the probable cost of the required rehabilitation even if it had no intention of carrying out any sort of cost/benefit analysis. Thus, the only figures requiring special calculation are those needed to adjust the market price of unemployed or partially unemployed resources downward. It will frequently be the case that no such adjustment is appropriate. However, in those instances where it is appropriate, it may be necessary to call on experts from outside the agency or department to make the necessary forecasts and calculate the appropriate adjustment factors.[h]

Benefits

There are a number of different ways of classifying the benefits to be gained from the project. It is convenient here to classify them according to the type of recipient. In subsequent paragraphs each of the following is discussed in turn: relocatees, consumers of the new or improved housing, neighbors, taxpayers.

Chronologically, the first group to be affected by a housing project consists of those who have to be evicted from the site of the project and relocated elsewhere. Obviously, not all types of housing projects will require a significant amount of relocation. The most common instances where this occurs are the public housing and urban renewal projects built on land formerly occupied by slum neighborhoods.

The "benefits" that relocatees receive are generally negative since they suffer a reduction in both their monetary and "psychic" income as a result of the move that they are forced to make.[i] The first of these occurs because some income is typically expended searching for and then moving into a new dwelling unit. In addition, relocatees may end up spending significantly more for the new housing than the old, even if the quality remains the same.[j] To the extent that such expenditures are compensated for by payments from a higher level of government (as is partially the case for urban renewal relocatees) they do not enter into

---

[h]Another way of handling the problem of unemployed resources is simply to ignore it when carrying out the cost/benefit calculations. The total cost figure arrived at will then be based completely on out-of-pocket costs (approximately discounted). When it comes time for a local official to make a decision, however, he will in this case have to take into consideration both the excess of benefits over costs and the extent to which the projects under consideration increase local employment. A decision criterion based exclusively on the former is no longer appropriate.

[i]Recall that negative benefits are possible because our definition of project costs includes only those cost elements directly attributable to the construction, maintenance, or administration of the project.

[j]The reverse may also be true, in which case the benefits are "positive." For two conflicting studies dealing with this issue see Chester W. Hartman [334] and Janet Rothenberg Pack [656].

the cost/benefit calculations; otherwise, they are properly included. If they are included, probably the most effective way of gathering the data needed for the calculations is to interview individuals who were forced to relocate by earlier projects.[k]

The psychic costs of relocation are much more difficult to quantify. Indeed, as a practical matter the measurement problems are so severe that such costs are essentially never included in any formal accounting of costs and benefits. However, this does not mean they are insignificant. As Marc Fried [247] and Barrie Barstow Greenbie [295] have suggested, an individual's relocation to a new neighborhood lacking the supportive social environment of the old can have a significant adverse effect on his mental and even physical health. This is a consideration that public officials should keep in mind even though it cannot be adequately incorporated into a cost/benefit analysis.

The second group of individuals whose welfare is affected by the implementation of a project are those who directly consume the new or improved housing that it brought into existence. In the case of public housing or urban renewal that includes residential redevelopment, this group is made up of the occupants of the new buildings constructed on the site. In the case of a code enforcement or urban homestead project, it is made up of the occupants, who may be either owners or renters, of the housing that has been upgraded. As a first approximation, the value to a recipient of a government-provided good or service is the price it would bring on the private market. This means that to calculate the annual occupant-benefits of a project one must estimate the rent each of the affected units would receive were it offered on the private market. In the case of newly constructed units, the total benefit to occupants is then obtained simply by adding up these estimated rents.[l] In the case of rehabilitated units, this total must be adjusted by subtracting total annual rents earned before the rehabilitation occurred.

Conceptually, such calculations are straightforward. However, in practice difficulties sometimes appear. If the cost/benefit study is antecedent to the completion of the project or the affected units are offered at subsidized rents, no actual market data is available for them. This means estimates have to be made based on the known market rents of existing unsubsidized units. There is more than one way of doing this. A sophisticated procedure employing multiple

---

[k]If retail establishments and other firms, both on the project site and in the surrounding neighborhood, are forced to move by the project, their search and moving costs should also be included as negative benefits. (Stores in the neighborhood may have to leave because a large number of their regular customers are relocatees.)

[l]When the units in question are constructed on the site of an urban renewal project, this aggregate rent figure will necessarily include all gains in land productivity brought about by the assembly of many small parcels into a single large one. The significance of such gains has been much stressed (probably excessively so) by urban renewal theorists. See, for example, Otto A. Davis and Andrew B. Whinston [175]. A useful summary and critique of their basic arguments may be found in James Heilbrun [349], Chap. 11.

regression techniques is available (see Bagby [37] and Kain and Quigley [401]). If it is used properly, one can obtain highly accurate and mutually consistent estimates. A less expensive and less time-consuming method, which is perfectly adequate in many cases, is to match the project units with closely comparable private market units whose rents are known. A major problem in either case is estimating rents for future years when market conditions may be very different from those prevailing in the year the project was completed.

The third category of benefit recipients is made up of the neighbors of the individuals who occupy the new or improved housing brought into existence by the project. It is a commonplace that one of the factors that households take into consideration when making a residential site choice is the quality of the neighborhood. Typically, they will scrutinize both its physical characteristics (the age, size, and condition of nearby structures, the number of trees, the amount of traffic, etc.) and the social characteristics (the age, income, ethnicity, etc.) of its inhabitants.

Given these facts, a government project that leads to the replacement or improvement of a limited number of the residential structures in a neighborhood is likely to confer benefits on the inhabitants of the remaining structures. Such benefits are examples of what are known as "neighborhood effects." These effects are often cited as a major source of the benefits to be obtained from urban renewal (see Davis and Whinston [175] and Rothenberg [735]). Clearly, other types of housing programs—zoning, for example—may also yield benefits of this sort. These effects may be negative as well as positive. A public housing project in a high income neighborhood will undoubtedly be perceived as a detriment rather than an asset.

The ultimate sources of the neighborhood effects generated by a project are manifold. The most obvious effect is the improved appearance of the neighborhood brought about by the presence of new or rehabilitated structures and any amenities provided with them. These might include landscaping, improved street lighting, new playground equipment etc.[m] In addition, the social complexion of the neighborhood may be affected. The occupants of the new housing may be different from those of the old. Urban homestead projects, for example, seek to substitute owner occupants for renters with the explicit intention of making the neighborhood more stable and hence more attractive as a residential location. Even when there is no turnover in the neighborhood population, the physical transformation of the environment may lead, by itself, to a reduction in antisocial behavior by both its inhabitants and strangers.[n]

Regardless of which of these specific mechanisms is operating the cost/benefit analyst faces the problem of quantifying their effects. The standard procedure here is to examine rents and property values in the neighborhood before and

---

[m]The costs of these amenities should of course be included as part of the project cost in any cost/benefit analysis.

[n]For some evidence on this point see Oscar Newman [611].

after the project is completed. Any differences that cannot be ascribed to exogenous effects, such as the general inflation of real estate prices over time, can then be taken as dollar measures of the degree of neighborhood improvement. Thus, to obtain an aggregate figure for annual project benefits to neighbors the analyst need only calculate these differences for each of the structures in the neighborhood and then add them up.

Before this calculation can be made, one must delimit the boundaries of the project "neighborhood." There is no technically correct way of doing this. Instead, the analyst must rely on common sense and his knowledge of the project area in question. Once a set of boundaries has been chosen, it remains only to isolate the project effect from all of the other influences on neighborhood rents. One procedure that has been used (see Nourse [627]) is to compare rent levels in the project neighborhood with those in an otherwise identical counterpart. The principal difficulty here is finding another neighborhood that is just like the project neighborhood but without the project. If this proves impossible, one can resort to multiple regression techniques essentially identical to those alluded to earlier. These techniques enable the analyst to control statistically for exogenous influences on rents and thus isolate the project effect.

The final group of individuals who may receive benefits from the project are the taxpayers of the municipality. Such benefits arise because the improved housing brought about by the project may reduce certain public service requirements in the neighborhoods where the housing is located. The two public services most often mentioned in this connection are fire and police protection—with reductions in expenditure for the former typically expected to be the more significant.

Consider a residential neighborhood in which a number of blighted residential structures are torn down and then replaced by a public housing project containing the same number of dwelling units and inhabited by the same tenants. Such a transformation is likely to reduce the neighborhood's demand for fire department resources. There will almost surely be fewer serious fires because the new structures are more fireproof than the old and also possess better fire alarm systems. There may even be fewer false alarms if the presence of the project engenders any increased sense of neighborhood or civic responsibility among its inhabitants or its neighbors. Reduced claims on police resources might also be expected if the design of the project and its relationship to the neighborhood were such as to reduce the local crime rate.[o]

Conceptually, the inclusion of such benefits creates few real difficulties. As usual, however, there are measurement and estimation problems—particularly

---

[o]If the decrease in the number of criminal acts or false alarms is due solely to the turnover in the local population brought about by the project, it is not proper to include the associated savings in the benefit calculation. This is because those acts that would have been perpetrated in the neighborhood had the project not been undertaken are presumably being carried out elsewhere by those in the original population who were displaced.

when the project being examined is still only on the drawing boards. In the latter case about all one can do is look at the experience of other neighborhoods in which projects were built and try to determine how much police and fire expenditures have declined over what they otherwise would have been. (For an example of such a calculation, see James C.T. Mao [517]). This data can then be used to forecast the probable expenditure reductions for the project under consideration.

Discounting

Most of the benefits just discussed, as well as some of the costs, will accrue over a sequence of years rather than at a single point in time. This means that the discounting procedure briefly mentioned earlier will have to be used. The purpose of this subsection is to explain this procedure in more detail.

Consider an individual who has M dollars in his savings account today and who wishes to know how much he will have in t years, given that the interest rate is i and that he makes no more deposits. At the end of the first year he will have

$$M_1 = (1 + i)M$$

At the end of the second year he will have

$$M_2 = (1 + i)M_1 = (1 + i)^2 M$$

And thus at the end of t years he will have

$$M_t = (1 + i)^t M$$

Suppose now we turn the problem around and ask what the present value (usually called *present discounted value* or PDV) to him is of M_t dollars to be received t years in the future. A moment's reflection reveals that this present value must be M since this is the amount of money that if invested today at compound interest will yield exactly M_t dollars in t years. Thus,

$$PDV = M = \frac{M_t}{(1 + i)^t}$$

Note that in this formulation M_t will always be greater than M because the denominator of the fraction on the right will always be greater than one. This is just a formal way of expressing an elementary point made earlier, namely, that a dollar to be received in the future is worth less than a dollar received today.

Let us now go further and take an individual who has an investment that will pay him M_t dollars in t years and M_s dollars in s years. The present discounted value of the investment to the individual is

$$PDV = PDV_t + PDV_s = \frac{M_t}{(1+i)^t} + \frac{M_s}{(1+i)^s}$$

the sum of the present values of the two separate payoffs. Clearly this procedure can be extended to an investment that yields a return in any number of years.

The relevance of all of this to cost/benefit analysis should be apparent. To make things concrete, let us suppose that a city government is contemplating a rigorous code enforcement program for a particular neighborhood. A cost/benefit analysis is performed and the following stream of costs and benefits is estimated for an n year time horizon:[p]

$$B_1, B_2, B_3, \ldots, B_n$$

$$C_1, C_2, C_3, \ldots, C_n$$

B_1 represents the total benefit accruing in year 1 to the occupants of the improved structure, their neighbors, and possibly taxpayers. C_1 represents the total cost of project in year 1. It includes the administrative costs to the city for that year and all costs borne by private landlords in the form of expenditures for rehabilitation or increased maintenance.

To make these two streams directly comparable, their present values must be calculated. Thus

$$PDV_B = \frac{B_1}{1+i} + \frac{B_2}{(1+i)^2} + \ldots + \frac{B_n}{(1+i)^n}$$

and

$$PDV_C = \frac{C_1}{1+i} + \frac{C_2}{(1+i)^2} + \ldots + \frac{C_n}{(1+i)^n}$$

must be obtained. Tables that give the value of $1/(1+i)^n$ for a large number of (i,n) combinations are readily available. Once these calculations are performed, decisions can then be made on the basis of either the difference between PDV_B and PDV_C or their ratio. These are the total benefit/total cost comparisons discussed informally in the first section of this appendix.

---

[p]The choice of n is a somewhat arbitrary one. The usual practice is to choose a period—say, ten years—within which costs and benefits can reasonably be foreseen. Costs and benefits occurring more than ten years in the future are thus ignored on grounds that they are too uncertain to be used as a basis for present decisions.

A problem of much theoretical interest to professional economists is that of choosing the appropriate interest rate (usually known as the social discount rate) for the preceding calculations. There are at least two separate questions that have been debated here. First, given that a market interest rate is appropriate to use, which market rate ought to be chosen? Should it be the short-term bond rate, the long-term bond rate, or something else? Second, and more fundamentally, should a market rate be used at all? Perhaps market rates are biased upward from a social point of view because they reflect only the time horizon of the current population, a horizon that is necessarily limited because of the finiteness of human life. Unfortunately, there is not room here for an extended treatment of these matters. For a further discussion of them, the reader should consult Richard Musgrave and Peggy B. Musgrave [570]. In practice, analysts frequently calculate both PDV_B and PDV_C several times over using different plausible discount rates each time. If all of the subsequent cost/benefit comparisons point to the same decision, this is the end of the matter. If not, the various candidate rates must be reexamined and the one most appropriate to the problem at hand selected. A reasonable choice here is often the rate of interest at which the municipality can borrow money.

Equity Problems

Let us now set aside all of the conceptual and measurement problems discussed in the preceding subsections and turn to an altogether different set of issues. These concern the distribution or incidence of the benefits and costs of a project among individuals or groups in the target population. Consider a public project whose total benefits are known to exceed its total costs. Assuming this project is not being compared to others whose benefit/cost ratio is even greater, the recommendation coming out of a standard cost/benefit analysis will be that the project should be undertaken. Suppose, however, it is discovered that all of the benefits of the project accrue to very wealthy individuals and all of the costs fall on the very poor. That is, suppose it turns out that the income distributional impact of the project is highly regressive. Should these new facts affect the decision to undertake or not undertake the project? The problem being posed here is not a purely hypothetical one. It will be recalled that much of the criticism leveled at urban renewal over the past ten or fifteen years has focused on its enrichment of the upper and middle classes at the expense of the poor.[q]

The first thing to observe about income distributional effects is that they do not pose a very serious problem if adequate compensation mechanisms exist. Almost by definition, the completion of a project whose benefits exceed its costs leads to an increase in the total real income collectively received by the target population. The size of the pie available to the target population for

---
[q]On this point see Martin Anderson [22].

consumption thus gets larger. In such a situation it is clearly possible to make everyone in this population better off by appropriate redistribution. If, for example, the project increased total annual real income by 5 percent, the local government could both tax those who benefited from the project and subsidize those who were hurt in such a way that when the dust settled every member of the target population had a real income that was 5 percent higher than before.

As a practical matter, however, such comprehensive compensation mechanisms do not exist. Partial compensation, however, is occasionally achieved through the use of such devices as tax rebates to landlords or moving-cost subsidies to relocatees. In the absence of such mechanisms, what is a local decision maker to do when faced with an otherwise desirable project that has an adverse income distributional effect? There is no clear-cut answer to this question. A hard-line view is that income distributional effects should be ignored on grounds that they will eventually be at least partially corrected by other governmental action whose explicit aim is to redistribute income from rich to poor. Practical political considerations would seem to dictate a more flexible approach, however. In the end, about all that can be said is that the local decision maker should be aware of the income distributional impacts of different projects and somehow take these into account when the final decisions have to be made.[r] Operationally, this implies that many cost/benefit studies will have to be supplemented with an analysis showing where the costs and benefits fall within the target population.

Postscript: Cost/Benefit Analysis and Comprehensive Urban Models

The preceding five sections attempt to give the reader a preliminary understanding of the steps that have to be taken when preparing a complete cost/benefit study of a local government housing project. A thoughtful critic may very well object to this syllabus on grounds that the procedures described in it do not seem to be based ultimately on any systematic model of how the local urban economy operates. Instead, they appear to be (and indeed they are) little more than ad hoc techniques designed to measure the significance of various "effects" that a project seems likely to have.

Ideally, a local government official would have at his disposal a fully calibrated computer model of the particular urban economy with which he is concerned. Such a model could be used to generate accurate and detailed forecasts of the future state of the economy under alternative public policy scenarios. Thus, for example, if the official had to choose among several urban renewal projects, he could feed their parameters (size, location, number and type of housing units constructed, etc.) into the model and out of it would come a set

---
[r]For a further discussion of these issues see E.S. Mishan [553], Chap. 4.

of forecasts, one for each project. Each forecast would contain estimates of rents, land values, vacancy rates, public service requirements, housing conditions, demographic characteristics, etc. for every neighborhood in the city. A decision could then be made among the projects by performing the requisite number of cost/benefit analyses using the data thus generated.

The advantage of using an urban model is that, if properly designed, it will take into account all of the secondary and "feedback" effects of the project, many of which will be very elusive and complex. An example will help illustrate this point.

Suppose a particular neighborhood in a city is subjected to a rigorous code enforcement campaign. If a cost/benefit analysis, following the steps outlined earlier in this section, is performed and it is discovered that the benefits exceed the costs by a significant amount, does it then follow that similar campaigns should necessarily be carried out in other neighborhoods? The answer is no, and one reason is that conventional cost/benefit techniques do not fully take into account the possibility that the upgrading of the project neighborhood led to the downgrading of another neighborhood somewhere else in the city. To the extent that this occurred, the measured net benefits from the original campaign should be adjusted downward, thereby making further such campaigns look relatively less attractive. Without a reasonably comprehensive urban model, however, it is virtually impossible to get a quantitative estimate of the true strength of this effect. The causal connections involved are too complicated to be followed through using only educated guesswork.

Unfortunately, we do not live in a social scientific utopia where such models are in fact available. A number of reasonably complex urban models have been constructed (for a partial survey, see Brown et al. [97]), but their ultimate worth is a matter of great controversy among planners and housing experts (see Lee [463] and Harris et al. [324]). The principal objection to them is that their theoretical and empirical foundations are extremely shaky. The National Bureau of Economic Research is currently sponsoring the construction of a highly sophisticated, dynamic housing market model [377] whose completion date lies somewhere in the indefinite future. Whether it will prove more useful than its predecessors to city government officials actively engaged in policy making remains to be seen.

In conclusion, all that can be said is that the value of cost/benefit analysis in the housing field depends in the end on the state of scientific knowledge about how urban systems operate. At the moment this knowledge is somewhat limited. As a result, analysts evaluating housing projects are forced to rely on their professional instincts in conjunction with seat-of-the-pants measurement techniques more than they would wish. This situation will undoubtedly improve as further housing research is completed and new urban models are built.

Making Intelligent Use of Cost/Benefit Analysis

Introduction

One of the principal objectives of this appendix was to explain the procedures that are followed when cost/benefit analysis is used to evaluate local government projects aimed at upgrading a community's housing stock. This task has been accomplished. What remains to be examined is a somewhat broader issue and one that does not lend itself nearly as well to the rather technical, point-by-point exposition of the previous section. In particular, given that a local decision maker understands the rudiments of the cost/benefit procedure, when and how should he make use of it? This section considers two different types of situations in which this question comes up. The first occurs when a cost/benefit study must be done under conditions of uncertainty; the second when the resources available to do a study are limited. Each of these cases is discussed separately below.

Cost/Benefit Analysis and Uncertainty

Consider a local government official who has before him three or four alternative projects among which he has to make a choice. If he and his staff dutifully follow the procedures sketched in the previous section, they will end up with a tabulation of estimated benefits and costs for each project (and, possibly, one or more measures of its income distributional impact). On the basis of what has been said so far, these figures would appear to be all that the official needs to look at to make his decision. While this is essentially correct, it is important to note that the whole process of arriving at and then interpreting them has been described in terms that ignore the fact that the official is operating in an environment that is constantly subject to change, often in unforeseen directions. The significance of this is that the official must make all of his decisions under conditions of uncertainty.

The ultimate sources of this uncertainty are two-fold. The first is the dynamic quality of the urban system on which the project will have its impact. As was mentioned at the end of the previous section, cost/benefit analysts have no reliable comprehensive models of this system. Consequently, their estimates of costs and benefits (particularly the latter) will necessarily be subject to a variety of measurement and forecasting errors. In general, the further into the future these costs and benefits occur, the greater such errors are likely to be. The second source of uncertainty faced by the local government official derives from the instability of the political climate in which he functions and to which he must at least occasionally respond. Even if all the forecasts made by his staff are accurate, he is still subject to the changing perceptions and concerns of his constituents.

There is no doubt that the presence of a significant amount of uncertainty makes cost/benefit analysis a less useful tool than it otherwise would be. An extreme reaction to this state of affairs might be to abandon it altogether and rely only on guesswork and good luck. This may be a rational thing to do in some cases, but certainly not always. There are in fact a variety of ways in which the standard cost/benefit procedures can be modified to take uncertainty into account. All of these modifications are rather inelegant, but their use does help preserve the intellectual framework that cost/benefit analysis provides and that in many ways is its most fundamental contribution to rational decision making.

Let us return to the official who must choose among a set of competing projects. One way of dealing with the uncertainty that he faces is to weight the raw cost and benefit figures according to their perceived reliability. Operationally this means giving those costs and benefits that are believed to be reasonably certain more weight than those that are not. Obviously such adjustments will affect the final outcome only if some projects have benefits and costs that appear to be much more uncertain than those of other projects. The main difficulty with this procedure is that the choice of a set of weights is usually a somewhat arbitrary one. In practice, what is frequently done is to exclude categorically those benefits and costs that are perceived to be the most uncertain (i.e., give them a weight of zero) and then include all of the rest.

Further options are available to the official if the individual projects under consideration may be altered in one way or another as new or revised information comes in. In such a case cost/benefit analysis may be employed in a sequential or iterative fashion. The first step would be to use the tool to make a tentative choice among the original set of alternatives. The usual cost/benefit procedures would be applied to accomplish this. The only new wrinkle would be that a project's flexibility or convertibility now becomes an important factor influencing the final choice. Thus, the official will no longer necessarily wish to choose the project with the greatest excess of benefits over costs, even if income distributional factors are ignored. A project with smaller net benefits, but one that promises a broader range of options should events begin to go contrary to expectations, may well be favored.

Once a preliminary choice has been made, cost/benefit analysis can be reapplied at various decision points in the evolution of the project. One can imagine, for example, it being used first to select a public housing site, then later to select the type of housing units to be constructed on the site, and still later to select the proper number of security and maintenance personnel to be employed once the housing is actually occupied. Clearly the various decision "stages" here are not independent of one another. When choosing a site, for example, one will typically want to have some tentative idea of the type of housing that is most likely to be constructed at each of the candidate locations. Nonetheless, it is true that the final decision about these units can be made later than the final decision about the site. As a result the decision maker has an opportunity to modify the original plan if the arrival of new information renders the original cost and benefit calculations obsolete.

Clearly, it is not always going to be possible to do repeated cost/benefit studies of a single project. For one thing, if the period between a project's initiation and completion is short, there will be no time to complete them. For another, if the resources available for conducting such studies are limited, it may be feasible to do only one, thus precluding the extended dialogue between decision maker and analyst, which is the real heart of the process described in the previous paragraph.[5] In either case other methods of coping with uncertainty must be relied upon.

The Costs and Benefits of Cost/Benefit Analysis

To an academic economist, doing a cost/benefit analysis means spending a significant amount of time and money first identifying the various costs and benefits of a project and then using ingenious measurement procedures to determine their quantitative significance. The end product is a report that is very detailed and very complete. In the second section of this appendix it was implicitly assumed that the hypothetical local decision maker discussed there wished to obtain just such a report from his technical staff.

If this were the only type of cost/benefit study possible, the procedure would not be of very much practical significance to public officials. The reason is that complete cost/benefit studies are likely to be costly relative to the value of the information obtained from them. There are a number of reasons for this. For one thing, proper use of some of the measurement techniques discussed earlier may require technical expertise (and computer facilities) that are not available within the department or agency in charge of the project. If so, outside consultants (economists, appraisers, computer programmers, etc.) have to be hired to do the work and they are usually expensive. Furthermore, unless large sums of money are expended, the time frame within which a local official has to make a decision is often too short to permit the completion of one or more full-scale cost/benefit studies. Finally, as was mentioned in the preceding subsection, the estimates of the benefits and costs required for a complete study will always be subject to significant measurement errors. This means that a rational decision maker may not want such estimates calculated even if he could afford them because they would be too unreliable to use.

---

[5]A sequence of partial studies is a possible alternative to a single complete one when funds are scarce. The value of studies that do not attempt to achieve a full accounting of all costs and benefits is discussed in the next subsection.

In some cases, of course, the project may be of sufficient importance to justify the allocation of significant amounts of money and staff time to its evaluation. If, for example, a community has completed one large urban renewal project and is thinking about embarking on others, it may be very desirable to do a really careful analysis of the first project to see precisely what the community put into it and what it got out. Such an instance may be more the exception than the rule, however, particularly in the case of small- or medium-sized cities.

What then of the more typical choice situations where a complete accounting of all costs and benefits is out of the question due to its high cost? The answer is that the cost/benefit framework, if not always the full panoply of measurement procedures and techniques, can still play an important role in the decision-making process.

The first thing to observe in this connection is that knowledge of cost/benefit analysis can help local officials organize their own thinking about the project and help them come to a decision about it even in situations where resources for project evaluation are virtually nonexistent. Simply sitting down and attempting to identify all sources of benefits and costs can be a great aid to rational decision making. Obviously, competent local officials always do this in one way or another, but an official or staff member with some experience in cost/benefit analysis will be able to do the job more quickly and more systematically. A further payoff from this procedure is that it may suggest the use of already existing data that have been gathered for other purposes. In many public agencies project data are scattered through a variety of different departments. A knowledge of cost/benefit analysis can help the local official choose among this data and then make use of the information thus gathered in a rational fashion.

An intermediate situation is one where some funds are available for data collection and analysis (unlike the situation in the previous paragraph), but one where these funds are insufficient to finance a complete examination and evaluation of the project's consequences. Here too a knowledge of cost/benefit analysis can be useful. Experience with this tool can enable the decision maker to allocate his limited funds in a manner that will maximize the utility of the information gathered. He will know, for example, what the most important cost and benefit items are likely to be. He will also know the techniques for measuring them. He thus may well be in a position to conduct a partial cost/benefit study whose informational value is only slightly inferior to that of a complete study.

Summing up, we may say that the use of cost/benefit analysis has its own costs and benefits. The costs are the governmental resources that must be allocated to information gathering and analysis. The benefits are the increases in social welfare brought about by the more efficient use of those resources that remain. There is nothing that necessarily prevents these costs from exceeding the benefits in any decision-making situation. However, the burden of the previous paragraphs (and indeed of this whole essay) is that this is probably not the typical case. It may very well be true that the cost of a complete cost/benefit study exceeds the benefits derived from it most of the time. This fact becomes of limited relevance, however, once it is recognized that doing a cost/benefit study is not an all-or-nothing proposition. Thus, the possibility exists that the benefits from a partial or preliminary study will exceed its cost even while the reverse is true for a significantly more comprehensive study of the same project. There is, of course, nothing that guarantees this result and in the end some risks must always be taken.

Appendix C:
Sample Evaluation Forms

SUMMARY PAGE
NSF EVALUATION FORM

Disposition:
Starting time: _____   Accept _____
Ending time: _____   Reject _____
Time spent: _____   Marginal _____
                          _____
                          _____
                          _____

(Fill this part out first. Be sure that author, title, and publication data are complete and precise, as this will be used to correct our bibliography cards.)

AUTHOR: _____

TITLE: _____
_____
_____

PUBLICATION DATA: _____
_____
_____
_____

LENGTH: _____ TOPIC IN PRELIMINARY BIBLIOGRAPHY
                   (SEE FILE CARD OR BIBLIOGRAPHY): _____

SUMMARILY REJECTED BECAUSE: _____
_____

(The remaining items should be filled in upon completion of the evaluation form.)

TOPIC (See item IIIa, next page): _____

FLAGGED AT (Numbers of the problematic items, and short descriptions of the problems):
_____
_____
_____
_____
_____
_____
_____
_____

STOPPED AT (Number of terminal item):_____
   (Short description of the problem):_____

FURTHER ACTION REQUIRED:_____
_____
_____

STAPLE TO SUMMARY FORM   AUTHOR: _____
                              TITLE: _____
BASIC FORM

NSF EVALUATION FORM

I. Published before 1964? (If yes, stop; or FLAG if this seems a crucial
   study.)   FLAG _____

II. Where found (for future access): _____
   _____

III. Does study deal with housing development and services, promotion of
     housing development, preservation of existing stock?
        a. Yes, clearly _____
        b. No, clearly _____
        c. Perhaps, tangentially, cannot say . . . .   FLAG _____
           (explain, if c): _____
           _____
           _____

IIIa. To which of the following topics does the study seem appropriate (to
      judge from its contents, not from its title)? (If a lengthy study
      and appropriate to more than one topic, try to indicate the pages
      relevant to each.)

      A. Housing development and services – in general

         _____ 1. Impact of alternative forms of subsidies by function: acquisition
                   development, occupancy, operating and tax; and by method –
                   direct and indirect (tax exemption, etc.)
         _____ 2. Alternative forms of sponsorship and development (includes public
                   and private cooperation)
         _____ 3. Housing demand and location patterns
         _____ 4. Housing goals and policy
         _____ 5. Mortgage finance
         _____ 6. Housing supply
      B. Promotion of housing development – new construction
         _____ 1. Federal and state assistance programs: financial and technical
                   services
         _____ 2. Municipal codes and regulations (including exclusionary zoning)
         _____ 3. Municipal property tax policies
         _____ 4. Municipal site acquisition, land banking, development programs
                   (includes effects of other building and construction on housing)
         _____ 5. New construction and industrialized housing techniques (including
                   Operation Breakthrough)
         _____ 6. Public housing
         _____ 7. New towns and planned communities
      C. Preservation of existing housing stock – conservation and rehabilitation
         _____ 1. Federal and state assistance programs: financial and technical
                   services
         _____ 2. Municipal code enforcement

_____ 3. Municipal data systems: housing condition and occupancy data
_____ 4. Municipal property tax and assessment policies
_____ 5. Housing deterioration, abandonment and homesteading
_____ 6. Filtering
_____ 7. Relocation
_____ 8. Rent control
_____ 9. Private rehabilitation programs and repair programs

IIIb. Has this study any relevance for municipal policy makers (as contrasted, for example, with studies of strictly academic or technical interest)?
Yes, clearly_____
No, clearly_____(Go to XII.)
Perhaps, indirectly, cannot say . . . . FLAG_____

IV. In this work from a popular journal addressed to a general audience?
Yes_____(Go to XII)
No_____
Unclear_____ . . . . FLAG_____

V. Does this work deal mainly with legal case analysis, statutory construction, judicial remedies, etc. — intended primarily for lawyers and judges?
Yes_____(Go to XII)
No_____
Unclear_____ . . . . FLAG_____

VI. Is this work primarily expository and/or historical in nature?
Yes_____(Go to XII)
No_____
Unclear_____ . . . . FLAG_____

VII. Affiliations.
A. Who sponsored this study?_____

B. What is the intended audience for this study?_____

C. What is the affiliation of the author?_____

VIII. Type of work.
A. Evaluative (of the literature in general or of other works in particular)?
Yes, including no new research_____(Note works evaluated below, then skip to XII)
Yes, including new research_____(Note works evaluated below, then continue)
No_____

B. Theoretical treatment?
   Yes, including no new research_____Skip to XII, unless this
      seems an "important" theoretical advance, in which case . . . . FLAG_____
   Yes, including new research_____
   No_____
C. Methodological treatment?
   Yes, including no new research_____Skip to XII, unless this
      seems an "important" methodological advance, in which case . . FLAG_____
   Yes, including new research_____
   No_____
D. A report of new research addressed primarily to substantive questions?
   Yes_____   No_____
E. If "no" to A, B, C, D: what then is it? Describe:_____
   _____

F. If an evaluation, note here the works evaluated:_____
   _____
   _____
   _____

IX. Focus of the Research
   A. Level of government to which the study is relevant:
      1. Primarily municipal_____
      2. Of limited relevance to municipal_____
      3. Of no possible relevance to municipal_____ (Explain why, then
         skip to XII.)_____
         _____
         _____

   B. Geographic:
      1. Primarily New England cities_____
      2. Includes one or more NE cities_____
      3. General, theoretical, etc., with some possible relevance to
         NE cities_____
      4. Of no possible relevance to NE cities_____
         (Explain why, then skip to XII)_____
         _____
         _____

   C. Size of city:
      1. All medium-size cities_____
      2. One or more medium-size cities_____
      3. General, theoretical, etc., of possible relevance to medium-
         size cities_____
      4. Of no possible relevance to medium-size cities_____
         (Explain why, then skip to XII)_____
         _____
         _____

X. Is this a case study?
      No_____   Yes_____ . . . . FLAG_____
      If it is a case study, are its conclusions specific only to the case studied?
      _____(If "yes", go to XII.)

XI. How readable would you say this study is for the "interested" reader? (Not for a general audience, that is, but also not for the technically sophisticated.)
_____ A. Very readable, almost entertaining
_____ B. Readable
_____ C. Readable with some difficulty
_____ D. Pretty stiff going:
  _____ 1. Requires technical skills
  _____ 2. Just plain incompetent writing

XII. Are there any special features in this work worth noting? (e.g., bibliography, extensive footnotes, data presented in such a fashion as to make them potentially useful to other studies, any other features?)
_____
_____
_____

XIII. Using the footnotes and bibliography for this work, prepare index cards for any studies cited that seem possibly relevant to the topics listed under topic IIIa.

If you skipped to XII from an earlier topic because this study did not meet some of our criteria, return to the summary page and complete it.

Otherwise, continue to the full form of the NSF EVALUATION FORM.

FULL FORM
NSF EVALUATION FORM   AUTHOR:_____
                                             TITLE:_____

(UPON COMPLETION OF THIS FORM, STAPLE IT TO THE BASIC FORM AND THE SUMMARY PAGE.)

XIV. Objective of the study
   A. How stated: Explicit_____ Implicit_____ (If the latter)   FLAG_____
   B. List the objectives:_____
      _____
      _____
      _____
      _____
      _____

   C. Evaluate the objectives:
      1. Clear, well-formulated (Note which objectives if only some)
         _____
      2. A bit vague (Note which objectives if only some) . . . . FLAG_____
         _____
      3. Very unclear. (Note which objectives if only some) . . . . FLAG_____
         _____

XV. Theoretical backing for the study
   A. Is the study based explicitly on some well-developed and appropriate
      empirical theory or model?_____ If yes, describe:_____
      _____
      _____

   B. Is the study evidently based on a theory or model that is left implicit?
      _____ If yes, describe it below and . . . . FLAG_____
      _____
      _____

   C. Is the study theoretically naive?_____ If yes, ... FLAG_____
      Does this seem a serious drawback to the study?_____ If yes, FLAG_____
      Give reasons in either case:_____
      _____
      _____

XVI. Source of Data, in short.
   (If more than one type of course is used, note for each type whether
   it is principal – the basic type, used to support the major conclusions –
   supporting – used to support important points, but not the most important
   type – or minor – used to support conclusions which are distinctly
   minor points in the context of the study. Obviously, there may be more
   than one of each of these.)

A. Type of source
   1. Interviews:
      a. Depth, few:_____
      b. Survey, many:_____
   2. Aggregate data analysis:_____
   3. Individual data from public records, etc.:_____
   4. Other original data:_____
      (describe if 3 or 4):_____
      _____
      _____

   5. Secondary analysis of others' data:_____
      (describe):_____
      _____
      _____

   6. Simulation approaches (as a source of "data"):_____
      a. Machine simulation:_____
      b. Human simulation (gaming): _____
      c. Any mix of a and b: _____
   7. Other types of sources of data:_____
      (describe them):_____
      _____
      _____

   8. No data:
      a. Theoretical analyses, logical:_____
      b. Methodological analyses, logical:_____
B. Are the sources of data relevant to the stated objectives of the study?
   No, clearly_____(Stop.)
   Yes, clearly_____
   Problematic_____ . . . . FLAG_____
   Comment:_____
   _____
   _____

XVII. The Data Universe
   A. Describe the universe(s) from which the data were drawn.
   _____
   _____
   _____

   B. Is the universe pertinent to the stated objectives of the study?
      Yes_____
      No, clearly_____ (Stop.)
      Problematic . . . . FLAG_____
      Comment:_____
      _____
      _____

   C. If the reasons for the choice of this particular universe are not
      stated or are not obvious . . . . FLAG_____
      Comment:_____
      _____
      _____

XVIII. The Sample
    A. Is the sample explicitly stated?_____If not .... FLAG_____
    B. Type of sample
        1. Universal sample (i.e., includes the entire universe):_____
        2. True sample:
           a. Stratified sample:_____
               (1) Describe the principles of stratification:_____

               (2) Do the principles seem relevant and adequate to the study's objectives?

               (3) By what method were the units selected within the strata?_____

                  If the selection process seems wanting or problematic .. FLAG_____
                  Possible biases introduced by the selection process?

           b. Nonstratified sample
              (1) random sample_____
                  Describe the sampling process briefly:_____

                  Does the process seem adequate and reasonable?_____
                  If not, or if problematic .... FLAG_____
                  Possible biases introduced by the selection process?

        2. Nonrandom sample (Opportunity samples, etc.)_____
           Describe the process briefly:_____

           Is the process adequate and reasonable?_____

           If not, or if problematic .... FLAG_____
           Possible biases introduced by the process?_____

    C. Size of the sample:
        1. Number of units initially drawn:_____
        2. Number of actual respondents:_____
           Does this seem an adequate number of respondents?

3. If this is a stratified sample, does the N in each stratum seem adequate or not?
_____
_____

D. Duration and time:
   1. Is the study one-shot?_____
   2. Or of longer duration?_____
      To what time period does the study apply?_____
_____

E. Are the data presented in such a way as to make them useful to someone else's analysis?_____
_____
_____

F. Any further comments on the sample?_____
_____
_____

XIX. Reliability of the Research Methods.
   A. If interviews.
      1. Are the survey instruments presented?_____
      2. Are the interviewers described?_____Describe them briefly (by type):
         _____
         _____
         a. Do their qualifications seem good?_____
            If not, or problematic .... FLAG_____
         b. Are tests for interviewer reliability presented?_____
            Does the study at least indicate an awareness of the problem?_____
      3. Would a pretest or pilot study have been appropriate?_____
         Comment:_____
         _____
         Was one carried out?_____
         Describe briefly:_____
         _____
         If a pilot study would have been appropriate but one was not carried out
         .... FLAG_____
   B. If aggregate data analysis:
      1. Data at what level of aggregation?_____
         _____
         If this level seems inappropriate, given the study's objectives ..... FLAG_____
      2. From what sources are the data derived? Describe:_____
         _____
         _____
         Are there reasons for thinking these sources unreliable?
         _____
         If yes, ... FLAG_____

C. If reanalysis of others' data:
   1. What are the sources of the data? Describe: _____
   _____
   _____

   2. Are there reasons for thinking these sources unreliable? _____
   _____
   _____

   If yes, or problematic .... FLAG ____

D. If other types of original data:
   1. Comment on the appropriateness _____
   _____

   If problematic .... FLAG ____
   2. Comment on the reliability: _____
   _____

   If problematic .... FLAG ____

E. If the study is not based on empirical data, i.e., is essentially theoretical or methodological:
   1. Is the approach appropriate? _____
   _____

   If this is problematic .... FLAG ____
   2. Does the approach seem well-done? _____
   _____

F. Is a technical "expert's" opinion needed to evaluate this study?
   _____

   If so, note under "further action required" on the summary page and
   .... FLAG ____

XX. What basic assumptions does this study rely upon? (Note whether this reliance is explicit or implicit.)
_____
_____

Do these assumptions seem reasonable? _____
Comment: _____
_____

Do these assumptions appear to bias the conclusions of the study? _____
_____
_____

Does the author indicate an awareness of this bias? _____
Attempt to account for it? _____
_____ If so, how? _____
_____
_____

XXI. The Type of Analysis
(Note whether the type is principal, supporting, or minor, using the guides to these categories presented under XVI above.)
A. Anecdotal_____ If principal, stop; or FLAG_____
(Explain why we would want to consider this study if this is the principal type of analysis, and if you have only flagged this study rather than stopping at this point.)
_____
_____

B. Case study_____ If principal .... FLAG_____
(Case studies with no generalizable conclusions should have been eliminated by the basic evaluation. If this is one that has sneaked through, stop.)

C. Comparative analysis_____
What is compared with what?_____
_____
_____

D. Statistical:
  1. Type of approach:
     a. Hypothesis testing_____

     b. Simply descriptive_____

     c. Something else (describe):_____
     _____
     _____

  2. Style of analysis:
     a. Uses illustrative numbers only_____

     b. Uses descriptive statistics (frequency distributions, etc.)_____

     c. Uses cross-tabulations
        (1) With summary measures of association_____

        (2) Without summary measures_____

     d. Uses summary measures of association, with tests of statistical significance
     _____

     e. Uses more sophisticated techniques_____

        (1) Regressions_____

        (2) Others (describe):_____
        _____

3. Is the style of analysis appropriate to the data?_____
_____

If not, why not (e.g., level of measurement problems, distribution problems, randomness assumptions, normality and so forth)?
_____
_____
_____

If not, or if problematic .... FLAG_____
Do the data seem adequately analyzed_____or underanalyzed_____
4. Cautionary statements:
   a. Would measures of statistical significance (or confidence intervals) be appropriate?_____
   _____

   b. Are they used?_____

   c. Are other means of relating the strength of the conclusions to the data base used (e.g., literary, rule of thumb, etc.)?_____
   _____

   d. If "yes" on 4a, but not on 4b and not on 4c .... FLAG_____
E. Other types of analysis (describe them):_____
_____
_____
_____

XXII. Is the type of analysis used
   A. Appropriate for the objectives of the study?_____
      If not, or if problematic........................... .... FLAG_____
      Comment on the reasons:_____
      _____
      _____

XXIII. The Variables considered in the study.
   A. The Dependent variables:
      1. List them:

      2. Are these variables relevant to the study's objectives?_____
         If not, or if problematic.... .... FLAG_____
         Comment on the reasons:_____
         _____

      3. Are these variables adequate to the study's objectives?_____
         If not, or if problematic............................. FLAG_____
         Comment on the reasons:_____
         _____
         _____

4. Are these variables well-operationalized? _____
   If not, or if problematic .... FLAG _____
   Comment on the reasons: _____
   _____
   _____

B. Independent variables:
   1. List them:

   2. Are these variables relevant to the study's objectives? _____
      If not, or if problematic .... FLAG _____
      Comment: _____
      _____

   3. Are these variables adequate to the objectives? _____
      If not, or if problematic .... FLAG _____
      Comment: _____
      _____

   4. Are these variables well-operationalized? _____
      If not, or if problematic .... FLAG _____
      Comment: _____
      _____

C. Control variables:
   1. List them:

   2. Are these variables relevant to the study's objectives? _____
      If not, or if problematic .... FLAG _____
      Comment: _____
      _____

   3. Are these variables adequate to the objectives? _____
      If not, or if problematic .... FLAG _____
      Comment: _____
      _____

   4. Are the variables well-operationalized? _____
      If not, or if problematic .... FLAG _____
      Comment: _____
      _____

   5. In what manner does the researcher account for control variables?
      _____
      _____
      _____

XXIV. Conclusions.
(List the main conclusions with an evaluation of how well-founded they are. If they seem poorly founded, reference the problem by the number of the item on this form where the problem is described.)

XXV. Objectives in light of the conclusions of the study.
   A. Are all of the objectives of the study satisfied by the conclusions drawn from the study?_____
   If some are not satisfied, note which ones:_____
   _____
   _____

   B. Do you recall other studies that have reached contrary conclusions?
   If yes,   FLAG_____
   List any that you recall, or any cited by the author, referencing the conclusions here:

   C. Does the author indicate areas or questions on which further research and evidence are needed? (Note the areas.)_____
   _____

   Do his conclusions (or lack of conclusions) suggest such gaps in the literature to you? (Note the areas.)_____
   _____
   _____
   _____

XXVI. Interdependence in the literature.
   List the works cited in this study that are used to make or support some major point. (Skip "see also" citations, and other minor citations.) For each work cited note whether this study:
   A. Uses some of its conclusions. Note which conclusions.
   B. Uses some of its data. Note which data.
   C. Uses some of its methods. Note which methods.
   D. Uses some of its theory. Note which theory.
   Under each of these, note whether this study:
      1. Accepts as given
      2. Supports (adds new weight to)
      3. Refines
      4. Disputes or rejects
   the conclusions, data, methods, theory; and note briefly on what basis—e.g., new data, logical analysis, better methods.

XXVI. Interdependence in the literature (continued. See directions for this item on the previous page.)

XXVII. Preliminary Policy Utility Criteria
    A. Physical Accessibility
       Is this study readily available?
       Yes_____ No_____ Can't say_____
       Explain in any case:_____
       _____

    B. Lexical and Organizational Accessibility
       1. Is this study written in a language that a policy maker can understand?
          Yes_____ No_____ Marginal_____
       2. Are the arguments developed in such a way that a policy maker can understand them?
          Yes_____ No_____ Not sure_____
          Explain:_____
          _____

       3. Are explicit, policy-oriented recommendations made?
          Yes_____ No_____ Not clear_____
          Explain:_____
          _____

       3a. If they are made, are they presented prominently (e.g., at the beginning of the work, or set off in boxes, or in bold-face type)?
           Yes_____ No_____
       3b. If no recommendations are made, are the findings or conclusions at least set off in a prominent fashion?
           Yes_____ No_____
           Explain:_____
           _____

    C. Administrative feasibility—includes such programmatic considerations as ease of understanding, staffing, managing, implementing, evaluating, modifying, and terminating a program based on the study recommendations.
       1. Does the study pay explicit attention to administrative feasibility questions?
          Yes_____ No_____
          If so, does it seem convincing on this point?
          Yes_____ No_____ Problematic_____
          Explain:_____
          _____
          _____

2. If not, are its recommendations, if any, feasible from an administrative viewpoint?
   Not applicable_____
   This may be a problem_____
   This is probably not a problem_____
   I cannot say_____
   Explain:_____
   _____

D. Political feasibility—includes such considerations as controversiality, potential conflict with other agencies and institutions—public or private, immediacy of results, permanency of the program, sallience of benefits, impact on the official's chances of reelection, impact on his control over patronage, relative political weights of those who receive benefits and those who have to pay for the program.
   1. Does the study take political considerations explicitly into account?
      Yes_____ No_____ Problematic_____
      Explain:_____
      _____

   2. If not, are its recommendations, if any, reasonable from a political point of view?
      Not applicable_____
      This may be a problem_____
      This is probably not a problem_____
      I cannot say_____
      Explain:_____

E. Cost—includes such considerations as the size of the direct outlay, the cost of administration, the time horizon of the cost (do benefits come early and costs later?), the nature of the payment (from general funding or through bonding?), the interdependence or severability of sub-items (could it be treated incrementally?).
   1. Does this study take cost explicitly into account?
      Yes_____ No_____
      If so, does it seem convincing on this point?
      Yes_____ No_____ Problematic_____
      Explain:_____
      _____

   2. If not, are its recommendations, if any, reasonable taking costs into consideration?
      Not applicable_____
      This may be a problem_____
      This is probably not a problem_____
      I cannot say_____
      Explain:_____
      _____

F. Equity—includes such considerations as the relation of costs and benefits to ability to pay and to need, the recipients of benefits (those who need housing or those who build or finance housing?), progressive or regressive incidence of the program.

1. Does this study pay explicit attention to questions of equity?
   Yes_____ No_____
   If so, does it seem convincing on this point?
   Yes_____ No_____ Problematic_____
   Explain:_____
   _____
   _____

2. If the study gives little or no attention to questions of equity, do the distributional effects of its recommendations, if any, seem likely to satisfy reasonable criteria or equity?
   Not applicable_____
   This may be a problem_____
   This is probably not a problem_____
   I cannot say_____
   Explain:_____
   _____
   _____

COMPLETE THE SUMMARY PAGE, AND STAPLE THE SUMMARY PAGE, THE BASIC FORM, AND THE FULL FORM TOGETHER.

XXVIII. Comment on any major problems in this study for which space has not been previously provided. If necessary,   FLAG_____

Appendix D:
NSF Research Program Note

A large body of research on municipal systems, operations, and services has been created over the last quarter century. However, its usefulness to decision makers has been limited because it has not been evaluated comprehensively with respect to technical quality, usefulness to policy makers, and potential for codification and wider diffusion. In addition, this research has been hard to locate and not easily accessible. Therefore, systematic and rigorous evaluations of this research are required to provide syntheses of evaluated information for use by public agencies at all levels of government and to aid in the planning and definition of research programs.

Recognizing these needs, the Division of Social Systems and Human Resources issued a Program Solicitation in January 1973 for proposals to evaluate policy-related research in 17 categories in the field of municipal systems, operations, and services. This competition resulted in 19 awards in June 1973.

Each of the projects was to: (1) evaluate the internal validity of each study by determining whether the research used appropriate methods and data to deal with the questions asked; (2) evaluate the external validity of the research by determining whether the results were credible in the light of other valid policy-related research; (3) evaluate the policy utility of specific studies or sets of studies bearing on given policy instruments; (4) provide decision makers, including research funders, with an assessed research base for alternative policy actions, in a format readily interpretable and usable by decision makers.

Each report was to include an analysis of the validity and utility of research in the field selected, a synthesis of the evidence, and a discussion of what, if any, additional research is required.

The following is a list of the awards showing the research area evaluated, the organization to which the award was made, and the principal investigator.

1. Fire Protection: Georgia Institute of Technology, Department of Industrial and Systems Engineering, Atlanta, Georgia 30332; D.E. Fyffe
2. Fire Protection: New York RAND Institute, 545 Madison Avenue, New York, New York 10022; Arthur J. Swersey
3. Emergency Medical Services: University of Tennessee, Bureau of Public Administration, Knoxville, Tennessee 37916; Hyrum Plaas
4. Municipal Housing Services: Cogen, Holt and Associates, 956 Chapel Street, New Haven, Connecticut 06510; Harry Wexler
5. Formalized Pre-Trial Diversion Programs in Municipal and Metropolitan Courts: American Bar Association, 1705 DeSales Street, N.W., Washington, D.C. 20036; Roberta-Rovner-Pieczenik
6. Parks and Recreation: National Recreation and Park Association, 1601 North Kent Street, Arlington, Virginia 22209; The Urban Institute, 2100 M Street, N.W., Washington, D.C. 20037; Peter J. Verhoven
7. Police Protection: Mathematica, Inc., 4905 Del Ray Avenue, Bethesda, Maryland 20014; Saul I. Gass
8. Solid Waste Management: Massachusetts Institute of Technology, Department of Civil Engineering, Cambridge, Massachusetts 02139; David Marks
9. Citizen Participation Strategies: The RAND Corporation, 2100 M Street, N.W., Washington, D.C. 20037; Robert Yin
10. Citizen Participation: Municipal Sub-systems: The University of Michigan, Program in Health Planning, Ann Arbor, Michigan 48104; Joseph L. Falkson

11. Economic Development: Ernst & Ernst, 1225 Connecticut Avenue, N.W., Washington, D.C. 20036; Lawrence H. Revzan
12. Goal of Economic Development: University of Texas-Austin, Center for Economic Development, Department of Economics, Austin, Texas 78712; Niles M. Hansen
13. Franchising and Regulation: University of South Dakota, Department of Economics, Vermillion, South Dakota 57069; C.A. Kent
14. Municipal Information Systems: University of California, Public Policy Research Organization, Irvine, California 92664; Kenneth L. Kraemer
15. Municipal Growth Guidance Systems: University of Minnesota, School of Public Affairs, Minneapolis, Minnesota 55455; Michael E. Gleeson
16. Land Use Controls: University of North Carolina, Chapel Hill, Center for Urban and Regional Studies, Chapel Hill, North Carolina 17514; Edward M. Bergman
17. Land Use Controls: The Potomac Institute, Inc., 1501 Eighteenth Street, N.W., Washington, D.C. 20036; Herbert M. Franklin
18. Municipal Management Methods and Budgetary Processes: The Urban Institute, 2100 M Street, N.W., Washington, D.C. 20037; Wayne A. Kimmel
19. Personnel Systems: Georgetown University, Public Services Laboratory, Washington, D.C. 20037; Selma Mushkin

A complementary series of awards were made by the Division of Social Systems and Human Resources to evaluate the policy-related research in the field of human resources. For the convenience of the reader, a listing of these awards appears below:

1. An Evaluation of Policy Related Research on New Expanded Roles of Health Workers: Yale University, School of Medicine, New Haven, Connecticut 06520; Eva Cohen
2. An Evaluation of Policy Related Research on the Effectiveness of Alternative Allocation of Health Care Manpower: Interstudy, 123 East Grant Street, Minneapolis, Minnesota 55403; Aaron Lowin
3. An Evaluation of Policy Related Research on Effects of Health Care Regulation: Policy Center, Inc., Suite 500, 789 Sherman, Denver, Colorado 80203; Patrick O'Donoghue
4. An Evaluation of Policy Related Research on Trade-Offs Between Preventive and Primary Health Care: Boston University Medical Center, Boston University, School of Medicine, Boston, Massachusetts 02215; Paul Gertman
5. An Evaluation of Policy Related Research on Effectiveness of Alternative Programs for the Handicapped: Rutgers University, 165 College Avenue, New Brunswick, New Jersey 08901; Monroe Berkowitz
6. An Evaluation of Policy Related Research on Effects of Alternative Health Care Reimbursement Systems: University of Southern California, Department of Economics, Los Angeles, California 90007; Donald E. Yett
7. An Evaluation of Policy Related Research on Alternative Public and Private Programs for Mid-Life Redirection of Careers: RAND Corporation, 1700 Main Street, Santa Monica, California 90406; Anthony H. Pascal
8. An Evaluation of Policy Related Research on Relations between Industrial Organization, Job Satisfaction, and Productivity: Brandeis University Florence G. Heller Graduate School for Advanced Studies in Social Welfare, Waltham, Massachusetts 02154; Michael J. Brower
9. An Evaluation of Policy Related Research on Relations between Industrial Organization, Job Satisfaction and Productivity: New York University, Department of Psychology, New York, New York 10003; Raymond A. Katzell

10. An Evaluation of Policy Related Research on Productivity, Industrial Organization and Job Satisfaction: Case Western Reserve University, School of Management, Cleveland, Ohio 44106; Suresh Srivastva
11. An Evaluation of Policy Related Research on Effectiveness of Alternative Methods to Reduce Occupational Illness and Accidents: Westinghouse Behavioral Safety Center, Box 948, American City Building, Columbia, Maryland 21044; C. Michael Pfeifer
12. An Evaluation of Policy Related Research on the Impact of Unionization on Public Institutions: Contract Research Corporation, 25 Flanders Road, Belmont, Massachusetts 02178; Ralph Jones
13. An Evaluation of Policy Related Research on Projection of Manpower Requirements: Ohio State University, Center for Human Resource Research, Columbus, Ohio 43210; S.C. Kelley
14. An Evaluation of Policy Related Research on Effectiveness of Alternative Pre-Trial Intervention Programs: ABT Associates, Inc., 55 Wheeler Street, Cambridge, Massachusetts 02138; Joan Mullen
15. An Evaluation of Policy Related Research on the Effectiveness of Pre-Trial Release Programs: National Center for State Courts, 1660 Lincoln Street, Denver, Colorado 80203; Barry Mahoney
16. An Evaluation of Policy Related Research on Effectiveness of Volunteer Programs in the Area of Courts and Corrections: University of Illinois, Department of Political Science, Chicago Circle, Box 4348, Chicago, Illinois 60680; Thomas J. Cook
17. An Evaluation of Policy Related Research on Effectiveness of Juvenile Delinquency Prevention Program: George Peabody College for Teachers, Department of Psychology, Nashville, Tennessee 37203; Michael C. Dixon
18. An Evaluation of Policy Related Research on Exercise of Discretion by Law Enforcement Officials: College of William and Mary, Metropolitan Building, 147 Granby Street, Norfolk, Virginia 23510; W. Anthony Fitch
19. An Evaluation of Policy Related Research on Exercise of Police Discretion: National Council on Crime and Delinquency Research Center, 609 2nd Street, Davis, California 95616; M.G. Neithercutt
20. An Evaluation of Policy Related Research on Post Secondary Education for the Disadvantaged: Mercy College of Detroit, Department of Sociology, Detroit, Michigan 48219; Mary Janet Mulka

Copies of the above cited research evaluation reports for both municipal systems and human resources may be obtained directly from the principal investigator or from the National Technical Information Service (NTIS), U.S. Department of Commerce, 5285 Port Royal Road, Springfield, Virginia 22151 (Telephone: 703-321-8517).

Bibliography

The bibliography that follows represents a listing of works deemed to be relevant to the policy-related literature on municipal housing services, based on a preliminary assessment of their titles and the books or journals in which they are published.

Those items that are asterisked (*) were not evaluated by our staff for one or more of the following reasons: (1) their focus is tangential to our study; (2) they were published prior to 1964 or after January 1974; (3) they were unavailable in the several resource libraries used by the evaluation staff (Yale University Library System; Library of Congress, Washington, D.C.; Library of the U.S. Department of Housing and Urban Development; among others); (4) they are out-of-print. Consequently, we cannot vouch for the completeness or accuracy of the publication data provided for these asterisked entries, although every possible effort has been made to verify this information.

*[1] Aaron, Henry J. "A New View of Property Tax Incidence," *American Economic Review*, LXIV (2) (May 1974), 212-221.

[2] _____. "Federal Housing Subsidies," *The Economics of Federal Subsidy Programs.* Washington, D.C.: U.S. Government Printing Office, 1972, 571-596. (A compendium of papers submitted to the Joint Economic Committee, Congress of the United States. Part 5—Housing Subsidies. October 9, 1972.)

*[3] _____. "Income Taxes and Housing," *American Economic Review*, LX (5) (December 1970), 789-806.

[4] _____. *Shelter and Subsidies: Who Benefits from Federal Housing Policies?* Washington, D.C.: The Brookings Institution, 1972.

[5] _____. "What do Circuit-Breaker Laws Accomplish?" in George E. Peterson (ed.). *Property Tax Reform.* Washington, D.C.: The Urban Institute, 1973, 53-64.

*[6] _____ and George M. von Furstenberg, "The Inefficiency of Transfers in Kind: The Case of Housing Assistance," *Western Economic Journal*, IX (June 1971), 184-191.

*[7] Abrams, Charles. *The City is the Frontier.* New York: Harper and Row, 1965.

[8] _____. *Home Ownership for the Poor: A Program for Philadelphia.* New York: Praeger Publishers, 1970.

[9] Achtenberg, Emily J. *Rehabilitation Loans and Grants in Boston.* Cambridge, Massachusetts: Joint Center for Urban Studies of the Massachusetts Institute of Technology and Harvard University, 1970. (Abstract no. 12.)

[10] Ackerman, Bruce. "Regulating Slum Housing Markets on Behalf of the

Poor: Of Housing Codes, Housing Subsidies and Income Redistribution Policy," *The Yale Law Journal*, LXXX (6) (May 1971), 1093-1197.
*[11] Adamson, R.T. "Housing Policy and Urban Renewal," in Lithwick, N. Harvey and Gilles Paquet (eds.). *Urban Studies: A Canadian Perspective.* Toronto: Methuen, 1968, 222-239.
[12] Agapos, A.M. and Paul R. Dunlap. "Elimination of Urban Blight Through Inverse Proportional Ad Valorem Property Taxation," *The American Journal of Economics and Sociology*, XXXII (2) (April 1973), 143-152.
[13] Aiken, Michael and Robert R. Alford. "Community Structure and Innovation: The Case of Public Housing," *The American Political Science Review*, LXIV (3) (September 1970), 843-864.
*[14] Alberts, William W. and Allen F. Jung. "Some Evidence of the Intra-Regional Structure of Interest Rates on Residential Mortgage Loans," *Land Economics*, XLVI (2) (May 1970), 208-213.
[15] Almy, Richard R. "Rationalizing the Assessment Process," in George E. Peterson (ed.). *Property Tax Reform.* Washington, D.C.: The Urban Institute, 1973, 175-188.
*[16] Aloi, Frank A., Arthur Abba Goldberg, and James M. White. "Racial and Economic Segregation by Zoning: Death Knell for Home Rule?" *University of Toledo Law Review* (Winter 1969), 65.
*[17] Alonso, William. *Information on and Evaluations of Innovations in Housing Design and Construction Techniques as Applied to Low-Cost Housing.* Berkeley: University of California Press, 1969.
[18] _____. *Location and Land Use: Toward a General Theory of Land Rent.* Cambridge, Massachusetts: Harvard University Press, 1964.
[19] Altshuler, Alan A. *The City Planning Process: A Political Analysis.* Ithaca, New York: Cornell University Press, 1965.
*[20] _____. "The Potential of 'Trickle Down'," *The Public Interest* (15) (Spring 1969).
[21] American Society of Planning Officials. *Problems of Zoning and Land-Use Regulation.* Washington, D.C.: National Commission on Urban Problems, 1968. (Research report no. 2.)
*[22] Anderson, Martin. *The Federal Bulldozer: A Critical Analysis of Urban Renewal 1949-1962.* Cambridge, Massachusetts: The Massachusetts Institute of Technology Press, 1964.
[23] Anderson, Paul E. *Tax Planning of Real Estate.* Philadelphia: Joint Committee on Continuing Legal Education of the American Law Institute and the American Bar Association, 1970.
[24] Anderson, Theodore R. "Social and Economic Factors Affecting the Location of Residential Neighborhoods," *Papers and Proceedings, Regional Science Association*, IX (1962), 161-170.
*[25] APHA Committee on the Hygiene of Housing. *Planning the Home for Occupancy.* Washington, D.C.: APHA Committee on the Hygiene of Housing, 1950.

*[26] Arcadia, California Planning Department. *A Statistical Comparison of Multiple-Family Dwelling Units and Elementary School Enrollment.* Arcadia, California: Arcadia Planning Department, 1970.

*[27] Arcelus, Francisco and Allan H. Meltzer. "The Markets for Housing and Housing Services," *Journal of Money, Credit and Banking*, V (Part I) (February 1973), 78-99.

 [28] Arthur D. Little, Incorporated. *A Study of Property Taxes and Urban Blight.* Cambridge, Massachusetts: Arthur D. Little, Inc., 1973. (Prepared for the U.S. Department of Housing and Urban Development.)

 [29] _____. *Project Infill: An Experiment in Housing Technology.* Cambridge, Massachusetts: Arthur D. Little, Inc., 1971. (Report to the Department of Community Affairs under contract with the Connecticut Research Commission. C-72892.)

*[30] _____. *Project Rehabilitation Monitoring Report Overview.* Cambridge, Massachusetts: Arthur D. Little, Inc., 1971.

 [31] _____. *San Francisco Community Renewal Program, Final Report to the City Planning Commission, City and County of San Francisco.* Cambridge, Massachusetts: Arthur D. Little, Inc., 1965.

 [32] _____. *State Programs of Community Development Assistance: A Comparative Assessment of Programs in Three States.* Cambridge, Massachusetts: Arthur D. Little, Inc., 1971. (Prepared for U.S. Department of Housing and Urban Development, HUD contract no. H-1296.)

*[33] Askari, Hossein. "Federal Taxes and the Internal Rate of Return on Owner Occupied Housing," *National Tax Journal*, XXV (1) (March 1972), 101-105.

*[34] Associated General Contractors of America. *Housing Survey of the Houston Metropolitan Area: The Impact of Codes, Regulations and Industry Practices on the Cost of Housing.* Houston, Texas: National Commission on Urban Problems, 1968. (Background paper no. 30.)

 [35] Babcock, Richard F. *The Zoning Game: Municipal Practices and Policies.* Madison, Wisconsin: The University of Wisconsin Press, 1966.

 [36] _____ and Fred P. Bosselman. "Suburban Zoning and the Apartment Boom," *University of Pennsylvania Law Review*, CXI (8) (June 1963), 1040-1091.

 [37] Bagby, D. Gordon. *Housing Rehabilitation Costs.* Lexington, Massachusetts: Lexington Books, D.C. Heath and Co., 1973.

 [38] Bahl, Roy W. "A Land Speculation Model: The Role of the Property Tax as a Constraint to Urban Sprawl," *Journal of Regional Science*, VIII (2) (Winter 1968), 199-208.

*[39] Bailey, Martin J. "Effects of Race and Other Demographic Factors on the Values of Single Family Homes," *Land Economics*, XLII (2) (May 1966), 215-220.

 [40] _____. "Note on the Economics of Residential Zoning and Urban Renewal," *Land Economics*, XXXV (3) (August 1959), 288-292.

[41] Bails, Dale. "An Alternative: The Land Value Tax: The Argument for Continued Use of Part of the General Property Tax," *The American Journal of Economics and Sociology*, XXXII (3) (July 1973), 283-294.

[42] Ball, Michael J. "Recent Determinants of Relative Housing Values," *Urban Studies*, X (2) (June 1973), 213-233.

[43] Bancroft, Raymond. *American's Mayors and Councilmen: Their Problems and Frustrations*. NLC Research Report. Washington, D.C.: National League of Cities, 1974.

[44] Banfield, Edward. *Political Influence*. New York: Free Press of Glencoe, 1961.

[45] Banfield, Edward and James Q. Wilson. *City Politics*. Cambridge, Massachusetts: Harvard University Press, 1963.

*[46] Banfield, Edward C. *Unheavenly City: The Nature and Future of our Urban Crisis*. Boston: Little, Brown and Company, 1970.

*[47] Barton-Aschman Associates. *The Barrington, Illinois Area: A Cost-Revenue Analysis of Land Alternatives*. Chicago: Barton-Aschman Associates, 1970.

[48] Beck, Morris. "Determinants of the Property Tax Level: A Case Study of Northeastern New Jersey," *National Tax Journal*, XVIII (1) (March 1965), 74-77.

[49] _____. *Property Taxation and Urban Land Use in Northeastern New Jersey*. Washington, D.C.: Urban Land Institute, 1963. (Research monograph no. 7.)

*[50] _____. *Tax Policy and Urban Redevelopment: An Evaluation of Federal, State and Local Incentives for Investment in Urban Real Estate*. New Brunswick, New Jersey: Rutgers University, 1966.

[51] _____. "Urban Redevelopment: Influence of Property Taxation and Other Factors," *National Tax Association Proceedings*, 1964, 239-249.

*[52] Becker, Arthur P. "Arguments for Changing the Real Estate Tax to a Land Value Tax," *Tax Policy* XXXVII (9-12) (September-December 1970).

[53] _____ (ed.). *Land and Building Taxes: Their Effect on Economic Development*. Madison, Wisconsin: University of Wisconsin Press, 1969.

[54] _____. "Principles of Taxing Land and Buildings for Economic Development," in Arthur P. Becker (ed.), *Land and Building Taxes: Their Effect on Economic Development*. Madison Wisconsin: The University of Wisconsin Press, 1969, 11-47.

*[55] _____. "Urban Development and Federal Grants," *National Tax Association Proceedings* (1966), 112-133.

*[56] Becker, David M. "The Police Power and Minimum Lot Size Zoning," *Washington University Law Quarterly* (Summer 1969), 263.

[57] Beckmann, M.J. "On the Distribution of Urban Rent and Residential Density," *Journal of Economic Theory*, I (1) (June 1969), 60-67.

[58] Beeman, William Joseph. *The Property Tax and the Spatial Pattern of Growth Within Urban Areas.* Washington, D.C.: The Urban Land Institute, 1969. (Research monograph no. 16.)

*[59] Behman, Sara and Donald Codella. "Wage Rates and Housing Prices," *Industrial Relations* (February 1971), 86-104.

[60] Behrens, John O. *A Report on the Local Administration of Building Codes.* Chicago, Illinois: Public Administration Service, 1966. (National Commission on Urban Problems, background paper no. 40.)

[61] Bensky, M. *Report on the Development of a Sample Program Planning Memo for a Model City Agency.* Santa Barbara, California: TEMPO Center for Advanced Studies, General Electric Company, 1967.

*[62] Benson, George C.S., Sumner Benson, Harold McClelland, and Procter Thomson. *The American Property Tax: Its History, Administration and Economic Impact.* Claremont, California: Lincoln School of Public Finance, Claremont Men's College, 1965.

[63] Berger, Curtis, Eli Goldston, and Guido A. Rothrauff, Jr. "Slum Area Rehabilitation by Private Enterprise," *Columbia Law Review*, LXIX (5) (May 1969), 739-769.

[64] Berger, Miles. "Assessment Techniques in Urban Renewal Areas," *Assessment Administration, 1965: Proceedings of the Thirty-First International Conference on Assessment Administration*, 87-90.

[65] Berkman, Herman G. "The Game Theory of Land Use Determination," *Land Economics*, XLI (1) (February 1965), 11-19.

[66] Berney, Robert E. and Arlyn J. Larson. "Micro-analysis of Mobile Home Characteristics with Implications for Tax Policy," *Land Economics*, XLII (4) (November 1966), 453-463.

[67] Bernhardt, Kenneth (ed.). *Housing Market Opportunities: Industrialized Housing, New Towns, and Rehabilitation.* Ann Arbor, Michigan: Industrial Development Division, Institute of Science and Technology, The University of Michigan, 1972.

*[68] _____ (ed.). *Housing: New Trends and Concepts.* Ann Arbor, Michigan: Industrial Development Division, Institute of Science and Technology, University of Michigan, 1972.

*[69] Beyer, Glenn H. *Housing and Society.* New York: Macmillan, 1965.

[70] Bish, Robert L. "Public Housing: The Magnitude and Distribution of Direct Benefits and Effects on Housing Consumption," *Journal of Regional Science*, IX (3) (December 1969), 425-438.

[71] _____. *The Distribution of Housing Taxes and Subsidies and Effects on Housing Consumption of Low-Income Families.* Bloomington, Indiana: Ph.D. dissertation, Indiana University, 1968.

*[72] Bloomberg, Warner, Jr. and H.J. Schmandt. *Power, Poverty and Urban Policy.* Beverly Hills, California: Sage Publishers, 1968. (Urban Affairs Annual Reviews, volume II.)

*[73] Bonham, Gordon Scott. "Discrimination and Housing Quality," *Growth and Change*, III (4) (October 1972), 26-34.

[74] Bosselman, Fred P. *Alternatives to Urban Sprawl: Legal Guidelines for Governmental Action.* Washington, D.C.: National Commission on Urban Problems, 1968. (Research report no. 15.)

[75] Boston, Helen S. *Housing for Low-Income Families.* Washington, D.C.: U.S. Department of Housing and Urban Development, 1966. (Paper prepared for a seminar on the low-income family.)

[76] Boston, John et al. "The Impact of Race on Housing Markets: A Critical Review," *Social Problems*, XIX (Winter 1972), 382-393.

[77] Boston Municipal Research Bureau. *Costs and Other Effects on Owners and Tenants of Repairs Required Under Housing Code Enforcement Programs.* Boston, Massachusetts: Boston Municipal Research Bureau, 1968.

*[78] Bourne, L.S. "Location Factors in the Redevelopment Process: A Model of Residential Change," *Land Economics*, XLV (2) (May 1969), 183-193.

*[79] _____. "A Spatial Allocation—Land Use Conversion Model of Urban Growth," *Journal of Regional Science*, IX (2) (1969), 261-272.

*[80] Bowe, William J. "Regional Planning vs. Decentralized Land Use Control—Zoning for the Megalopolis," *De Paul Law Review*, XVIII (Autumn 1968), 144.

*[81] Bradford, D.F. "An Econometric Simulation Model of Intra-Metropolitan Housing Location: Housing, Business, Transportation and Local Government: Discussion," *American Economic Review*, LXII (2) (May 1972), 99-102.

*[82] Brady, Eugene A. "A Sectoral Econometric Study of the Postwar Residential-Housing Market," *Journal of Political Economy*, LXXV (April 1967), 147-158.

*[83] _____. "A Sectoral Econometric Study of the Postwar Residential Housing Market: An Opposite View: Reply," *Journal of Political Economy*, LXXVIII (March-April 1970), 268-278.

[84] Brandenburg, John G. *The Industrialization of Housing: Implications for New Town Development.* Chapel Hill, North Carolina: Center for Urban and Regional Studies, University of North Carolina, 1970.

[85] Branfman, Eric J., Benjamin I. Cohen, and David M. Trubek. *Fiscal and Other Incentives for Exclusionary Land Use Controls.* New Haven, Connecticut: Center for the Study of the City and its Environment, Institution for Social and Policy Studies, Yale University, 1972.

[86] _____. *Measuring the Invisible Wall; Land Use Controls and the Residential Patterns of the Poor.* New Haven, Connecticut: Center for the Study of the City and its Environment, Institution for Social and Policy Studies, Yale University, 1973. (Reprint R3-1. Reprinted from *The Yale Law Journal*, LXXXII (3) (January 1973), 483-508.)

*[87] Brazer, Marjorie Cahn. "Economic and Social Disparities between Central Cities and Their Suburbs," *Land Economics*, XLIII (3) (August 1967), 294-302.
*[88] _____. "Economic and Social Disparities between Central Cities and Their Suburbs: Rejoinder," *Land Economics*, XLVI (3) (August 1970), 349-350.
*[89] Break, George F. "Federal Loan Insurance for Housing," in George F. Break et al. *Federal Credit Agencies; A Series of Research Studies.* New York: Prentice-Hall, 1963.
 [90] Breger, G.E. "The Concept and Causes of Urban Blight," *Land Economics*, XLIII (4) (November 1967), 369-376.
 [91] Bridges, Benjamin, Jr. "The Elasticity of the Property Tax Base: Some Cross-Section Estimates," *Land Economics*, XL (4) (November 1964), 449-451.
*[92] Brigham, Eugene F. "The Determinants of Residential Land Values," *Land Economics*, XLI (November 1965), 325-334.
*[93] _____. *A Model of Residential Land Values.* Santa Monica, California: The RAND Corporation, 1964. (RM-4043-RC.)
*[94] Brodsky, Harold. "Residential Land and Improvement Values in a Central City," *Land Economics*, XLVI (3) (August 1970), 229-247.
*[95] _____. "Residential Land and Improvement Values in a Central City: A Reply (C.T. Haworth and D.W. Rassmussen) with Rejoinder," *Land Economics*, XLVIII (2) (May 1972), 198.
*[96] Brooks, Mary. *Exclusionary Zoning.* Chicago: American Society of Planning Officials, 1970. (Planning Advisory Service report no. 254.)
 [97] Brown, H. James et al. *Empirical Models of Land Use.* New York: National Bureau of Economic Research, 1972.
*[98] Brown, Samuel Lovitt. *Price Variations in New FHA Houses: A Report of Research Methods of Constructing Price Indexes, 1959-1961.* Washington, D.C.: U.S. Government Printing Office, 1971. (Working paper no. 31, Bureau of the Census, U.S. Department of Commerce.)
*[99] Brown, W.H., Jr. "Access to Housing: The Role of the Real Estate Industry," *Economic Geography*, XLVIII (January 1972), 66-78.
*[100] Browning, Clyde E. "Land Value Taxation: Promises and Problems," *Journal of the American Institute of Planners*, XXIX (4) (November 1963), 301-309.
 [101] _____. "Opening Pandora's Box: The Property Tax and Planning," *Proceedings of the 1964 Annual Conference, American Institute of Planners*, 168-174.
 [102] Brueggeman, William B. "The Impact of Federally Subsidized Housing Programs: The Columbus, Ohio Case," in Stephen D. Messner and Maury Selden (eds.). *Proceedings, American Real Estate and Urban Economics Association, 1970*, V (1971), 51-65.

*[103] Brueggeman, William B. *The Impact of Private Construction and Government Housing Programs in a Local Housing Market.* Ann Arbor, Michigan: Ph.D. dissertation, Ohio State University, University Microfilms, 1971.

*[104] _____ et al. "Multiple Housing Programs and Urban Housing Policy," *Journal of the American Institute of Planners,* XXXVIII (3) (May 1972), 160-167

[105] Buehler, Alfred G. "A Reconsideration of the Property Tax," in Tax Institute of America. *The Property Tax: Problems and Potential.* Princeton, New Jersey: Tax Institute of America, 1967, 5-16.

[106] "Building Codes and Residential Rehabilitation: Tilting at Windmills," *Columbia Journal of Law and Social Problems,* V (2) (August 1969), 88-98.

[107] Building Research Advisory Board. *Specification-Versus Performance-Type Building Codes.* Washington, D.C.: National Academy of Sciences—National Academy of Engineering, 1966. (National Commission on Urban Problems. Background paper no. 39.)

[108] Burchell, Robert W. (ed.). *Frontiers of Planned Unit Development: A Synthesis of Expert Opinion.* New Brunswick, New Jersey: Center for Urban Policy Research, Rutgers University, 1973.

[109] Bureau of Economic and Business Research, Temple University. *Financing Lower-Middle Income Housing.* Philadelphia: Bureau of Economic and Business Research, Temple University, 1964. (Demonstration project PA. D-3.)

[110] Burnham, James B. "Housing Starts, 1966 and 1969: A Comparison Using an Econometric Model," *Land Economics,* XLVIII (1) (February 1972), 88-89.

[111] Burns, Leland S. *Cost Benefit Analysis of Improved Housing: A Case Study.* Los Angeles: International Housing Productivity Study, Real Estate Research Program, Graduate School of Business Administration, Division of Research, University of California at Los Angeles, 1966. (Reprint no. IHPS-4.)

*[112] _____ . "Housing as Social Overhead Capital," *Essays in Urban Land Economics.* Los Angeles, University of California Press, 1966, 3-30.

*[113] _____ . "A Programming Model for Urban Development," *Regional Science Association, Papers and Proceedings,* XI (1963), 195-210.

[114] Burstein, Joseph. "New Techniques in Public Housing," *Law and Contemporary Problems,* XXXII (3) (Summer 1967), 529-549.

[115] Butler, Edgar W. and Edward J. Kaiser. "Prediction of Residential Movement and Spatial Allocations," *Urban Affairs Quarterly,* VI (4) (June 1971), 477-494.

[116] Buttel, Frederick H. *Correlates of Zoning Nonenforcement in South Central Connecticut Towns.* New Haven, Connecticut: Center for the

Study of the City and its Environment, Institution for Social and Policy Studies, Yale University, 1974.

[117] Byram, Richard W. "Comment. The HUD Interest Subsidy Housing Programs: Some Economic Realities Affecting Project Feasibility and Investor Participation," *UMKC Law Review*, XLI (1) (Fall 1972), 37-69.

[118] Cagle, Laurence T. and Irwin Deutscher. "Housing Aspirations and Housing Achievement: The Relocation of Poor Families," *Social Problems*, XVIII (2) (Fall 1970), 243-256.

[119] California Department of Housing and Community Development. *Demonstration in Low-Cost Housing Techniques.* Sacramento, California: California Department of Housing and Community Development, 1970. (Carried out with financial aid from the U.S. Department of Housing and Urban Development. Project California L.I.H.D. #3. Contract #H-650.)

*[120] Campbell, A.K. and J. Burkhear. "Public Policy for Urban America," in Harvey S. Perloff and Lowdon Wingo, Jr. (eds.). *Issues in Urban Economics.* Baltimore: The Johns Hopkins University Press, 1967, 577-647.

*[121] Carnegie, Christa Lew. "Homeownership for the Poor: Running the Washington Gauntlet," *Journal of the American Institute of Planners*, XXXVI (May 1970), 160-167.

[122] Carreiro, Joseph, Allen Bushnell, Joseph Koncelik, Charles Pearman, Howard Levirne, and Steven Mensch. *The New Building Block: A Report on the Factory-Produced Dwelling Module.* Ithaca, New York: Center for Urban Development Research, Cornell University, 1968.

[123] Case, Frederick E. "Code Enforcement in Urban Renewal," *Urban Studies*, V (3) (November 1968), 277-289. (Reprint no. 52, The Housing, Real Estate, and Land Studies Program, University of California at Los Angeles.)

*[124] _____. "Housing Demand Characteristics of Underhoused Families in the Inner City," *The Annals of Regional Science*, 111 (December 1969), 15-26.

[125] _____. "Housing the Underhoused in the Inner City," *The Journal of Finance*, XXVI (2) (May 1971), 427-444.

[126] _____ (ed.). *Inner-City Housing and Private Enterprise; Based on Studies in Nine Cities.* New York: Praeger Publishers, 1972. (Praeger Special Studies in U.S. Economic and Social Development.)

*[127] _____. "Prediction of the Incidence of Urban Residential Blight," *Regional Science Association, Papers and Proceedings*, LXXI (1963), 211-214.

[128] _____. *Tax Rates and Land Use in Los Angeles County.* Los Angeles: Real Estate Research Program, Graduate School of Business Administration, Division of Research, University of California at Los Angeles,

1964. (Reprint no. 40. Reprinted from *Papers and Proceedings of the Regional Science Association*, Third Annual Meeting, 1964.)

[129] Center for Community Change, The and The National Urban League. *The National Survey of Housing Abandonment.* New York: The Center for Community Change and The National Urban League, 1972. (Third edition.)

*[130] Center for National Policy Review (The), School of Law, Catholic University of America. *Shelter and Surplus Land: A Report on the Potential of Federal Surplus Property.* Washington, D.C.: The Center for National Policy Review, School of Law, Catholic University of America, June 1973.

*[131] Chapin, F. Stuart, Jr. "A Model for Stimulating Residential Development," *Journal of the American Institute of Planners*, XXXI (3) (May 1965), 120-125.

[132] _____ and Henry C. Hightower. "Household Activity Patterns and Land Use," *Journal of the American Institute of Planners*, XXXI (3) (August 1965), 222-231.

*[133] _____ and Shirley F. Weiss. *Some Input Refinements for a Residential Model.* Chapel Hill, North Carolina: Center for Urban and Regional Studies, University of North Carolina, 1965.

[134] Cheng, Pao Lun. "The Common Level of Assessment in Property Taxation," *National Tax Journal*, XXIII (1) (March 1970), 50-65.

[135] Childs, Gerald L. "Efficient Reallocation of Land in Urban Renewal," *Western Economic Journal*, VII (September 1969), 211-222.

*[136] Chinitz, Benjamin and C.M. Tiebout. "The Role of Cost-Benefit Analysis in the Public Sector of Metropolitan Areas," in Julius Margolis (ed.). *The Public Economy of Urban Communities.* Washington, D.C.: Resources for the Future, 1965. (Papers presented at Second Conference on Urban Public Expenditures, under sponsorship of Committee on Urban Economics of Resources for the Future.)

*[137] Christy, Lawrence C. and Peter W. Coogan. "Family Relocation in Urban Renewal," *Harvard Law Review*, LXXXII (4) (February 1969), 864-907.

[138] Chung, Hyung C. *The Economics of Residential Rehabilitation: Social Life of Housing in Harlem.* New York: Praeger Publishers, 1973.

[139] Cicarelli, James and Clifford Landers. "The Cost of Housing for the Poor: A Case Study," *Land Economics*, XLVIII (1) (February 1972), 53-57.

[140] Citizens League Committee on Rebuilding in the Central Cities. *Building Confidence in Older Neighborhoods; a "Pooled" Approach to the Maintenance, Management and Marketing of Houses to Help Preserve the Strength of Residential Areas in Minneapolis and St. Paul.* Minneapolis, Minnesota: Citizens League Committee in Rebuilding in the Central Cities, 1973.

[141] Clawson, Marion. *Suburban Land Conversion in the United States: An Economic and Governmental Process.* Baltimore and London: The Johns Hopkins University Press, 1971.

[142] _____. "Urban Sprawl and Speculation in Suburban Land," *Land Economics*, XXXVIII (2) (May 1962), 99-111.

*[143] Cohen, Benjamin I. "Another Theory of Residential Segregation," *Land Economics*, XLVII (3) (August 1972), 314-315.

[144] _____. *Public Land Use Controls and the Residential Location of the Poor.* New Haven, Connecticut: Center for the Study of the City and its Environment, Institution for Social and Policy Studies, Yale University, 1973. (A working paper.)

*[145] Cohn, Jules. "Is Business Meeting the Challenge of Urban Affairs?" *Harvard Business Review*, XLVIII (2) (March-April 1970), 68-82.

[146] Coke, James G. and John J. Gargan. *Fragmentation in Land-Use Planning and Control.* Washington, D.C.: National Commission on Urban Problems, 1969. (Research report no. 18.)

[147] Cole, John D. "The Role of the Appraiser," in Tax Institute of America. *The Property Tax: Problems and Potential.* Princeton, New Jersey: Tax Institute of America, 1967, 111-119.

[148] Coleman, Richard P. *Seven Levels of Housing: An Exploration in Public Imagery.* Cambridge, Massachusetts: Joint Center for Urban Studies, 1973. (Working paper no. 20.)

[149] Committee on Housing Research and Development. *Activities and Attitudes of Public Housing Residents: Rockford, Illinois.* Urbana, Illinois: Committee on Housing Research and Development, University of Illinois at Urbana-Champaign, 1971.

[150] Comptroller General of the United States. *Limited Success of Investor-Sponsor Cooperative Housing Program.* Washington, D.C.: Comptroller General of the United States, 1968.

[151] Congressional Research Service, Library of Congress. *The Central City Problem and Urban Renewal Policy.* Washington, D.C.: U.S. Government Printing Office, 1973. (Prepared for the Subcommittee on Housing and Urban Affairs, Committee on Banking, Housing and Urban Affairs, United States Senate.)

[152] Congressional Research Service. *Property Taxation: Effects on Land Use and Local Government Revenues.* Washington, D.C.: U.S. Government Printing Office, 1971. (A background study prepared for the Subcommittee on Intergovernmental Relations of the Committee on Government Operations, United States Senate, 92d Congress, 1st Session.)

[153] Cooper, James R. *Can the 1968-78 National Housing Goals be Achieved? An Examination of the Economic, Social and Political Forces which Affect the Efficient Production of Housing to Meet the Needs of All Americans.* Urbana, Illinois: Committee on Housing Research and Development, University of Illinois at Urbana-Champaign, 1971.

[154] Cord, Steven. "How Land Value Taxation would Affect Homeowners," *The American Journal of Economics and Sociology*, XXXII (2) (April 1973), 153-154.

[155] _____. "The Role of the Graded Tax in Urban Redevelopment: A Case Study of Lancaster, Pennsylvania," *The American Journal of Economics and Sociology*, XXIX (3) (July 1970), 321-328.

[156] _____. "Tax Reform and Urban Renewal," *American Journal of Economics and Sociology*, XXX (4) (October 1971), 395-396.

*[157] Crandall, R.W. and C.D. MacRae. "Economic Subsidies in the Urban Ghetto." *Social Science Quarterly* (December 1971), 492-507.

[158] Crecine, John P., Otto A. Davis, and John E. Jackson. "Urban Property Markets: Some Empirical Results and Their Implications for Municipal Zoning," *The Journal of Law and Economics*, X (October 1967), 79-99.

*[159] Cullingworth, J.B. "Housing and the State: The Responsibilities of Government," in A.A. Nevitt. *The Economic Problems of Housing*. New York: St. Martin's Press, 1967.

*[160] Cunningham, Roger A. "Land-Use Control—The State and Local Programs," *Iowa Law Review*, L (Winter 1965), 243.

[161] Curran, Donald J. "The General Property Tax and Residential Rehabilitation," *National Tax Association Proceedings*, 1964, 250-258.

[162] Curry, S. Leigh, Jr. "The Federal Role in Housing Code Enforcement," *The Urban Lawyer*, 111 (4) (Fall 1971), 567-573.

[163] Czamanski, Stanislaw. "Effects of Public Investments on Urban Land Values," *Journal of the American Institute of Planners*, XXXII (4) (July 1966), 204-217.

*[164] _____. "A Model of Urban Growth," *Regional Science Association, Papers and Proceedings*, XIII (1964), 177-200.

*[165] _____. "A Model of Urban Land Allocation," *Growth and Change*, IV (1) (January 1973), 43-48.

*[166] Dacy, Douglas C. "Productivity and Price Trends in Construction Since 1947," *Review of Economics and Statistics*, XLVII (4) (November 1965), 406-411.

*[167] Daicoff, Darwin W. *Capitalization of the Property Tax*. Ann Arbor, Michigan: Ph.D. dissertation, University Microfilms, University of Michigan, 1962.

*[168] Daly, Grover and D. Robert Papera. "The Sale and Financing of On-the-Lot Housing," *Land Economics*, XL (November 1964), 433-437.

[169] Dasso, Jerome. "An Evaluation of Rent Supplements," *Land Economics*, XLIV (4) (November 1968), 441-449.

*[170] Davidoff, Paul and Neil N. Gold. "Exclusionary Zoning," *Yale Review of Law and Society*, (1) (1971), 56.

*[171] Davis, J. Taft. "Middle Class Housing in the Central City," *Economic Geography*, XLI (July 1965), 238-251.

[172] Davis, Otto A. "Economic Elements in Municipal Zoning Decisions," *Land Economics*, XXXIX (4) (November 1963), 375-386.
[173] _____. "A Pure Theory of Urban Renewal," *Land Economics*, XXXVI (2) (May 1960), 220-226.
[174] _____ and Kenneth L. Wertz. "The Consistency of the Assessment of Property: Some Empirical Results and Managerial Suggestions," *Applied Economics*, 1 (2) (May 1969), 151-157.
[175] _____ and Andrew B. Whinston. "The Economics of Complex Systems: The Case of Municipal Zoning," *Kyklos*, XVII (3) (1964), 419-446.
[176] _____. "The Economics of Urban Renewal," *Law and Contemporary Problems*, XXVI (4) (Winter 1961), 105-117.
[177] Day, Kenneth C. "Municipal Corporations—Public Purpose—Taxation and Revenue Bonds to Finance Low-Income Housing," *North Carolina Law Review*, IL (4) (June 1971), 830-838.
*[178] Delafons, J. *Land Use Controls in the United States*. Cambridge, Massachusetts: The Massachusetts Institute of Technology Press, 1969.
*[179] DeLeeuw, Frank. *The Cost of Leased Housing*. Washington, D.C.: Urban Land Institute, 1971.
[180] _____. *Operating Costs in Public Housing; A Financial Crisis*. Washington, D.C.: The Urban Institute, 1969.
*[181] _____ and Nkanta F. Ekanem. *The Demand for Housing: A Review of Cross-Section Evidence*. Washington, D.C.: The Urban Institute, 1970. (Urban Institute working paper 112-114.)
[182] _____. "The Supply of Rental Housing," *American Economic Review*, LXI (5) (December 1971), 806-817.
*[183] _____. *Time Lags in the Rental Housing Market*. Washington, D.C.: The Urban Institute, 1970.
[184] DeLeeuw, Frank and Sam H. Leaman. "The Section 23 Leasing Program," *The Economics of Federal Subsidy Programs*. Washington, D.C.: U.S. Government Printing Office, 1972, 642-659. (A compendium of papers submitted to the Joint Economic Committee, Congress of the United States. Part 5—Housing Subsidies. October 9, 1972.)
[185] _____ and Helen Blank. *The Design of a Housing Allowance*. Washington, D.C.: The Urban Institute, 1970. (UI 112-25.)
*[186] Delson, Jerome K. "Correction on the Boundary Conditions in Beckmann's Model on Urban Rent and Residential Density," *Journal of Economic Theory*, II (September 1970), 314-318.
*[187] Deming, Frederick W. "The Federal Government and The Mortgage Lender," *Real Estate Review*, 1 (Summer 1971).
*[188] Denton, John H. (ed.). *Race and Property*. Berkeley, California: Diablo Press, 1964.
*[189] Derthick, Martha. *New Towns in-Town: Why a Federal Program Failed*. Washington, D.C.: The Urban Institute, 1972.

[190] DeSalvo, Joseph S. *Effects of the Property Tax on Operating and Investment Decisions of Rental Property Owners.* Santa Monica, California: The RAND Corporation, 1970.

[191] _____. *A Methodology for Evaluating Housing Programs.* Santa Monica, California: The RAND Corporation, 1970. (P-4364-1.)

[192] _____. "Reforming Rent Control in New York City: Analysis of Housing Expenditures and Market Rentals," *Papers and Proceedings of the Regional Science Association,* XXVII (1971), 195-227.

[193] Devine, Richard J., Winston O. Rennie, and N. Brenda Sims. *Where the Lender Looks First: A Case Study of Mortgage Disinvestment in Bronx County, 1960-1970.* New York: National Urban League, Inc., 1973.

*[194] Dick, Brett R. and John S. Pfarr. "Detroit Housing Code Enforcement and Community Renewal: A Study in Futility," *Prospectus: A Journal of Law Reform,* 111 (December 1969), 61.

*[195] Dickerman, John M. "Housing, A Social Paradox: Facing A Twin Challenge," in Melvin R. Laird (ed.). *Republican Papers.* New York: Praeger, 1968.

[196] Donnison, D.V. "The Political Economy of Housing," in Adela A. Nevitt (ed.). *The Economic Problems of Housing.* New York: MacMillan and Company, 1967.

[197] Dougharty, L.A. *Forces Shaping Urban Development: The Property Tax.* Santa Monica, California: The RAND Corporation, 1973. (P-5022.)

*[198] Downs, Anthony. "Are Subsidies the Best Answer for Housing Low and Moderate Income Households?" *The Urban Lawyer,* IV (Summer 1972), 405-416.

[199] _____. *Federal Housing Subsidies: How Are They Working?* Chicago: Real Estate Research Corporation, 1972.

*[200] _____. "Home Ownership and American Free Enterprise," in Anthony Downs (ed.). *Urban Problems and Prospects.* Chicago: Markham, 1970.

[201] _____. "Housing the Urban Poor: The Economics of Various Strategies," *American Economic Review,* LIX (September 1969), 646-651.

[202] _____. "Moving Toward Realistic Housing Goals," in Kermit Gordon (ed.). *Agenda for the Nation.* Washington, D.C.: The Brookings Institution, 1968.

[203] _____. *Summary Report. Federal Housing Subsidies: Their Nature and Effectiveness and What We Should Do About Them.* Washington, D.C.: The National Association of Home Builders, 1972.

[204] _____. *Summary Report; Federal Housing Subsidies: Their Nature and Effectiveness and What We Should Do About Them.* Washington, D.C.: The National Association of Home Builders, 1972.

*[205] Drury, Margaret J. *Mobile Homes: The Unrecognized Revolution in American Housing.* New York: Praeger Publishers, 1970.

*[206] Ducey, John McMullen and K.R. Berlient. *Loan Closing Costs on Single Family Homes in Six Metropolitan Areas.* Washington, D.C.: The Institute of Urban Life, 1965.

*[207] Duhl, Leonard J. (ed.). *The Urban Condition.* New York: Basic Books, 1963.

[208] Duncan, Joseph W. "New Approaches to Low-Cost Housing," *Business Economics*, IV (1) (January 1969), 53-56.

*[209] Eacret, David T. *The Economics of Industrialized Housing: Effects of Modular Production on the Residential Construction Industry.* Ann Arbor, Michigan: Ph.D. dissertation, Colorado State University, University Microfilms, 1972.

*[210] Eastburn, D.P. "Housing in the 1970's—What Can the Federal Reserve Do About It?" *Federal Reserve Bank of Philadelphia Business Review* (April 1970), 4-8.

*[211] Eaves, Elsie. *How the Many Costs of Housing Fit Together.* Washington, D.C.: U.S. Government Printing Office. (National Commission on Urban Problems, research report no. 16.)

*[212] _____. *The Multi-Layer Housing Dollar.* Washington, D.C.: U.S. Government Printing Office, 1966. (National Commission on Urban Problems background paper.)

[213] Ecker-Racz, L.L. "Limitations on the Taxation of Property," *Assessment Administration, 1965: Proceedings of the Thirty-First International Conference on Assessment Administration*, 14-20.

[214] Edel, Matthew. "Urban Renewal and Land Use Conflicts," *The Review of Radical Political Economics*, 111 (3) (Summer 1971), 76-89.

[215] Edgley, Charles K., W.G. Steglich, and Walter J. Cartwright. "Rent Subsidy and Housing Satisfaction: The Case of Urban Renewal in Lubbock, Texas," *The American Journal of Economics and Sociology*, XXVII (2) (April 1968), 113-124.

[216] Edson, Charles L. *Home Ownership for Low-Income Families.* Chicago: National Legal Aid and Defender association, 1969.

*[217] _____. "Housing Abandonment—The Real Problem and a Proposed Solution," *Real Property, Probate and Trust Journal*, VII (Summer 1972), 382.

[218] Eichler, Edward P. and Marshall Kaplan. *The Community Builders.* Berkeley and Los Angeles: University of California Press, 1967.

[219] Eisenstadt, Karen M. *Factors Affecting Maintenance and Operating Costs in Private Rental Housing.* New York: The New York City RAND Institute, 1972. (R-1055-NYC.)

*[220] Eldridge, Mark T. *Explorations into Decision Factors in the Rental Market.* Chapel Hill, North Carolina: Center for Urban and Regional Studies, University of North Carolina, 1967. (Environmental Policies and Urban Development Thesis Series #9.)

*[221] Eley, Lynn W. and Thomas W. Casstevens. *The Politics of Fair-Housing Legislation: State and Local Case Studies.* San Francisco: Chandler Publishing Company, 1968.

[222] Elias, C.E., Jr. and James Gillies. *Some Observations on the Role of Speculators and Speculation in Land Development.* Los Angeles. Graduate School of Business, University of California at Los Angeles, 1965. (Reprint no. 38.)

[223] Ellickson, Robert. "Government Housing Assistance to the Poor," *The Yale Law Journal*, LXXVI (3) (January 1967), 508-545.

*[224] "Enforcement of Municipal Housing Codes," *Harvard Law Review*, LXXVIII (Fall 1965), 801.

[225] Engle, Robert F., III, Franklin M. Fisher, John R. Harriss, and Jerome Rothenberg. "An Econometric Simulation Model of Intra-Metropolitan Housing Location: Housing, Business, Transportation, and Local Government," *Papers and Proceedings, American Economic Association* (May 1972), 87-97.

*[226] Fairfax County Planning Division. *Student Contribution from Apartments and Mobile Homes.* Fairfax, Virginia: Fairfax County Planning Division, 1966.

[227] Falk, Karl. "Property Tax Reform: A Revitalized Property Tax Could Help Develop Better Housing, Better Cities," *Journal of Housing*, XXIV (1) (January 1967), 39-42.

[228] Farley, William and Michael Liechenstein. *Improving Public Safety in Urban Apartment Dwellings: Security, Concepts and Experimental Design for New York City Housing Authority Buildings.* New York: The New York City RAND Institute, 1971. (R-655-NYC.)

[229] "Federal Aids for Enforcement of Housing Codes," *New York University Law Review*, XL (5) (November 1965), 948-977.

*[230] Feiler, Michael H. "Metropolitanization and Land Use Parochialism— Toward a Judicial Attitude," *Michigan Law Review*, LXIX (March 1971), 655.

[231] Field, Charles G. and Francis T. Ventre. "Local Regulation of Building: Agencies, Codes, and Politics," in International City Management Association. *The Municipal Year Book 1971.* Washington, D.C.: International City Management Association, 1971, 139-165.

[232] Fielding, Byron. "How Useful Are Rent Supplements in Meeting Low-Income Housing Needs," *The Journal of Housing*, XXVI (1) (January 1969), 12-17.

[233] Finn, Joseph T. "Labor Requirements for Public Housing," *Monthly Labor Review*, XCV (4) (April 1972), 40-41.

*[234] Fischer, Donald E. and Keith D. Johnson. *The Residential Mortgage Market in Southeastern Connecticut: A Survey.* Storrs, Connecticut: University of Connecticut School of Business Administration, 1969. (Real estate report no. 9.)

*[235] Fisher, Ernest M. "Twenty Years of Rent Control in New York City," *Essays in Urban Land Economics in Honor of the Sixty-fifth Birthday of Leo Grebler*. Los Angeles: Real Estate Research Program, University of California at Los Angeles, 1966, 31-67.

*[236] Fisher, H. Benjamin. *Evaluation of Alternative Plans for New Communities: Toward Application of the Competition-For-Benefits Model*. Chapel Hill, North Carolina: University of North Carolina, 1971.

*[237] Fisher, Robert Moore. "Monetary Policy: Its Relation to Mortgage Lending and Land Economics," *Land Economics*, XLV (November 1969), 418-424.

*[238] Fishman, Joshua A. "Some Social and Psychological Determinants of Inter-group Relations in Changing Neighborhoods: An Introduction to the Bridgeview Study," *Social Forces* (October 1961), 42-51.

[239] Forrester, Jay W. *Urban Dynamics*. Cambridge, Massachusetts: The Massachusetts Institute of Technology Press, 1969.

*[240] Foster, Howard G. "Unions, Residential Construction, and Public Policy," *Quarterly Review of Economics and Business* XII (Winter 1972), 45-55.

[241] Franklin, Herbert M. *Controlling Urban Growth—But for Whom?* Washington, D.C.: The Potomac Institute, Inc., 1973.

*[242] _____. "The Federal Government as 'Houser of Last Resort': A Policy for Democratic Urban Growth," *Urban Law Annual*. St. Louis, Missouri: School of Law, Washington University, 1972, 23-24.

*[243] _____ "Federal Power and Subsidized Housing," *The Urban Lawyer*, III (Winter 1971), 61.

[244] Freedman, Leonard. *Public Housing; The Politics of Poverty*. New York: Holt, Rinehart and Winston, Inc., 1969.

[245] Freeman, Elsa S. "HUD's Library: A National Resource," *HUD Challenge* (March 1974), 15-17.

*[246] Fried, Joseph. *Housing Crisis U.S.A.* New York: Praeger Publishers, 1971.

*[247] Fried, Marc. "Grieving for a Lost Home: Psychological Costs of Relocation," in James Q. Wilson (ed.). *Urban Renewal*. Cambridge, Massachusetts: The Massachusetts Institute of Technology Press, 1966.

[248] Frieden, Bernard J. *The Future of Old Neighborhoods: Rebuilding for a Changing Population*. Cambridge, Massachusetts: The Massachusetts Institute of Technology Press, 1964. (Published for the Joint Center for Urban Studies of the Massachusetts Institute of Technology and Harvard University.)

*[249] _____. "Housing and National Urban Goals: Old Policies and New Realities," in James Q. Wilson (ed.). *The Metropolitan Enigma: Inquiries into the Nature and Dimensions of America's Urban Crisis*. Cambridge, Massachusetts: Harvard University Press, 1968.

[250] _____. *Improving Federal Housing Subsidies: Summary Report*. Cam-

bridge, Massachusetts: Massachusetts Institute of Technology, 1972. (Prepared for Housing Subcommittee, House Committee on Banking and Currency, U.S. Congress.)

*[251] Friedlander, Ann. *The Interstate Highway System: A Study in Public Investment.* Amsterdam: North-Holland Publishing Company, 1975.

[252] Friedman, Lawrence Meir. "Government and Slum Housing: Some General Considerations." *Law and Contemporary Problems*, XXXII (2) (Spring 1967), 357-370.

[253] _____ and James E. Krier. *A New Lease on Life: Section 23 Housing and the Poor.* Madison, Wisconsin: Institute for Research on Poverty, The University of Wisconsin, 1967.

*[254] Furstenthal, Joseph, John L. Lineweaver, and Richard H. Reel, Jr. *Federally Assisted Low Income Housing Programs—Three Case Studies.* Berkeley: The Center for Real Estate and Urban Economics, University of California, 1972.

[255] Gaffney, Mason. "An Agenda for Strengthening the Property Tax," in George E. Peterson (ed.). *Property Tax Reform.* Washington, D.C.: The Urban Institute, 1973, 65-84.

[256] _____. "Containment Policies for Urban Sprawl," in Richard L. Stauber (ed.). *Approaches to the Study of Urbanization.* Lawrence, Kansas: Governmental Research Center, University of Kansas, 1964, 115-133.

[257] _____. "Land Planning and the Property Tax," *Journal of the American Institute of Planners*, XXXV (3) (May 1969), 178-183.

[258] _____. "Land Rent, Taxation, and Public Policy: The Sources, Nature and Functions of Urban Land Rent," *The American Journal of Economics and Sociology*, XXXI (3) (July 1972), 241-257.

[259] _____. "Land Rent, Taxation and Public Policy: Taxation and the Functions of Urban Land Rent," *The American Journal of Economics and Sociology*, XXXII (1) (January 1973), 17-34.

[260] _____. "Policies and Practices Affecting Urban Land Costs as an Element of Housing Costs," in Mason Gaffney et al. *Land as an Element of Housing Costs: The Effects of Public Policies and Practices; The Effects of Housing Demand.* Arlington, Virginia: Institute for Defense Analysis, 1968, 1-37.

[261] _____. "Property Taxes and the Frequency of Urban Renewal," *National Tax Association Proceedings*, 1964, 272-285.

[262] _____. "What is Property Tax Reform?" *The American Journal of Economics and Sociology*, XXXI (2) (April 1972), 139-152.

[263] Gallagher, John R. III, and John J. O'Donnell, Jr. *Nonprofit Housing: Rent Supplement Program Under Section 221(d)(3).* Washington, D.C.: Nonprofit Housing Center, Urban America, Inc., 1968.

[264] Gallaway, Lowell E. "Urban Decay and the Labor Market," *The*

Quarterly Review of Economics and Business, VII (4) (Winter 1967), 7-16.
*[265] Gans, Herbert J. "The Human Implications of Current Redevelopment and Relocation Planning," *Journal of American Institute of Planners*, XXV (1961).
*[266] _____. *The Urban Villagers: Group and Class in the Life of Italian-Americans.* New York: The Free Press, 1962.
*[267] Garrity, Paul G. "Community Economic Development and Low-Income Housing Development," *Law and Contemporary Problems*, XXXVI (2) (Spring 1971), 191-204.
 [268] Geddes, Robert L. et al. *Cooperation of the Public and Private Sectors in Housing.* Princeton, New Jersey: School of Architecture, Princeton University, 1968.
*[269] Gelfand, Jack E. *Financing Lower-Middle Income Housing.* Philadelphia: Bureau of Economic and Business Research, Temple University, 1964.
 [270] _____. "Mortgage Credit and Lower-Middle Income Housing Demand," *Land Economics*, XLVI (2) (May 1970), 163-170.
 [271] _____. "The Credit Elasticity of Lower-Middle Income Housing Demand," *Land Economics*, XLII (4) (November 1966), 464-472.
 [272] Genung, George R., Jr. "Public Housing—Success or Failure," *The George Washington Law Review*, XXXIX (4) (May 1971), 734-763.
 [273] George Schermer and Associates. *More Than Shelter; Social Needs in Low- and Moderate-Income Housing.* Washington, D.C.: National Commission on Urban Problems, 1968. (Research report no. 8.)
*[274] Georgia Institute of Technology, Graduate City Planning Program. *Report of a Study of Housing Developments and Their Effect on County Fiscal Capacity.* Atlanta: Georgia Institute of Technology, Graduate City Planning Program, 1970.
 [275] Getz, Malcolm. *A Model of the Impact of Transportation Investment on Land Rents.* New Haven, Connecticut: Institution for Social and Policy Studies, Yale University, 1973. (Working paper W3-1.)
*[276] Gibson, Constance B. *Policy Alternatives for Mobile Homes.* New Brunswick, New Jersey: Center for Urban Policy Research, Rutgers University, 1972.
*[277] Gillies, J. "The Future of Federal Housing Policies in the U.S.," in A.A. Nevitt (ed.). *The Economic Problems of Housing.* New York: St. Martin's Press, 1967.
 [278] Gilman, Marvin S. "Homeownership for Low-Income Families Under Section 235," in National Urban Coalition. *Private Capital and Low-Income Housing.* Washington, D.C.: National Urban Coalition, 64-79.
*[279] Glazer, Nathan. "Housing Problems and Housing Policies," *The Public Interest* (Spring 1967), 21-56.
*[280] Goetze, Rolf. *Conserving the Urban Housing Stock: A Set of Case*

Studies on the Impact of Government Policy. Cambridge, Massachusetts: Ph.D. dissertation, Massachusetts Institute of Technology, 1970.

[281] Goldberg, Arthur Abba. "State Agencies: Housing Assistance at the Grass Roots," *Real Estate Review*, 1 (4) (Winter 1972), 14-19.

*[282] Goldberg, Michael A. "Transportation, Urban Land Values and Rents: A Synthesis," *Land Economics*, XLVI (2) (May 1970), 153-162.

*[283] Goldfinger, N. "Labor Costs and the Rise in Housing Prices," *Monthly Labor Review* XCIII (May 1970), 60-61.

[284] Gordon, R.J. "A New View of Real Investment in Structure, 1919-1966," *Review of Economics and Statistics*, L (4) (November 1968), 417-428.

*[285] Gottschalk, Shimon. "Citizen Participation in the Development of New Towns: A Cross-National View," *Social Service Review*, XLV (June 1971), 194-204.

*[286] "Government Housing Assistance to the Poor," *Yale Law Journal*, LXXVI (January 1967), 508.

*[287] "Government Programs to Encourage Private Investment in Low Income Housing," *Harvard Law Review*, LXXXI (April 1968), 1295.

[288] Grad, Frank P. *Legal Remedies For Housing Code Violations.* Washington, D.C.: National Commission on Urban Problems, 1968. (Research report no. 14.)

*[289] Gramlich, Edward and Dwight M. Jaffee. *Savings Deposits, Mortgages, and Housing.* Lexington, Massachusetts: Lexington Books D.C. Heath and Co., 1972.

*[290] Grebler, Leo. "The Housing Inventory: Analytic Concept and Quantitative Change," *American Economic Review* (May 1951), 555-568.

[291] _____. "Land Reform in Urban Renewal Programs: A Comparative Analysis," *The Western Economic Journal*, 1 (2) (Spring 1963), 93-102.

[292] _____. *Production of New Housing: A Research Monograph on Efficiency in Production.* New York: Social Science Research Council, 1950.

[293] Greenberg, Stanley B. *The Etiology of Poor Neighborhoods.* New Haven, Connecticut: Institution for Social and Policy Studies, Yale University, 1973 (Working paper W3-5.)

[294] Greenbie, Barrie Barstow. "New House or New Neighborhood? A Survey of Priorities Among Home Owners in Madison, Wisconsin," *Land Economics*, XLV (3) (August 1969), 359-365.

*[295] _____. "Social Territory, Community Health, and Urban Planning," *Journal of the American Institute of Planning*, XL (2) (March 1974) 74-82.

*[296] Greenleigh Associates. *An Evaluation of the Urban Observatory Program* (January 1974).

[297] Greenstein, Abraham J. "Federally Assisted Code Enforcement: Problems and Approaches," *The Urban Lawyer*, III (4) (Fall 1971), 629-642.

*[298] Greer, Scott. *Urban Renewal and American Cities*. Indianapolis: Bobbs-Merrill, 1965.

[299] Grey, Arthur L., Jr. "Urban Renewal and Land Value Taxation," in Arthur P. Becker (ed.). *Land and Building Taxes: Their Effect on Economic Development*. Madison, Wisconsin: University of Wisconsin Press, 1969, 81-96.

[300] Gribetz, Judah and Frank P. Grad. "Housing Code Enforcement: Sanctions and Remedies," *Columbia Law Review*, LXVI (7) (November 1966), 1254-1290.

[301] Grier, Eunice S. *Large Family-Rent Subsidy Demonstration Program*. Washington, D.C.: National Capital Housing Authority, 1965.

*[302] _____ and George Grier. *The Impact of Race on Neighborhoods in the Metropolitan Setting*. Washington, D.C.: Washington Center for Metropolitan Studies, 1961.

*[303] Grier, George C. "The Negro Ghettos and Federal Housing Policy," *Law and Contemporary Problems*, XXXII (3) (Summer 1967), 550-560.

[304] Grigsby, William G. "Economic Aspects of Code Enforcement," *The Urban Lawyer*, 111 (4) (Fall 1971), 533-537.

*[305] _____. *Housing Markets and Public Policy*. Philadelphia: University of Pennsylvania Press, 1963.

[306] _____. *Possible Impacts of the Guaranteed Annual Income on Urban Housing*. Philadelphia: Institute for Environmental Studies, University of Pennsylvania, 1969.

[307] Groberg, Robert P. *Centralized Relocation: A New Municipal Service*. Washington, D.C.: National Association of Housing and Redevelopment Officials, 1969. (Publication no. N533.)

[308] Groves, Harold M. "Property Tax—Effects and Limitations," in Tax Institute of America. *The Property Tax: Problems and Potential*. Princeton, New Jersey: Tax Institute of America, 1967, 17-27.

*[309] Gruen, Claude. *The Socio-Economic Determinants of Urban Residential Housing Quality*. Ann Arbor, Michigan: Ph.D. dissertation, University of Cincinnati, University Microfilms, 1964.

[310] _____. "Urban Renewal's Role in the Genesis of Tomorrow's Slums," *Land Economics*, XXXIX (3) (August 1963), 285-291.

[311] Gruen, Nina Jaffe and Claude Gruen. *Low and Moderate Income Housing in the Suburbs: An Analysis for the Dayton, Ohio Region*. New York: Praeger Publishers, 1972. (Praeger Special Studies in U.S. economic and social development.)

*[312] Guandolo, Joseph. "Housing Codes in Urban Renewal." *George Washington Law Review*, XXV (October 1956), 15.

*[313] Guido, Kenneth J., Jr. "The Impact of the Tax Reform Act of 1969 on the Supply of Adequate Housing," *Vanderbilt Law Review*, XXV (March 1972), 289.

*[314] Gurko, Stephen. "Federal Income Taxes and Urban Sprawl," *Denver Law Journal*, XLVIII (1972), 329.

[315] Hagman, Donald G. "The Single Tax and Land-use Planning: Henry George Updated," *UCLA Law Review*, XII (3) (March 1965), 762-788.

*[316] Hale, Carl W. "Optimality of Local Subsidies in Regional Development Programs," *Quarterly Review of Economics and Business*, IX (Autumn 1969) 35-50.

[317] Halperin, Jerome Y. "Analysis of a 236 Project," in National Urban Coalition. *Private Capital and Low-Income Housing.* Washington, D.C.: National Urban Coalition, 79-94.

[318] Hamilton, Bruce W. *The Impact of Zoning and Property Taxes on Urban Structure and Housing Markets.* Princeton, New Jersey, Ph.D. dissertation, Princeton University, 1972.

[319] _____, "Property Taxation's Incentive to Fiscal Zoning," in George E. Peterson (ed.). *Property Tax Reform.* Washington, D.C.: The Urban Institute, 1973, 125-139.

[320] Hammer, Greene, Siler Associates. *Regional Housing Planning; A Technical Guide.* Washington, D.C.: The American Institute of Planners, 1972. (Under contract to the U.S. Department of Housing and Urban Development.)

*[321] Hanke, Byron R. "Planned Unit Development and Land Use Intensity," *University of Pennsylvania Law Review*, CXIV (3) (November 1965).

[322] Harberger, Arnold C. "The Incidence of the Corporation Income Tax," *The Journal of Political Economy*, LXX (3) (June 1962), 215-240.

*[323] Harris, Britton. *The Location and Structure of Housing Demand and Supply.* Philadelphia: Institute for Environmental Studies, University of Pennsylvania, 1973.

*[324] Harris, Britton, Douglas Lee, Jr., and J.B. Schneider. "A Review Forum." *Journal of the American Institute of Planners*, XL (3) (May 1974), 212-215.

*[325] _____, Joseph Nathanson, and Louis Rosenburg. *Research on an Equilibrium Model of Metropolitan Housing and Locational Choice, Interim Report.* Institute for Environmental Studies, Graduate School of Fine Arts, University of Pennsylvania, March 1966.

*[326] Harris, Curtis C., Jr. "A Stochastic Process Model of Residential Development," *Journal of Regional Science*, VIII (1) (1968), 29-40.

*[327] Harris, R.N.S., G.S. Tolley, and C. Harrell. "The Residence Site Choice," *Review of Economics and Statistics* (August 1968), 241-247.

[328] Harris, Robert. *Policy Analysis and Policy Development.* Washington, D.C.: The Urban Institute, 1973.

*[329] Harrison, Gilbert Warner. "The FHA Condominium, Use as a Means of Meeting the Need for Moderate Income Housing," *New York Law Forum* (Fall 1965), 458-502.

[330] Harriss, C. Lowell. "Economic Evaluation of Real Property Taxes," *Proceedings of the Academy of Political Science*, XXVIII (4) (January 1968), 489-512.

[331] _____ et al. "Land Value Taxation: Pro and Con," *Tax Policy*, XXXVII (9-12) (September-December 1970), 3-56.
[332] _____. *Property Taxation: Economic Aspects*. New York: Tax Foundation, Inc., 1968. (Government finance brief no. 13.)
[333] _____. "Property Taxes: Outlook and Effects," in Tax Institute of America. *The Property Tax: Problems and Potential*. Princeton, New Jersey: Tax Institute of America, 1967, 28-42.
[334] Hartman, Chester W. "The Housing of Relocated Families," *Journal of the American Institute of Planners*, XXX (4) (November 1964), 266-286.
[335] _____ and Gregg Carr. "Housing Authorities Reconsidered," *Journal of the American Institute of Planners*, XXXV (1) (January 1969), 10-21.
[336] _____. *Local Public Housing Administration: An Appraisal*. Berkeley, California: Institute of Urban and Regional Development, University of California, 1970. (Working paper no. 137.)
[337] Hartshorn, Truman A. "Inner City Residential Structure and Decline," *Annals of the Association of American Geographers* LXI (1) (March 1971), 72-96.
*[338] Harvard University Graduate School of Design. *Comparative Housing Study: Analyses of Housing Types and Comparative Designs of Dense Urban Residential Sectors*. Cambridge: Harvard University Graduate School of Design, 1958.
*[339] Harvard University Program on Technology and Society. *Technology and the City*. Cambridge, Massachusetts: Harvard University Press, 1970. (Research review no. 5.)
[340] Harvey, Robert O. and W.A.V. Clark. "The Nature and Economics of Urban Sprawl," *Land Economics,* XLI (1) (February 1965), 1-9.
[341] Haskell, Mark A. and Stephen Leshinski. "Fiscal Influences on Residential Choice: A Study of the New York Region," *The Quarterly Review of Economics and Business* IX (4) (Winter 1969), 47-55.
*[342] Haugen, Robert A. and A. James Heins. "A Market Separation Theory of Rent Differentials in Metropolitan Areas," *Quarterly Journal of Economics*, LXXXIII (November 1969), 660-672.
*[343] Hauser, Philip M. and M.B. Wirth. "Relocation: Opportunity or Liability?" in Margaret S. Gordon (ed.). *Poverty in America: Proceedings of a National Conference*. San Francisco: Chandler Publishing Co., 1965, 349-366. (Institute of Industrial Relations, University of California, Berkeley.)
*[344] Hausman, Leonard J. *Integrating Housing Allowances with AFDC, FAP and Other Transfer Programs*. Waltham, Massachusetts: The Florence Heller Graduate School for Advanced Studies in Social Welfare, Brandeis University, 1973.
[345] Heideman, M. Lawrence, Jr. "Public Implementation and Incentive Devices for Innovation and Experiment in Planned Urban Development," *Land Economics*, XLV (2) (May 1969), 262-267.

*[346] Heilbrun, James. *The Effects of Alternative Real Estate Taxes on the Maintenance and Rehabilitation of Urban Rental Housing.* Ann Arbor, Michigan: Ph.D. dissertation, Columbia University, University Microfilms, University of Michigan, 1964.
 [347] _____. *Real Estate Taxes and Urban Housing.* New York: Columbia University Press, 1966.
 [348] _____. "Reforming The Real Estate Tax to Encourage Housing Maintenance and Rehabilitation," in Arthur P. Becker (ed.). *Land and Building Taxes: Their Effect on Economic Development.* Madison, Wisconsin: The University of Wisconsin Press, 1969, 63-79.
*[349] _____. *Urban Economics and Public Policy.* New York: St. Martin's Press, 1974.
*[350] Heinberg, John D. *Housing Policy and Economic Stabilization; A Review and Analysis of the Evidence.* Washington, D.C.: The Urban Institute, 1969.
*[351] _____. "Housing Policy Goals and the Turnover of Housing," *Journal of the American Institute of Planners*, XXXI (3) (August 1965), 232-245.
 [352] _____. *Income Assistance Programs in Housing: Conceptual Issues and Benefit Patterns.* Washington, D.C.: The Urban Institute, 1970. (Working paper no. 112-18.)
 [353] _____. *Reply to HUD Draft Proposal on Rehabilitation Research.* Washington, D.C.: The Urban Institute, 1969. (Working paper no. 112-3.)
 [354] _____ and W.E. Oates. "The Incidence of Differential Property Taxes on Urban Housing: A Comment and Some Further Evidence," *National Tax Journal*, XXIII (1) (March 1970), 92-98.
*[355] Hempel, Donald J. *A Comparative Study of the Home Buying Process in Two Connecticut Housing Markets.* Storrs, Connecticut: Center for Real Estate and Urban Economic Studies, University of Connecticut, 1970. (CREUES real estate report no. 10.)
*[356] Herbert, John D. and B.H. Stevens. "A Model for the Distribution of Residential Activity in Urban Areas," *Journal of Regional Science*, II (Fall 1960), 21-36.
*[357] Herzog, John P. and James S. Earley. *Home Mortgage Delinquency and Foreclosure.* New York: National Bureau of Economic Research, 1970.
*[358] Higgins, Warren J. *Impact of Federal Taxation on Real Estate Decisions.* Storrs, Connecticut: Center for Real Estate and Urban Economic Studies, University of Connecticut, 1971. (CREUES report no. 11.)
 [359] Hills, Stuart L. "The Planned Suburban Community," *Land Economics*, XLV (2) (May 1969), 277-282.
*[360] Hirsch, Werner Z. "Administrative and Fiscal Considerations in Urban Development," in Robert B. Mitchell (ed.). *Urban Revival: Goals and*

Standards, American Academy of Political and Social Sciences, CCCLII (March 1964), 48-61.

*[361] Hodge, Patricia Leavey and Philip M. Hauser. *The Challenge of America's Metropolitan Outlook, 1960-1985*. New York: Praeger Publishers, 1968.

[362] Hoffman, Bernard Benjamin, Jr. *Forced Home Ownership: A Study of a Hypothesis which claims that Involuntary Ownership, Blighted Neighborhoods and Inordinate Property Taxation are Associated with Elderly and Single Owners in Older Suburbia and the Rural Urban Fringe.* Syracuse, New York: Syracuse University, 1967.

*[363] Hohn, P. "A Disaggregated Housing Market Model," in A.A. Nevitt (ed.). *The Economic Problems of Housing.* New York: St. Martin's Press, 1967.

[364] Holden, Arthur C. "The Interest Rate, Mortgage Debt, and Rent," *Land Economics*, XLII (1) (February 1966), 103-107.

*[365] Holley, Paul. *School Enrollment by Housing Type.* Chicago: American Society of Planning Officials, 1966. (Planning Advisory Service report no. 210.)

*[366] Hoskins, W. Lee. "Housing the Poor: A Frontal Attack," *Federal Reserve Bank Business Review* Philadelphia (November 1970), 6-16.

[367] Housing and Community Research Groups (The). *Community Housing Development Corporations; The Empty Promise.* Cambridge, Massachusetts: Urban Planning Aid, Inc., 1973.

[368] *Housing in the Seventies*, Department of Housing and Urban Development, National Housing Policy Review, Washington, D.C., 1973.

[369] *Housing Survey of the Houston Metropolitan Area; The Impact of Codes, Regulations and Industry Practices on the Cost of Housing.* Houston, Texas: School of Architecture, Rice University, 1968. (Prepared for the National Commission on Urban Problems.)

[370] Howards, Irving. "Property Tax Rate Limits in Illinois and Their Effects upon Local Government," *National Tax Journal*, XVI (3) (September 1963), 285-293.

*[371] Huang, David and Michael D. McCarthy. "Simulation of the Home Mortgage Market in the Late Sixties," *Review of Economics and Statistics*, XLIX (4) (November 1967), 441-450.

*[372] Hudson Institute. *The Future of Housing and Urban Development Policy.* Groton-on-Hudson, New York, Hudson Institute, Inc., September 1972.

[373] Hudson, James, Patricia Mathews and The Urban Institute Housing Group. *Variations in Operations: Housing for Lower-Income Households.* Washington, D.C.: The Urban Institute, 1969. (Working paper.)

[374] Hughes, James W. *Urban Indicators, Metropolitan Evolution, and Public Policy.* New Brunswick, New Jersey: Center for Urban Policy Research, Rutgers University, 1973.

[375] Hyman, David N. and E.C. Pasour, Jr. "Real Property Taxes, Local Public Services, and Residential Property Values," *Southern Economic Journal*, XXXIX (4) (April 1973), 601-611.

*[376] Ingram, Gregory K. and John F. Kain. "A Simple Model of Housing Production and the Abandonment Problem," *Proceedings of the American Real Estate and Urban Economics Association*, V (June 1972), 79-107.

*[377] Ingram, Gregory K., John F. Kain, and J. Royce Ginn. *The Detroit Prototype of the NBER Urban Simulation Model.* New York: National Bureau of Economic Research, 1972.

[378] Institute of Public Administration. *Rapid Rehabilitation of Old Law Tenements; An Evaluation.* New York: Institute of Public Administration, 1968.

*[379] Interfaith Housing Corporation. *The Suburban Noose—A Story of Non-profit Housing Development for the Modest-Income Family in Metropolitan Boston.* Boston: Interfaith Housing Corporation, December 1969.

[380] International and Social Studies Division, Institute for Defense Analysis. *Constraints on the Aggregation of Federally Subsidized, Low-Cost Housing.* Arlington, Virginia: Institute for Defense Analysis, 1968. (AD 682 893.)

[381] International Association of Assessing Officers. *Assessing and the Appraisal Process.* Chicago: International Association of Assessing Officers, 1969. (Third edition.)

[382] Isler, Morton L. *Thinking About Housing: A Policy Research Agenda.* Washington, D.C.: The Urban Institute, 1970. (Working paper no. 112-6. Formerly titled "A Housing Perspective and Research Strategy.")

[383] Jacobs Company, Inc., The. *A Study of Small Community Needs as Related to Federal Housing and Community Development Assistance.* Chicago: The Jacobs Company, Inc., 1970.

*[384] Jacobs, Jane. "Strategies for Helping Cities," *American Economic Review*, LIX (September 1969), 652-656.

*[385] Jaffee, Dwight M. "The Implications of the Proposals of the Hunt Commission for the Mortgage and Housing Markets," *Policies for a More Competitive Financial System*. Boston: Federal Reserve Bank of Boston. (Conference series no. 8, Federal Reserve Bank of Boston.)

[386] Johnson, Byron L. "Is Housing Productive?" *Land Economics*, XL (1) (February 1964), 92-94.

[387] Johnson, Ernest H. "Fractional Ratios and their Effect on Achievement of Uniform Assessment," in Tax Institute of America. *The Property Tax: Problems and Potential.* Princeton, New Jersey: Tax Institute of America, 1967, 209-215.

[388] Johnson, Thomas F. "Federal Aid for Urban Renewal: Help or Hind-

rance?" in Helmut Schoeck and J.W. Wiggins (eds.). *Central Planning and Neo-Mercantilism.* Princeton, New Jersey: D. Van Nostrand Co., Inc., 1964, 125-137.

*[389] Johnson. Verle. "Housing: Can It Last?" *Federal Reserve Bank of San Francisco Review* (September 1971), 165-170.

*[390] Johnston, John D. "Developments in Land Use Control," *Notre Dame Law Journal,* XL (Spring 1970), 399.

*[391] Joiner, Robert C. "Trends in Home Ownership and Rental Costs," *Monthly Labor Review,* XCIII (7) (July 1970), 26-31.

[392] Joint Committee on Building Codes. *Report on Model Codes.* Washington, D.C.: National Commission on Urban Problems, 1966. (Background paper no. 22.)

[393] Joint Economic Committee, Congress of the United States. *The Economics of Federal Subsidy Programs.* Washington, D.C.: U.S. Government Printing Office, 1972. (A compendium of papers submitted to the Joint Economic Committee, Congress of the United States. Part 5— Housing Subsidies. October 9, 1972.)

*[394] Jones & Laughlin Steel Corporation. *New Concepts in Low-Cost Residential Housing.* Pittsburgh: Jones & Laughlin Steel Corporation, 1967.

[395] Kain, John F. "An Alternative to Rent Control." Cambridge, Massachusetts: mimeograph, Harvard University, 1969. (Lecture on rent control, Cambridge League of Women Voters.)

*[396] _____. "A Contribution to the Urban Transportation Debate: An Econometric Model of Urban Residential and Travel Behaviour," *Review of Economic Statistics,* XLVI (February 1964), 55-64.

*[397] _____. "Housing Segregation, Negro Employment, and Metropolitan Decentralization," *Quarterly Journal of Economics,* LXXXII (May 1968), 175-197.

*[398] _____. "The Journey to Work as a Determinant of Residential Location." Berkeley, California: Ph.D. dissertation, Department of Economics, University of California, 1961.

[399] _____. "Postwar Metropolitan Development: Housing Preferences and Auto Ownership," *The American Economic Review,* LVII (2) (May 1967), 223-235.

*[400] _____ and John M. Quigley. "Housing Market Discrimination, Home-Ownership, and Saving Behavior," *The American Economic Review,* LXII (3) (June 1972), 263-277.

[401] _____. "Measuring the Value of Housing Quality," *Journal of the American Statistical Association,* LXV (330) (June 1970), 532-548.

[402] Kaiser, Edward J. *A Producer Model for Residential Growth: Analyzing and Predicting the Location of Residential Subdivisions.* Chapel Hill, North Carolina: Center for Urban and Regional Studies, Institute for Research in Social Sciences, University of North Carolina, 1968.

*[403] Kaiser, Edward J. and Shirley F. Weiss, "Decision Agent Models of the Residential Development Process—A Review of Recent Research," *Traffic Quarterly*, (October 1969), 597-632.

*[404] _____. "Local Public Policy and the Residential Development Process," *Law and Contemporary Problems*, XXXII (2) (Spring 1967), 232-249.

[405] Kaiser Engineers. *In Cities Experimental Housing Research and Development Project*. Oakland, California: Kaiser Engineers, 1971. (Prepared under contract no. H-1011 with the U.S. Department of Housing and Urban Development.)

*[406] Kaminow, I. "Should Housing be Sheltered from Tight Credit?" *Federal Reserve Bank Business Review, Philadelphia* (November 1970), 24-35.

[407] Kamm, Sylvia. *Land Banking: Public Policy Alternatives and Dilemmas*. Washington, D.C.: The Urban Institute, 1970.

[408] Kaplan, Abraham. *The Conduct of Inquiry: Methodology for Behavioral Science*. San Francisco: Chandler Publishing Co., 1964.

*[409] Kartman, Arthur E. "Demand for Housing: The Neglected Supply Side," *University of Washington Business Review*, XXX (3) (Spring 1971), 59-64.

[410] _____. "New Evidence on the Demand for Housing," *The Southern Economic Journal*, XXXVIII (4) (April 1972), 525-530.

*[411] Kaufman, Jerome L. and Mary Vance. *Community Renewal Programs: A Bibliography*. Urbana, Illinois: Department of Urban Planning and Landscape Architecture, University of Illinois, 1965.

*[412] Kaufman, Richard F. (ed.). *Urban America: Goals and Problems*. Washington, D.C.: U.S. Government Printing Office, 1967.

[413] Keating, William Dennis. *Emerging Patterns of Corporate Entry Into Housing*. Berkeley, California: Ph.D. dissertation, The Center for Real Estate and Urban Dynamics, Institute of Urban and Regional Development, University of California at Berkeley, 1973.

[414] Keith, John H. *Property Tax Assessment Practices: A Reference Book for the Assessor, Appraiser, Accountant, Attorney and the Student*. Monterey Park, California: Highland Publishing Company, 1966.

*[415] Keith, Nathaniel. "An Assessment of National Housing Needs," *Law and Contemporary Problems*, XXXII (2) (Spring 1967), 209-219.

[416] _____. *Housing America's Low- and Moderate-Income Families; Progress and Problems Under Past Programs; Prospects Under Federal Act of 1968*. Washington, D.C.: The National Commission on Urban Problems, 1968. (Research report no. 7.)

[417] Keller, Suzanne. "Friends and Neighbors in a Planned Community," in Robert W. Burchell (ed.). *Frontiers of Planned Unit Development: A Synthesis of Expert Opinion*. New Brunswick, New Jersey: Center for Urban Policy Research, Rutgers University, 1973, 228-240.

*[418] Kempner, Paul S. "A Look at Single Tenant Net Leased Properties," *Real Estate Review*, 1 (Spring 1971), 50-53.
[419] Kenower, John. *MICAH: A Case Study in Housing Rehabilitation Through Non-Profit Sponsorship.* Providence, Rhode Island: Rhode Island Department of Community Affairs, 1969.
[420] Kent, T.J. Jr. *The Urban General Plan.* San Francisco: Chandler Publishing Co., 1964.
[421] Kessler, Robert P. and Chester W. Hartman. "The Illusion and The Reality of Urban Renewal: A Case Study of San Francisco's Yerba Buena Center," *Land Economics*, XLIV (4) (November 1973), 440-453.
*[422] Key, William H. *When People Are Forced to Move: Final Report of a Study of Forced Relocation.* Washington, D.C.: 1967.
[423] Keyes, Langley Carleton, Jr. *The Boston Rehabilitation Program: An Independent Analysis.* Cambridge, Massachusetts: Joint Center for Urban Studies of the Massachusetts Institute of Technology and Harvard University, 1970.
[424] _____. *The Rehabilitation Planning Game: A Study in the Diversity of Neighborhood.* Cambridge, Massachusetts: The Massachusetts Institute of Technology Press, 1969.
*[425] _____. *The Role of Nonprofit Sponsors in the Production of Housing.* Washington: D.C.: U.S. Government Printing Office, 1971, 159-181. (Submitted to Subcommittee on Housing Panels on Housing Production, Housing Demand and Developing a Suitable Living Environment, Part I.)
[426] Keyserling, Leon H. *The Coming Crisis in Housing: And Its Adverse Impact upon Economic Growth and Employment.* Washington, D.C.: Conference on Economic Progress, 1972.
*[427] Kilbridge, Maurice, D., R.P. O'Block, and P.V. Teplitz. *Urban Analysis.* Boston: Graduate School of Business Administration, Harvard University, 1970, 332.
*[428] King, Alvin T. *Land Values and the Demand for Housing: A Micro-Economic Study.* Ann Arbor, Michigan: Ph.D. dissertation, Yale University, University Microfilms, 1972.
[429] Kinnamon, David L. "The Uniformity Clause, Assessment Freeze Laws, and Urban Renewal: A Critical View," *Wisconsin Law Review*, (4) (Fall 1965), 885-909.
*[430] Kirwan, R.M. and D.B. Martin. "Some Notes on Housing Market Models for Urban Planning," *Environment and Planning*, III (3) (1971), 243-252.
*[431] Klaassen, Leo H. "Some Theoretical Considerations for the Structure of the Housing Market," *Essays in Urban Land Economics.* Los Angeles: University of California Press, 1966, 68-75.

*[432] Klaman, Saul B. "Public/Private Approaches to Urban Mortgage and Housing Problems," *Law and Contemporary Problems*, XXXII (2) (Spring 1967), 250-265.
*[433] Knight, R.E. "The Quality of Mortgage Credit: Part I," *Federal Reserve Bank of Kansas City, Monthly Review* (March 1969), 13-20.
*[434] _____. "The Quality of Mortgage Credit: Part II," *Federal Reserve Bank of Kansas City, Monthly Review* (April 1969), 10-18.
*[435] Koenker, Roger. "An Empirical Note on the Elasticity of Substitution Between Land and Capital in a Monocentric Housing Market," *Journal of Regional Science*, XII (2) (August 1972), 299-305.
[436] Kolodny, Robert. *Self Help in the Inner City: A Study of Lower Income Cooperative Housing Conversion in New York*. New York: United Neighborhood Houses of New York, Inc., 1973.
[437] Kosoff, Allen. "Incentives for Urban Apartment Construction," *The American Journal of Economics and Sociology*, XXXII (3) (July 1973), 295-305.
[438] Kraemer, Kenneth L. *Policy Analysis in Local Government: A Systems Approach to Decision-Making*. Washington, D.C.: The International Management Association, 1973.
*[439] Krasnowiecki, Jan Z. *Cases and Materials on Housing and Urban Development*. St. Paul: West Publishing Co., 1969.
*[440] _____. *Legal Aspects of Planned Unit Residential Development with Suggested Legislation*. Washington, D.C.: Urban Land Institute, 1965.
*[441] _____. "Model Land Use and Development Planning Code," *Maryland Planning and Zoning Law Study Commission Final Report: Legislation Recommendations*, 1969, 113-116.
*[442] _____. "Planned Unit Development: A Challenge to Established Theory and Practice of Land Use Control," *University of Pennsylvania Law Review*, CXIV (3) (November 1965).
[443] Kristof, Frank S. "Federal Housing Policies: Subsidized Production, Filtration and Objectives: Part I," *Land Economics*, XLVIII (4) (November 1972), 309-320.
[444] _____. "Federal Housing Policies: Subsidized Production, Filtration and Objectives: Part II," *Land Economics*, XLIX (2) (May 1973), 163-174.
*[445] _____. "Housing Policy Goals and the Turnover of Housing," *Journal of the American Institute of Planners*, XXXI (4) (August 1965), 232-245.
[446] _____. *A Study and Report on: Urban Needs and Economic Factors in Housing Policy*. Washington, D.C.: National Commission on Urban Problems, 1968. (Contract no. H. 899.)
*[447] _____. *Urban Housing Needs Through the 1980's: An Analysis and

Projection. Washington, D.C.: U.S. Government Printing Office, 1968. (National Commission on Urban Problems, research report no. 10.)

*[448] Krooth, David L. and Jeffrey G. Spragens. "The Interest Assistance Programs—A Successful Approach to Housing Problems," *George Washington Law Review*, XXXIX (1971), 789-817.

*[449] Kuminek, E. "Changes in the Output of the Building Industry as a Factor in the Development of Home-Building," in A.A. Nevitt (ed.). *Economic Problems of Housing.* New York: St. Martin's Press, 1967, 228-235.

*[450] Ladd, W.M. "The Effect of Integration on Property Values," *American Economic Review*, (September 1962), 801-808.

*[451] Laidler, David. "Income Tax Incentives for Owner-Occupied Housing," in Arnold C. Harberger and Martin J. Bailey (eds.). *The Taxation of Income from Capital.* Washington, D.C.: The Brookings Institution, 1969, 50-76.

[452] Land, Alan E. "Toward Optimal Land Use: Property Tax Policy and Land Use Policy," *California Law Review*, LV (August 1967), 856-897.

*[453] Lansing, John B. *Residential Location and Urban Mobility: The Second Wave of Interviews.* Ann Arbor: Survey Research Center, Institute for Social Research, University of Michigan, 1966.

*[454] _____ and Nancy Barth. *Residential Location and Urban Mobility: A Multivariate Analysis.* Ann Arbor: Survey Research Center of Institute for Social Research, University of Michigan, 1964.

*[455] Lansing, John B., C.W. Clifton, and James N. Morgan. *New Homes and Poor People: A Study of Chains of Moves.* Ann Arbor: Survey Research Center, Institute for Social Research, University of Michigan, 1969.

*[456] Lansing, John B., Robert W. Marans, and Robert B. Zehner. *Planned Residential Environments.* Ann Arbor, Michigan: Institute for Social Research, University of Michigan, 1970.

*[457] Lapham, Victoria Cannon. "Do Blacks Pay More For Housing?" *Journal of Political Economy*, LXXIX (6) (November-December 1971), 1244-1257.

[458] Latcham, Franklin C. and Roger W. Findley. "The Influence of Taxation and Assessment Policies on Open Space," in Frances W. Herring (ed.). *Open Space and The Law.* Berkeley, California: Institute of Governmental Studies, University of California at Berkeley, 1965, 53-72.

*[459] Laurenti, Luigi. *Property Values and Race: Studies of Seven Cities.* Berkeley: University of California Press, 1960.

*[460] Lebergott, Stanley. "Slum Housing: A Proposal," *Journal of Political Economy*, LXXVIII (November 1970), 1362-1366.

*[461] _____. "Slum Housing: A Further Word," *Journal of Political Economy*, LXXX (5) September-October 1972), 1067-1068.

[462] Ledbetter, William H., Jr. "Public Housing—A Social Experiment Seeks

Acceptance," *Law and Contemporary Problems*, XXXII (3) (Summer 1967), 490-527.
*[463] Lee, Douglas, Jr. "Requiem for Large Scale Models," *Journal of the American Institute of Planners*, XXIX (3) (May 1973).
*[464] Lee, Tong Hun. "Demand for Housing: A Cross-Section Analysis," *Review of Economics and Statistics*, May 1963, 190-196.
*[465] _____. "Housing and Permanent Income; Tests Based on Three Year Reinterview Survey," *Review of Economics and Statistics*, L (4) (November 1968), 480-490.
*[466] _____. "More on the Stock Demand Elasticities of Non-Farm Housing," *Review of Economics and Statistics*, XLIX (November 1967), 640-642.
*[467] _____. "The Stock Demand Elasticities of Non-Farm Housing," *Review of Economics and Statistics*, XLVI (February 1964), 82-89.
*[468] Lehman. "Building Codes, Housing Codes and the Conservation of Chicago's Housing Supply," *University of Chicago Law Review*, XXXI (Autumn 1963), 180.
[469] Lempert, Richard and Kiyoshi Ikeda. "Evictions from Public Housing: Effects of an Independent Review," *American Sociological Review*, XXXV (5) (October 1970), 852-860.
[470] Levin, Jack and Gerald Taube. "Bureaucracy and the Socially Handicapped: A Study of Lower-Status Tenants in Public Housing," *Sociology and Social Research*, LIV (2) (January 1970), 209-219.
*[471] Levin, Melvin (ed.). *Innovations in Housing Rehabilitation.* Boston: Boston University Urban Institute, 1969. (Monograph no. 2.)
[472] Levin, Michael S. "Some First Returns on Planned Unit Development," in Robert W. Burchell (ed.). *Frontiers of Planned Unit Development: A Synthesis of Expert Opinion.* New Brunswick, New Jersey: Center for Urban Policy Research, Rutgers University, 1973, 241-250.
[473] Levine, Rosalie B. "The Real Estate Tax and Housing," *Financing Government in New York City* New York: Graduate School of Public Administration, New York University, 1966, 693-717. (Final research report to the Temporary Commission on City Finances, City of New York, New York.)
[474] Lewis, Jordan D. and Lynn Lewis (eds.). *Industrial Approaches to Urban Problems; Discussions of Housing, Transportation, Education, and Solid Waste Management Issues.* New York: Praeger Publishers, 1972.
*[475] Lichfield, Nathaniel and Julius Margolis. "Benefit-Cost Analysis as a Tool in Urban Government Decision-Making," in Howard G. Schaller (ed.). *Public Expenditure Decisions in the Urban Community.* Baltimore: The Johns Hopkins University Press, 1963.
[476] Lieberman, Barnet. "Administrative Provisions of Housing Codes," in Eric W. Mood, Barnet Lieberman and Oscar Sutermeister. *Housing Code*

Standards: Three Critical Studies. Washington, D.C.: National Commission on Urban Problems, 1969. (Research report no. 19.)

[477] _____. *Local Administration and Enforcement of Housing Codes: A Survey of 39 Cities.* Washington, D.C.: National Association of Housing and Redevelopment Officials, 1969.

[478] Lindbeck, Assar. "Rent Control as an Instrument of Housing Policy," in Adela Adam Nevitt (ed.). *The Economic Problems of Housing.* New York: St. Martin's Press, 1967, 53-72.

[479] Lindemen, Bruce. *Low Income Housing Subsidies and the Housing Market; An Economic Analysis.* Atlanta: Bureau of Business and Economic Research, School of Business Administration, Georgia State University, 1969. (Research paper no. 50.)

[480] Lindholm, Richard W. (ed.). *Property Taxation, USA.* Madison, Wisconsin: The University of Wisconsin Press, 1967.

[481] _____. "Twenty-one Land Value Taxation Questions and Answers," *The American Journal of Economics and Sociology*, XXXI (2) (April 1972), 153-163.

[482] Linton, Mields and Coston, Incorporated. *A Study of the Problems of Abandoned Housing.* Springfield, Virginia: National Technical Information Service, U.S. Department of Commerce, 1971.

[483] Listokin, David. *The Dynamics of Housing Rehabilitation; Macro and Micro Analyses.* New Brunswick, New Jersey: Center for Urban Policy Research, Rutgers University, 1973.

[484] Loshbough, Bernard E. "Rehabilitation of Housing: Federal Programs and Private Enterprise," *Law and Contemporary Problems*, XXXII (3) (Summer 1967), 416-438.

[485] _____. "Social Action Programs in Urban Renewal," in Margaret S. Gordon (ed.). *Poverty in America.* San Francisco: Chandler Publishing Company, 1965, 335-348.

*[486] Lowry, Ira S. "Filtering and Housing Standards: A Conceptual Analysis," *Land Economics*, XXXVI (1960), 362-370.

[487] _____. *Housing Assistance for Low-Income Urban Families: A Fresh Approach.* New York: New York City RAND Institute, 1971. (RAND publication no. P-4645.)

[488] _____. *Reforming Rent Control in New York City: The Role of Research in Policy Making.* New York: The New York City RAND Institute, 1970.

[489] _____ (ed.). *Rental Housing in New York City; Volume 1: Confronting the Crisis.* New York: The New York City RAND Institute, 1970. (RM-6190-NYC.)

[490] _____. *Research on New York City's Housing Problems.* Santa Monica, California: The RAND Corporation, 1968.

[491] _____, Joseph S. DeSalvo, and Barbara M. Woodfill. *Rental Housing*

in New York City; Volume II: The Demand for Shelter. New York: The New York City RAND Institute, 1971. (R-649-NYC. Abridged.)

[492] Lozano, Eduardo. "Housing Costs and Alternative Cost-Reducing Policies," *Journal of the American Institute of Planners*, XXXVIII (3) (May 1972) 176-181.

*[493] Ly, J.J. "The Manipulation of Property Tax as a Determinant in Changing Land Use Patterns in the Urban Fringe," *The Annals of Regional Science*, 1 (December 1967), 102-113.

[494] Lym, Glenn Robert. "Effect of a Public Housing Project on a Neighborhood: Case Study of Oakland, California," *Land Economics*, XLIII (4) (November 1967), 461-466.

*[495] Lynn, Arthur D., Jr. (ed.). *The Property Tax and Its Administration.* Madison: University of Wisconsin Press, 1969.

[496] MacDonald, Gordon D. and Rosalind Tough. "New York: Social Action in Urban Renewal," *Land Economics*, XLII (4) (November 1966), 514-522.

[497] Mace, Ruth L., Charles L. Weill, Jr., and Gustav M. Ulrich. "Trends in the Market Value of Real Property in the Central Areas of Two North Carolina Cities," *Land Economics*, XLII (1) (February 1966), 85-94.

*[498] Mace, Ruth L., and Sumner Meyers. "Outdoor Recreation," in Robert Dorfman (ed.) *Measuring Benefits of Government Investments.* Washington, D.C.: The Brookings Institution, 1965.

[499] Mace, Ruth L. and Warren J. Wicker. *Do Single-Family Homes Pay Their Way? A Comparative Analysis of Costs and Revenues for Public Services.* Washington, D.C.: Urban Land Institute, 1968. (Research monograph 15.)

[500] Mahaffey, Charles T. *A Special Study on Building Codes.* Washington, D.C.: National Commission on Urban Problems, 1968. (Background paper no. 18.)

*[501] Maisel, Sherman. *California Housing Studies: Land Costs for Single Family Housing.* Berkeley, California: Center for Planning and Development Research, University of California, 1963.

[502] _____. "The Economic Aspects of Housing," *International Encyclopedia of the Social Sciences* (1968), 521-526.

*[503] _____. *Financing Real Estate: Principles and Practices.* New York: McGraw-Hill, 1965.

[504] _____. "The Relationship of Residential Financing and Expenditures on Residential Construction," in Michael A. Stegman (ed.). *Housing and Economics: The American Dilemma.* Cambridge, Massachusetts: The Massachusetts Institute of Technology Press, 1970, 39-50. (Reprinted with the permission of The United States Savings and Loan League, 1965 Proceedings, Conference on Savings and Residential Financing, Chicago, 1966.)

*[505] _____ and John S. Austin Burnham. "The Demand for Housing: A Comment," *Review of Economics and Statistics*, LIII (4) (November 1971), 410-413.

*[506] Maisel, Sherman J. and Louis Winnick. "Family Housing Expenditures: Elusive Laws and Intrusive Variances," *Proceedings of the Conference on Consumption and Saving.* Philadelphia, Pennsylvania: University of Pennsylvania, 1960. (Volume I.)

*[507] Malone, John R. "Capital Expenditure for Owner-Occupied Housing: A Study of Determinants," *Journal of Business*, XXXIX (July 1966), 359-366.

[508] Mandelker, Daniel R. "The Comprehensive Planning Requirement in Urban Renewal," *University of Pennsylvania Law Review*, CXVI (1) (November 1967), 25-73.

*[509] _____. *Controlling Planned Residential Development.* Chicago: American Society of Planning Officials, 1966.

[510] _____. "Housing Codes, Building Demolition, and Just Compensation: A Rationale for the Exercise of Public Powers over Slum Housing," *Michigan Law Review*, LXVII (4) (February 1969), 635-678.

[511] _____. "The Local Community's Stake in Code Enforcement," *The Urban Lawyer*, III (4) (Fall 1971), 601-608.

*[512] Mandelstamm, Allan B. "The Effects of Unions on Efficiency in the Residential Construction Industry: A Case Study," *Industrial and Labor Relations Review*, XVIII (July 1965), 503-521.

*[513] Mankin, Wyatt. "New Look at the Muth Model," *American Economic Review*, LXII (December 1972), 980-981.

*[514] Manvel, Alan D. *Housing Conditions in Urban Poverty Areas.* Washington, D.C.: U.S. Government Printing Office, 1968. (National Commission on Urban Problems, research report no. 9.)

[515] _____. *Local Land and Building Regulation. How Many Agencies? What Practices? How Much Personnel?* Washington, D.C.: National Commission on Urban Problems, 1968. (Research report no. 6.)

[516] Mao, James C.T. *Efficiency in Public Renewal Expenditures through Capital Budgeting.* Berkeley, California: The Center for Real Estate and Urban Economics, Institute of Urban and Regional Development, University of California at Berkeley, 1965.

[517] _____. "Efficiency in Public Urban Renewal Expenditures Through Benefit-Cost Analysis," in Wallace F. Smith (ed.). *Land Using Activities: Theoretical Issues in Land Economics.* Berkeley, California: The Center for Real Estate and Urban Economics, Institute of Urban and Regional Development, University of California at Berkeley, 1970. (Reprinted from *Journal of the American Institute of Planners*, XXXII (2) (March 1966).)

[518] _____. "Quantitative Analysis of Urban Renewal Investment Decisions," *The Journal of Finance*, XXII (2) (May 1967), 195-207.

[519] Mao, James C.T. "Relocation and Housing Welfare: A Case Study," *Land Economics*, XLI (4) (November 1965), 365-370.

[520] _____ and Roger L. Wright. "A Chance-Constrained Approach to Urban Renewal Decisions," *Journal of Financial and Quantitative Analysis*, III (June 1968), 135-150.

*[521] Marcuse, Peter. "Comparative Analyses of Federally-Aided Low- and Moderate-Income Housing Programs," *Journal of Housing* (October 1969), 536-539.

[522] _____. "Homeownership for Low Income Families: Financial Implications," *Land Economics*, XLVIII (2) (May 1972), 134-143.

[523] _____. "Social Indicators and Housing Policy," *Urban Affairs Quarterly*, VII (2) (December 1971), 193-218.

[524] Marshall Kaplan, Gans, and Kahn. *Public Housing Conversion: A Feasibility Study*. San Francisco: Marshall Kaplan, Gans, and Kahn, 1973. (Prepared for the Cambridge Model Cities Administration.)

*[525] Martin, Preston. "Aggregate Housing Demand: Test Model, Southern California," *Land Economics* XLII (4) (November 1966), 503-513.

[526] Massachusetts Special Commission on Low-Income Housing. *Final Report*. Boston, Massachusetts: Wright & Potter Printing Co., Legislative Printers, 1965.

[527] Massell, Benton F. "Maintenance of Slum Housing: Optimal Policy Subject to a Political Constraint," *Journal of Political Economy*, LXXX (5) (September/October 1972), 1060-1066.

*[528] McFarland, M. Carter. "The Rising Tide of Housing Allowances," *AIA Journal*, (October 1972), 26-28.

[529] McFarland, M. Carter and Walter K. Vivrett (eds.). *Residential Rehabilitation*. Minneapolis, Minnesota: University of Minnesota, 1965. (A compilation of papers presented at the Training Institute in Residential Rehabilitation, University of Minnesota, Minneapolis, Minnesota, July 19-30, 1965.)

*[530] McKean, Roland N. *Public Spending*. New York: McGraw-Hill, 1968.

*[531] _____. *Efficiency in Government Through Systems Analysis*. New York: John Wiley and Sons, 1958.

*[532] McKee, David L. and Gerald H. Smith. "Environmental Diseconomies in Suburban Expansion," *American Journal of Economics and Sociology*, XXXI (2) (April 1972), 181-188.

[533] McKie, Robert and W.K. Kumar. "House Improvement and Rateable Values," *Urban Studies*, VIII (2) (June 1971), 147-150.

*[534] McKim, Bruce T. "Economic and Psychological Limits of the Property Tax," in David. R. Doerr and Raymond R. Sullivan (eds.). *Major Tax Study: Part 5–Taxation of Property in California*. Sacramento: California Assembly Interim Committee on Revenue and Taxation, 1964, 284-331.

[535] McKinsey & Company, Inc. *Initiating Rehabilitation in the State of Illinois.* Springfield, Illinois: The Illinois Housing Development Authority, 1973.

[536] McMahan, John W. "An Opportunity for Private Capital in the Housing Market," in National Urban Coalition. *Private Capital and Low-Income Housing.* Washington, D.C.: National Urban Coalition, 8-27.

*[537] Megee, Mary. "Statistical Prediction of Mortgage Risk," *Land Economics*, XLIV (November 1968), 461-470.

[538] Meinster, David R. "Property Tax Shifting Assumptions and Effects on Incidence Profiles," *The Quarterly Review of Economics and Business*, X (4) (Winter 1970), 65-83.

[539] Melamed, Anshel. "The Gray Areas: Unutilized Potentials and Unmet Needs," *Land Economics*, XLI (2) (May 1965), 151-158.

*[540] Melnyk, M. "The Problem of Long Cycles in Residential Construction," *Land Economics*, XLIV (November 1968), 480-491.

[541] Merz, Paul E. "The Income Tax Treatment of Owner-Occupied Housing," *Land Economics*, XLI (3) (August 1965), 247-255.

[542] Messner, Stephen D. "Urban Redevelopment in Indianapolis: A Benefit-Cost Analysis," *Journal of Regional Science*, VIII (2) (Winter 1968), 149-158.

[543] Metro Metrics, Inc. *The Economics of Urban Growth: Costs and Benefits of Residential Construction.* Washington, D.C.: Metro Metrics, Inc., 1971.

*[544] Meyerson, Martin and Edward C. Banfield. *Politics, Planning and the Public Interest: The Case of Public Housing in Chicago.* New York: The Free Press of Glencoe, 1955.

*[545] Miami Valley Regional Planning Commission. *Housing Needs in the Miami Valley Region, 1970-75.* Dayton, Ohio: Miami Valley Regional Planning Commission, 1970.

[546] Michigan State Housing Development Authority. *The Primary Economic Impact at the State and Local Levels of State-Financed Housing.* Lansing, Michigan: Michigan State Housing Development Authority, 1972. (DDS Publication 166 (Rev. 3-73).)

[547] Mields, Hugh, Jr. *Federally Assisted New Communities: New Dimensions in Urban Development.* Washington, D.C.: Urban Land Institute, 1973.

[548] Mieszkowski, Peter. "The Property Tax: An Excise Tax or a Profits Tax," *Journal of Public Economics*, 1 (1972), 73-96.

*[549] Miller, Glenn H., Jr. "Housing in the 60's: A Survey of Some Nonfinancial Factors," *Federal Reserve Bank of Kansas City, Monthly Review* (May 1969), 3-10.

[550] Miller, L. Charles, Jr. *The Economics of Housing Code Enforcement.* New Haven, Connecticut: Center for the Study of the City and its

Environment, Institution for Social and Policy Studies, Yale University, 1972.

[551] Miller, L. Charles, Jr. *Housing Markets, Standards, and Needs.* New Haven, Connecticut: Center for the Study of the City and its Environment, Institution for Social and Policy Studies, Yale University, 1972. (Working paper.)

[552] Milliman, J.W. and W.G. Pinnell. "Economic Redevelopment for Evansville, Indiana: A Case Study of a Depressed City," in Committee for Economic Development. *Community Economic Development Efforts: Five Case Studies.* New York: Committee for Economic Development, 1964, 239-309. (Supplementary paper no. 18.)

*[553] Mishan, E.S. *Economics for Social Decisions.* New York: Praeger Publishers, 1972.

[554] Mitre Corporation, The. *The In-Cities Project; Some Initial Results.* McLean, Virginia: The Mitre Corporation, 1969.

[555] Mittelbach, Frank G., Donald M. McAllister, and Demetrius D. Gasparis. *The Role of Removals from the Inventory in Regional Housing Markets.* Los Angeles: Division of Research, Graduate School of Business Administration, University of California at Los Angeles, 1970. (Occasional paper no. 4.)

[556] _____ and Leland S. Burns. *Housing Codes—Selected Economic Implications.* Los Angeles: Graduate School of Business Administration, University of California at Los Angeles, 1970. (Occasional paper no. 5.)

[557] Moffitt, Leonard C. "Planning and Assessment Practice," *Land Economics*, XLII (3) (August 1966), 371-378.

[558] Mollenkopf, John and Jon Pynoos. "Boardwalk and Park Place: Property Ownership, Political Structure, and Housing Policy at the Local Level," in Jon Pynoos, Robert Schafer, and Chester Hartman (eds.). *Housing Urban America.* Chicago: Aldine Publishing Company, 1973, 55-74.

*[559] _____. "Property, Politics and Local Housing Policy," *Politics and Society* (Summer 1972), 407-429.

*[560] Montesano, Aldo. "A Restatement of Beckmann's Model on the Distribution of Urban Rent and Residential Density," *Journal of Economic Theory*, IV (April 1972), 329-354.

[561] Mood, Eric W. "The Development, Objective and Adequacy of Current Housing Code Standards," in Eric W. Mood, Barnet Lieberman, and Oscar Sutermeister. *Housing Code Standards: Three Critical Studies.* Washington, D.C.: National Commission on Urban Problems, 1969. (Research report no. 19.)

*[562] Mooney, Joseph D. "Housing Segregation, Negro Employment, and Metropolitan Decentralization: An Alternative Perspective," *Quarterly Journal of Economics*, LXXXIII (May 1969), 299-311.

[563] Moorhouse, John C. "Optimal Housing Maintenance under Rent Control," *Southern Economic Journal*, XXXIX (1) (July 1972), 93-106.

*[564] Morgan, James N. "Housing and Ability to Pay," *Econometrica*, XXXIII (2) (April 1965), 289-306.

[565] Moses, Stephen D. "Rental Housing for Low-Income Families under Section 236," in National Urban Coalition. *Private Capital and Low-Income Housing*. Washington, D.C.: National Urban Coalition, 28-63.

[566] Moynihan, Daniel P. "Policy vs. Program in the 70's," *The Public Interest* (Summer 1970).

*[567] Muller, Thomas and Grace Dawson. *The Fiscal Impact of Residential and Commercial Development: A Case Study*. Washington, D.C.: The Urban Institute, 1972.

[568] Murray, Barbara B. "Central City Expenditures and Out-Migration to the Fringe," *Land Economics*, XLV (4) (November 1969), 471-474.

*[569] Musgrave, Richard. "Is the Property Tax on Housing Regressive," *American Economic Review*, LXIV (2) (May 1974), 222-229.

*[570] Musgrave, Richard and Peggy B. Musgrave. *Public Finance in Theory and Practice*. New York: McGraw-Hill, 1973.

*[571] Muth, Richard F. *Cities and Housing, The Spatial Pattern of Urban Residential Land Use*. Chicago: University of Chicago Press, 1969.

[572] _____. "The Demand for Housing and the Demand for Land," in Mason Gaffney et al. *Land As An Element of Housing Costs: The Effects of Public Policies and Practices; The Effects of Housing Demand*. Arlington, Virginia: Institute for Defense Analysis, 1968, 39-66.

*[573] _____. "The Demand for Non-Farm Housing," in A.C. Harberger (ed.). *The Demand for Durable Goods*. Chicago: University of Chicago Press, 1960.

*[574] _____. "The Demand for Non-Farm Housing: Comment," in Alfred N. Page and Warren R. Seyfried (eds.). *Urban Analysis; Readings in Housing and Urban Development*. Glenview, Illinois: Scott Foresman, 1970, 146-165.

*[575] _____. "The Derived Demand for Urban Residential Land," *Urban Studies*, VIII (3) (October 1971), 245-254.

[576] _____. *Public Housing: An Economic Evaluation*. Washington, D.C.: American Enterprise Institute for Public Policy Research, 1973.

[577] _____. "Slums and Poverty," in Adela A. Nevitt (ed.). *The Economic Problems of Housing*. New York: MacMillan & Company, 1967.

*[578] _____. "The Stock Demand Elasticities of Non-Farm Housing: Discussion," *Review of Economics and Statistics*, XLVII (November 1965), 447-449.

*[579] _____. "Urban Residential Land and Housing Markets," in H.S. Perloff and L. Wingo (eds.). *Issues in Urban Economics*. Baltimore: The Johns Hopkins University Press, 1968.

[580] Muth, Richard F. and Elliot Wetzler. *Effects of Constraints on Single-Unit Housing Costs.* Arlington, Virginia: Institute for Defense Analysis, 1968.

[581] Myers, Will S., Jr. "General Appraisal of the Effect of Exemptions on Tax Base," in Tax Institute of America. *The Property Tax: Problems and Potential.* Princeton, New Jersey: Tax Institute of America, 1967, 267-282.

*[582] Nachbaur, Elizabeth Hirsch. *An Exploratory Analysis of the Proposed National Housing Allowance Program.* Washington, D.C.: Master's thesis, The George Washington University, 1971.

[583] Nachbaur, William T. "Empty Houses: Abandoned Residential Buildings in the Inner City," *Howard Law Journal*, XVII (1) (1971), 3-68.

[584] Nash, William W. *Residential Rehabilitation: Private Profits and Public Purposes.* New York: McGraw-Hill, 1959.

[585] National Academy of Sciences Summer Study Center. *New City in City: A Summer Study on Science and Urban Development.* Woods Hole, Massachusetts: National Academy of Sciences Summer Study Center, 1966.

*[586] National Association of Housing and Redevelopment Officials. *Critical Urban Housing Issues, 1967. A Selection of Papers from NAHRO National Housing Policy Forum.* Washington, D.C.: NAHRO, 1967.

[587] National Center for Housing Management, Inc. *Report of the Task Force on Improving the Operation of Federally Insured or Financed Housing Programs. Volume II: Public Housing.* Washington, D.C.: National Center for Housing Management, Inc., 1973.

[588] National Commission on Urban Problems. *Building The American City. Report of the National Commission on Urban Problems to the Congress and to the President of the United States.* Washington, D.C.: U.S. Government Printing Office, 1968, 254-321.

[589] _____. "Public Housing," "Publicly Assisted or Subsidized Housing," "Housing Program Recommendations," *Building the American City: Report of the National Commission on Urban Problems to the Congress and to the President of the United States.* Washington, D.C.: U.S. Government Printing Office, 1968, 108-133, 143-151, 180-197.

*[590] National Committee Against Discrimination in Housing. *How the Federal Government Builds Ghettos.* New York: National Committee Against Discrimination in Housing, 1968.

*[591] _____. *Jobs and Housing: A Study of Employment and Housing Opportunities for Racial Minorities in the Suburban Areas of the New York Metropolitan Region.* New York: National Committee Against Discrimination in Housing, 1970.

[592] National Urban Coalition, The. *Proposal for Action Research in Urban Homesteading.* Washington, D.C.: The National Urban Coalition, 1973.

[593] _____. *Urban Homesteading: Process and Potential; An Exploration into Options for Urban Stabilization by the National Urban Coalition.* Washington, D.C.: The National Urban Coalition, 1974.

[594] Natoli, Salvatore J. "Zoning and the Development of Urban Land Use Patterns," *Economic Geography*, XLVII (2) (April 1971), 171-184.

*[595] Naylor, Thomas H. "The Impact of Fiscal and Monetary Policy on the Housing Market," *Law and Contemporary Problems*, XXXII (3) (Summer 1967), 384-396.

*[596] Needleman, Lionel. "The Comparative Economics of Improvement and New Building," *Urban Studies*, VI (2) (1969), 196-209.

*[597] _____. *The Economics of Housing.* London: Staples Press, 1965.

*[598] Nelson, Richard. *Technology, Economic Growth, and Public Policy.* Washington, D.C.: The RAND Corporation and Brookings Institution Study, 1967.

*[599] Nelson, Robert Henry. "Housing Facilities, Site Advantages, and Rent," *Journal of Regional Science*, XII (August 1972), 249-259.

*[600] Nenno, Mary K. *Housing in Metropolitan Areas: Roles and Responsibilities of Five Key Actors.* Washington, D.C.: National Association of Housing and Redevelopment Officials, 1973.

*[601] Netzer, Dick. *Economics and Urban Problems: Diagnoses and Prescriptions.* New York: Basic Books, 1970.

[602] _____. *Economics of the Property Tax.* Washington, D.C.: The Brookings Institution, 1966.

[603] _____. *Impact of the Property Tax: Effect on Housing, Urban Land Use, Local Government Finance.* Washington, D.C.: National Commission on Urban Problems, 1968. (Supplied to the Joint Economic Committee of the United States Congress.)

[604] _____. "Is there too much Reliance on the Local Property Tax?" in George E. Peterson (ed.). *Property Tax Reform.* Washington: D.C.: The Urban Institute, 1973, 13-23.

[605] _____. "Some Alternatives in Property Tax Reform," in Tax Institute of America. *The Property Tax: Problems and Potential.* Princeton, New Jersey: Tax Institute of America, 1967, 386-401.

*[606] Neutze, Max. "The Cost of Housing," *Economic Record*, XLVIII (123) (September 1972), 357-373.

[607] _____. "Property Taxation and Multiple-Family Housing," in Arthur P. Becker (ed.). *Land and Building Taxes: Their Effect on Economic Development.* Madison, Wisconsin: The University of Wisconsin Press, 1969, 115-128.

[608] _____. *The Suburban Apartment Boom: Case Study of a Land Use Problem* Baltimore, Maryland: The Johns Hopkins University Press, 1968.

*[609] Nevitt, A.A. (ed.). *The Economic Problems of Housing.* New York: St. Martin's Press, 1967.

[610] New Jersey (State of), County and Municipal Government Study Commission. *Housing and Suburbs: Fiscal and Social Impact of Multi-family Development.* Trenton: New Jersey County and Municipal Government Study Commission, October 1974.

*[611] Newman, Oscar. *Defensible Space.* New York: Doubleday, 1973.

[612] Nicholson, R.J. and N. Topham. "The Determinants of Investment in Housing by Local Authorities: An Econometric Approach," *Journal of the Royal Statistical Society, Series A (General),* CXXXIV (3) (1971), 273-320.

*[613] Nicol, Robert E.G. et al. "An Alternative in Mortgage Lending," *Quarterly Review of Economics and Business*, XII (Spring 1972), 31-42.

*[614] Niebanck, Paul L. *Relocation in Urban Planning: From Obstacle to Opportunity.* Philadelphia: University of Pennsylvania Press, 1968.

*[615] _____. *Rent Control and the Rental Housing Market, New York City, 1968.* New York: Housing and Development Administration, 1970.

*[616] _____ with John B. Pope. *The Elderly in Older Urban Housing: Problems of Adaptation and the Effects of Relocation.* Philadelphia: Institute for Environmental Studies, University of Pennsylvania, 1965.

[617] _____. *Residential Rehabilitation: The Pitfalls of Non-Profit Sponsorship.* Philadelphia: Institute for Environmental Studies, University of Pennsylvania, 1968.

[618] Niedercorn, John H. "A Negative Exponential Model of Urban Land Use Densities and its Implications for Metropolitan Development," *Journal of Regional Science*, XI (3) (December 1971), 317-326.

*[619] _____ and John F. Kain. "An Econometric Model of Metropolitan Development," *Regional Science Association, Papers and Proceedings*, XI (1963), 122-143.

*[620] Niskanen, W.A. "The Use of Intrametropolitan Data," in Werner Z. Hirsch (ed.). *Elements of Regional Accounts.* Baltimore: The Johns Hopkins University Press, 1964.

[621] Nordhaus, William D. "Tax Incentives for Low Income Housing," in National Tax Association, *Proceedings of the Sixty-First Annual Conference on Taxation* (1968), 396-414.

[622] Northam, Ray M. "Vacant Urban Land in the American City," *Land Economics*, XLVII (4) (November 1971), 345-355.

*[623] Nourse, Hugh O. "Economic Analysis of Standard Quality Housing," in Hugh O. Nourse (ed.). *The Effect of Public Policy on Housing Markets.* Lexington, Massachusetts: Lexington Books, D.C. Heath and Co., 1973, 128.

[624] _____. "The Economics of Urban Renewal." *Land Economics*, XLII (1) (February 1966), 65-74.

*[625] _____. "The Effect of Air Pollution on House Values," *Land Economics*, XLIII (May 1967), 181-189.

[626] _____. "The Effect of a Negative Income Tax on the Number of Substandard Housing Units," *Land Economics*, XLVI (4) (November 1970), 436-446.

*[627] _____. "The Effect of Public Housing on Property Values in St. Louis," *Land Economics*, XXXIX (4) (November 1963). (Reprinted in Hugh O. Nourse (ed.). *The Effects of Public Policy on Housing Markets*. Lexington, Massachusetts: Lexington Books, D.C. Heath and Co., 1973, 3-13.)

*[628] _____. *The Effects of Public Policy on Housing Markets*. Lexington, Massachusetts: D.C. Heath and Company, 1973.

[629] _____. "Redistribution of Income from Public Housing," *National Tax Journal*, XIX (11) (March 1966). (Reprinted in Hugh O. Nourse (ed.). *The Effects of Public Policy on Housing Markets*. Lexington, Massachusetts: Lexington Books, D.C. Heath and Co., 1973, 29-42.)

*[630] _____, Martin J. Bailey and Richard F. Muth. "Regression Method for Real Estate Price Index Construction," *Journal of the American Statistical Association*, LVIII (December 1963), 993-1010. (Reprinted in Hugh O. Nourse (ed.). *The Effects of Public Policy on Housing Markets*. Lexington, Massachusetts: Lexington Books, D.C. Heath and Co., 1973, 15-27.)

*[631] Nourse, Hugh O. and Donald Guy. "The Filtering Process: The Webster Groves and Kankakee Cases," *Proceedings of the American Real Estate and Urban Economics Association*, V (December 1970). (Reprinted in Hugh O. Nourse (ed.). *The Effects of Public Policy on Housing Markets*. Lexington, Massachusetts: Lexington Books, D.C. Heath and Co., 1973, 91-105.)

*[632] Nourse, Hugh O., Donald Phares and John Stevens. "The Effect of Aging and Income Transition on Neighborhood House Values," in Hugh O. Nourse (ed.). *The Effects of Public Policy on Housing Markets*. Lexington, Massachusetts: Lexington Books, D.C. Heath and Co., 1973, 107-119.

[633] Oakland, William H. "Using the Property Tax to Pay for City Government: A Case Study of Baltimore," in George E. Peterson (ed.). *Property Tax Reform*. Washington, D.C.: The Urban Institute, 1973, 141-173.

[634] Oates, Wallace E. "The Effects of Property Taxes and Local Public Spending on Property Values: An Empirical Study of Tax Capitalization and the Tiebout Hypothesis," *Journal of Political Economy*, LXXVII (6) (December 1969), 957-971.

*[635] Oates, W.E. et al. "The Analysis of Public Policy in Dynamic Urban Models," *Journal of Political Economy*, LXXXIX (1) (January 1971), 142-153.

*[636] O'Block, Robert P. and R.H. Kuehn, Jr. *An Economic Analysis of the*

Housing and Urban Development Act of 1968. Boston: Graduate School of Business Administration, 1970.

[637] Odell, Carolyn J. *Code Enforcement and Housing Maintenance in New York City: A Strategy for Change.* New York: Community Service Society, 1972.

[638] Oldman, Oliver and Henry Aaron. "Assessment-Sales Ratio Under the Boston Property Tax," *National Tax Journal,* XVIII (1) (March 1965), 36-49.

*[639] Olken, Charles E. "Economic Development in the Model Cities Program," *Law and Contemporary Problems,* XXXVI (1) (Spring 1971), 205-226.

[640] Olsen, Edgar O. *Can Public Construction and Rehabilitation Increase the Quantity of Housing Service Consumed by Low-Income Families?* Santa Monica, California: The RAND Corporation, 1969.

*[641] _____. "Competitive Theory of the Housing Market," *American Economic Review,* LIX (September 1969), 612-622.

[642] _____. "An Econometric Analysis of Rent Control," *Journal of Political Economy,* LXXX (6) (November/December 1972), 1081-1100.

[643] _____. *The Effects of a Simple Rent Control Scheme in a Competitive Housing Market.* Santa Monica, California: The RAND Corporation, 1969.

[644] _____. *An Efficient Method of Improving the Housing of Low Income Families.* Santa Monica, California: The RAND Corporation, 1969.

[645] _____. "Subsidized Housing in a Competitive Market: Reply," *The American Economic Review,* LXI (1) (March 1971), 220-224.

[646] _____. *A Welfare Economic Evaluation of Public Housing.* Houston, Texas: Ph.D. dissertation, Rice University, 1968.

[647] _____ and James R. Prescott. *An Analysis of Alternative Measures of Tenant Benefits of Government Housing Programs with Illustrative Calculations from Public Housing.* Santa Monica, California: The RAND Corporation, 1969.

[648] Ophek, Eli. "On Samuelson's Analysis of Land Rent," *The American Journal of Economics and Sociology,* XXXII (3) (July 1973), 306-310.

*[649] Organization for Social and Technical Innovation. *Self-Help Housing in the U.S.A.* Cambridge, Massachusetts: Organization for Social and Technical Innovation, 1969.

*[650] Ornati, Oscar. *Poverty Amid Affluence: A Report on a Research Project Carried Out at the New School for Social Research.* New York: Twentieth Century Fund, 1966.

*[651] _____. "Poverty in the Cities," in Harvey S. Perloff and Lowdon Wingo, Jr. *Issues in Urban Economics.* Baltimore: The Johns Hopkins University Press, 1967, 335-362.

[652] Orr, Larry L. "The Incidence of Differential Property Taxes on Urban Housing," *National Tax Journal*, XXI (3) (September 1968), 253-262.

[653] _____. "The Incidence of Differential Property Taxes: A Response," *National Tax Journal*, XXIII (1) (March 1970), 99-101.

[654] _____. *The Welfare Economics of Housing for the Poor*. Madison, Wisconsin: Institute for Research on Poverty, The University of Wisconsin—Madison, 1968. (Discussion paper 33-69.)

[655] O'Toole, William J. "A Prototype of Public Housing Policy—The USHC," *Journal of the American Institute of Planners*, XXXIV (3) (May 1968), 140-152.

*[656] Pack, Janet Rothenberg. *Household Relocation: The New Haven Experience*. Fels Center of Government Research Report, March 1973.

*[657] Page, Alfred, N. "Regional Residential Construction Cycles," *Land Economics*, XLI (February 1965), 66-69.

*[658] _____ and W.R. Seyfried (eds.). *Urban Analysis: Readings in Housing and Urban Development*. Glenview, Illinois: Scott Foresman, 1970, 139-145.

*[659] Paldam, Martin. "What is Known About the Housing Demand?" *Swedish Journal of Economics*, LXXII (June 1970), 130-148.

*[660] Papageorgiou, George J. "The Population Density and Rent Distribution Models Within a Multicentre Framework," *Environment and Planning*, III (1971), 267-282.

*[661] _____ and Emilio Casetti. "Spatial Equilibrium Residential Land Values in a Multicenter Setting," *Journal of Regional Science*, (December 1971), 385-389.

[662] Parsons, Kermit C., Harriet L. Budke, Simone Clemhout, Paul B. Farrell, James L. Prost, Ernest F. Roberts. *Public Land Acquisition for New Communities and the Control of Urban Growth: Alternative Strategies*. Ithaca, New York: Center for Urban Development Research, Cornell University, 1973.

*[663] Pascal, Anthony Henry. *The Economics of Housing Segregation*. Santa Monica, California: The RAND Corporation, 1967. (Memorandum RM-5510-RC.)

*[664] Paulus, Virginia. *Housing: A Bibliography, 1960-1972*. New Brunswick, New Jersey: Center for Urban Policy Research, Rutgers University, 1974.

[665] Peavy, John Jr. "Section 236 and Other Housing Programs," *Urban Lawyer*, IV (2) (Spring 1972), 312-314.

[666] Pechman, Joseph A., et al. *Financing State and Local Governments*. Boston: Federal Reserve Bank of Boston, 1970. (Proceedings of a conference, June 1970.)

[667] Penner, Rudolph G. and William L. Silber. "Federal Housing Credit Programs: Costs, Benefits, and Interactions," *The Economics of Federal*

Subsidy Programs. Washington, D.C.: U.S. Government Printing Office, 1972, 660-675. (A compendium of papers submitted to the Joint Economic Committee, Congress of the United States. Part 5—Housing Subsidies. October 9, 1972.)

*[668] Perloff, Harvey S. and Lowdon Wingo, Jr. (eds.). *Issues in Urban Economics*. Washington, D.C.: The Johns Hopkins University Press, 1968.

[669] Peterson, George E. "The Issues of Property Tax Reform," in George E. Peterson (ed.). *Property Tax Reform*. Washington, D.C.: The Urban Institute, 1973, 1-12.

[670] _____. "The Property Tax and Low-Income Housing Markets," in George E. Peterson (ed.). *Property Tax Reform*. Washington, D.C.: The Urban Institute, 1973, 107-124.

[671] _____, Arthur P. Solomon, Hadi Madjid, and William C. Apgar, Jr. *Property Taxes, Housing, and the Cities*. Lexington, Massachusetts: Lexington Books, D.C. Heath and Co., 1973.

*[672] Phillips, Kenneth F. and David Z. Bryson. "Refinancing: A First Step Toward a Realistic Housing Program for the Poor," *George Washington Law Review*, XXXIX (1971), 835.

[673] Pickard, Jerome P. "Adapting the Property Tax to Social and Economic Change," *Urban Land*, XXIV (11) (December 1965), 1 ff.

*[674] _____. *Changing Urban Land Values as Affected by Taxation*. Washington, D.C.: Urban Land Institute, 1962.

[675] _____. "Evaluating Tax Concessions for Urban Renewal," in Tax Institute of America. *The Property Tax: Problems and Potential*. Princeton, New Jersey: Tax Institute of America, 1967, 295-306.

[676] _____. *Taxation and Land Use in Metropolitan and Urban America*. Washington, D.C.: Urban Land Institute, 1966. (Research monograph no. 12.)

[677] _____. "Using the Property Tax to Achieve Social and Economic Change," *Assessment Administration, 1965. Proceedings of the Thirty-First International Conference on Assessment Administration*, 33-38.

[678] Piven, Frances Fox and Richard A. Cloward. "The Case Against Urban Desegregation," in Jon Pynoos, Robert Schafer, and Chester Hartman (eds.). *Housing Urban America*. Chicago: Aldine Publishing Company, 1973, 97-107. (Reprinted from *Social Work*, XII (1) (January 1967), 12-21.)

*[679] Pleeter, Saul. *The Effects of Public Housing on Neighboring Property Values and Rents in Buffalo, New York*. Ann Arbor, Michigan: Ph.D. dissertation, State University of New York at Buffalo, University Microfilms, 1971.

*[680] Plott, Charles R. "Some Organizational Influences on Urban Renewal Decisions," *Papers and Proceedings, American Economic Association*, LVIII (May 1968), 306-321.

[681] Polaha, Stephen J. "Housing Codes and the Prevention of Urban Blight—Administrative and Enforcement Problems and Proposals," *Villanova Law Review*, XVII (3) (February 1972), 490-523.

*[682] Pollock, Richard. "Supply of Residential Construction: A Cross-Section Examination of Recent Housing Market Behavior," *Land Economics*, IL (1) (February 1973), 57-66.

[683] Popp, Dean O. and Frederick D. Sebold. "Redistribution of Tax Liabilities Under Site Value Taxation: A Survey of San Diego County," *The American Journal of Economics and Sociology*, XXXL (4) (October 1972), 413-426.

*[684] Poulsen, Roy G. "Central City Land Use and Suburban Financial Support," *Land Economics*, XLVI (4) (November 1970), 497-502.

*[685] Powers, Mary G. "Age and Space Aspects of City and Suburban Housing," *Land Economics*, XL (November 1964), 381-387.

[686] Prescott, James Russell. *The Economics of Public Housing: A Normative Analysis*. Cambridge, Massachusetts: Ph.D. dissertation, Harvard University, 1964.

[687] _____. "Rental Formation in Federally Supported Public Housing," *Land Economics*, XLIII (3) (August 1967), 341-345.

[688] President's Committee on Urban Housing (The). *A Decent Home—The Report of the President's Committee on Urban Housing*. Washington, D.C.: U.S. Government Printing Office, 1968.

*[689] _____. *Housing Costs, Production, Efficiency, Finance, Manpower, Land. Technical Study Volume II*. New York: Marketing Research Department, McGraw-Hill, 1968.

*[690] President's Task Force on Low Income Housing. *Toward Better Housing for Low Income Families*. Washington, D.C.: President's Task Force on Low Income Housing, 1970.

[691] Price Waterhouse and Company. *A Study of the Effects of Real Estate Property Tax Incentive Programs upon Property Rehabilitation and New Construction*. Sacramento, California: Price Waterhouse & Company, 1973. (Prepared for the Department of Housing and Urban Development; distributed by NTIS–PB-220 409.)

*[692] Princeton University School of Architecture, Research Center for Urban and Environmental Planning. *Cooperation of the Public and Private Sectors in Housing*. Princeton, New Jersey: School of Architecture conference no. 88, 1968.

[693] "Property Tax Debate," *American Journal of Economics and Sociology*, XXXI (April 1972), 113-163.

[694] Public Affairs Counseling. *HUD Experimental Program for Preserving Declining Neighborhoods: An Analysis of the Abandonment Process*. Washington, D.C.: U.S. Department of Housing and Urban Development, 1973.

[695] "Public Housing and Urban Policy: Gautreaux v. Chicago Housing Authority," *The Yale Law Journal*, LXXIX (4) (March 1970), 712-729.

*[696] "Public Landlords and Private Tenants: The Eviction of 'Undesirables' from Public Housing Projects," *Yale Law Journal*, LXXVII (April 1968), 988.
*[697] Pynoos, Jon, Robert Schafer, and Chester W. Hartman (eds.). *Housing Urban America*. Chicago: Aldine Publishing Co., 1973.
[698] Quigley, John M. *The Influence of Workplaces and Housing Stocks upon Residential Choice: A Crude Test of the "Gross Price" Hypothesis*. New Haven, Connecticut: Institution for Social and Policy Studies, Yale University, 1972. (Working paper W3-12.)
[699] Rafsky, William L. *Public Assisted Housing*. 1966. (Prepared for the Study Group of New York Housing and Neighborhood Improvement.)
[700] Rainwater, Lee. "Fear and the House-as-Haven in the Lower Class," *Journal of the American Institute of Planners*, XXXII (1) (January 1966), 23-31.
[701] _____. *Public Responses to Low Income Policies: FAP and Welfare*. Cambridge, Massachusetts: Joint Center for Urban Studies, 1972 (Working paper no. 8.)
[702] Ramsey, David and George Vredeveld. *A Rationale for Government Intervention in Housing: Impact of Government Non-Housing Policies on the Housing and Mortgage Markets*. Columbia, Missouri: College of Administration and Public Affairs, Department of Economics, University of Missouri, 1973.
[703] Rapkin, Chester. "New Towns for America: From Picture to Process," *Journal of Finance*, XXII (2) (May 1967), 208-219.
[704] _____. *The Private Rental Market in New York City, 1965: A Study of Some Effects of Two Decades of Rent Control*. New York: The City of New York, The City Rent and Rehabilitation Administration, 1966.
*[705] _____ and William G. Grigsby. *The Demand for Housing in Racially Mixed Areas; A Study of the Nature of Neighborhood Change*. Berkeley: University of California Press, 1960.
[706] Raymond and May Associates. *Zoning Controversies in the Suburbs: Three Case Studies*. Washington, D.C.: National Commission on Urban Problems, 1968. (Research report no. 11.)
[707] _____ and the staffs of the Nassau County and Suffolk County Planning Departments. *Housing: Better Homes for Better Communities*. Hauppauge, New York: Nassau-Suffolk Regional Planning Board, 1968.
[708] Raymond, Parish & Pine, Inc. *Draft Technical Memoranda Bethlehem Housing Study Bethlehem, Pennsylvania*. Tarrytown, New York: Raymond, Parish & Pine, Inc. 1973.
*[709] Reach, Barbara. *Social Aspects of Cooperative and Non-Profit Housing: New and Rehabilitated*. New York: Community Service Society of New York, 1968. (Background paper for the National Commission on Urban Problems.)

[710] Real Estate Research Corporation. *Program Potentials in Housing: A Regional Action Program (A Study of Housing Conditions and Needs in the Six State New England Region).* Boston: New England Regional Commission, 1971.

[711] Reed, Ella W. and Ellery F. Reed. *A Demonstration Study for Creating "Standard" Housing from Substandard Housing Through Parallel Activity of Code Enforcement Accompanied by Guidance to the Resident Families.* Cincinnati, Ohio: The Better Housing League of Greater Cincinnati, 1966.

[712] Reeves, Marilyn Langford. *Philadelphia's Rent Subsidy Program: A Local Approach Using Private Market Housing.* Ithaca, New York: Center for Urban Development Research, Cornell University, 1969. (Misc. paper no. 8.)

[713] Regional Planning Agency of South Central Connecticut. *Regional Housing Needs: Recommendations.* New Haven, Connecticut: Regional Planning Agency of South Central Connecticut, 1972.

[714] _____. *Regional Housing Needs: A Summary of Existing and Projected Housing Needs for South Central Connecticut.* New Haven, Connecticut: Regional Planning Agency of South Central Connecticut, 1972.

*[715] Reid, Margaret G. *Housing and Income.* Chicago: University of Chicago Press, 1962.

[716] Rein, Martin. *Welfare and Housing.* Cambridge, Massachusetts: Joint Center for Urban Studies of the Massachusetts Institute of Technology and Harvard University, 1972. (Working paper no. 4. Prepared as background materials for the Subcommittee on Housing of the Committee on Banking and Currency, House of Representatives, 92d Congress, 1st Session, June 1971.)

*[717] Reiss, Albert J., Jr. and Howard Aldrich. "Absentee Ownership and Management in the Black Ghetto: Social and Economic Consequences," *Social Problems*, XVIII (Winter 1971), 319-339. (Yale ISPS reprint RI-1.)

[718] "Residential Rent Control in New York City," *Columbia Journal of Law and Social Problems*, III (5) (June 1967), 30-65.

[719] Rhode Island Department of Community Affairs. *Memorandum for the Governor: Title V of H.R. 9688–"Housing Block Grants to State and Metropolitan Housing Agencies"–Analysis and Recommendations.* Providence: Rhode Island Department of Community Affairs, 1972.

[720] _____. *Utilization of the Existing Housing Stock in the Ten Year Period 1960 to 1970–An Analysis of the Trends Affecting the Vacant Housing Stock of the State of Rhode Island.* Providence: Rhode Island Department of Community Affairs, 1971. Research monograph no. 2.

[721] Richman, Raymond L. "The Incidence of Urban Real Estate Taxes

Under Conditions of Static and Dynamic Equilibrium," *Land Economics*, XLIII (2) (May 1967), 172-180.

[722] Richman, Raymond L. "The Theory and Practice of Site-Value Taxation in Pittsburgh," *National Tax Association Proceedings*, 1964, 259-271.

[723] Ricks, Bruce. "New Town Development and the Theory of Location," *Land Economics*, XLVI (1) (February 1970), 5-11.

*[724] Ridker, Ronald. *Economic Costs of Air Pollution*. New York: Praeger Publishers, 1967.

[725] Ritter, Lawrence S. "A Capital Market Plan for the Urban Areas," *California Management Review*, XI (4) (Summer 1969), 37-46.

[726] Rivkin/Carson Inc. *Chapter IV–Policy Recommendations of USA: The Third Century; Guiding the Growth of a Metropolitan Nation*. Washington, D.C.: Rivkin/Carson Inc., 1968. (A draft prepared for the National Urban Coalition.)

[727] Rivkin, Steven R. "Courting Change: Using Litigation to Reform Local Building Codes," *Rutgers Law Review*, XXVI (4) (Summer 1973), 774-802.

[728] Robert R. Nathan Associates, Inc. *The Need and Feasibility of a National Housing Policy for the United States*. Washington, D.C.: Robert R. Nathan Associates, Inc., 1968.

*[729] Robin, R.S. "Taxpayer's Choice Incentive System: An Experimental Approach to Community Economic Development Tax Incentives," *Law and Contemporary Problems*, XXXVI (1) (Winter 1971), 99-118.

*[730] Roegge, Frank E., Gerard J. Talbot, and Robert M. Zinman. "Real Estate Equity Investments and the Institutional Lender: Nothing Ventured, Nothing Gained," *Fordham Law Review*, XXXIX (May 1971), 579.

*[731] Ronfelt, Stephen F. and Denis J. Clifford. "Judicial Enforcement of the Housing and Urban Development Act," *Hastings Law Journal*, XXI (January 1970), 317.

*[732] Rosen, Albert. "Receivership: A Useful Tool for Helping to Meet the Housing Needs of Low Income People," *Harvard Civil Rights Law Review*, III (Spring 1968), 311.

[733] Rosenblatt, Joel. *Discretion as a Variable in Housing Code Enforcement*. Washington, D.C.: The Urban Institute, 1970. (Working paper no. 9.)

[734] Ross, Hardies, O'Keefe, Babcock, McDugald & Parsons. *The Conflict Between Regional Goals and Local Land Use Controls*. Chicago: National Commission on Urban Problems, 1966. (Background paper no. 3.)

[735] Rothenberg, Jerome. *Economic Evaluation of Urban Renewal; Conceptual Foundation of Benefit-Cost Analysis*. Washington, D.C.: The Brookings Institution, 1967.

[736] _____. "Urban Renewal Programs," in Robert Dorfman (ed.). *Measuring Benefits of Government Investments*. Washington, D.C.: The Brookings Institution, 1965, 292-366.

[737] Rothenstein, Guy G. *Investment of Potential Savings in Total Building Cost of Multi-Family Housing Built by Industrialized Building Systems.* Washington, D.C.: National Commission on Urban Problems, 1968. (Research report no. 31.)

[738] Rothschild, Michael. "Models of Market Organization with Imperfect Information," Harvard Institute of Economic Research, Discussion on paper #224, December 1971.

*[739] Royer, Donald M. *Attitudes of White and Negro Residents Towards Living in Integrated Neighborhoods in Thirteen Indiana Communities.* Indianapolis, Indiana: Civil Rights Commission, 1964.

[740] Rybeck, Walter. *How the Property Tax Can be Modernized to Encourage Housing Construction, Rehabilitation and Repair.* Washington, D.C.: The Urban Institute, 1969. (Working paper no. 112-13.)

[741] _____ (ed.). *A Symposium: Property Taxation, Housing, and Urban Growth.* Washington, D.C.: The Urban Institute, 1970.

[742] Rydell, C. Peter. *Factors Affecting Maintenance and Operating Costs in Federal Public Housing Projects.* New York: The New York City RAND Institute, 1973.

[743] _____. *The Landlord Reinvestment Model: A Computer Based Method of Evaluating the Financial Feasibility of Alternative Treatments for Problem Buildings.* New York: The New York City RAND Institute, 1970.

[744] _____. "Review of Factors Affecting Maintenance and Operating Costs in Public Housing," *Papers and Proceedings of the Regional Science Association*, XXVII (1971), 229-245.

[745] Sabella, Edward M. "The Effects of Property Taxes and Local Public Expenditures on the Sales Prices of Residential Dwellings," *The Appraisal Journal*, XLII (1) (January 1974), 114-125.

[746] Sadacca, Robert, Suzanna B. Loux, Morton L. Isler, Margaret J. Drury. *Management Performance in Public Housing.* Washington, D.C.: The Urban Institute, 1974.

[747] Sagalyn, Lynne B. and George Sternlieb. *Zoning and Housing Costs; The Impact of Land-Use Controls on Housing Price.* New Brunswick, New Jersey: Center for Urban Policy Research, Rutgers University, 1973.

*[748] Sager, Lawrence Gene. "Tight Little Islands: Exclusionary Zoning, Equal Protection and the Indigent," *Stanford Law Review*, XXI (April 1969), 767.

[749] Sanoff, Henry et al. *Low Income Housing Demonstration.* Berkeley, California: Department of Architecture, University of California at Berkeley, 1965. (Prepared for the U.S. Department of Housing and Urban Development.)

[750] Sause, George G. "Appraisal of the Property Tax," *The American Journal of Economics and Sociology*, XXIX (1) (January 1970), 97-108.

[751] Sazama, Gerald W. "Equalization of Property Taxes for the Nation's

Largest Central Cities," *National Tax Journal*, XVIII (2) (June 1965), 151.

[752] Schaaf, A.H. *Economic Aspects of Urban Renewal: Theory, Policy, and Area Analysis*. Berkeley, California: Real Estate Research Program, Institute of Business and Economic Research, University of California at Berkeley, 1960.

[753] _____. "Economic Feasibility Analysis for Urban Renewal Housing Rehabilitation," *Journal of the American Institute of Planners*, XXXV (6) (November 1969), 399-404.

[754] _____. "Effect of Federal Mortgage Underwriting on Residential Construction," *The Appraisal Journal* (January 1967), 54-69.

[755] _____. "Effects of Property Taxation on Slums and Renewal: A Study of Land Improvement Assessment Ratios," *Land Economics*, XLV (1) (February 1969), 111-117.

[756] _____. *The Potential of Subsidized Housing Rehabilitation*. Berkeley, California: Center for Real Estate and Urban Economics, University of California at Berkeley, 1970. (Reprint no. 69. Reprinted from *Proceedings*, American Real Estate and Urban Economics Association, V (1970), 105-116.)

[757] _____. "Public Policies in Urban Renewal: An Economic Analysis of Justifications and Effects," *Land Economics*, XL, (1) (February 1964), 67-78.

[758] _____. "Rising Vacancy Rates Aren't Always Bad," *Real Estate Review* II (4) (Winter 1973), 101-104.

*[759] _____. "Some Theory and Policy Implications of the Postwar Housing Boom," *Land Economics*, XLII (May 1966), 179-187.

*[760] Schafer, Robert and Charles G. Field. "Section 235—National Housing Act: Homeownership for Low-Income Families," *Journal of Urban Law*, XLVI (1968), 667.

[761] Schechter, Henry B. "Federal Housing Subsidy Programs," *The Economics of Federal Subsidy Programs*. Washington, D.C.: U.S. Government Printing Office, 1972, 597-630. (A compendium of papers submitted to the Joint Economic Committee, Congress of the United States. Part 5—Housing Subsidies. October 9, 1972.)

*[762] _____ and Marion K. Schlefer. "Housing Needs and National Goals," *Papers Submitted to Subcommittee on Housing Panels on Housing Production, Housing Demand, and Developing a Suitable Living Environment: Part I*. Washington, D.C.: U.S. Government Printing Office, 1971, 1-139.

*[763] Schermer, George and Arthur J. Levin. *Housing Guide to Equal Opportunity: Affirmative Practices for Integrated Housing*. Washington, D.C.: The Potomac Institute, Inc., 1968.

[764] Schmandt, Henry J. "Municipal Control of Urban Expansion," *Fordham Law Review*, XXIX (4) (April 1961), 637-656.

[765] Schmenner, Roger W. *Urban Redevelopment: Can It Pay Its Own Way?* New Haven, Connecticut: Institution for Social and Policy Studies, Yale University, 1973. (Working paper W3-2.)

*[766] Schmitt, Robert C. "Implications of Density in Hong Kong," *Journal of the American Institute of Planners*, XXXIX (3) (August 1963).

[767] Schoenbrod, David S. "Large Lot Zoning," *Yale Law Journal*, LXXVIII (8) (July 1969), 1418-1441.

[768] Schorr, Alvin L. *Slums and Social Insecurity: An Appraisal of the Effectiveness of Housing Policies in Helping to Eliminate Poverty in the United States.* Washington, D.C.: U.S. Government Printing Office. (U.S. Department of Health, Education, and Welfare, Social Security Administration, Division of Research and Statistics. Research report no. 1.)

[769] Schreiberg, Sheldon L. "Abandoned Buildings: Tenant Condominiums and Community Redevelopment," *The Urban Lawyer*, II (2) (Spring 1970), 186-218.

[770] Sears, Gregory H. *Shelter and Surplus Land; A Report on the Potential of Federal Surplus Property.* Washington, D.C.: The Center for National Policy Review, School of Law, Catholic University of America, 1973.

*[771] Sengstock, Frank S. and M.C. Sengstock. "Homeownership: A Goal for All Americans," *Journal of Urban Law*, XLVI (1967), 317.

[772] Shannon, John. "The Property Tax: Reform or Relief?" in George E. Peterson (ed.). *Property Tax Reform.* Washington, D.C.: The Urban Institute, 1973, 25-52.

*[773] Shelton, John P. "The Cost of Renting Versus Owning a Home," *Land Economics*, XLIV (February 1968), 59-72.

*[774] Shenkel, William L. "Self-Help Housing in the United States," *Land Economics*, XLIII (2) (May 1967), 190-201.

*[775] Shinn, A.M. "Measuring the Utility of Housing: Demonstrating a Methodological Approach," *Social Science Quarterly*, LII (June 1971), 88-102.

*[776] Shoup, Donald C. "Advance Land Acquisition by Local Governments: A Cost-Benefit Analysis," *Yale Economic Essays*, IX (2) (Fall 1969), 147-207.

[777] Shuman, Howard E. "The Role of Housing Code Enforcement in Meeting the Housing Needs of the Low-Income Family," *Journal of Housing*, XXV (11) (December 1968), 568-570.

[778] Siegel, Richard A. "Stability of Input-Output Production Coefficients for the Residential Construction Industry," *Land Economics*, XL (3) (August 1964), 331-335.

*[779] Sigsworth, E.M. and R.K. Wilkinson. "The Measurement of Deficiencies in the Housing Stock," *Yorkshire Bulletin of Economic and Social Research*, XXII (November 1970), 143-163.

[780] Sims, Christopher A. "Efficiency in the Construction Industry," *Report of the President's Committee on Urban Housing, Technical Studies, Volume II*, (1968), 149-174.

[781] Slavet, Joseph S. and Melvin R. Levin. *New Approaches to Housing Code Administration.* Washington, D.C.: National Commission on Urban Problems, 1969. (Research report no. 17.)

*[782] Slitor, Richard E. *The Federal Income Tax in Relation to Housing.* Washington, D.C.: U.S. Government Printing Office, 1969. (National Commission on Urban Problems, research report no. 5.)

[783] Smart, Walter, Walter Rybeck, Howard E. Shuman. *The Large Poor Family—A Housing Gap.* Washington, D.C.: Communication Service Corporation, 1968. (National Commission on Urban Problems, research report no. 4.)

*[784] Smith, Lawrence B. "A Bi-Sectoral Housing Market Model," *Canadian Journal of Economics*, II (November 1969), 557-569.

*[785] _____. "A Sectoral Econometric Study of the Postwar Residential Housing Market: An Opposite View," *Journal of Political Economy*, LXXIII (March-April 1970), 268-278.

[786] Smith, R. Stafford. "Property Tax Capitalization in San Francisco," *National Tax Journal*, XXIII (2) (June 1970), 177-193.

[787] Smith, Theodore Reynolds. "Land Value Versus Real Property Taxation: A Case Study Comparison," *Land Economics*, XLVI (3) (August 1970), 305-313.

[788] _____. *Real Property Taxation and the Urban Center: A Case Study of Hartford, Connecticut.* Hartford, Connecticut: John C. Lincoln Institute, 1972.

[789] Smith, Wallace F. "Filtering and Neighborhood Change," in Michael A. Stegman (ed.). *Housing and Economics: The American Dilemma.* Cambridge, Massachusetts: The Massachusetts Institute of Technology Press, 1971, 64-89.

[790] _____. *Housing: The Social and Economic Elements.* Berkeley: University of California Press, 1970.

*[791] _____. "The Income Level of New Housing Demand," *Essays in Urban Land Economics.* Los Angeles: University of California Press, 1966, 143-178.

*[792] _____. *Land Using Activities.* Berkeley, California: The Center for Real Estate and Urban Economics, University of California at Berkeley, 1970. (Research report no. 33.)

[793] _____. "The Implementation of the Rent Supplement Program—A Staff View," *Law and Contemporary Problems*, XXXII (3) (Summer 1967), 482-489.

[794] Smolensky, Eugene. "Public Housing or Income Supplements: The Economics of Housing for the Poor," *Journal of the American Institute of Planners*, XXXIV (2) (March 1968), 94-101.

[795] _____ et al. *The Economics of Anti-Poverty Programs Involving Income-in-Kind, Phase I: The Public Housing Case.* Chicago: The Center for Urban Studies, The University of Chicago, 1967.

[796] _____ and J. Douglas Gomery. *Efficiency and Equity Effects in the Benefits from the Federal Housing Program in 1965.* Madison, Wisconsin: Institute for Research on Poverty, University of Wisconsin—Madison, 1973. (Reprint no. 88. Reprinted from "Benefit-Cost Analyses of Federal Programs," a Joint Economic Committee Print, 92d Congress, 2d Session, U.S. Government Printing Office, January 2, 1973, 144-181.)

[797] _____, Selwyn Becker, and Harvey Molotch. "The Prisoner's Dilemma and Ghetto Expansion," *Land Economics*, XLIV (4) (November 1968), 419-430.

[798] Solomon, Arthur P. *The Cost Effectiveness of Subsidized Housing.* Cambridge, Massachusetts: Joint Center for Urban Studies, 1971. (Working paper no. 5.)

[799] _____. *Housing Allowances: Their Meaning for the Urban Poor.* Cambridge, Massachusetts: Joint Center for Urban Studies, 1973. (Submitted for presentation to the American Institute of Planners Conference, 1973.)

[800] _____. *Housing and Public Policy Analysis.* Cambridge, Massachusetts: Joint Center for Urban Studies, 1972. (Working paper no. 12.)

[801] _____. *Housing the Urban Poor.* Cambridge, Massachusetts: Joint Center for Urban Studies, 1974.

[802] _____ and George E. Peterson. *Property Taxes and Populist Reform.* Cambridge, Massachusetts: Joint Center for Urban Studies, 1972. (Working paper no. 16.)

*[803] Sparks, Gordon R. "A Model of the Mortgage Market and Residential Construction Activity," in American Statistical Association. *Proceedings of the Business and Economics Statistics Section's Annual Meeting, 1967.* Washington, D.C.: American Statistical Association, 1967, 77-83.

*[804] Spengler, Joseph J. "Population Pressure, Housing, and Habitat," *Law and Contemporary Problems*, XXXII (2) (Spring 1967), 191-208.

*[805] Spohn, Richard B. "The Owner-Builder: Analysis and Recommendations," *Harvard Journal on Legislation*, IX (1972), 424.

*[806] "Sponsorship of Subsidized Housing for Low and Moderate Income Families Under the National Housing Act," *George Washington Law Review*, XXXVIII (1970), 1973.

*[807] Sporn, Arthur D. "Empirical Studies in the Economics of Slum Ownership," *Land Economics*, XXXVI, (November 1960), 333-340.

[808] _____. "Some Contributions of the Income Tax Law to the Growth and Prevalence of Slums," *Columbia Law Review*, LIX (7) (November 1959), 1026-1064.

*[809] Stahl, I. "Some Aspects of a Mixed Housing Market," in A.A. Nevitt (ed.). *The Economic Problems of Housing.* New York: St. Martin's Press, 1967, 73-84.

[810] Stanford Research Institute. *A Capital Improvement Program for Rehab-*

ilitation of Three Public Multifamily Housing Projects and Analysis of Alternative Future Prospects for the Housing Authority. Menlo Park, California: Stanford Research Institute, 1969.

[811] Staples, John H. "Urban Renewal: A Comparative Study of Twenty-Two Cities, 1950-1960," *Western Political Quarterly*, XXIII (2) (June 1970), 294-304.

*[812] Starr, Roger. "Housing the City's People," *Proceedings of the Academy of Political Science*, XXIX (August 1969), 133-147.

[813] Stegman, Michael A. (ed.). *Housing and Economics; The American Dilemma.* Cambridge, Massachusetts and London: The Massachusetts Institute of Technology Press, 1970.

[814] _____. *Housing Investment in the Inner City: The Dynamics of Decline; A Study of Baltimore, Maryland; 1968-1970.* Cambridge, Massachusetts: The Massachusetts Institute of Technology Press, 1972.

[815] _____. "Low-Income Ownership; Exploitation and Opportunity," *Journal of Urban Law*, L (3) (February 1973), 371-402.

*[816] _____. "The New Mythology of Housing," in Susan S. Fainstein and Norman I. Fainstein, *The View from Below: Urban Politics and Social Policy.* Boston: Little, Brown and Company, 1972.

*[817] _____. "Slum Housing: Case Flow, Maintenance and Management," in Stephen D. Messner (ed.). *Proceedings, American Real Estate and Urban Economics Association*, IV (1970), 231-252.

*[818] _____. "Slumlords and Public Policy," *Journal of the American Institute of Planners*, XXXIII (6) (November 1967), 419-424.

*[819] Stern, Andrew. "Fluctuations in Residential Construction: Some Evidence from the Spectral Estimates," *Review of Economics and Statistics*, LIV (2) (August 1972), 328-332.

[820] Sternberg, Arnold C. "A Guide to Collaboration with Private Developers in Subsidized Housing," *Using Joint Ventures in Model Cities.* Washington, D.C.: Model Cities Service Center, National League of Cities, U.S. Conference of Mayors, 1971.

[821] Sternlieb, George. "The Abandoned Building as a Clue to the Future of the American City," in George Sternlieb. *Some Aspects of the Abandoned House Problem.* New Brunswick, New Jersey: Center for Urban Policy Research, Rutgers University, 1970. Testimony Prepared for the U.S. Senate Subcommittee on Housing and Urban Affairs of the Banking and Currency Committee, July 23, 1970.

*[822] _____. "Abandoned Housing—What is to be Done?" *Urban Land*, XXXI (3) (March 1972), 6.

*[823] _____. "Abandonment and Rehabilitation: What Is To Be Done?" *Papers*, 315. New Brunswick, New Jersey: Center for Urban Policy Research, Rutgers University.

[824] _____. "The City as Sandbox," *The Public Interest* (25) (Fall 1971), 14-21.

*[825] _____. *The Garden Apartment Development: A Municipal Cost-Revenue Analysis.* New Brunswick, New Jersey: Bureau of Economic Research, Rutgers University, 1964.

[826] _____. *The Tenement Landlord.* New Brunswick, New Jersey: Center for Urban Policy Research, Rutgers University, 1966.

[827] _____. "Slum Housing: A Functional Analysis," *Law and Contemporary Problems*, XXXII (2) (Spring 1967), 349-356.

[828] _____. *The Urban Housing Dilemma: The Dynamics of New York City's Rent Controlled Housing.* New York: The City of New York, Housing and Development Administration, Department of Rent and Housing Maintenance, Office of Rent Control, 1972.

[829] _____, W. Patrick Beaton, Robert W. Burchell, James W. Hughes, Franklin J. James, David Listokin, and Duane Windsor. *Housing Development and Municipal Costs.* New Brunswick, New Jersey: Center for Urban Policy Research, Rutgers University, 1973.

[830] Sternlieb, George and Robert W. Burchell. *Residential Abandonment; The Tenement Landlord Revisited.* New Brunswick, New Jersey: Center for Urban Policy Research, Rutgers University, 1973.

*[831] _____ and James W. Hughes. *Housing Costs and Housing Restraints.* New Brunswick, New Jersey: Center for Urban Policy Research, Rutgers University, 1970.

[832] Sternlieb, George and Bernard Indik. "Housing Vacancy Analysis," *Land Economics*, XLV (1) (February 1969), 117-121.

*[833] Sternlieb, George and Virginia Paulus (eds.). *Housing, 1971-1972.* New Brunswick, New Jersey: Center for Urban Policy Research, Rutgers University, 1974.

[834] Stickney, Lawrence E. "Coming of Age in America: The Need for Property Tax Reform," *The Administrative Law Review*, XXI (3) (April 1969), 325-345.

*[835] Stigler, George J. "The Economics of Information," *Journal of Political Economy*, LXIX (6) (June 1961), 213-225.

[836] Stinchcombe, Arthur L. "Bureaucratic and Craft Administration of Production," *Administrative Science Quarterly* (September 1959), 168-187.

[837] Stockfish, J.A. *An Investigation of the Opportunities for Reducing the Cost of Federally Subsidized Low-Income Families.* Arlington, Virginia: Institute for Defense Analysis, 1968. (AD 782 897.)

*[838] Straszheim, Mahlon R. *The Demand for Residential Housing Services.* Cambridge, Massachusetts: Harvard Institute of Economic Research, Harvard University, 1971. (Discussion paper no. 192.)

*[839] _____. *Modeling Urban Housing Markets and Metropolitan Change: An Econometric Approach.* New York: National Bureau of Economic Research, 1972.

*[840] Stuart, Darwin G. and Robert B. Teska. "Who Pays for What: A Cost

Revenue Analysis of Suburban Land Use Alternatives," *Urban Land*, XXX (3) (March 1971).
[841] Subcommittee on Intergovernmental Relations of the Committee on Government Operations, United States Senate. *Status of Property Tax Administration in the States; Compilation of State Responses to Survey.* Washington, D.C.: U.S. Government Printing Office, 1973.
[842] Subcommittee on Legal and Monetary Affairs, Committee on Government Operations, House of Representatives, 92nd Congress, 2nd Session. *Defaults on FHA-Insured Home Mortgages–Detroit, Michigan.* Washington, D.C.: U.S. Government Printing Office, 1972. (House report no. 92-1152.)
[843] Subcommittee on Urban Affairs, United States Congress. *Urban America: Goals and Problems.* Washington, D.C.: U.S. Government Printing Office, 1967.
[844] Sullivan, Donald G. *Cooperative Housing and Community Development: A Comparative Evaluation of Three Housing Projects in East Harlem.* New York: Praeger Publishers, 1969.
*[845] Sullivan, L.A. "Flexibility and the Rule of Law in American Zoning Administration," in Charles M. Haar, *Law and Land: Anglo-American Planning Practice.* Cambridge, Massachusetts: Harvard and The Massachusetts Institute of Technology Press, 1964.
*[846] Surrey, Stanley S. "Federal Income Tax Reform: The Varied Approaches Necessary to Replace Tax Expenditures with Direct Governmental Assistance," *Harvard Law Review*, LXXXIV (December 1970), 352-408.
*[847] _____. *Pathways to Tax Reform; The Concept of Tax Expenditures.* Cambridge, Massachusetts: Harvard University Press, 1973.
[848] _____. "Tax Incentives as a Device for Implementing Government Policy: A Comparison with Direct Government Expenditures," *Harvard Law Review*, LXXXIII (4) (February 1970), 705-738.
*[849] Sussna, Stephen. "Apartment Zoning Trends," *Connecticut Bar Journal*, XLVI (December 1972), 688.
[850] _____. "Bulk Control and Zoning: The New York City Experience," *Land Economics*, XLIII (2) (May 1967), 158-171.
[851] _____. *Land Use Control–More Effective Approaches.* Washington, D.C.: Urban Land Institute, 1970. (Research monograph no. 17.)
[852] Sutermeister, Oscar. "Inadequacies and Inconsistencies in the Definition of Substandard Housing," in Eric W. Mood, Barnet Lieberman, and Oscar Sutermeister. *Housing Code Standards: Three Critical Studies.* Washington, D.C.: National Commission on Urban Problems, 1969. (Research report no. 19.)
*[853] Swan, Craig E. "Homebuilding: A Review of Experience," *Brookings Papers on Economic Activity*, I (1) (1970), 48-70.

*[854] _____. "Labor and Material Requirements for Housing," *Brookings Papers on Economic Activity*, I (2) (1971), 347-387.

[855] Szanton, Peter L. "Systems Problems in the City." The RAND Corporation, April 1972.

[856] Szego, G.C. *Cost-Reducing Condominium Systems for Low-Cost Homes.* Arlington, Virginia: Institute for Defense Analysis, 1968. (AD 682 896.)

*[857] Tabb, William K. "A Cost-Benefit Analysis of Location Subsidies for Ghetto Neighborhoods," *Land Economics*, XLVIII (1) (February 1972), 45-52.

[858] Taggart, Robert III. *Low-Income Housing: A Critique of Federal Aid.* Baltimore and London: The Johns Hopkins University Press, 1970.

[859] Taube, Gerald and Jack Levin. "Public Housing as Neighborhood: The Effect of Local and Non-Local Participation," *Social Science Quarterly*, LII (3) (December 1971), 534-542.

[860] Taubman, P. and R. Rasche. "Subsidies, Economic Lives, and Complete Resource Misallocation," *The American Economic Review*, LXI (5) (December 1971), 938-945.

[861] Teitz, Michael B. "Some Observations on Policy Analysis in New York City." *Papers of the Regional Science Association*, 27, 247-56.

[862] TEMPO Center for Advanced Studies. *Selecting Urban Renewal Projects in Small Cities.* Santa Barbara, California: TEMPO Center for Advanced Studies, General Electric Company, 1972. (Prepared for Redevelopment Agency, City of Santa Maria, California under HUD Demonstration Project California D-9. GE72TMP-21(1).)

*[863] _____. *U.S. Housing Needs: 1968-1978.* Santa Barbara, California: TEMPO Center for Advanced Studies, General Electric Company, 1968.

[864] Teplitz, Paul, David Birch, and Bernard J. Frieden. *Forecasting Metropolitan Housing Needs.* Cambridge, Massachusetts: Joint Center for Urban Studies of the Massachusetts Institute of Technology and Harvard University, 1973. (Working paper no. 19.)

[865] Thiokol Chemical Corporation, Economic Development Operations. *Forest Heights Low Income Homeownership Program: Research and Final Report.* Ogden, Utah: Thiokol Chemical Corporation, 1970.

[866] Thorndike, Samuel L., Jr. "Some Theoretical Aspects of Building Value Tax Burdens on Landowners," *Land Economics*, XLVI (1) (February 1970), 59-67.

*[867] Tondro, Terry J. "Urban Renewal Relocation: Problems on Enforcement of Conditions of Federal Grants to Local Agencies," *University of Pennsylvania Law Review*, CXVII (December (1968), 83.

[868] Touche Ross & Co. *Study on Tax Considerations in Multi-Family Housing Investments.* Washington, D.C.: U.S. Government Printing Office, 1972. (Prepared for the U.S. Department of Housing and Urban Development.)

[869] Tullock, Gordon. "Subsidized Housing in a Competitive Market; Comment," *The American Economic Review*, LXI (1) (March 1971), 218-219.

*[870] Uhler, Russell Shelley. "The Demand for Housing: An Inverse Probability Approach," *Review of Economics and Statistics*, L (1) (February 1968), 129-134.

[871] Ukeles, Jacob B. *The Consequences of Municipal Zoning.* Washington, D.C.: Urban Land Institute, 1964.

*[872] United States Department of Housing and Urban Development. *A Compendium of Report Resulting From HUD Research and Technology Funding.* Washington, D.C.: HUD-RT-26, December 1972.

*[873] _____. Abandoned Housing Research: A Compendium. Washington, D.C.: U.S. Government Printing Office, to be published.

*[874] _____. *Code Enforcement.* Washington, D.C.: U.S. Department of Housing and Urban Development, 1972. (Community development evaluation series no. 5.)

[875] _____. *Housing in the Seventies.* Washington, D.C.: U.S. Government Printing Office, 1973.

*[876] _____. *Neighborhood Conservation and Property Rehabilitation Bibliography.* Washington, D.C.: U.S. Government Printing Office, 1969.

*[877] Urban Planning Aid, Incorporated. *Evaluation of the Boston Rehabilitation Program.* Cambridge, Massachusetts: Tenants Association of Boston, 1969.

[878] Urban Research Center, Hunter College of the City University of New York. *The Relationship of Zoning to Housing Adequacy and Availability for those of Low and Moderate Incomes.* New York: Urban Research Center, Hunter College of the City University of New York, 1968. (Background paper prepared for the National Commission on Urban Problems.)

*[879] Valore, Joseph A. "Product Liability for a Defective House," *Insurance Law Journal* (558) (July 1969), 395-405.

[880] Van Alstyne, Carol (ed.). *Land Bank Handbook; Advance Acquisition of Sites for Low and Moderate Income Housing.* Greensboro, North Carolina: Piedmont Triad Council of Governments, 1972.

*[881] Van Hoorn, Elisabeth. *Code Enforcement for Multiple Dwellings in New York City: A Survey with Recommendations*, Parts I and II. New York: Community Service Society, 1962 and 1965.

[882] Vine, James R. "The Role and Responsibility of the Assessor," in Tax Institute of America. *The Property Tax: Problems and Potential.* Princeton, New Jersey: Tax Institute of America, 1967, 95-102.

[883] von Borries, Hans-Wilkin. "Local Finance and Community Development," *Journal of the American Institute of Planners*, XXX (1) (February 1964), 34-45.

[884] von Furstenberg, George M. "Default Risk on FHA-Insured Home Mortgages as a Function of the Terms of Financing: A Quantitative Analysis," *The Journal of Finance*, XXIV (3) (June 1969), 459-477.

[885] _____. "The Distribution of Federally Assisted Rental Housing Services by Regions and States," *The Economics of Federal Subsidy Programs*. Washington, D.C.: U.S. Government Printing Office, 1972, 631-641. (A compendium of papers submitted to the Joint Economic Committee, Congress of the United States. Part 5–Housing Subsidies. October 9, 1972.)

[886] _____. "Improving the Feasibility of Homeownership for Lower-Income Families Through Subsidized Mortgage Financing," in The President's Committee on Urban Housing. *Technical Studies, Volume I*, Part II. Washington, D.C.: U.S. Government Printing Office, 1967.

[887] _____. "Interstate Differences in Mortgage Lending Risks: An Analysis of the Causes," *Journal of Financial and Quantitative Analysis*, V (2) (June 1970), 229-242.

[888] _____. "The Investment Quality of Home Mortgages," *Journal of Risk and Insurance*, XXXVII (3) (September 1970), 437-445.

[889] _____. "Risk Structures and the Distribution of Benefits within the FHA Home Mortgage Insurance Program," *Journal of Money, Credit and Banking*, II (3) (August 1970), 303-322.

[890] _____. *Technical Studies of Mortgage Default Risk: An Analysis of the Experience with FHA and VA Home Loans During the Decade 1957-1966*. Ithaca, New York: Center for Urban Development Research, Cornell University, 1971.

*[891] _____ and Howard R. Moskof. "Federally Assisted Rental Housing Programs: Which Income Groups Have They Served or Whom Can They Be Expected to Serve?" in *The Report of the President's Committee on Urban Housing: Technical Studies*, I. Washington, D.C.: U.S. Government Printing Office, 1967.

*[892] Wallace, A. "Forecasting Housing Starts: A Disaggregated Model," *Business Economics*, IV (3) (May 1969), 29-31.

[893] Wallace, James E. "Federal Income Tax Incentives in Low- and Moderate-Income Rental Housing," *The Economics of Federal Subsidy Programs*. Washington, D.C.: U.S. Government Printing Office, 1972, 676-705. (A compendium of papers submitted to the Joint Economic Committee, Congress of the United States. Part 5–Housing Subsidies. October 9, 1972.)

[894] Weaver, Robert C. "Poverty In America–The Role of Urban Renewal," in Margaret Gordon (ed.). *Poverty in America*. San Francisco: Chandler Publishing Co., 1965, 323-334. (Published for the Institute of Industrial Relations, University of California at Berkeley.)

*[895] Webber, Melvin. "The Roles of Intelligence Systems in Urban-Systems

Planning," *Journal of American Institute of Planners*, XXXI (6) (November 1965).

[896] Wehner, Harrison G., Jr. *Sections 235 and 236; An Economic Evaluation of HUD's Principal Housing Subsidy Programs.* Washington, D.C.: American Enterprise Institute for Public Policy Research, 1973. (Evaluative studies no. 8.)

*[897] Weicher, John C. "The Effect of Urban Renewal on Municipal Service Expenditures," *Journal of Political Economy*, LXXX (January 1972), 86-101.

*[898] Weimer, Arthur M. "Future Factors in Housing Demand: Some Comments," *Essays in Urban Land Economics.* Los Angeles: University of California Press, 1966, 179-187.

[899] Weiner, Neil S. *Supply Conditions for Low-Cost Housing Production.* Arlington, Virginia: Institute for Defense Analysis, 1968. (AD 682 895.)

*[900] Weinstein, Bernard L. "State Tax Incentives to Promote Private Investment in Urban Poverty Areas: An Evaluation," *Land Economics*, XLVII (4) (November 1971), 421-423.

*[901] Weisbrod, Burton A. "Preventing High School Dropouts," in Robert Dorfman (ed.). *Measuring Benefits of Government Investments*, Washington, D.C.: The Brookings Institution, 1965, 117-167.

*[902] Weiss, Shirley F., Thomas G. Donnelly, and Edward J. Kaiser. "Land Values and Land Development Influence Factors: An Analytical Approach for Examining Policy Alternatives," *Land Economics*, XLII (May 1966), 230-233.

*[903] Weiss, Shirley F., Edward J. Kaiser, and Raymond J. Burby III (eds.). *New Community Development: Planning Process, Implementation, and Emerging Social Concern.* Chapel Hill, North Carolina: Center for Urban and Regional Studies, University of North Carolina, 1971. (Volumes I and II.)

*[904] Weissbourd, Bernard. "Satellite Communities; A Proposal for a New Housing Program," *Urban Land*, XXXI (9) (October 1972), 1-18.

[905] Welfeld, Irving H. "Rent Supplements and the Subsidy Dilemma: The Equity of a Selective Subsidy System," *Law and Contemporary Problems*, XXXII (3) (Summer 1967), 465-481.

[906] Wendell, Frana Summa. *Code Enforcement: Patterns and Consequences of Landlord Response to Housing Codes.* Bronx, New York: Ph.D. dissertation, Fordham University, 1971.

[907] Wendt, Paul F. "The Determination of National Housing Policies," *Land Economics*, XLV (3) (August 1969), 323-332.

[908] Wheaton, William L.C. "Public and Private Agents of Change in Urban Expansion," in Webber (ed.). *Explorations into Urban Structure.* Philadelphia: University of Pennsylvania Press, 1963.

*[909] Wheaton, William L.C., William C. Baer, and David M. Vetter. *Housing,*

Renewal and Development Bibliography. Monticello, Illinois: Council of Planning Librarians, 1968. (Exchange bibliography no. 46.)

[910] _____, Peter Bass, Donald Grainek, Robert Frank, and Margaret F. Wheaton. *Housing Needs and Urban Development, with Special Reference to Local and Federal Incentives for a More Equitable Distribution of Low Income Families*. Berkeley, California: College of Environmental Design, University of California, 1971. (Report to Housing Subcommittee, Committee on Banking and Currency, U.S. House of Representatives.)

*[911] _____, Grace Milgram and Margy Ellin Meyerson. *Urban Housing*. New York: Free Press, 1966.

*[912] Wheeler, James O. "Work-Trip Length and the Ghetto," *Land Economics*, XLIV (1) (February 1968), 107-112.

*[913] White, Melvin and Anne White. "Horizontal Inequality in the Federal Income Tax Treatment of Homeowners and Tenants," *National Tax Journal*, XVIII (September 1965), 225-239.

[914] Whittlesey, Robert B. *The South End Row House and its Rehabilitation for Low-Income Residents*. Boston, Massachusetts: South End Community Development, Inc., 1969.

*[915] Whyte, William H. *Cluster Development*. New York: American Conservation Association, 1964.

[916] Wicks, John H., Robert A. Little, and Ralph A. Beck. "A Note on the Capitalization of Property Tax Changes," *National Tax Journal*, XXI (3) (September 1968), 263-265.

[917] Wightman, James W. *The Impact of State and Local Fiscal Policies on Redevelopment Areas in the Northeast*. Boston: Federal Reserve Bank of Boston, 1968. (Research report no. 40.)

[918] Wilbur, D. Elliott, Jr. *Housing: Expectations and Realities; A Guide to the Intricacies of Providing Shelter*. Washington, D.C.: Gryphon House, 1971.

*[919] Wilkinson, R.K. "House Prices and the Measurement of Externalities," *Economic Journal*, LXXXIII (March 1973), 72-86.

*[920] Williams, J. Allen, Jr. "The Effects of Urban Renewal Upon a Black Community: Evaluation and Recommendations," *Social Science Quarterly*, L (3) (December 1969), 703-712.

*[921] _____. "The Multifamily Housing Solution and Housing Type Preference," *Social Science Quarterly*, LII (December 1971), 543-549.

[922] Williams, Lawrence A., Eddie M. Young, and Michael A. Fischetti. *Survey of the Administration of Construction Codes in Selected Metropolitan Areas*. Washington, D.C.: National League of Cities, 1968. (National Commission on Urban Problems. Background paper no. 28.)

*[923] Williams, Norman, Jr. "The Three Systems of Land Use Control (or Exclusionary Zoning and Revision of Enabling Legislation)," *Rutgers Law Review*, XXV (1970), 80.

*[924] Williams, Norman, Jr. and Edward Wacks, "Segregation of Residential Areas Along Economic Lines: Lionshead Lake Revisited," *Wisconsin Law Review*, (1969), 827.

[925] Wilner, Daniel M. and Rosabelle Price Walkley. "Some Special Problems and Alternatives in Housing for Older Persons," in John C. McKinney and Frank T. de Vyver (eds.). *Aging and Social Policy*. New York: Appleton-Century-Crofts, Division of Meredith Publishing Company, 1966, 221-259.

[926] _____, Thomas C. Pinkerton, and Matthew Tayback. *The Housing Environment and Family Life; A Longitudinal Study of the Effects of Housing on Morbidity and Mental Health*. Baltimore: The Johns Hopkins Press, 1962.

*[927] Wilson, James Q. *Urban Renewal, The Record and the Controversy*. Cambridge, Massachusetts: The Massachusetts Intsitute of Technology Press, 1966.

*[928] Winger, Alan R. "An Approach to Measuring Potential Upgrading Demand in the Housing Market," *The Review of Economics and Statistics*, LXV (August 1963), 239-244.

*[929] _____. "Demand and Residential Fluctuations," *Nebraska Journal of Economics and Business*, X (Summer 1971), 51-61.

*[930] _____. "Housing Tenure Preferences in the 1970's," *Economic Business Bulletin*, XXIII (2) (Winter 1971), 32-36.

[931] _____. "Inter-Area Variations in Vacancy Rates," *Land Economics*, XLIII (1) (February 1967), 84-90.

*[932] _____. "Regional Growth Disparities and the Mortgage Market," *Journal of Finance*, XXIV (September 1969), 659-662.

*[933] _____. "Short-Term Activity in Residential Construction Markets: Some Regional Considerations," *Southern Economic Journal*, XXXVI (April 1970), 390-403.

*[934] _____. "Short-Term Fluctuations in Residential Construction: An Overview of Recent Research," *Mississippi Valley Journal of Business Economics*, V (3) (Spring 1970), 39-51.

*[935] _____. "Trade-Offs in Housing," *Land Economics*, XLV (4) (November 1969), 413-417.

[936] _____ and John Madden. "The Application of the Theory of Joint Products: The Case of Residential Construction," *The Quarterly Review of Economics and Business*, X (2) (Summer 1970), 61-69.

*[937] _____. "Residential Construction, Acceleration, and Urban Growth," *Journal of Regional Science*, XI (April 1971), 91-100.

*[938] Wingo, Lowdon, Jr. "An Economic Model of the Utilization of Urban Land for Residential Purposes," *Papers and Proceedings of Regional Science Association*, VII (1961), 191-205.

*[939] _____. "Issues in a National Urban Development Strategy for the United States," *Urban Studies*, IX (1) (February 1972), 3-27.

*[940] _____. "Urban Renewal: Objectives, Analysis, and Information Systems," in Werner Z. Hirsh (ed.). *Regional Accounts for Policy Decisions, Papers Presented at the conference on Regional Accounts.* Baltimore: The Johns Hopkins University Press, 1966.
*[941] Winnick, Louis. *Rental Housing: Opportunities for Private Investment.* New York: McGraw-Hill, 1958.
*[942] _____. "Rental Housing Problems for Private Investment," in Marshall D. Ketchum and Leon T. Kendall (eds.). *Readings in Financial Institutions.* Boston: Houghton Mifflin Company, 1965.
[943] Winthrop, Henry. "Yield Insurance and Low-Cost Housing: A Contribution to the Anti-Poverty Program," *Land Economics*, XLIV (2) (May 1968), 141-152.
[944] Wittman, Dennis L. "Property Tax Relief: A Viable Adjunct to Housing Policy?" *Urban Law Annual* (1972), 171-196.
[945] Wood, Elizabeth. In D.J. Bogue (ed.). *Needed Urban and Metropolitan Research.* Chicago: Scripps Foundation Studies in Population Distribution, no. 7, 1953.
[946] Woodard, F.O. and Ronald W. Brady. "Inductive Evidence of Tax Capitalization," *National Tax Journal*, XVIII (1) (March 1965), 193-201.
[947] Woodruff, Archibald M. "Land Value Taxation: A 1966 Evaluation," in Tax Institute of America. *The Property Tax: Problems and Potential.* Princeton, New Jersey: Tax Institute of America, 1967, 427-428.
[948] _____. "Practical Limits of Property Taxation," *Proceedings of the Academy of Political Science*, XXVIII (4) (January 1968), 513-526.
[949] Woodruff, Archibald, Jr. "The Property Tax: Some Urgent Problems," *Urban Land*, XXIII (5) (May 1964), 2 ff.
*[950] Wright, Colin. "Residential Location in a Three-Dimensional City," *Journal of Political Economy*, LXXIX (November-December 1971), 1378-1387.
[951] Yancey, William L. "Architecture, Interaction, and Social Control: The Case of a Large-Scale Public Housing Project," *Environment and Behavior,* III (1) (March 1971), 3-21.
[952] Young, Charles E. "Residential Building Before the Boom," *American Statistical Association, Proceedings of Business and Economics Section's Annual Meeting,* 1966, 273-275.
*[953] Young, Milton. "Private Investment in Low and Moderate Income Housing," *Criminal Law and Urban Problems Course Handbook Series No. 6.* New York: Practicing Law Institute, 1969.
*[954] Zelder, Raymond E. "Poverty, Housing and Market Processes," *Urban Affairs Quarterly* (September 1972).
*[955] _____. "Racial Segregation in Urban Housing Markets," *Journal of Regional Science*, X (1) (April 1970), 93-105.

Acquisition of Housing Studies

This addendum to the bibliography is intended to assist the reader in obtaining specific studies and in updating the foregoing bibliography. The list reflects those institutions and services that proved to be most helpful to the project team in compiling the bibliography and in obtaining studies for evaluation.

Abstracts and Book Reviews

Journal of Housing
National Association of Housing and Redevelopment Officials
2600 Virginia Avenue, N.W.
Washington, D.C. 20037

    Abstracts bibliographies and research reports on housing, prepared by NAHRO Librarian. Items cited in this monthly publication are available from publishers whose addresses are provided.

Land Use Abstracts
Urban Land Institute
1200 18th Street, N.W.
Washington, D.C. 20036

    A quarterly summary of new publications, prepared by the Library Staff of the ULI. Publications listed must be requested from the publishers, whose addresses are given.

Planning
American Society of Planning Officials
1313 60th Street
Chicago, Illinois 60637

    Similar to the *Journal of Housing*, this monthly publication includes a "Planner's Library" section that has book reviews and lists according to classification all books and reports ASPO receives.

Urban Affairs Abstracts
National League of Cities and U.S. Conference of Mayors
1620 Eye Street, N.W.
Washington, D.C. 20006

    Published weekly. NLC and USCM cannot furnish copies of items abstracted. Requests must be directed to the journal in which the article appears. Journal addresses are provided.

Urban Land
Urban Land Institute
1200 18th Street, N.W.
Washington, D.C. 20036

A newsletter, published 11 times per year, containing book reviews, summaries of research done by the ULI, articles by guest academicians on urban matters and reports of research.

Urban Technology
Weekly Government Abstracts
NTIS (National Technical Information Service)
U.S. Department of Commerce
P.O. Box 1553
Springfield, Virginia 22151

This publication describes most unclassified, federally funded housing research as it is completed. An annual subscription includes an order form that can be used to request all items cited in the publication.

Bibliographies and Indexes to Periodical Literature

Council of Planning Librarians Exchange Bibliographies
Mrs. Mary Vance, Editor
P.O. Box 229
Monticello, Illinois 61856

A compilation of bibliographies prepared by planning students, faculty, and professionals. A list of the bibliographies is available from the council, and individual bibliographies can be purchased. The individual bibliographies include no ordering information.

The Dictionary Catalog of the U.S. Department of Housing and Urban Development Library and Information Division
U.S. Department of Housing and Urban Development
Washington, D.C. 20410

Published by G.K. Hall of Boston in 1972, this 19-volume catalog mirrors the card catalog of the HUD Library in Washington, D.C. The entire 19-volume catalog is available for purchase from G.K. Hall.

Housing and Planning References
Prepared by The Library
U.S. Department of Housing and Urban Development
Washington, D.C. 20410

Issued bi-monthly, it arranges books, documents, and pertinent periodical articles by subject. Subscriptions available from the Superintendent of Documents.

Index to Legal Periodicals
Published by the H.W. Wilson Company
950 University Avenue
Bronx, New York

Compiled in cooperation with the American Association of Law Libraries. Indexes by subject and author articles that appear in legal periodicals, yearbooks, law institutes, and annual law reviews. Indexes are published monthly, and bound cumulative indexes are published at intervals of three years. Various subject headings relate to housing, for example, abatement, city planning, real property, renewal planning, zoning.

Journal of Economic Literature
American Economic Association
1313 21 Avenue South
Nashville, Tennessee 37212

A bibliography of recent books and journal articles. Section 930 of the index is Urban Economics and Section 932 is Housing Economics.

Publications Lists

Many university, private, and governmental research institutions will provide extensive lists of works published under their own auspices. Most of the studies cited can be obtained directly from the institution providing the publication list. A few commercial publishing houses have extensive research listings as well. The sources provided here are by no means a complete listing, but rather those that provided material most helpful to us.

Publishing Houses and Research Institutions

Arthur D. Little, Inc.
Acorn Park
Cambridge, Massachusetts 02140

Center for Real Estate and Urban Economics
260 Stephens Hall
University of California
Berkeley, California 94720

Center for Urban Development Research
Cornell University
726 University Avenue
Ithaca, New York 14850

Center for Urban Policy Research
Rutgers University
Building 4051
Kilmer Area Campus
New Brunswick, New Jersey 08903

Center for Urban and Regional Studies
The University of North Carolina at Chapel Hill
108 Battle Lane
Chapel Hill, North Carolina 27514

The Housing, Real Estate and Urban Land Studies Program
Graduate School of Management
University of California
Los Angeles, California 90024

Institute for Defense Analysis
400 Army-Navy Drive
Arlington, Virginia 22202

Institute for Research on Poverty
Social Science Building
1180 Observatory Drive
University of Wisconsin
Madison, Wisconsin 53706

Institute of Urban and Regional Development
316 Wurster Hall
University of California
Berkeley, California 94720

Joint Center for Urban Studies of the Massachusetts Institute of Technology and Harvard University
66 Church Street
Cambridge, Massachusetts 02138

The Johns Hopkins University Press
Baltimore, Maryland 21218

Lexington Books
D.C. Heath and Company
125 Spring Street
Lexington, Massachusetts 02173

The Massachusetts Institute of Technology Press
28 Carleton Street
Cambridge, Massachusetts 02142

National Housing and Economic Development Law Project
Earl Warren Legal Institute
2313 Warring Street
Berkeley, California 94704

Praeger Publishers, Inc.
111 Fourth Avenue
New York, New York 10003

The RAND Corporation
1700 Main Street
Santa Monica, California 90406

The Urban Institute
2100 M Street, N.W.
Washington, D.C. 20037

Public Agencies, Services, and Information Exchanges

CBT Publications
U.S. Department of Commerce
National Bureau of Standards
Washington, D.C. 20234
 This list of publications includes NBS publications and articles in scientific and technical journals on building codes.

A Compendium of Reports Resulting from HUD Research and Technology Funding
U.S. Department of Housing and Urban Development
Washington, D.C. 20410
 Lists the names and affiliations of persons or groups currently under contract to HUD, including expected dates of publication and project titles. No addresses

or ordering information provided. Last published in 1972, HUD intends to update this listing annually.

HUD Weekly News Summary
U.S. Department of Housing and Urban Development
Washington, D.C. 20410

Lists all releases, notices of publication, speeches, and other information announced by HUD every week. Copies of any of the items mentioned are available from HUD.

Library of Congress Photoduplication Service
Washington, D.C. 20540

Makes photoduplicates of materials in its collections for research use. In making an inquiry, it is necessary to give an accurate and complete identification of the document desired.

NTIS Special Interest Publications
National Technical Information Service
U.S. Department of Commerce
P.O. Box 1553
Springfield, Virginia 22151

A central source for the public sale of government-sponsored research reports and other analyses prepared by federal agencies, their contractors or grantees. It is helpful to reference the NTIS accession number, if known, when ordering. Items sent promptly.

Smithsonian Science Information Exchange
Room 300
1730 M Street, N.W.
Washington, D.C. 20036

Indexes short summaries of ongoing and recently completed research and compiles information packages, by topic, for public sale. Packages are reviewed and updated every 90 days and the latest packets that are available are listed in the SSIE Science Newsletter.

Superintendent of Documents
U.S. Government Printing Office
Washington, D.C. 20402

A long waiting period, usually up to several months, is required to obtain studies from the Superintendent of Documents. However, regional offices generally process orders more quickly.

U.S. Department of Housing and Urban Development
Washington, D.C. 20410

Photocopies of documents up to 50 pages can be obtained through the librarian. Requests for documents held by the HUD Library in Washington, D.C. can be made to the many regional offices, most of which have their own libraries.

Indexes

Name Index

Aaron, Henry, 70
Achtenberg, Emily, 105
Ackerman, Bruce, 58, 73
Agapos, A.M., 84
Altshuler, Alan, 28, 134
Anderson, Martin, 196
Arthur D. Little, Inc., 37, 70, 75, 77, 125, 131

Bagby, D. Gordon, 103, 123, 192
Bails, Dale, 84
Banfield, Edward, 27
Beck, Morris, 81
Becker, Arthur P., 82
Bish, Robert L., 94, 112
Branfman, Eric J., 52, 77
Brown, H. James, 198
Burchell, Robert W., 37, 80, 129
Buttel, Frederick H., 51, 67

Carr, Gregg, 132
Case, Frederick E., 58, 130
Cohen, Benjamin I., 52, 77
Cord, Steven, 84, 130

Davis, Otto A., 31, 51, 70, 130, 191
de Leeuw, Frank, 99
Dougharty, L.A., 75
Downs, Anthony, 49, 93, 96, 101, 130, 134, 153
Dunlap, Paul R., 84

Eichler, Edward P., 147

Fisher, Ernest M., 63, 64
Forrester, Jay, 153
Freeman, Elsa S., 157
Fried, Marc, 191
Frieden, Bernard J., 128
Friedlander, Ann, 182

Gaffney, Mason, 84
Gans, Herbert J., 34
George, Henry, 9, 84
Greenbie, Barrie Barstow, 191
Grey, Arthur L., 84
Grigsby, William G., 37

Hamilton, Bruce W., 78
Harberger, Arnold, 72
Harris, Robert, 137, 198
Hartman, Chester W., 34, 132, 190
Heilbrun, James, 75, 82
Heinberg, John D., 74

Isler, Morton, 151, 153

Kain, John F., 192
Kaplan, Abraham, 118, 123
Kaplan, Marshall, 147
Kemper, Peter, 181
Kenower, John, 107, 129
Kent, T.J., Jr., 25
Kessler, Robert P., 34
Keyes, Langley Carleton, Jr., 104-106, 108, 125, 134
Kilbridge, Maurice D., 153
Kolodny, Robert, 111, 113

Leaman, Sam H., 99
Lee, Douglas, Jr., 198
Lindholm, Richard W., 84
Lindsay, John V., 138-140
Linton, Mields and Coston, Inc., 37, 60, 70, 76, 126, 128, 132
Listokin, David, 106
Long, Norton, 108
Lowry, Ira S., 98, 138-139, 155

Mace, Ruth L., 78, 130
McKean, Roland N., 182
Manvel, Alan D., 49
Mao, James C.T., 33, 194
Messner, Stephen D., 33-34, 125
Meyerson, Martin, 27
Mishan, E.S., 185, 197
Mollenkopf, John, 49
Moorhouse, John C., 65, 123
Musgrave, Peggy B., 196
Musgrave, Richard, 196
Muth, Richard F., 54, 93-94, 95, 112, 125

Nachbaur, William T., 38
Needleman, Lionel, 103

303

Netzer, Dick, 69-70, 75, 80, 82-83, 86
Neutze, Max, 33, 50-51, 67, 125, 132
Newman, Oscar, 192
Niebanck, Paul L., 107, 130
Nourse, Hugh O., 125, 193

Oates, W.E., 74
O'Block, R.P., 153
Oldman, Oliver, 70
Olsen, Edgar O., 61, 63, 66, 94-95, 98, 123
Orr, Larry L., 74, 95, 125

Pack, Janet Rothenberg, 181, 190
Paulus, Virginia, 19, 156
Peterson, George E., 75, 76, 77, 81, 82, 90
Phares, Donald, 125
Pope, John, 107
Popp, Dean O., 84, 125
Prescott, James R., 94-95, 123
Price Waterhouse and Company, 70, 81-82, 85-86
Pynoos, Jon, 49

Quigley, John M., 192

Rapkin, Chester, 63, 64
Reeves, Marilyn Langford, 98, 125
Rothenberg, Jerome, 33
Rybeck, Walter, 84

Sabella, Edward M., 74, 124, 129
Sadacca, Robert, 126, 132
Sagalyn, Lynne, 50, 52, 54
Schaaf, A.H., 70, 85, 87, 103-104, 130
Sebold, Frederick D., 84, 125
Smith, T.R., 70, 84, 85, 129, 130
Smolensky, Eugene, 94, 95, 112
Solomon, Arthur P., 93, 95, 98-99, 112, 125, 129
Stegman, Michael A., 37, 64, 76
Sternlieb, George, 33, 37, 50, 52, 54, 63, 64, 65, 73, 75-76, 77, 78, 80, 90, 126, 129
Stevens, John, 125
Stull, William J., 181
Sullivan, Donald G., 125
Szanton, Peter L., 139

Teplitz, P.V., 153
Trubek, David M., 52, 77
Tullock, Gordon, 98

Wehner, Harrison G., Jr., 98
Wendell, Frana Summa, 129
Wertz, Kenneth L., 70, 130
Wetzler, Elliot, 54, 125
Wexler, Harry, 181
Wheaton, William, 26
Whinston, Andrew B., 31, 51, 191
Wicker, Warren J., 78, 130
Wood, Elizabeth, 159
Wood, Robert, 140

Subject Index

Abandoned housing, 35-45
  causes, 37
  gaps in research on, 38
  policy-related research on, 36-38
  property tax effects, 75-77
  property taxes, 37-38
  urban blight, 37-38
American Public Health Association, 57
American Society of Planning Officials, 49, 156
Arlington, Virginia
  site-value tax system, 85

Baltimore housing market study, 37
Bedrooms, 78, 90
Benefit vs. cost. *See* Cost/benefit analysis
Boston
  leased-housing subsidies, 99
  tax abatement programs, 81-82
Boston Municipal Research Bureau, 59, 105, 128
Boston Rehabilitation Program, 101, 104-106
Boston West End survey, 34-35
Building codes
  administration, 55
  effect on costs, 53-55
  effect on housing quality, 55
  functions, 47
  influences on, 9
  purpose, 53

Camden Housing Improvement Projects, 106-107
Center for Community change, 37, 59, 76, 126, 128, 132
Center for Urban Policy Research, 117, 140, 156
Chicago Housing Authority, 27
City Managers. *See* Policy makers
Committee on Urban Housing, 134
Community-based development corporations, 106-107
Community Development Act, 3
Comprehensive planning
  studies relating to, 25-29

Condominiums, 110
Construction standards, 15
Cooperative apartments, 10, 110
Cost/benefit analysis
  generally, 181-186: benefit calculation, 183-184; building code studies, 56; cost calculation, 183, 185-186; cost/revenue, 185-186; equity issues addressed to, 136; history, 181-182; limitations, 183; procedure, 182-185
  housing programs, 187-203: benefit calculation, 190-194, negative benefits, 190-191; benefit distribution problems, 196-197; Boston leased housing program, 99; cost calculation, 188-190, psychic costs, 190-191; discounting procedure, 194-196; limitations, 187-188; neighborhood effects, 192-193
  New York City rent control, 64
  policy related research, 31-35
  rehabilitation programs, 103
  techniques, 33-35
  uncertainty, problems of, 199-201
  urban models, use of, 197-198
  urban renewal problems, 31-35
  use of, 199-203
Cost/effectiveness analysis, 182
Cost/revenue analysis, 185-186
Costs. *See* Finance

Decision making. *See* Policy makers; Policy-making; Policy-related research
Design standards, 15
Development planning. *See* Housing
Discounting procedure, 184, 194-196
Douglas Commission, 47, 49, 55, 105, 134
  code enforcement, 57-58
  study on building codes, 53-54

Eminent domain, 29, 30
Exclusionary zoning, 77
  causes and effects, 51-52
  defined, 48

Exclusionary zoning *(cont.)*
  racial factors, 52

Fairhope, Alabama
  site-value tax study, 85
Federal aid, 3, 30, 91ff
  assistance programs, 3, 9-10
  housing assistance programs, 91ff
  See also Housing assistance programs
Finance
  cost analysis of rehabilitation vs.
    new construction, 103-104
  cost/benefit analysis, 31-33, 181ff
  cost calculations in cost/benefit analysis, 183, 185, 188-190
  costs of rent control, 64
  effect of property tax on cash flow, 76
  effect of site-tax on costs, 86
  effects of zoning on, 50
  federal aid, 3, 30
  human costs, 34-35
  land write-down, 30, 31, 32
  production costs, 15, 16
  revenue from site-value taxation, 88
  subsidies. *See* Subsidies
  See also Property taxation; Subsidies
Flood Control Act, 181

Game theory, 31-33
Grants. *See* Loans and grants
Greenleigh Evaluation Report, 141-142

Honolulu
  site-value tax system, 85, 86, 88
Housing
  defined, 5
  demographic factors, 50
  effect of tax abatement on, 80-82
  effect of urban renewal on, 29-30
  incentive programs, 80
  information channels, 168f, 169-172f
  information sources, 165-168f, 169-179f
  use by policy makers, 178, 179f, 180
  information systems, 8
  planning, 25-29: analyzed by Banfield, 27; comprehensive planning, 8; middle range, 29

rehabilitation problems. *See* Rehabilitation
suburban apartments, 50
supply and demand studies, 73
tax abatement programs, 80-82
See also Local housing; Public housing; Rehabilitation
Housing Act, 1949, 29
Housing Act, 1965, 101
Housing and community research groups, 107
Housing assistance programs
  federal, 91ff
  local administration, 92
Housing codes
  enforcement, 57-59
  functions, 47
  multiple dwelling, 9
  purpose, 56-57
  subsidy suggestion, 58-59
  See also Urban renewal
Housing market
  slum housing study, 58-59
  variables for research on, 39, 40t, 41-44, 45t, 46
Housing process, 5-6f
Housing regulatory system, 47ff
Housing stock
  maintenance problems, 3-4
  See also Housing
Housing studies. *See* Policy-related research
Housing subsidy programs, 3. *See also* Subsidies

Incentive programs, 80
  to private developers, 9
Information systems
  housing market analysis, 39, 40t, 41-44, 45t
  theory, lack of, 35-36, 46
  utility of, 36
Institute of Public Administration, 107
International City Management Association, 55, 157

Joint Center for Urban Studies, 104-106, 117

Kansas City housing allowance experiment, 98

Land use regulations, 47ff
  evaluation of studies on, 48-49
Land write-down, 30, 31
Landlords
  effect of property tax on, 76-77
Loans and grants, 10
Local government
  influence on housing policy, 7-8
  role in housing, 3
Local housing
  characteristics, 5, 6f, 7
  complexity of, 5
  dynamics of, 5
  economics, effect on, 5-6
  influences on, 7-8
  instruments, 7-9; analysis, 11, 13ff, coordinated use of, 13ff, 14
  officials, 5
  problems of, 11f, 15ff
  See also Housing; Public housing; Urban renewal
Local policy making. See Policy making

Mayors. See Policy makers
Methodology
  assumptions, use of, 123
  concretization, 120
  data analysis, techniques, 126-127
  defined, 118
  designs, 120, 131-132
  external validity: analysis, 127-130; sampling problems, 127-131
  generalizability, 130-133
  informants, use of, 126
  internal validity analysis, 121-127
  problems in, analysis, 121ff
  sampling, problems of, 125-126; cases, validity of, 128-129; "opportunity" sample, 128; reporting weakness, 130; size, 129
  steps, 118, 119t, 121
  variables: operationalization, 124-125; specification of, 119-120, 123-125
Metro metrics, 79
Miami Valley Regional Commission, 29
MICAH, 107
Mortgage insurance, 101
Municipal Finance Officers Association, 157
Municipal housing. See Local housing

Municipal Yearbook, 55

National Association of Home Builders, 93, 97
National Association of Housing and Redevelopment Officials, 156, 157, 179-180
National Association of Mutual Savings Banks, 93, 97
National Bureau of Economic Research, 198
National Commission on Urban Problems. See Douglas Commission
National Housing Act of 1968, 91, 96
National Housing Policy Review, 96
National League of Cities, 140-142, 156, 157, 158-159
National Science Foundation, xiii, 4, 151
  research program, 223-225
National Technical Information Service, 156
National Urban Coalition, 111
National Urban League, 37, 59, 76, 126, 128, 132
New Jersey
  "bedroom multipliers" study, 78
  municipal tax policy study, 52
  zoning study, 52
New Jersey County and Municipal Government Study Commission, 140, 154
New Jersey Department of Community Affairs, 140
New York City
  abandonment study, 37
  cooperative conversions, 111
  Housing and Development Administration, 138-140
  Project Rehab, 107-108
  rent control in. See Rent control
  tax abatement programs, 81-82
New York City-RAND Institute, 63, 64, 65, 94-95, 117, 138-140, 154
Newark
  Sternlieb's studies, 73
Northern Alameda County, Calif., 70, 85
Northern Virginia Builders Association, 79

Philadelphia rehabilitation program, 103, 107

Pittsburgh
   site-value tax system, 85, 86, 88
Planning. *See* Housing
Policy framework. *See* Policy makers; Policy making for policy makers, 16-17
Policy makers. *See* Policy making
   advisers, use of, 166t, 167t, 168, 173
   characteristics, 158-160
   information sources used by, 171, 172f, 173-176, 179f
   local administration of federal programs, 52
   local policy-makers, survey of, 20, 21f, 22, 165ff
   relationship to researchers, 136-138
   training, 173-174f
   use of research studies by, 133-136, 147ff, 153-162: survey technique and findings, 165-167, 168f, 169-179f, 180
Policy making. *See* Policy makers
   conflicts in, 16
   federal aid to, 3
   instruments, analysis of, 16-17
   research, effect on, 67-68
   research, use in, 21f, 22, 27-28, 165-180
Policy-related research
   abandonment studies, 35-39, 40t, 41-45
   administrative problems addressed by, 135
   bibliographic search, 17-19: evaluation, 19-20, 205-222
   building codes studies, 53-56
   comprehensive planning: influence on, 25-29; questions, 26-27; research, 25-29
   cost/benefit analysis. *See* Cost/benefit analysis
   data analysis techniques, 126-127
   data availability, 124-125
   decision-making related to, 158-162
   defined, 13
   demand subsidies, 98-100
   dissemination of studies, problems and recommendations, 133-134, 155-158
   effect on policy makers, 67-68. *See also* Policy makers; Policy making
   equity problems addressed by, 136
   evaluation, 3, 4: forms, 205-222
   expectations, 136-143
   financial support needs, 150-153
   fiscal zoning studies, 78-79
   game-theory analysis, 31-33
   generalizability requirement, 130-133
   housing assistance programs, 91
   housing codes, 56-60
   information systems, analysis, 35-36
   institutional support recommended, 152-153
   interdependence, lack of, 155-156
   methodology. *See* Methodology
   National Science Foundation evaluations, 223-225
   paucity of literature on, 27-29
   practical problems addressed by, 135-136
   property taxation: gaps, 79; studies, 69-71, 75
   quality and reliability analyzed, 148, 149t, 150-153
   rehabilitation programs, 100-112: self-help programs, 111-112. *See also* Rehabilitation
   rent control studies, 60-68
   site-value taxation studies, 82-89
   studies, 10-11f, types: policy analysis, 12-13; pure social science, 11f-13
   tax abatement programs, 80-81
   theory, lack of, 143, 148-152; problems, 122-124
   unavailability, 133-134; recommendations for change, 155-158
   urban renewal planning: influence on, 29-35; questions, 30-31. *See also* Urban renewal
   use of: by policy makers, 133-136, 147ff, 153-162; in decision making, 21f, 22, 176, 177f, 178f, 179; survey technique and findings, 165-167, 168t, 169-179t. *See also* Policy makers; Policy making
   weaknesses, 117-118
   welfare-economics theories, 94
   zoning studies, 48-53: need for, 52-53
Politics
   in city planning, 27-29

in local policy, 49
policy-related research addressed to, 135-136
Project design, 17-22
flow chart, 18f
local policy makers, survey of, 20, 21f, 22
Project Rehab, 101ff
New York City, 107, 113
Property taxation
administration, 69-71
as sales tax on housing, 73-75
as tax on owner's capital, 75-76
defects, 71
disincentive effect, 75-76
effect on cash flow, 76
effect on housing, 69, 71, 89-90
effects in central city, 73-74, 76-77
generalizability of A.D. Little study, 131-132
public services related to, 74
reform programs, 80-82
regressivity analysis, 71-73
site-value tax. See Site-value taxation
studies, 70
theoretical studies, 71
See also Finance
Public housing. See Subsidies
case study, 27-28
consumer oriented programs, 95
leased housing, 95, 98-100
politics in, analyzed, 27-28
subsidies, 93-97
Public interest, 27

Quality (of housing), 15
Quantity (of research), 148, 149t, 150-153
Quantity (of housing), 15
Queens Village, Inc., 107

Real property taxation. See Property taxation
Rehabilitation (of housing), 100-112
advantages, 101-102
community-based housing development corporations, 106-107
cost analysis, 103-104
research on, 102ff
technology, effect on, 107-108
Rehabilitation (of neighborhoods), 10, 108-110

Rent control, 47
alternatives, 66-67
effect on maintenance, 65
effect on noncontrolled housing, 66
effect on space allocation, 64
effectiveness studies, 62-63
history, 60-61
New York City experience, 9, 61-67: benefits, distribution of, 63; description, 62; Sternlieb's study, 37; theoretical studies, 61-62; withdrawal efforts, 65-66

St. Paul comprehensive plan, 28
Self-help programs
local government assistance, 10
rehabilitation programs, 110-112
Site-value taxation, 9, 69
effect on central city, 88
effect on costs, 86
effect on low-income projects, 88-89
effect on property values, 88
effect on revenue, 88
effectiveness studies, 84-86
equity effects, 86-88
graded-tax system, 85, 88
purposes, 84
theories, 82-84
as wealth tax, 87-88
Subdivision codes
effect on housing costs, 50
purpose, 47
Subsidies
below-market rate, 31
cash grant, 95-96
demand, 73, 93, 97-100: advantages, 97-98; cash grants, 95-96
federal assistance, 91ff
for housing code enforcement, 58-59
interest-reduction, 96-97
land write-down, 30, 31, 32
mortgage-insurance programs, 101
priorities, studies on, 101-102
public housing, 93-97
rehabilitation loans, 31
rent control as, 62-63
supply, 73, 92-96
See also Finance
Supply and demand studies. See Subsidies

Taxation
  incentive programs, 9, 80
  tax abatement programs, 9
  See also Property taxation; Site-value taxation
Tenant groups
  to rehabilitate declining dwellings, 10

U.S. Bureau of the Budget, 139
U.S. Bureau of the Census, xiii, 61, 121
U.S. Department of Commerce, 156
U.S. Department of Housing and Urban Development, xiii, 17, 37, 58, 91, 94, 140-143, 151, 156
  Housing and Urban Development Library and Information Division, 157
  Housing Assistance Administration, 91
U.S. Federal Housing Administration, 91, 105
U.S. Office of Equal Opportunity, 151
U.S. Office of Management and Budget, xiii, 151
U.S. President's Commission on Income Maintenance, 151
U.S. President's Committee on Urban Housing, 5, 49, 134
U.S. Public Health Service, 57
United States Conference of Mayors, 156, 157
United States Savings and Loan League, 93, 97
Urban Affairs Abstracts, 156
Urban blight, 37-38
Urban homesteading, 10, 186

Urban Institute, 100, 117, 151
Urban Land Institute, 156
Urban models, 197-198
Urban Observatory Program, 138, 140-143, 154
  structure, 141-142
Urban Planning Aid, 104-106
Urban Planning Research and Demonstration Program, 143
Urban renewal
  cost/benefit analysis, use of. *See* Cost/benefit analysis
  defined, 29, 30
  human costs, 34-35
  planning, 29-31
  "prisoner's dilemma," resolution of, 32
  purposes, 30
  self-help programs, 110-112
  tools, 8
  urban models, use of, 197-198

Washington, D.C.
  apartment building, 50

Yerba Buena urban renewal project, 34

Zoning
  fiscal competition, land use, 77
  fiscal factors, 52, 77-78
  history, 14
  policy-related research on, 51-53
  public plans, 51
  racial factors, 52, 77
Zoning codes
  effects on housing costs, 50, 51-52
  functions, 47
  surveys, 48ff

About the Authors

Harry J. Wexler graduated from Harvard College in 1957. In 1962 he received the LLB from Yale Law School and the M.A. in American Studies. After several years practicing law, Wexler returned to Yale as a member of the faculty of city planning where he taught from 1965 through 1972. From 1971 through 1973 he was executive director and general counsel of a nonprofit housing development corporation. He is currently a partner at Cogen, Holt and Associates, an urban consulting firm based in New Haven.

Richard L. Peck graduated from the University of California (Berkeley) in 1966. After college, Peck entered Yale Graduate School where he received the M.A. in international relations in 1968, the M. Phil. in political science in 1969, and is presently a Ph.D. candidate in political science. Peck is Assistant Professor of International Relations at Lewis and Clark College. He was a research associate at Cogen, Holt and Associates in 1973-74.

Related Lexington Books

Birch, David; Atkinson, Reilly; Sandström, Sven; and Stack, Linda, *Patterns of Urban Change: The New Haven Experience*, 160 pp., 1974

Field, Charles G. and Rivkin, Steven R., *The Building Code Burden*, 240 pp., 1975

Lineberry, Robert L. and Masotti, Louis H., eds., *Perspectives on Urban Policy*, In Press

Mills, Edwin S. and Oates, Wallace E., eds., *Fiscal Zoning and Land Use Controls*, 224 pp. 1975

Schussheim, Morton J., *The Modest Commitment to the Cities*, 256 pp., 1974

Tabors, Richard D.; Rogers, Peter; and Shapiro, Michael, *Land Use and the Pipe: The Effects of Sewer Extension*, In Press

Czamanski, Daniel Z., *The Cost of Preventive Services: The Case of the Fire Department*, 128 pp., 1975

Nourse, Hugh O., *The Effects of Public Policy on Housing Markets*, 140 pp., 1973

Morris, Peter, *State Housing Finance Agencies*, 192 pp., 1974

Wolman, Harold L., *Housing and Housing Policies in the U.S. & U.K.*, 144 pp., 1975

Schafer, Robert, *The Suburbanization of Multifamily Housing*, 176 pp., 1974

Downs, Anthony, *Federal Housing Subsidies*, 160 pp. 1973

Bagby, Gordon, *Housing Rehabilitation Costs*, 128 pp., 1973